Effective
School
Consultation

AN INTERACTIVE APPROACH

Effective School Consultation

AN INTERACTIVE APPROACH

George M. Sugai 1951-
Gerald A. Tindal
UNIVERSITY OF OREGON

BROOKS/COLE PUBLISHING COMPANY
PACIFIC GROVE, CALIFORNIA

Brooks/Cole Publishing Company
A Division of Wadsworth, Inc.

Printed in the United States of America.

10   9   8   7   6   5   4   3   2   1

Library of Congress Cataloguing-in-Publication Data

Sugai, George M.
    Effective school consultation : an interactive approach / George
M. Sugai, Gerald A. Tindal.
       p.   cm.
    Includes bibliographical references and index.
    ISBN 0-534-19302-1
    1. Educational counseling. 2. Problem children—Counseling of.
3. Problem children—Education. I. Tindal, Gerald A.
II. Title.
LB1027.5.S8537 1993
371.4′6—dc20   92-36198
                                                                        CIP

Sponsoring Editor: *Vicki Knight*
Marketing Representative: *Tammy Stenquist*
Editorial Associate: *Heather L. Graeve*
Production Editor: *Penelope Sky*
Manuscript Editor: *Robin Witkin*
Permissions Editor: *May Clark*
Interior and Cover Design: *E. Kelly Shoemaker*
Cover Artwork: *Laura Militzer Bryant*
Art Coordinator: *Susan Haberkorn*
Interior Illustration: *Laurel Mueller and Bill Bokermann*
Indexer: *Lois Oster*
Typesetting: *Graphic World Inc.*
Printing and Binding: *Arcata Graphics, Fairfield*

Credits continue on page 445.

To
James and Kikue Sugai
and
Tom Tindal

ABOUT THE AUTHORS

GEORGE SUGAI is an associate professor in the College of Education at the University of Oregon. His current training and research activities use applied behavior analysis principles and procedures to improve social skills instruction, resolve social behavior problems, and enhance the consultation process. George received his Ph.D. in Special Education from the University of Washington in 1980. Before coming to the University of Oregon in 1985 he filled a variety of professional roles: (a) teacher trainer at the University of Kentucky, (b) special education teacher in the public schools, (c) treatment director in a residential program, and (d) counselor in camping programs for individuals with disabilities.

George is a productive member of the professional community. He has published numerous articles in professional journals and presented at state, national, and international conferences. His book *Effective Teaching: Principles and Procedures of Applied Behavior Analysis with Exceptional Students* (written with Mark Wolery and Don Bailey) is widely used in teacher training programs across the country and internationally. George is also active in the schools, where he consults, provides inservice training, and conducts research.

GERALD TINDAL received his Ph.D. from the University of Minnesota in 1982 and is an associate professor currently on the faculty in the College of Education at the University of Oregon, where he provides training and conducts research in classroom assessment and consultation. With a strong focus on monitoring student progress, Jerry has written many research articles on using assessment systems to make effective and useful educational decisions. In *Classroom-Based Assessment* (written with Doug Marston), Jerry discusses how the assessment system can be applied effectively and efficiently in school and classroom contexts. Jerry has recently extended his work on classroom assessment from the elementary to the middle school curriculum. This research provides an in-depth examination of content area curricula and how to facilitate student acquisition of science and social studies concepts.

Jerry is an active member of the professional community. He directs a resource consultation program in the College of Education, manages the Oregon Conference on current topics in education, and is editor of *Diagnostique,* an assessment journal.

PREFACE

Visit any classroom and you will see an incredible place where opportunities for teaching and learning flourish at every turn. Teachers are learning from students as well as educating them, and students are learning from each other. Although many of these interactions are carefully orchestrated and enacted, many are unplanned and frequently undetected by their participants.

Teachers must be fluent across a seemingly impossible range of areas. For example, not only must Miss Phillips be an expert in third grade reading, math, spelling, and social studies, she also must be skilled at teaching art, physical education, and career education. Not only must Mr. Chaney be fluent at freshman biology, he also must be skilled at teaching sophomore general chemistry and intermediate physics. Mr. Spivey uses his skills to teach four periods of seventh grade English literature; however, he also must manage two periods of eighth grade study hall and 45 minutes of cafeteria duty. Every day, Mrs. Wilson must teach her kindergartners how to read a calendar, tell time, and discriminate between numbers and letters, in addition to helping them learn to brush their teeth, use the toilet appropriately, play cooperatively, and tie their shoes. The examples go on and on, and these responsibilities represent only the tip of the proverbial iceberg. Teachers must also promote their students' social development, make sure they follow rules, correct misbehavers, find and evaluate new curricula and modify current materials, and adjust instructional activities for students with learning and behavioral deficits or culturally diverse backgrounds.

Given these conditions, we believe that all teachers will encounter an academic situation or social behavior problem with which they will need assistance. We believe that consultation has begun when teachers look to others for creative solutions to classroom challenges.

In this book, we show how the process of consultation can be applied to persistent academic and social behavior problems. We emphasize a behavior-analytic, best-practices approach to solving student, classroom, and school challenges, demonstrating the learned nature and lawfulness of behavior and the importance of the immediate environment. Consultation is defined as a structured series of problem-solving steps or interactions that occur between two or more individuals. We emphasize the development and modification of solutions from information that is systematically obtained and analyzed within the context of the immediate problem. We view collaboration as the outcome of a successful consultation in which educators engage in a coordinated or united effort to solve a problem.

Fluency in the steps and substeps of consultation requires systematic practice and access to meaningful performance feedback. We have compiled the practices that can best increase a consultant's accountability, effectiveness, and efficiency, if they are applied in a responsible manner. To assist practitioners, we provide many examples set in schools; we also include templates and forms to structure information gathering and promote functional interactions.

ORGANIZATION

This book is divided into four sections. The introductory Part I includes an overview of consultation in Chapter 1; the characteristics and importance of the initial request for assistance are discussed in Chapter 2. Social behavior problems are emphasized in Part II. Chapter 3 contains strategies for identifying and describing problems and collecting information related to those problems. We describe specific, direct observation procedures and data and problem analysis strategies in Chapter 4, and offer guidelines for selecting and developing the working features of interventions in Chapter 5. Additional intervention programming considerations and strategies are covered in Chapter 6. In Chapter 7 we discuss guidelines for implementing, monitoring, and evaluating interventions designed by teachers and consultants for solving social behavior problems.

In Part III we move from social behavior to academic instruction problems. We discuss guidelines for determining what to teach in Chapter 8, and analyze how teaching is conducted in Chapter 9. In Chapter 10 we consider several strategies for evaluating how these academic interventions benefit learning and achievement.

Part IV, the conclusion, contains Chapter 11, in which we discuss assessment and intervention strategies for solving problems and managing conflicts when working with others. We believe that this book as a whole will help you develop strategies for engaging in interactive and analytic school consultation.

ACKNOWLEDGMENTS

We completed this book with the support and assistance of a large team of players. We are deeply indebted to our families (Bets, Kiyoshi, and Reiko, and Linda, Sevrina, and Karston) who were always supportive, tolerant, and accommodating, and to the teachers and students who have taught us how to be better educators and consultants. We express our gratitude to Vicki Knight, our editor, for giving us this opportunity and for guiding, prodding, and reinforcing us throughout the project.

We also thank the staff at Brooks/Cole, including Penelope Sky, Robin Witkin, and May Clark, who gently maneuvered us toward the final product. The following reviewers offered kindly worded suggestions and comments: Carol Gearheart, University of Northern Colorado; Nancy Glomb, Southern Utah University; Earle Knowlton, University of Kansas; Sandra Lloyd, University of Texas at El Paso; Peter R. Matthews, Lock Haven University; Terry Overton, Longwood College; Marleen Pugach, University of Wisconsin, Milwaukee; and Judy Wood, Virginia Commonwealth University. Dave Knox, Jerry Marr, Linda Mauricio, Anne Scott, and Darlene Scott provided us with invaluable local assistance by "finding that last missing reference," "fixing that funny-looking figure," and "mailing that chapter ASAP." Finally, we acknowledge the encouragement and professional models provided by Jane Carter, Ed Kameenui, and David Evans, and the high-quality training we received from B. and R. Davidson.

GEORGE M. SUGAI
GERALD A. TINDAL

BRIEF CONTENTS

CONTENTS

PART II
SOCIAL BEHAVIOR PROBLEMS   **53**

CHAPTER THREE
Problem Identification and Information Collection   **55**

CHAPTER FOUR
Direct Observation Procedures and Problem Analysis   **81**

CHAPTER SEVEN

Intervention Implementation, Monitoring, and Evaluation

213

PART III

ANALYSIS OF INSTRUCTION

255

CHAPTER EIGHT

What to Teach

257

CHAPTER NINE
How to Teach
300

CHAPTER TEN
Evaluating Academic Outcomes
341

INTRODUCTION

Introduction to Consultation

When the bell rings marking the beginning of another school day, teachers are confronted by a multitude of challenges, routines, and responsibilities. For example, they must review their daily schedule, greet their students, read announcements, take attendance, and collect homework. Once they actually begin teaching, there are materials to distribute, assessments to conduct, lessons to review, new material to present, errors to correct, learning to reinforce, and appropriate and inappropriate behavior to manage. Needless to say, the life of a teacher is active and often quite demanding. Shaping their students' academic and social character is an important and challenging responsibility.

Unfortunately, not all classroom routines go smoothly and not all students learn as efficiently as their teachers would like. Sometimes these classroom challenges become chronic, and even the best teachers exhaust their repertoire of standard remedies. At this point, they look to others for creative solutions. When this search begins, they have initiated a series of steps collectively called consultation. For example, Mr. Wannaroo teaches sixth-grade biology. He is a highly respected teacher with a reputation for reaching even the most difficult student using consistent and positive interpersonal skills and effective teaching strategies. A month ago, Reiko transferred to Mr. Wannaroo's third-hour biology class. Reiko is unlike any student he has ever had. She is openly noncompliant, disrupts other students as they are working, and is generally unresponsive to standard classroom management strategies. To Mr. Wannaroo's surprise, she turns in all her assignments on time, scores in the top 5% of the class on all exams, and rarely misses a day of school. He has tried a number of interventions but each has failed to improve Reiko's behaviors. Mr. Wannaroo has tried writing behavioral contracts, modifying the curriculum, meeting with her parents, assigning in-school suspensions, and scheduling weekly visits with the counselor.

After consulting with Reiko's other teachers, Mr. Wannaroo discovers that they too have experienced similar problems and have been unsuccessful. He decides to request assistance from the special education teacher who is also the building resource consultant, thus initiating the process or interaction known as consultation.

In this chapter, we explore what consultation is and how an analytic approach might be used to solve applied educational problems. Specifically, we provide a working definition of consultation, examine the characteristics of a behavioral approach to consultation, and then present an application of this approach that emphasizes problem identification and analysis and serves as the basis for this text.

A WORKING DEFINITION OF CONSULTATION

In our example, Mr. Wannaroo asks for assistance in solving a perplexing classroom problem. Most of us would agree that he has initiated a process called consultation. However, defining this process is not an easy task. A review of the literature indicates that there are as many definitions of consultation as there are approaches to it. Therefore, before defining what we mean by consultation, we discuss four general approaches to consultation.

Approaches to Consultation

Four general approaches to consultation are commonly practiced and described in the literature: organizational, advocacy, mental health, and behavioral. In the following sections, we describe the major features of each approach.

Organizational consultation.   Some consultants use a process called *organizational consultation* to bring about change in the way systems operate. As facilitators of change, these consultants focus on interventions that enhance the communication and interpersonal skills of the individual or consultee who, in turn, makes changes that accommodate the system, not the individual. For Schmuck, Murray, Smith, Schwartz, and Runkel (1975), the key question is, "What processes of organizational change will produce actual improvement in the classroom?" (p. 2). For example, an organizationally based consultant might be asked to provide advice and assistance on the way teachers and administrators make decisions (e.g., supervision, staff development, curriculum development), or on the way referrals to special education are managed by general and special educators, building administrators, and related services staff. The primary outcome of organizational consultation is an evaluation of and/or a change in how a unit's programs relate and interact with one another.

An organizational approach to consultation is based on the following assumptions: (a) schools are organizations, (b) as organizations, schools have "behavioral and programmatic regularities" that are not individual or person-specific, (c) organizational context must be considered for successful reform, and (d) major instructional innovations are associated with changes in the school's behavioral and programmatic regularities (Alpert & Meyers, 1983).

Based on these assumptions, the organizationally based consultant works toward helping groups to (a) develop clearer and more open communication skills,

(b) build increased trust and understanding in personal communications, (c) increase involvement and information sharing in decision making, (d) collaboratively identify and solve problems, (e) analyze and improve group-processing procedures, and (f) identify and arrange conflicts in a systematic manner (Schmuck et al., 1975). Therefore, the organizational-based consultant must attend to "interpersonal relations and the organizational context in which the reforms have been attempted. Any major innovation in curriculum or instructional technique implies a change in the 'culture' of the school" (Schmuck et al., 1975, p. 360). To accomplish this objective, intervention focuses on four steps: "improving communication skills through simulation," "changing norms through problem-solving in groups," instituting "structural changes through group agreements," and making "curricular and instructional changes" (Schmuck et al., 1975, p. 362).

Advocacy consultation.   A second general approach to consultation is termed *advocacy consultation.* In this approach, the consultant acts as a "collaborative peer" or expert who serves as an ombudsman for any disenfranchised group whose main objective is to reform the social system and promote social justice (Parsons & Meyers, 1984). For example, an advocacy-based consultant might be involved in seeing that the concerns of a particular special interest group (for example, parents of medically fragile children) are heard and acted on by a district policy-making group or that a unique class of students (such as Native Americans with developmental disabilities or elementary-age children with attention deficit–hyperactivity disorder) is served equitably within a district or program.

The focus of intervention is any planned action that increases political activity and knowledge. Based on "conflict theory," advocacy consultation makes the following assumptions:

1. The continuing conflict between the advantaged and the disadvantaged groups is a natural aspect of social integration;
2. In organizations such as schools or hospitals, a variety of groups disagree, and the source of these differences is embedded in social class, race, age, and sex backgrounds;
3. It is assumed, generally by institutions in society, that harmony is the natural order and that problems based on issues of class, sex, race, or economics do not exist; and
4. The acceptance of conflict as a preeminent dynamic in organizations is essential if change, resulting in a reduction of injustice and oppression, is to be affected. [Parsons & Meyers, 1984, p. 9]

Mental health consultation.   In the *mental health consultation,* the consultant assumes the role of a counselor in order to solve specific client-related problems by increasing the consultee's skill and knowledge level. Using an intrapsychic, process-oriented approach to behavior change, the consultant must help teachers resolve their own deeply rooted feelings before successful client change can be achieved. They achieve this resolution by building a relationship with the consultee and enlarging his or her perceptions and understanding of the problem.

For example, a mental health–based consultant might assist a frustrated teacher, who has a classroom of students who display noncompliant, disrespectful behaviors, by first acknowledging and confirming the teacher's feelings of defeat. Once a trusting relationship is established, the consultant can help the teacher develop a realistic understanding of the problem. According to this approach, if this change in perception does not occur, changes in teacher behavior and ultimately in student behavior are not possible.

This mental health consultation model is based on four assumptions:

1. The consultant can alter the consultee's perceptions.
2. A change in perceptions will result in a change in behavior.
3. A change in the consultee's behavior will affect the client's behavior.
4. A change in the consultee's behavior will generalize to other problem situations.

Behavioral consultation.   *Behavioral consultation,* the fourth common approach to consultation, is based on behavioral and social learning theories, which focus on behavior—that is, what the participants in the consultation process do and what products they generate. Behavior is viewed as dependent or functionally related to factors associated with the immediate environment. These interactions between learned behavior and environmental stimuli are emphasized. The "goal of behavioral consultation is to change the consultee's behavior in handling a particular client or work-related problem" (Kuehnel & Kuehnel, 1983, pp. 85–86).

The behavioral consultant is viewed as a teacher and manipulator of contingencies. To solve specific client-related problems, the consultant must increase the consultee's specific skill and knowledge level through teaching (for example, modeling, rehearsing, coaching). The consultant helps the consultee use specific behavioral interventions: (a) observing behavior and setting, (b) establishing a baseline, (c) analyzing data, (d) setting objectives, (e) implementing intervention, (f) evaluating outcomes, and (g) using systematic decision-making procedures to adjust programs. Kuehnel and Kuehnel (1983) indicate that the behavioral consultant pinpoints problem behaviors, teaches the consultee to handle the problem behaviors differently, and assumes that the consultee's perceptions and expectations will change as a result of behavior change.

Because this approach serves as the underpinnings for the approach to educational consultation taken in this book, it is discussed in detail later in this chapter.

Definition of Consultation

We might describe consultation, in its simplest form, as a general strategy used by two or more individuals to cope with or handle classroom problems. Others characterize consultation as any collaborative or joint effort to provide support or indirect service to educators that results in improved solutions to student-related problems (Alpert & Meyers, 1983; Friend, 1985; Gutkin, Singer, & Brown, 1980; Lilly & Givens-Ogle, 1981). Focusing on interpersonal and collaborative aspects, Idol, Paolucci-Whitcomb, and Nevin (1986) define consultation as "an interactive process which enables people with diverse expertise to generate creative solutions to mutually defined problems" (p. 1). These definitions emphasize "mutuality" or "shared ownership of a common issue or problem" (West, 1990, p. 27) and "reciprocity" or "equal access to information and the opportunity to participate in problem identification, discussion, decision making, and all final outcomes" (West, 1990, p. 27).

In their examination of the consultation field, Bergan and Kratochwill (1990) generally define consultation as "a problem-solving activity between the psychologist-consultant and one or more consultees (usually teachers or parents) who take the primary responsibility for providing services to a client (usually a child)" (pp. 381–382). They base this definition on their belief that most consultation is "an indirect mode of service delivery, in which the consultant works through the consultee to deliver psychological services" (p. 382). However, Bergan and Kratochwill indicate that in more behavioral approaches to intervention, programs "are delivered directly by a trained professional or with the direct assistance of the professional who works along with the service provider to help the child client" (p. 382).

To add further to this problem of definition, Meyers, Parsons, and Martin (1979) describe consultation as a technique that has six characteristics:

1. It is a helping or problem-solving process.
2. It occurs between a professional helpgiver and a helpseeker who has responsibility for the welfare of another person.
3. It is a voluntary relationship.
4. The helpgiver and helpseeker share in solving the problem.
5. The goal is to help solve a current work problem of the helpseeker.
6. The helpseeker profits from the relationship in such a way that future problems may be handled more sensitively and skillfully. (p. xii)

We define consultation as a structured series of interactions or problem-solving steps that occur between two or more individuals. Structure refers to the specific behaviorally oriented steps that must be present. Typically, these steps are sequenced around the problem-solving process (for example, problem identification, information collection and problem analysis, intervention development). Emphasis is placed on the development and modification of solutions based on information obtained from the systematic, ongoing analysis of the immediate problem context. We subscribe to a behavioral perspective that places importance on observable events and performance. In addition, we see collaboration as an outcome of a successful engagement among individuals in the operation of problem analysis and intervention development and implementation.

In this book, we use the term *consultant* to refer to any individual who is responsible for responding systematically to a request for assistance. Given our school-based focus, this individual could be a resource teacher, school psychologist, program specialist, behavioral consultant, school counselor, and so on. Although we refer to the classroom teacher as the consultee and use teacher and consultee interchangeably, the "consultee" could be any one of a variety of individuals—for example, a teacher, teaching assistant, bus driver, cafeteria worker, secretary, administrator, or parent. The consultant interacts directly with the consultee or teacher during the consultation process. Although we sometimes use the term *client,* we prefer *student* to refer to the individual at the center of the consultation process. *Student* does not imply student ownership of the problem and makes it easier to reinforce the interactive nature of problem ownership, behavior change, and intervention planning.

Narrowing the Focus

Although a teacher's immediate concern is often centered on identifying effective ways of responding to or solving a problem, most consultation approaches emphasize prevention; that is, catching the problem early and/or assisting the consultee so that similar problems can be solved successfully in the future. Our emphasis is also on prevention, which can be characterized along a continuum of three levels of prevention (Parsons & Meyers, 1984).

Primary prevention level.   The primary prevention level focuses on averting or preventing the occurrence of a problem. The emphasis is placed on larger populations of individuals or systems. For example, a new superintendent wants to implement an attendance motivation program that will prevent the high truancy and absenteeism reported by neighboring school districts. To help build this program, building principals request the assistance of a consultant who has experience in developing attendance improvement programs in public schools. Together, the consultant, building principal, and teaching staff develop an attendance motivation program that includes incentives for participation in school activities, a daily attendance data monitoring system, and an absenteeism follow-up strategy. By implementing this program, teachers hope to prevent the problem experienced by other school districts. In this example, consultation is used to "pre-correct" or avert a potential problem before it has an opportunity to develop.

Secondary prevention level.   The secondary prevention level focuses on the signs or early indicators of problems. Shortening the duration or lessening the impact of a problem before it becomes more severe is stressed at this level. For example, Ms. Hanover notices that Karsten's reading and math performance has dropped dramatically over the last four-week period and that he has isolated himself from his peers during recess and other play activities. To avoid the possible negative consequences that might result if this performance pattern is not remedied, Ms. Hanover meets with the school psychologist. Together, they develop a plan to assess whether Karsten can do the current reading and math tasks, has any physical abnormalities, or is experiencing any difficulties at home or with his peers. Using the data collected, they develop an intervention. They also decide to reserve the option of referring the problem to the building teacher assistance team for further problem solving. In this example, Ms. Hanover and the school psychologist establish an intervention based on behavioral signs that are clearly different from Karsten's usual behavior patterns. By developing such an intervention, more serious and potentially lasting consequences (such as academic failure, skill deficits, or negative peer relations) might be averted or minimized.

Tertiary prevention level.   At the tertiary level of prevention, consultation activities focus on minimizing the immediate consequences of an existing severe problem. Emphasis is placed on regaining control over a situation so remediation and prevention strategies can be developed, implemented, and evaluated. For example, the principal at Olympia High School is distressed by the 178 in-school suspensions that have been assigned over the past six months. Staff and student morale is low, and parents are demanding a change. With the assistance of a district discipline specialist, the principal schedules a series of staff meetings to assess what kinds of student misbehavior are occurring, whether teachers are responding consistently to current discipline procedures, and what might be done to reverse the current trend. Based on this information, a team of teachers develops a set of recommendations for reducing the number of in-school suspensions and preventing student misbehavior. In this illustration, the principal and her staff are experiencing a severe problem. A consultant—the district discipline specialist—facilitates a series of activities designed to minimize the immediate effects of the problem and prevent any recurrence.

These prevention levels illustrate the proactive nature of consultation. Parsons and Meyers (1984) indicate that "regardless of the immediate effects on the client or consultee, the most important goal is to provide generalized effects that help similar clients in the present and the future" (p. 10).

Consultation Service Delivery Categories

Although people's reactions to problem signs or outcomes typically initiate the process of consultation, it should be viewed as a preventive, systematic response in which individuals work together to solve a problem. However, since the focus of consultants efforts vary with the type of problem and how services are provided, the process can take many forms and can serve many different functions. These variations further characterize how consultation is defined and operationalized. Four basic consultation service delivery categories have been delineated (Caplan, 1970; Meyers, Parsons, & Martin, 1979; Parsons & Meyers, 1984).

Category I: Direct service to client.   In this category, the emphasis is placed on modifying the specific "behavior, attitudes, and feelings" of the *client* (that is, student) who is presenting a problem. The consultant is primarily responsible for collecting data and implementing interventions. For example, after interviewing Eden and observing her social interactions with peers at recess, an educational consultant might teach an interpersonal social skills group that would include Eden. Her teacher would not be asked to change. However, as Eden's skills improve, the consultant would reduce her participation in the support group.

Category II: Indirect service to client.   In this category, the emphasis is the same as in Category I, except someone other than the consultant (usually the teacher) collects performance data on the student and implements interventions. In Eden's case, the consultant would set up ways for her teacher to watch and evaluate the kinds of interactions she has with peers and to develop and implement a simple incidental teaching strategy in which the teacher would coach and give specific performance feedback to Eden whenever an interaction opportunity occurs. Within this level of consultation, the consultant provides the consultee with *specific* strategies that can be applied directly to a specific problem.

Category III: Service to the consultee.   This category is similar to Category II, but the consultant concentrates on modifying the *teacher's* general "behavior, attitudes, and feelings." The goal is "to increase knowledge, to develop skills, to promote self-confidence, and to maintain an objective view of the work situation" (Parsons & Meyers, 1984, pp. 5–6). Mr. Frankfort says that he is an ineffective teacher because he is unsuccessful at managing individual student behavior in large group contexts. A consultant helps him implement some simple group management techniques so he can be more successful. In this category, the consultant focuses on providing Mr. Frankfort with a general class of strategies that can be applied across a number of situations.

Category IV: Service to the system.   Unlike the other categories, here the emphasis is on improving the organizational functioning of a system as a whole. The Olympia High School problem that was illustrated previously is an example of a Category IV service delivery type. Due to the high number of in-school suspensions, the consultant helped the principal and her teachers rewrite their school discipline policies, establish clear roles and responsibilities for students and staff with respect to the implementation of the policy, and develop a mechanism for working with parents and other district administrative staff. In this category, the emphasis is placed on policy, administration, and system-level functioning.

Determining the service category.   A careful analysis of the problem (that is, a request for assistance and problem analysis) is necessary to determine the initial category of consultation service. Initially, more than one category might be involved, and they might change over time as progress is made. It is more efficient to think of the categories as place markers along a continuum of service delivery options. The following questions should be asked: (a) Is the problem client- or situation-specific, or is it generalized across contexts? (b) Does the organizational system function effectively? (c) Whose behaviors need to be modified? The system's, the consultee's, or the client's? (d) Who should change those behaviors? The consultee or the consultant? and (e) Is the problem experienced by others? The flow chart in Figure 1.1 shows the relationship between these questions and the consultation service categories.

CHARACTERISTICS OF A BEHAVIORAL APPROACH TO CONSULTATION

The mental health and organizational approaches to consultation are similar in that the focus is on the collaborative process of consultation rather than on its behaviors or outcomes. For our purposes, we refer to these approaches collectively as process or collaborative approaches. We will no longer be discussing the advocacy approach

FIGURE 1.1

Flow chart for determining consultation category

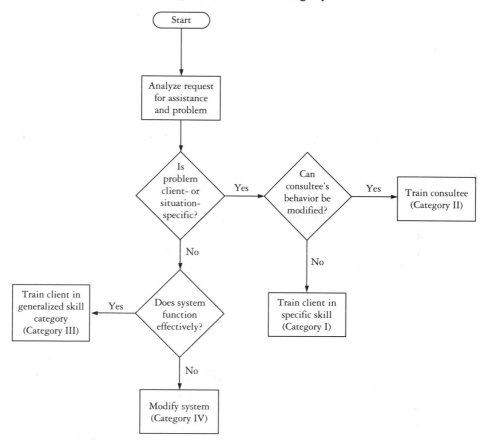

in this book because it is not typically and directly applied in classrooms and is generally not focused on teacher and student behaviors.

The literature describes many variations of the collaborative approach (e.g., Idol, Paolucci-Whitcomb, & Nevin, 1986; Sileo, Rude, & Luckner, 1988), but they all focus on evaluating and modifying how consultants and consultees view themselves and others and their relationships. The chief goal is to foster more collaborative, trusting relationships, because if this kind of relationship does not exist, consultation cannot occur.

Proponents of the collaborative approaches address classroom problems by stressing interactive communication, equal participation, and shared planning (Sugai & Carter, 1989; West, 1990). According to West and Idol (1987), this interactive process "enables teams of people with diverse expertise to generate creative solutions to mutually defined problems" (p. 389). Although a collaborative approach provides a logical and appealing process for consultation, it lacks a strong empirical base. Thus, for the purposes of this book, we focus our attention on the behavioral approach to consultation. This is not to say that collaborative approaches are not behavioral. Idol, Plaoucci-Whitcomb, and Nevin (1986), for example, include data-based decision making and functional analysis of problem situations as important features of collaborative consultation. However, the behavioral perspective plays a central role in this textbook. The major assumptions, foundations, and influences of behavioral consultation are discussed in the following sections.

Assumptions of a Behavioral Perspective

Unlike process approaches, behavioral approaches to consultation are rooted in the behavioral or behavior analytic perspective (Bergan & Kratochwill, 1990). Although process and organization are important, they are the secondary outcomes of the analysis and modification of what individuals do—that is, their actual behaviors. The focus is on what the consultee can do, as a result of training, and what changes are observed in the client's behaviors. This approach is premised on three major assumptions about behavior: it is learned, it is lawful, and it can be changed by manipulating the environment.

Behavior is learned.   Although their genetic (for example, physiology, physical attributes, temperament) and learning histories may predispose individuals to behave and learn in certain ways, they also acquire responses by interacting with their environment; that is, behavior is learned (Kuehnel & Kuehnel, 1983; Skinner, 1953; Wolery, Bailey, & Sugai, 1988). Learning can be defined "as an enduring change in behavior as a result of experience" (Wolery, Bailey, & Sugai, 1988, p. 3). Human beings learn specific ways to act, respond, and talk, for example, by watching, being told, and trying new responses. Then based on the feedback they receive, they either engage in the behaviors more or less often or modify them so they will be more useful. These behaviors become building blocks for more complex behaviors and skills, some appropriate and some inappropriate.

The child who hits others when she is angry or the teacher who raises his voice when one of his students fails to follow his directions the first time were not "born" with these behaviors. The child may have seen other children hit when they were angry, and when she tried it, she found that many people in her environment rushed to her. The teacher may have learned that speaking softly had no effect on his students, but by speaking a little louder, he could get their attention and achieve compliance.

By assuming that behavior is learned, the behavioral consultant must determine what environmental contingencies are maintaining the learned response, so that he or she can make the appropriate manipulations to change the consultee and/or client's targeted behavior. This assumption applies to both the adaptive *and* maladaptive behaviors of the teacher *and* student; that is, all behaviors are similarly acquired, maintained, and modified. For example, students learn to swear in the same way they learn to compliment. They learn how to express anger by running from the room in the same way that other students learn to express anger by asking to talk to an adult. Similarly, teachers learn to verbally reprimand students for inappropriate behavior in the same way they learn to verbally praise students who follow the rules. They also learn to attend to talkative students who disrupt lessons in the same way that they learn to ignore other students who display similar behaviors.

Behavior is lawful.   Behavior is assumed to be lawful (that is, predictable) and related to immediate social and environmental factors. Other approaches, however, attach greater importance to what goes on inside the person's mind ("black box"). Process-oriented approaches assume that learning has a distinct neurological basis that requires the individual to attend to sensory input, organize it, attach meaning to it, and integrate it with prior knowledge in order to respond (Wolery, Bailey, & Sugai, 1988). Although there may be some inherent logic to this premise, it fails to account for the influence of antecedents that set the occasion or "the stage" for responding and of consequences that affect the probability of that behavior recurring.

Since behavior is assumed to operate in a predictable manner, if environmental factors are systematically assessed, greater predictive control can be developed. In turn, the greater the predictive power, the greater the opportunity to manipulate the controlling antecedent or consequent events to affect the occurrence of the behavior. Behavioral consultants focus on assessing and manipulating these events. For example, after watching Kiyoshi interact with his teacher, we notice that he is more likely to give a correct verbal response when the teacher prompts him that a question is about to be presented (for example, "Here's your question . . ." "Now it's your turn for a question . . ."). When the teacher does not give this simple verbal precorrect, Kiyoshi will often answer incorrectly.

Behavior can be changed by manipulating the environment.   Because internal states are difficult to observe and because it is difficult to rely confidently on verbal reports of internal states, emphasis is placed on what the individual does—that is, his or her specific actions. Unlike more process-oriented perspectives that assume a change must occur *within* the individual (through communication style, cognitions, perceptions, or attitudes) before a change can be produced in observed behavior, the behavioral position assumes that behavior can be directly affected by manipulating relevant environmental factors. In Kiyoshi's case, a simple verbal cue or hint about an ensuing question has a foreseeable effect on occasioning a correct verbal response.

The active, conscious act of systematically manipulating pertinent antecedent and consequent events is called *teaching.* The better we understand how these antecedents and consequences are related to the behavior's occurrence, the greater the opportunity to facilitate learning—that is, change behavior. If meaningful change is to take place, changes in behavioral contingencies must occur (Kuehnel & Kuehnel, 1983). Thus, in the behavioral approach to consultation, teaching is a key element in changing teacher and student behavior (learning).

Foundations and Influences

Tharp and Wetzel (1969) provided one of the earliest applications of the behavioral consultation approach in their classic text *Behavior Modification in the Natural*

Environment. Using resources from school, home, and community settings, they promoted triadic relationships between consultant, consultee, and client and employed behavior analysis and behavioral contracting strategies to improve the social behaviors of young predelinquent youth. Since 1969, the behavioral consultation approach has been applied in a wide range of settings (such as schools, homes, mental hospitals, juvenile correctional facilities, public areas, residential treatment schools, community mental health centers, nursing homes, and industrial settings) and across a wide range of populations, including children, adolescents, adults, and senior citizens (Vernberg & Reppucci, 1986). In all contexts, the focus has been on the application of such behavioral principles as positive reinforcement, extinction, timeout, token economies, and contracting.

Bergan (1977) developed one of the most widely recognized applications of the behavioral approach to the consultation process. He emphasized the behaviors (especially verbal behaviors) and outcomes of consultation rather than the process variables emphasized in the collaborative approaches. Social learning principles, such as social reinforcement, modeling, and coaching, (Bandura, 1969, 1976) provide the foundation for enabling teachers to learn new skills and solve classroom-based problems (Idol & West, 1987) and to introduce specific classroom interventions that produce improvements in student performance (Reschly, 1976).

Since Bergan (1977) views consultation as "largely a matter of verbal interchange between a consultant and a consultee" (p. 29), he emphasizes measuring the type and frequency of verbal behavior. In his approach, verbal utterances are tools for assessment and the focus of behavior change. Specifically, four main verbal statement or message categories are evaluated: (a) source, such as the consultant or consultee, (b) content, such as background environment, behavior setting, behavior, or individual characteristics, (c) process, such as specification, evaluation, or inference, and (d) control, such as the elicitor or emitter. Bergan provides a detailed set of definitions, instructions, and forms for coding and evaluating these message categories, which can be used for both applied and research purposes. (For more information, see J. Bergan, *Behavioral Consultation,* Columbus, Ohio: Merrill; and J. R. Bergan & T. R. Kratochwill, *Behavioral Consultation and Therapy,* New York: Plenum, 1990.)

In his analysis and manipulation of verbal interchange, Bergan uses a four-stage problem-solving model as the basis for the process of behavioral consultation. Since these stages are included within the analytic approach, we give brief descriptions here and more detailed ones in later chapters:

1. *Problem identification* involves specification of the problem or problems to be solved in consultation, development of a measurement procedure to assess the current baseline level of the problem behavior, and determination of the size of the discrepancy between the actual and expected performance levels of the problem behavior.
2. *Problem analysis* includes identification of variables that might facilitate achievement of a solution and development of a plan to solve the problem specified in the first stage.

3. *Plan implementation* involves consultee implementation of the plan or supervision of the implementation and continued measurement of targeted behaviors.
4. *Problem evaluation* involves determination of the degree of progress toward reaching goal and plan effectiveness and includes strategies for modification, maintenance, or termination of the consultation (Bergan, 1977).

The Bergan consultation problem-solving model has a number of key features: (a) the teacher or consultee is an active participant in the problem-solving process, (b) the student or client can be involved in the problem-solving process, (c) structure is provided for meeting the knowledge and skill needs of the consultee in a variety of ways, (d) opportunities are available to make data-based (empirical) decisions, (e) problems are defined from a perspective outside of the client, (f) the controlling role of environmental factors on behavior is emphasized, and (g) evaluation of goal achievement and intervention effectiveness is stressed rather than characteristics of the client or consultee. The behavioral consultation process is organized around a series of structured interviews (that is, the problem-identification interview, the problem-analysis interview, the problem-evaluation interview), which increase opportunities to assess and evaluate the verbal behaviors of the consultation process.

The triadic and Bergan consultation models share two common features found in the behavioral consultation approach. First, the consultant directly guides and expedites all participant movements through the consultation process. In many cases, the consultant is responsible for all four stages of the process and frequently recommends a specific intervention for the consultant or teacher to try (Reschly, 1976). Second, decision making and evaluation are focused on observed improvement (or lack of improvement) in the student behavior (that is, problem resolution). Relatively little attention is given to how smooth, collaborative, or supportive the interaction between the consultant and consultee.

Although the behavioral consultation approach has accrued the greatest empirical support of all other forms of consultation (Alpert & Yammer, 1983), relatively little is known about its efficacy. For example, it is unclear to what extent each of the major steps in the model contributes to the effectiveness of the process (Fuchs & Fuchs, 1989). However, the behavioral approach provides a definable set of procedures and strategies that can function as a foundation for solving educational problems in applied settings.

FEATURES OF AN ANALYTIC APPROACH TO EFFECTIVE SCHOOL CONSULTATION

The behaviorally based "analytic" approach to consultation stressed in this textbook is not a new model, but rather the outcome of our attempt to consolidate a wide range of best practices into a comprehensive package that increases accountability, is student focused, and is highly structured. The major aspects of the analytic approach are (a) rationale, (b) key features, (c) steps in the problem-solving process, and (d) assumptions; they are described in the following paragraphs.

Rationale

The behaviorally based analytic approach to consultation described in this textbook was developed in response to deficiencies associated with other approaches to consultation. For example, process models lack objective definitions of consultant skills and fail to specify consultant behaviors. As a result, it is difficult to train consultants in the skills required to engage in collaboration (Alioa, 1983; Idol & West, 1987). Haight (1984) and Huefner (1988) also indicate that special educators are ill equipped to use those skills required for effective consultation (such as assessment, communication, intervention development and implementation, and evaluation).

In addition, other authors indicate that collaborative consultation is time consuming for both the consultant and consultee (Idol & West, 1987; Huefner, 1988; Piersel & Gutkin, 1983; Reisberg & Wolf, 1986). Since building equal and collaborative relationships (West & Cannon, 1988) is emphasized, the consultant must spend time using an assortment of communication skills, such as active listening, paraphrasing, and questioning. Idol-Maestas and Ritter (1985) reported that in-service teacher consultants named "lack of time to engage in consultation" as one of the main impediments to effective consultation. In fact, as little as 4.9% of the resource teacher's time is spent in consultation activities (Evans, 1980). Consultees or teachers may also resent the encroachment of additional consultation demands on their already limited planning time.

Last, the collaborative consultation approach is often incompatible or in conflict with the usual classroom problem in which one person (a teacher with a problem) wants what another person (a trained and experienced consultant) can provide (a novel solution) (Sugai & Carter, 1989). The actual relationship is not collaborative and nonhierarchial as Parsons and Meyers (1984) portray but is hierarchial and facilitative (Idol & West, 1987).

Key Features

A behaviorally based analytic approach to consultation has a number of defining features: a behavioral perspective, applied behavior analysis principles and procedures, a focus on outcomes, and a structured and prescribed approach to problem solving.

Behavioral perspective.   As indicated earlier, the analytic approach is built on a behavioral perspective and reflects many of the essential features of Bergan's original behavioral consultation model (1977): (a) it is focused on the behavior of the individual, (b) it emphasizes the measurement of observable behavior, and (c) it examines the relationships between observed behaviors and associated environmental factors (that is, antecedents and consequences).

Applied behavior analysis principles and procedures.   The tools of an analytic approach to consultation are derived from applied behavior analysis, which is "the process of applying and evaluating the effects of behavioral procedures" (Wolery, Bailey, & Sugai, 1988, p. 21). The applied behavior analytic approach is based on seven fundamental attributes (Baer, Wolf, & Risley, 1968):

1. *It is applied:* focuses on socially important and relevant problems.
2. *It is behavioral:* focuses on observable behavior.
3. *It is analytic:* incorporates assessment (measurement) and evaluation (decisions, rules) procedures for determining intervention effectiveness.
4. *It is technological:* emphasizes clear and detailed descriptions of interventions and teaching procedures.
5. *It is conceptually systematic:* uses procedures that originated in learning theory.
6. *It searches for effective procedures:* investigates procedures that produce useful change in student behavior.
7. *It searches for generalizable effects:* investigates procedures that facilitate the use of a skill across contexts.

When we assume that a given teaching or intervention strategy may or may not be effective for an individual, we must have the tools to assess and evaluate performance and to design and modify interventions. An applied behavior analytic perspective is useful because it enables us to define functional relationships between behavior (student, teacher, and/or consultant) and environmental events. Understanding these relationships increases our ability to predict behavior and to rearrange the environment to change the behavior. More important, the principles and procedures of applied behavior analysis provide a theoretical position and set of procedures that accommodate individual differences.

Focus on outcomes.   The analytic approach to educational consultation attempts to expand on Bergan's work and build collaborative relationships as an *outcome* of consultation. Emphasis is placed on operationalizing what consultants and consultees must do to be successful. The intricacies of the classroom environment are not ignored (Witt & Martens, 1988), rather there is a directed effort to concentrate the teacher's attention on those variables that are immediately available and can be manipulated. The analytic approach has been described as "prescriptive" (Sugai & Carter, 1989) and as an attempt to

> resolve the disadvantages associated with the collaborative model in three important ways: (a) collaboration is defined objectively and consultant behavior is described specifically, (b) prescriptiveness is increased so steps in the consultation process are completed as quickly as possible, and (c) both the consultant and consultee are reinforced positively for engaging in a time-efficient process. [p. 4]

Change in behavior (that is, the degree to which change in the student's behavior is significant) is the basis for determining success or failure. "Significant change" is determined by comparing the student's performance (outcome) against one or more standards: (a) previous baseline performance, (b) same age/grade peer performance, (c) criteria specified by important social agents, such as parents, teachers, administrators, (d) criterion specified in a behavioral objective, or (e) the social or cultural norms of the community.

Structured and prescribed approach to problem solving.   Analytic consultation is characterized by its highly organized and prescribed procedures and problem-solving format. Efficiency is emphasized in each step of the consultation process. For example, specifically designed forms are used, time limits are provided and followed, and consultants are taught to facilitate directly and lead all participants in the consultation process. Consultants take advantage of the fact that a chosen intervention is usually recommended by the consultee (Reschly, 1976) and direct the selection and development of an intervention. In addition, parsimonious and scripted intervention strategies are emphasized because of their effectiveness and the need to accommodate the working conditions of the classroom (Fuchs et al., 1990b). The analytic consultant acknowledges his or her "helpgiver" role, the "helpseeker" role of the consultee, and the "resistances" associated with individual consultations, such as time, resources, and responsibility (Piercel & Gutkin, 1983). In addition, Fuchs, Fuchs, Bahr, Fernstrom, and Stecker (1990a) support a more inclusive model of behavioral consultation because strong reductions in problem behavior are obscured.

Major Steps

The process aspect of analytic consultation is built around five major steps: (a) request for assistance, (b) information collection, (c) problem analysis, (d) intervention, (e) evaluation and follow-up. A detailed discussion of each step is covered in later chapters. These steps are defined and used to guide the consultant and teacher through a systematic and focused problem-solving process.

> **STEP 1** *Request for Assistance:* The consultant receives a request from a classroom teacher indicating a concern about a particular child or classroom problem.
>
> **STEP 2** *Information Collection:* The consultant conducts a structured interview with the teacher, directly observes the learning environment(s), and collects pertinent information.
>
> **STEP 3** *Problem Analysis:* The consultant and the teacher develop an objective definition of the problem that will be the focus of the intervention.
>
> **STEP 4** *Intervention:* The consultant and the consultee brainstorm and evaluate intervention solutions. They select an intervention, which the teacher implements.
>
> **STEP 5** *Evaluation and Follow-up:* The consultant and teacher review data, evaluate the effectiveness of the intervention, and develop maintenance strategies.

The consultant facilitates activities that result in movement through the five steps. This process is viewed as collaborative in that all outcomes are the result of cooperative efforts between the consultant and teacher. Specifically, the process provides (a) structured opportunities for exchanging information, (b) guided meetings with clearly defined and enforced time limits, purpose, and levels of participation, (c) regularly scheduled follow-up activities, and (d) specifically structured communication strategies (Sugai & Carter, 1989).

Assumptions

The analytic approach to consultation taken in this book is a structured, collaborative approach to solving educational problems. There is an overt emphasis on examining behavior and the relationships between behavior and environmental or setting factors. Efficient operation of this model is based on a number of assumptions about a behavioral and educational approach toward consultation.

First, we believe that a reliable way to conceptualize the "referral for services" is as a "request for assistance." When characterized in this way, consultation services become a service option rather than an automatic response. In the analytic approach, the explicit goal is to enhance the accuracy of assessing the problem and identifying, developing, and implementing the intervention.

Second, *collaboration* is defined as a coordinated or united effort among individuals to solve a problem rather than as a vague, poorly defined process in which the primary outcome is improved affiliations and perceptions between individuals. This definition of collaboration acknowledges the hierarchial relationship between the consultant and consultee, the need for an interaction directed by the consultant, and contingencies that influence the interactions of both the consultant and consultee. Collaboration is further characterized as a cooperative set of behaviors specifically directed at solving a problem. In addition, collaboration is viewed as the outcome of an effective problem-solving activity and interaction.

Third, a consultation "problem" exists when a teacher (consultee) engages in repeated unsuccessful attempts at remediating a student's learning and/or social behavior problem. In this context, the teacher has depleted his or her standard "bag of tricks" and must rely on the consultant's expertise, experience, and new outlook. Although this perspective tends toward an expert model of consultation, it is more appropriately characterized as a collaborative problem-solving approach that is "coached" or directed by the consultant.

Fourth, both academic and social behavior problems are "teaching problems" (Colvin, Sugai, & Patching, in press; Sugai, 1992). In most instances, academic problems are viewed as teaching problems. For example, when students have difficulty with a spelling rule, a math concept, or a reading skill, teachers give them the rule or strategy that will enable them to succeed. In contrast, social behavior problems are typically treated as compliance problems; the teacher assumes the student "knows" the right response but is "choosing" not to demonstrate it. For example, when students talk out without raising their hand, teachers typically react using negative consequences, such as verbal reprimands, to decrease the probability that the talk-out will occur in the future. In contrast, from a behavioral approach, social behavior problems are also regarded as teaching problems. As such we assess whether the student has the desired response—that is, raising his or her hand to get attention—and teach that response if it is absent.

Fifth, effective instructional procedures can serve as the foundation for effective behavior management. The literature is replete with demonstrations of the strong association between high academic achievement and low off-task behaviors. Numerous researchers (Berliner, 1985; Brophy & Good, 1986; Kounin, 1970; Rosenshine, 1983; Rosenshine & Stevens, 1986) have described the critical role played by high academic engaged time, curriculum that is delivered and aligned with the desired outcomes, meaningful feedback, effective transitions, high success rates, and careful allocation of time. Thus, the initial analysis of a social behavior problem focuses on the quality of (a) the curriculum, (b) instructional design, (c) delivery of the curriculum and instruction, (d) opportunities for students to engage and respond successfully, and (e) overall management of the instructional environment.

Sixth, measurement of performance and analysis of data are essential to the success of the problem-solving process. Although impressions, judgments, and other qualitative information provide a general "picture" or understanding of a problem or the course of an intervention program, they fail to provide the precision required for exact evaluation decisions. Precise data also facilitate communications, increase accountability, and provide a specific focus (objective) for consultation.

Finally, a goal- or outcome-oriented approach to problem solving is required to evaluate intervention success. Although the development of positive interpersonal relationships between the consultant and consultee is desirable, they are not viewed as the primary outcome of consultation. Rather the essential goals are an educationally relevant change in the student's behavior and an increase in the teacher's ability to solve similar problems independently (that is, maintenance and generalization).

SUMMARY

In this chapter, we gave a broad overview of consultation and consultation models. We presented a rationale for a behavioral and an analytic consultation approach and then described its distinguishing characteristics. A list of the chapter's key features follows:

1. The purpose of this chapter is to provide a context for understanding what consultation is and how to use an analytic approach to solve applied educational problems.

2. Consultation is a structured series of interactions or problem-solving steps that occur between two or more individuals. The process emphasizes the development and modification of solutions based on information obtained from the systematic, ongoing analysis of the immediate problem context.

3. Consultation is focused on prevention; that is, on solving problems before they become serious.

4. Consultation can consist of direct and/or indirect services to consultees and/or clients.

5. Four general approaches to consultation—organizational, advocacy, mental health, and behavioral—are described in the literature.

6. The organizational and mental health consultation approaches tend to be process or collaborative in their orientation; however, the behavioral approach focuses on the outcomes of the consultation process.

7. The behavioral approach is premised on three major assumptions: behavior is learned, behavior is lawful, and behavior can be changed through environmental manipulations.

8. Behavioral consultation is based on learning theory, systematic problem solving, and behavioral procedures.

9. A behaviorally based analytic approach to consultation tries to consolidate a wide range of best practices into a comprehensive package that increases accountability, focuses on the student, and is highly structured.

10. The analytic consultation approach is based on the behavioral perspective, uses applied behavior analysis procedures and principles, focuses on outcomes rather than process, and uses a structured and prescribed approach to problem solving.

11. The analytic consultation problem process consists of five major steps: request for assistance, information collection, problem analysis, intervention, and evaluation and follow-up.

12. The analytic approach is characterized by a number of assumptions associated with the following concepts: a request for assistance, collaboration, consultation problem, teaching problem, effective teaching procedures, measurement and data analysis, and goals and outcomes.

REFERENCES

ALIOA, G. F. (1983). Special educators' perceptions of their roles as consultants. *Teacher Education and Special Education, 6,* 83–87.

ALPERT, J. L., & MEYERS, J. (Eds.) (1983). *Training in consultation: Perspectives from mental health, behavioral and organizational consultation.* Springfield, IL: Charles C. Thomas.

ALPERT, J. L., & YAMMER, D. M. (1983). Research in school consultation: A content analysis of selected journals. *Professional Psychology, 14,* 604–612.

BAER, D. M., WOLF, M. M., & RISLEY, T. R. (1968). Some current dimensions of applied behavior analysis. *Journal of Applied Behavior Analysis, 1,* 91–97.

BANDURA, A. (1969). *Principles of behavior modification.* New York: Holt, Rinehart & Winston.

BANDURA, A. (1976). *Social learning theory.* Englewood Cliffs, NJ: Prentice–Hall.

BERGAN, J. R. (1977). *Behavioral consultation.* Columbus, OH: Charles Merrill.

BERGAN, J. R., & KRATOCHWILL, T. R. (1990). *Behavioral consultation and therapy.* New York: Plenum Press.

BERLINER, D. C. (1985). Effective classroom teaching: The necessary but not sufficient condition for developing exemplary schools. In G. R. Austin & H. Garber (Eds.), *Research on exemplary schools* (pp. 127–154). Orlando: Academic Press.

BROPHY, J., & GOOD, T. L. (1986). Teacher behavior and student achievement. In M. Wittrock (Ed.), *Third handbook of research on teaching* (pp. 328–375). Chicago: Rand McNally.

CAPLAN, G. (1970). *The theory and practice of mental health consultation*. New York: Basic Books.

COLVIN, G., SUGAI, G., & PATCHING, W. (In press). Pre-correction: A strategy for managing predictable behavior problems. *Intervention*.

EVANS, S. (1980). The consultant role of the resource teacher. *Exceptional Children, 46,* 402–404.

FRIEND, M. (1985). Training special educators to be consultants: Considerations for developing programs. *Teacher Education and Special Education, 8,* 115–120.

FUCHS, D., & FUCHS, L. S. (1989). Exploring effective and efficient prereferral interventions: A component analysis of behavioral consultation. *School Psychology Review, 18,* 260–283.

FUCHS, D., FUCHS, L. S., BAHR, M. W., FERNSTROM, F., & STECKER, P. M. (1990a). Prereferral intervention: A prescriptive approach. *Exceptional Children, 56,* 493–513.

FUCHS, D., FUCHS, L. S., GILMAN, S., REEDER, P., BAHR, M., FERNSTROM, P., & ROBERTS, H. (1990b). Prereferral intervention through teacher consultation: Mainstream assistance teams. *Academic Therapy, 25,* 263–276.

GUTKIN, T. B., SINGER, J. H., & BROWN, R. (1980). Teacher reactions to school-based consultation services: A multivariate analysis. *Journal of School Psychology, 18,* 126–134.

HAIGHT, S. L. (1984). Special education teacher consultant: Idealism versus realism. *Exceptional Children, 50,* 507–515.

HUEFNER, D. S. (1988). The consulting teacher model: Risks and opportunities. *Exceptional Children, 54,* 403–414.

IDOL, L., PAOLUCCI-WHITCOMB, P., & NEVIN, A. (1986). *Collaborative consultation*. Rockville, MD: Aspen.

IDOL, L., & WEST, F. (1987). Consultation in special education (part II): Training and practice. *Journal of Learning Disabilities, 21,* 474–494.

IDOL-MAESTAS, L. & RITTER, S. (1985). A follow-up study of resource/consulting teachers: Factors that facilitate and inhibit teacher consultation. *Teacher Education and Special Education, 8,* 121–131.

KOUNIN, J. (1970). *Discipline and group management in classrooms*. New York: Holt, Rinehart & Winston.

KUEHNEL, T. G., & KUEHNEL, J. M. (1983). Consultation training from a behavioral perspective. In J. L. Alperts & J. Meyers (Eds.), *Training in consultation: Perspectives from mental health, behavioral, and organizational consultation* (pp. 85–103). Springfield, IL: Charles C. Thomas.

LILLY, M.S., & GIVENS-OGLE, L. (1981). Teacher consultation: Present, past, and future. *Behavioral Disorders, 6*(2), 73–77.

MEYERS, J., PARSONS, R. D., & MARTIN, R. (1979). *Mental health consultation in the schools: A comprehensive guide for psychologists, social workers, psychiatrists, counselors, educators, and other human services professionals*. San Francisco: Jossey-Bass.

PARSONS, R. D., & MEYERS, J. (1984). *Developing consultation skills*. San Francisco: Jossey-Bass.

PIERSEL, W. C., & GUTKIN, T. B. (1983). Resistance to school-based consultation: A behavioral analysis of the problem. *Psychology in the Schools, 20,* 311–320.

REISBERG, L., & WOLF, R. (1986). Developing a consulting program in special education: Implementation and interventions. *Focus on Exceptional Children, 19*(3), 1–14.

RESCHLY, D. J. (1976). "School psychology consultation: Frenzied, faddish, or fundamental?" *Journal of Psychology, 14,* 105–113.

ROSENSHINE, B. V. (1983). Teaching functions in instructional programs. *Elementary School Journal, 83,* 335–351.

ROSENSHINE, B. V., & STEVENS, R. (1986).   Teaching functions. In M. C. Wittrock (Ed.), *Handbook of research on teaching* (3rd ed., pp. 376–391). New York: Macmillan.

SCHMUCK, R. A., MURRAY, D., SMITH, M. A., SCHWARTZ, M., & RUNKEL, M. (1975). *Consultation for innovative schools: OD for multiunit structure.* Eugene: University of Oregon, Center for Educational Policy and Management, College of Education.

SILEO, T. W., RUDE, H. A., & LUCKNER, J. L. (1988).   Collaborative consultation: A model for transition planning for handicapped youth. *Education and Training in Mental Retardation, 23,* 333–339.

SKINNER, B. F. (1953).   *Science and human behavior.* New York: Free Press.

SUGAI, G. M. (1992).   The design of instruction: Applications of teaching social behaviors. *Learning Disabilities Forum.*

SUGAI, G., & CARTER, J. F. (1989).   A prescriptive consultation approach. Unpublished manuscript. Eugene: University of Oregon.

THARP, R. G., & WETZEL, R. J. (1969). *Behavior modification in the natural environment.* New York: Academic Press.

VERNBERG, E. M., & REPPUCCI, N. D. (1986).   Behavioral consultation. In F. V. Mannino, E. J. Trickett, M. F. Shore, M. G. Kidder, & G. Levin (Eds.), *Handbook of mental health consultation* (pp. 49–80). Washington, D.C.: Department of Health and Human Services.

WEST, J. F. (1990).   Educational collaboration in the restructuring of schools. *Journal of Educational and Psychological Consultation, 1*(1), 23–40.

WEST, J. F., & CANNON, G. S. (1988).   Essential collaborative consultation competencies for regular and special educators. *Journal of Learning Disabilities, 21,* 56–63.

WEST, J. F., & IDOL, L. (1987).   School consultation (part I): An interdisciplinary perspective on theory, models, and research. *Journal of Learning Disabilities, 20,* 388–408.

WITT, J. C., & MARTENS, B. K. (1988).   Problems with problem-solving consultation: A re-analysis of assumptions, methods, and goals. *School Psychology Review, 17,* 221–226.

WOLERY, M. R., BAILEY, D. B., JR., & SUGAI, G. M. (1988). *Effective teaching: Principles and procedures of applied behavior analysis with exceptional students.* Boston: Allyn & Bacon.

CHAPTER TWO

Request for Assistance

School started a short six weeks ago and already Ms. Sargentti finds herself counting the days until the next school holiday. Although she has basically a good group of students, three boys make her days long and difficult. Marlin, in particular, acts out almost daily, and Ms. Sargentti is at a loss for ways to handle his behaviors. After further reflection, she begins to wonder why Marlin is even in her classroom. Maybe he is disturbed? After all, how many students crawl under their desks and hoot, or come to school smelling so badly that few students want to sit next to them or play with them during recess?

Ms. Sargentti wonders how much Marlin is learning under these conditions. The extra effort required to manage his behaviors significantly detracts from the amount of attention she can devote to other students who are equally deserving. Ms. Sargentti begins to think that the time has come to get help from someone, perhaps the counselor or special education teacher, but she is concerned that she has not tried everything that she can do.

This kind of scenario plays itself out daily in thousands of schools. Many teachers, like Ms. Sargentti, have students who challenge them to the limits of their teaching skills. Few teachers want to "give up" on a student, but frequently they do not have the means for determining when enough is enough. Although the circumstances change, the central questions remain the same: How do teachers know when they have done everything they can do? What should they do when they need assistance?

Three issues affect our ability to find solutions to these questions. First, students exhibit a range of problem behaviors; some are social and interactional, whereas others are academic and learning-oriented. Second, teachers implement many diverse programs; some help change student behavior, others fail. Finally, schools offer different ways for teachers to get help. In this chapter, we present a system that addresses these three issues under the rubric *Request for Assistance,* which is the first step in the consultation process.

24

After discussing terminology, rationale, and justification, we present a systems-level model for managing the Requests for Assistance. The chapter ends with a description of systems-level screening procedures that assist in early identification of students whose academic and/or social behaviors might cause them to fail in school. This discussion is premised on the need to

1. deliver a referral and consultation system that is overt, systematic, and organized,
2. specifically describe classroom behaviors so that an assessment system can be developed and implemented,
3. organize classroom interventions in a planned, structured, and precise manner to ensure that students receive the most effective and least restrictive program, and
4. view the consultation process from a systems-level perspective before moving into specified methods for actually assessing a particular problem behavior, or developing, implementing, and evaluating instructional programs for individual students.

TERMINOLOGY, RATIONALE, AND JUSTIFICATIONS

A *Request for Assistance* is what a teacher (or other member of the teaching staff) does when faced with a classroom problem that they have been unable to resolve. Regardless of the reason (for example, low problem tolerance, skill deficit, or lack of resources), the teacher is asking for help. He or she notifies someone that a problem exists and that additional assistance or resources are needed.

A Request for Assistance could be an informal oral solicitation made by one staff person to another or a written application to a formally established individual or body. No doubt, teachers ask each other daily for advice about materials, strategies, classroom activities, and management routines. For example, Ms. Sargentti could simply ask another teacher in that grade level for advice on how he or she has handled similar problems.

Informal consultations are valuable in building collaborative working relationships, solving many student and classroom problems, and contributing to the efficient operation of the classroom. However, we emphasize the application of more formal procedures because informal structures can be (a) highly variable and unsystematic, (b) limited in their generalized application to other similar problems, (c) limited in their educational impact for other teachers, and (d) lacking in procedural safeguards (such as accountability, documentation, or due process). We emphasize a well-documented, systematic approach to consultation, in which a specialist (or team of specialists) is responsible for helping others in the building. Formalizing the procedures facilitates quicker identification of commonalities across cases and more effective sharing of interventions with others in the building.

Although *referral* is a term commonly used for this procedure, we prefer Request for Assistance for two reasons. First, referral is widely used and firmly anchored to the special education process of refer-assess-place. Second, Request for Assistance highlights an effort to examine a problem and consider an array of solutions of which special education is one choice, *if* referral is deemed necessary.

A working model for requesting assistance is shaped by information from two important sources: special education referral research and legal mandates.

Special Education Referral Research

When building any working model, making improvements on past efforts is often useful. The data base from the special education referral research provides a wealth of information about the referral process. Consider the following findings presented by Thurlow, Christenson, and Ysseldyke (1984):

1. Procedures for referring students are generally unsystematic and highly variable, both within and between districts.
2. Low achievement alone is probably insufficient for warranting a referral and/or assessment; in many cases, behavior problems must accompany learning problems before teachers take notice and request assistance.
3. Referral decisions are quite subjective and often based on extraneous variables (such as the sex of the student or the teacher's tolerance for certain behaviors), thus increasing the variability in the decision-making system.
4. Most referred students are similar to other students who are not referred in many critical classroom behaviors.
5. Student difficulties are most often attributed to either student or home characteristics, rather than to the interaction of student, teacher, and school variables.
6. The current special education referral system is generally oriented toward a refer-to-place decision-making framework rather than a refer-to-intervene perspective. Referring teachers are rarely interested in getting help; rather they are requesting placement.
7. Systematic prereferral interventions are more the exception than the rule, and the decision-making procedure is long and often ineffective; that is, students end up in special education regardless of the data. In fact, of those students referred for assessment, 92% are actually assessed; 75% of these students, in turn, are placed in special education programs; the net effect is that 67% of all students referred are placed in special education.

The systems paradigm and structured strategies discussed in this chapter have been designed in response to these observations about the special education referral process. By attending to structured formats for operationalizing the Request for Assistance, consultants can participate in the development of a process that will result in (a) improved screening and evaluation procedures, (b) individualized instruction for students who are either difficult to teach or exhibit problem behaviors, (c) a communication system for special and general educators to use in their collaborative efforts, and (d) a cost-effective system resulting in improved student performance that costs less than traditional special education programs.

The Law

An essential characteristic of any Request for Assistance system must be attention to prevailing legal mandates. Although the law is somewhat vague in ascertaining student eligibility for special education services, two broad considerations should guide the decision-making process: the system should be fair and unbiased, and due process must be followed.

Bias and racial discrimination.   On an increasing basis over the past 20 years, schools and courts have been asked to clarify the mandates presented in law. Through many legal challenges brought primarily by parents, schools have had to ensure that all students are receiving the best education achievable in an integrated setting. One important issue to emerge from these challenges has been bias and racial discrimination. Separate but equal programs simply have not been vindicated. Any process for requesting assistance must demonstrate absolute regard for the insidious influence of biased decision making and racial discrimination. To address this concern, Heller, Holtzman, and Messick (1982) put forth the following seven guidelines:

1. It is the responsibility of teachers in the regular classroom to engage in multiple educational interventions and to note the effects of such interventions on a child experiencing academic failure before referring the child for special education assessment.
2. It is the responsibility of school boards and administrators to ensure that needed alternative instructional resources are available.
3. It is the responsibility of assessment specialists to demonstrate that the measures employed validly assess the functional needs of the individual child for which there are potentially effective interventions.
4. It is the responsibility of the placement team that labels and places a child in a special program to demonstrate that any differential label used is related to a distinctive prescription for educational practices and that these practices are likely to lead to improved outcomes not achievable in the regular classroom.
5. It is the responsibility of special education and evaluation staff to demonstrate systematically that high-quality, effective special instruction is being provided and that the goals of the special education program could not be achieved as effectively within the regular classroom.
6. It is the responsibility of the special education staff to demonstrate, on at least an annual basis, that a child should remain in the special education class. A child should be retained in the special education class only after it has been demonstrated that he or she cannot meet specified educational objectives and that all efforts have been made to achieve these objectives.
7. It is the responsibility of administrators at the district, state, and national levels to monitor on a regular basis the patterns of special education placements, the rates for particular groups of children or particular schools and districts, and the types of instructional services offered to affirm that

appropriate procedures are being followed or to redress inequities found in the system. [pp. 94–95]

Ensuring procedural safeguards.   The Request for Assistance process must give careful consideration and strict compliance to the due process and evaluation rules specified in Section 504 of the Rehabilitation Act of 1973. Citing from an Education for the Handicapped Law Report (353:238), West (1989) indicates that districts using Site Consultation Teams as the mechanism for administering referrals may be violating the procedural safeguards mandated by Section 504. Usually, these teams are established to provide interventions for students exhibiting a wide range of educational problems and often follow a fairly standard operating format. On referral to a team, information (other than formal testing) is collected and circulated among team members, who develop an "intervention plan" or recommend a full assessment for placement in special education. Although these procedures appear to be consistent with best practices and generally appropriate, the Office of Civil Rights indicates that many teams, in fact, operate in violation of required mandates. The most serious problem is often a lack of written provisions that clearly specify and detail parental involvement in the referral process.

A second problem is the inconsistent application of procedures across buildings within a district. School staffs vary in how they select team members, assign and define roles and responsibilities, and provide follow-up on team decisions and outcomes. Finally, a team's ability to provide interventions or refer for a full special education evaluation is often inconsistently applied to students within a school district. Frequently, assessment instruments and procedures are unreliable and invalid, used by untrained or poorly trained professionals, and not applied using documented procedures.

Requests for Assistance and other procedures that constitute prereferral procedures are legal, useful, and recommended. However, they are also an evaluation process and must follow procedural safeguards. Most importantly, parents must have opportunities for active involvement and participation, and procedures must be applied consistently and accurately across students, parents, teachers, and buildings.

For example, when making a Request for Assistance, Ms. Sargentti must have access to a procedure that is free of bias and discrimination, lawful and contains the appropriate due process safeguards, and consistently and accurately structured and applied. In the next section, we discuss a model that incorporates these recommendations.

A SYSTEMS-LEVEL MODEL FOR MANAGING THE REQUEST FOR ASSISTANCE

Although the focus of the classroom teacher and consultant's attention is the academic or social behavior performance of an individual student, we strongly believe that a systems-level delivery system must be in place. The actual behaviors we use to implement a procedure are only as effective and efficient as the system or structure that supports them. In fact, many classroom and student-level interventions will fail or be impossible to implement if they are designed in the absence of a systems-level support structure.

Although the building is probably the optimal unit for effective systems-level implementation, a district-level infrastructure is also needed to provide a guiding philosophy and an overall program structure for deploying services and resources. An elaboration of these assertions is beyond the scope of this discussion; however, we encourage careful consideration of their essential role in the effective and efficient operation of the consultation process. In this section, we discuss (a) aspects of developing the Request for Assistance at the systems level and (b) procedural components and guidelines for implementing the procedure at the building level.

Developing the Request for Assistance at the Systems Level

Four steps are required in developing a systems-level procedure for requesting assistance: (a) select a format, (b) operationalize the essential elements of the format, (c) develop supporting material and resources, and (d) train personnel on the format.

Select a format for the Request for Assistance.   The format or model for operationalizing the Request for Assistance may take a variety of forms. Although we stress a person- or consultant-based model, a team-based approach can also be used. Examples of person-based approaches include the Consulting Teacher (Egner & Lates, 1975; McKenzie, 1972; McKenzie et al., 1970) and the Resource/Consulting Teacher (Idol, 1983, 1989; Idol-Maestas, 1981; Idol-Maestas & Ritter, 1985). A variety of team-based models have been described in the literature, for example, Teacher Assistance Teams (Chalfant, Pysh, & Moultrie, 1979), Child Study Prereferral Intervention (Graden, Casey, & Christenson, 1985; Graden, Casey, & Bonstrom, 1985), and Mainstream Assistance Teams (Fuchs & Fuchs, 1990, 1989).

Although an informal interaction might initiate the process, a formal procedure should be used to make the actual Request for Assistance. Its operating features and procedures must be defined in functional terms and be in place before a Request for Assistance can be made to initiate the consultation process. Informal requests are frequently made. For example, Ms. Sargentti might discuss her predicament with a colleague during lunch, or she might mention it to a member of the building's teacher assistance team after a staff meeting.

We recommend a more formal format, one in which the teacher structures his or her request around a written statement containing specific kinds or categories of information and in which the student's parents are fully and appropriately informed and given the opportunity to consent. A written and guided format would increase accountability, decrease the influence of extraneous factors (such as personal emotions or biased interpretations), and standardize the request-making process within the building.

Operationalize the essential elements of the format.   When establishing an efficient format and process for making a Request for Assistance, the essential terms, elements, and outcomes must be clearly defined. The more observable and distinct these descriptions are, the easier it is to provide the information needed to initiate the request process. More important, the task of making the request should provide an opportunity for the teacher to self-evaluate the characteristics and severity of the problem. Therefore, completion of the Request for Assistance becomes the first evaluation point for determining the next step in the consultation process. For example, Ms. Sargentti may discover a simple solution, such as assigning a classroom peer tutor, for Marlin after describing his problem behaviors, assessing their severity, and identifying the conditions or contexts in which they are observed.

Operationalizing the essential elements of the format provides a specific language for making the request and initiating and completing later steps in the process; this language controls both the interactions of the participants and the procedural steps of implementation. Later in this chapter, we describe a comprehensive format that consists of four kinds of information about the problem: (a) identifying information, (b) identification and description of the problem behavior, (c) identification and description of problem context, and (d) description of previous interventions. This format is designed to initiate or set the occasion for the consultation process and enable the teacher and the consultant to conduct a preliminary evaluation of the problem.

Develop supporting material and resources.   After the components or kinds of information needed for a Request for Assistance are operationalized, a format for compiling or organizing the information must be developed. Instructions for making and completing a request and forms for writing the request must be developed. These materials should be written in a manner that minimizes open-ended responses and maximizes attainment of specific kinds of information. Closed-ended questions (for example, ''during what period of the day is the problem most severe?'') and checked or circled responses (such as ''Type of Problem: _____ Academic, _____ Social, _____ Self-Help, _____ Communication, _____ Health'') that structure the teacher's response are preferred to questions or items that leave detailing to the teacher (for example, ''Describe the problem behavior.'' ''How severe is the problem?'').

Instructions or explanations should be presented in a stepped or task-analyzed fashion. The following instructions are inadequate because they contain extraneous information.

> *Instructions:* The purpose of this form is to provide you with a structured means of making a Request for Assistance when you are faced with a classroom or student problem. Fill in each section succinctly, clearly, and completely. After you have completed each section, check to see that you have described the problem behavior in observable and measurable terms. After you have checked your responses, submit the original to the Teacher Assistance Team leader and keep a copy for yourself. After the team has reviewed your request, you will be asked to provide additional information and to meet with the team. . . .

Instructions should be simple and precise. Using a list format can make visual access to the information more efficient and effective.

1. Complete the Request for Assistance form.
2. Submit the original copy of the completed form to the Teacher Assistance Team leader.
3. Contact the team leader within three school days to set up a consultation meeting.

If the format is clearly stated, its elements are operationally defined, and all staff have directly been trained on the operation of the Request for Assistance procedure, instructions can be brief and efficient.

Train school personnel.   To increase access and ensure accurate and efficient use of the Request for Assistance process, users and participants must be trained in a systematic manner. Training should provide teachers with four aspects of the Request for Assistance procedure: (a) brief rationale and description of the assumptions and purpose behind the procedure, (b) definitions and detailed descriptions of the essential features of the procedure and the forms, (c) structured opportunities to model, rehearse, and practice the procedures for implementing the Request for Assistance, and (d) coaching and constructive feedback as the procedure is applied or implemented.

The consultant or members of the team who receive and process each Request for Assistance should provide this training. The primary goal is to ensure familiarity with and effective and efficient application of the Request for Assistance procedure.

Implementing the Procedure at the Building Level

Meyers (1973) has noted that the field of consultation would be advanced if attention were devoted to understanding the skills of the consultees as well as the skills of consultants and the process of their interactions with others. We approach consultation from an interactional and systemic framework in which the consultee or teacher must be fully informed. In part, we provide clarity by focusing only on a behavioral approach, which helps define the roles and expectations of all participants, and by describing the general steps in developing the Request for Assistance at the systems level.

However, more definition and detail are needed to operationalize the procedure at the building level; that is, how does the Request for Assistance actually function in a public school building? In this section, we further emphasize the procedural aspects of all Requests for Assistance; that is, the steps to complete in requesting assistance and the documentation needed for the system to function efficiently and effectively. We have outlined these steps in the form of questions, followed by a description of the issues. A checklist is also provided to help the consultant when assessing the completeness of each request.

Who should make a Request for Assistance?   Although most prereferral assessment and intervention systems assume that Requests for Assistance will come from teachers, we believe that all personnel are important members of the building and should be able to seek assistance for any persistent problem. For example, bus

drivers, cafeteria workers, secretaries, nurses, school psychologists, building administrators, counselors, custodians, and instructional assistants have regular
contact with students and should have access to the consultation process.

There are advantages to including everyone in the building from the beginning.
First, the complexity of and the shared responsibility for the problem and its
solution can be highlighted. Making a Request for Assistance is not a sign of
weakness. Rather it is a signal that the system is not providing an appropriate
educational experience for the student. Therefore, efforts to develop effective
programs for individual students and teachers is emphasized.

Second, when all building staff are involved, the full range of service delivery
options and strategies becomes available, not only at the Request for Assistance
phase, but also for information collection and analysis, development and implementation of interventions, and program evaluation. For too long, we have incorrectly assumed that students with behavior and learning problems are the sole
responsibility of specialists (for example, special education teachers and school
psychologists). In fact, more comprehensive problem identification (for example,
"child find") and more diverse educational programs can be developed if all school
personnel are involved. For example, a cafeteria worker sees Hailey stealing food
and lunch money from other children, the bus driver notices that Malcom sits alone
at the back of the bus with his jacket over his head, or the office secretary finds
Linda skipping physical education class and hiding in the office.

How should requests be framed?   Any Request for Assistance must be
premised on the assumptions that problem behaviors (a) are learned, (b) are
influenced by situational variables from the setting or context, and (c) can be
changed by teaching more appropriate and useful replacement responses and
manipulating the situational variables. Given these assumptions, we frame the
Request for Assistance from a situation-centered perspective rather than from a
person-centered approach (Deno, Mirkin, & Shinn, 1979).

In a person-centered approach, which is typical of most assessment perspectives in schools, the problem is seen as residing within the student. Teachers make
statements intended to interpret or explain the reasons for the student's behaviors.
Although many disabilities such as sensory impairments or physical disabilities,
reside within the person, considerable controversy exists over the validity of
person-centered interpretations for non-sensory-based disabilities (Tucker,
Stevens, & Ysseldyke, 1983).

In contrast, a situation-centered approach focuses on overt behaviors that are
visible in the classroom and are influenced and maintained by factors in the
immediate environment. These behaviors have developed interactively as a
function of the student's predisposition (namely, biological make-up and learning
history), the physical and social environment, and the teacher's interactions with
the student. Thus, rather than describing a student as learning disabled (a person-
centered label), only the specific academic behaviors and performance levels that
appear problematic are described. For example, Kelly reads orally 25 words per
minute and makes two errors per minute when reading a fourth-grade passage from
the Blue Plains Basal Reading Series; she spells 90% of her sixth-grade spelling
words correctly when allowed to spell the words out loud to a peer. Notice how

these abbreviated descriptions include both a behavior and the stimulus conditions—in this case, certain reading materials or response conditions—under which it is occurring.

A Request for Assistance should emphasize a situation-centered approach, thus focusing attention on the observable characteristics or dimensions of the problem behavior *and* the conditions under which the behavior is observed.

How should the Request for Assistance be actualized?   To help standardize the process, we advocate using a form that requests specific information about the problem from a situation-centered perspective. The sample Request for Assistance form illustrated in Figure 2.1 provides specific prompts for collecting or documenting certain types of information. Since the primary purpose of the request is to initiate the consultation process, teachers are asked to provide a general, objective description of the problem and the context in which it occurs. If deemed appropriate, a plan or structure for collecting more detailed information can be initiated based on this information.

Completion of a Request for Assistance also provides teachers with the opportunity to objectively assess the degree to which the presenting behaviors are problematic or identify new interventions. For example, while completing a request, a teacher may discover that the problem behavior is not as severe as the effects it has on his own tolerance level. Or, after completing the request, a teacher may develop a solution that does not require additional support or resources, thus temporarily sidestepping or completely avoiding the more formal consultation process.

The form should include several types of information about the problem. In our sample, the referring person is directed to provide information in five basic areas.

1. *Identifying information:* Information that identifies or distinguishes the referring teacher and the involved student.
   EXAMPLE:
   Referring Person: Ms. Sargentti
   Title: Teacher   Date: 10/25/90
   Student: Marlin
   Grade: 5th   DOB: 2/11/79   Sex: M

2. *Type of problem behavior:* The category and subcategory of problem.
   EXAMPLE:
   Social: x   Social Skills   x   Disruptive
   Self-Help: x   Hygiene

3. *Specific description of the problem:* Observable/measurable description of the problem behavior.
   EXAMPLE:
   Does his seatwork under his desk for 30–40 minutes at a time and at least twice per day. While under the desk, he gives a short (1–2 seconds) and loud hooting sound once every 5 minutes.
   Comes to school with strong body odor at least three of five school days. Few students will sit by him or play games with him.

FIGURE 2.1

Sample Request for Assistance form

REQUEST FOR ASSISTANCE FORM	Referring Person _____ Title _____ Date ___/___/____ Student _____ Grade _____ DOB ___/___/___ Sex: M F IEP: Y N

Check Type of Problem Behavior

Academic: ___Reading ___Math ___Spelling ___Writing ___Study Skills ___Other _____

Social: ___Aggressive ___Noncompliant ___Truant ___Tardy ___Withdrawn ___Disruptive
            ___Social Skills ___Self-Management ___Other_____

Communication: ___Language ___Fluency ___Articulation ___Voice ___Other _____

Self-Help: ___Dressing ___Hygiene ___Other_____

Health: ___Vision ___Hearing ___Physical ___Other _____

Provide Specific and Observable Description of Problem

Provide Specific Description of Problem Context

Where: _____

When: _____

With Whom: _____

Other: _____

Provide List of Previous Remediation Attempts

1. _____

2. _____

3. _____

4. *Specific description of problem context:* Observable/measurable description of the conditions, settings, and/or contexts in which the problem behavior is most often observed.
   EXAMPLE:
   > Where: In the classroom and occasionally in the lunchroom.
   > When: During independent seatwork, especially, during math and science.
   > With Whom: Any students, but especially with Goldie and Angel.

5. *List of previous remediation attempts:* List of strategies that have been attempted (successfully or unsuccessfully) to solve the presenting problem.
   EXAMPLE:
   > **1.** Telephone calls to parents.
   > **2.** Visits with the school nurse.
   > **3.** Verbally praising him when he is sitting in his chair.

To reiterate, the purpose of the Request for Assistance is to signal that a problem exists and that a different approach or solution is needed. The information requested on the form provides a general characterization of the problem and an opportunity for the referring person to engage in a systematic analysis of the situation. Ms. Sargentti's completed Request for Assistance form is presented in Figure 2.2. A more detailed analysis of the problem and its context occurs at the next consultation phase, Information Collection and Problem Analysis.

Who should receive the Request for Assistance? Although all building personnel should be active contributors and participants in any Request for Assistance, a specific person should be responsible for processing all requests. Three systems can be used to process requests. They can be received by (a) the building principal, (b) a member (frequently the chairperson) of a teacher assistance team, or (c) the consultant.

The advantage of having school principals receive the request is that they have a broad systems-level perspective of the building. They administer all program options, supervise the teaching staff, and are ultimately responsible for all activities and decisions that occur within the building. In some situations, however, the principal may not be the most appropriate choice because of the large number of responsibilities and tasks associated with being the administrator of a building, the considerable distance between the principal's daily duties and classroom activities, and the evaluative role principals have in their working relationships with teachers.

In contrast, in-house consultants or members of a teacher assistance team can receive requests as peers with equal status and specific knowledge of building options and classroom intervention alternatives. However, they may lack a building-level perspective. Consultants who are not part of a building staff can bring objective, outside perspectives and, possibly, fresh impressions to a Request for Assistance; however, they can also find it difficult to work efficiently with building staff until they can establish their own familiarity, competence, and trust.

Recently, more school buildings, districts, and state departments have established or recommended site-based management systems to respond to and manage problem situations (Carter & Sugai, 1989). As indicated earlier, these systems can take a variety of forms, including prereferral, teacher assistance, or

FIGURE 2.2

Ms. Sargentti's Request for Assistance for Marlin

REQUEST FOR ASSISTANCE FORM	Referring Person Ms. Sargentti
	Title _Teacher_ Date 10/25/90
	Student _marlin_
	Grade _5_ DOB _2/11/79_ Sex: (M) F IEP: Y (N)

Check Type of Problem Behavior

Academic: ___Reading ___Math ___Spelling ___Writing ___Study Skills ___Other _____

Social: ___Aggressive ___Noncompliant ___Truant ___Tardy ___Withdrawn ✓Disruptive ✓Social Skills ___Self-Management ___Other_____

Communication: ___Language ___Fluency ___Articulation ___Voice ___Other _____

Self-Help: ___Dressing ✓Hygiene ___Other_____

Health: ___Vision ___Hearing ___Physical ___Other _____

Provide Specific and Observable Description of Problem

- Crawls under desks and makes "hooting" noises.

- Does not bathe regularly.... body smells badly.

Provide Specific Description of Problem Context

Where: _In classroom_

When: _especially in reading group (after lunch)_

With Whom: _Teacher and peers_

Other: _Also occurs during math (after recess)._

Provide List of Previous Remediation Attempts

1. Ignoring   4. Telephone calls to parents
2. Parent conference   5. Visits with school nurse
3. Sent to office to talk with Vice-Principal   6. Verbal praise when seated in chair

consultation teams. These teams represent logical, efficient mechanisms for receiving and processing Requests for Assistance because of their local expertise and composition and related function and purpose in the building.

How should the Request for Assistance be handled?   After submitting a completed Request for Assistance form, the receiving person[1] should engage in a number of steps before initiating the next phase (Information Collection and Problem Analysis) in the consultation process. First and foremost, the teacher should be informed, preferably in writing, that the request was received and is being processed. If possible, the teacher should be given a specific timeline for completion of the review and, if appropriate, for initiation of the next step in the consultation process.

Next, the consultant should ensure the completeness and precision of the information provided. He or she should ask the following questions: (a) Has all identifying information been provided? (b) Has the problem type been checked? (c) Are problem descriptions presented in observable and measurable forms? (d) Has the problem context been described in observable and measurable terms? (e) Have previous remediation attempts been listed?

Finally, if the Request for Assistance is complete and accurate, the consultant should determine if the problem has been framed from a situation-centered perspective. The request should emphasize the behaviors displayed by the student and provide an objective description of the context within which the problem behaviors are observed.

A sample checklist for evaluating the completeness of a Request for Assistance is illustrated in Figure 2.3. If deficiencies are noted, the consultant should seek clarification or additional information before sending the request to the next phase. If the Request for Assistance is complete, the consultant should begin the Information Collection phase by scheduling a time to conduct a Problem Identification Interview (described in Chapter 3).

SYSTEMS-LEVEL SCREENING FOR CLASSROOM-BASED PROBLEMS

So far we have discussed the Request for Assistance from an individual, reactive perspective; that is, a person, typically a teacher, encounters a problem that causes him or her to seek help from colleagues. Usually, a student is presenting behaviors that cause him or her to be viewed so differently from peers that the teacher is compelled to respond. The teacher completes a Request for Assistance form, thus initiating the consultation or problem remediation process.

At this point, we recommend that personnel in school buildings and other systems examine ways to identify problem situations *before* they reach the level experienced by Ms. Sargentti and Marlin. Building staff should regularly and systematically screen or look for students who present academic or social behaviors that pose potential disaster if they are not confronted early and directly—that is,

---

[1] Although an administrator or team of individuals might be designated to receive a Request for Assistance, for simplicity, we refer to the individual consultant.

FIGURE 2.3
Sample checklist for evaluating the completeness of a Request for Assistance

REQUEST FOR ASSISTANCE CHECKLIST	Referring Person _____ Student _____ Consultant _____ Date ___/___/___

Y N   Has the referring person been informed that the request was received and is being processed, and if possible, been given a specific timeline?   Date ___/___/___

Y N   Is all identifying information provided?

Y N   Has problem type been checked?

Y N   Are problem descriptions presented in observable and measurable forms?

Y N   Has the problem context been described in observable and measurable terms?

Y N   Have previous remediation attempts been listed?

Y N   Has the problem been framed from a situation-centered perspective?

• Emphasis on behaviors displayed by the student.

• Provision of an objective description of the context within which the problem behaviors occurred.

Y N   Is the Request for Assistance complete?   Date ___/___/___

Y N   Has a Problem Identification Interview been scheduled?   Date ___/___/___

before the teacher's resources and skills are exhausted and a formal Request for Assistance must be made.

We suggest a preventive systems-level approach in which the emphasis is placed on systematic, formative, and efficient early intervention. It must provide a planned and comprehensive screening of the entire faculty and student enrollment. It must occur on a regular, ongoing basis. It must be compatible with the operation of classrooms and the administration of the larger school building and easy for teachers and administrators to implement. Walker and Fabre (1987) recommend that

> all children in regular classrooms should be screened regularly so that they have an equal chance to be identified for a variety of behavior problems that can interfere with their social and academic development. The teacher referral process, as it traditionally operates, does not accomplish this goal. Systematic screening procedures are needed which require the teacher to regularly evaluate all children in relation to criteria that affect their behavioral status and development. [p. 223]

We suggest three types of procedures for conducting systematic screening for problem behaviors: (a) classroom-based assessment, (b) systematic screening of social behaviors, and (c) risk factor tracking.

Classroom-Based Assessment

Generally, a systems-level approach to the assessment of academic performance and skills is restricted to the annual group administration of standardized achievement tests. Results are used to examine how large groups of students (that is, in classrooms or buildings) are performing relative to similar grade or age peer groups at the district, state, or national levels. These assessments have limited prescriptive or early identification function because they are given infrequently, do not test specific skills with much detail, and may not reflect how the student is performing in the curriculum used by the teacher.

To identify students who are having specific academic performance difficulties before a formal Request for Assistance must be made, teachers should conduct academic assessments that (a) test what is being taught, (b) are given frequently, and (c) provide prescriptive information about individual student performance. We refer to this approach as *classroom-based assessment.*

Classroom-based assessment can be very helpful as an early identification and systematic screening tool. Because the measures are brief, easy to administer, and have many alternate forms, classroom-based assessment is applicable at the systems level by teachers, trained paraprofessionals, and peer tutors. In many districts that use classroom-based assessment, full-scale norms have been established for use in eligibility decision making. However, in such applications, a normative standard is established during one year and then used in subsequent years to make comparisons with referred students. Typically, a random (or representative) group of students is assessed three times during this year, corresponding to the fall, winter, and spring academic calendar. Another variation is to screen students only once each year, in the fall. This assessment again becomes the standard against which individual student performance is compared. For additional information about this norming and standardization process, refer to Tindal and Marston (1990) or Shinn (1989).

When classroom-based assessment is used as a screener, the focus is on finding students who otherwise may not be referred because the intensity of the behavior has not reached a level that draws the teacher's attention. A typical profile is the compliant student who is quiet and well-behaved, tries hard, and is particularly fluent in oral communication skills. Her performance on written work and specific oral reading passages is well below average, but she manages to give the "right" answer or ask the appropriate questions when asked to respond orally. In this situation, the student's actual growth in reading, writing, math, and spelling is masked by her effective and appropriate social skills. Unless a standard task is administered, using a production response (that is, discrete and observable behavior) in which the student must actually read or write without prompts or assistance, she may not be identified until the problem reaches more distressful or noticeable levels.

We suggest two ways of using classroom-based assessment to systematically identify students with academic performance difficulties at an early stage: screening all students and rank ordering students. Although we present these procedures from the perspective of the consultant functioning as the administrator, any trained systems-level leader—such as the principal, curriculum specialist, or school psychologist—could oversee their implementation. The administration and scoring procedures are the same for both applications and are described in Chapter 10.

Screening all students.   This classroom-based assessment approach to screening involves creating a brief measure, such as a probe or test, that contains a wide range of items from the curriculum and is based on the difficulty or performance level at which most students in the class or grade function successfully. The general procedure consists of five steps: (a) sample the curriculum, (b) develop measures, (c) administer the measures, (d) score student performance, and (e) identify students whose performance is discrepant.

For example, Mr. Menke has three different groups of students who are functioning in three different books. Each book represents a different difficulty level (beginning, intermediate, or advanced) within the third-grade reading unit. Mr. Menke uses reading material from the advanced group's book because this group has the largest number of students. Within this book (or level), Mr. Menke selects a typical passage of 150–200 words that is most representative of the material in the entire book. Then he has each student read the passage aloud for one minute. As the student reads, Mr. Menke follows along on a copy of the passage, making specific notations for various error types. When the student finishes reading, Mr. Menke counts the number of errors and subtracts it from the total number of words read to obtain a measure of the student's rate correct. If the student's rate falls below 75 to 80 words per minute, Mr. Menke designates him or her as needing teacher attention.

In spelling and math, teachers would use similar procedural steps, although students are typically not grouped in these subject areas. In spelling, a list of words is generated that reflects high-utility words that are presented according to their frequency of usage in the English language or phonetic regularity. A sample consisting of approximately 15 to 20 words would provide an adequate number for screening students. A new word is presented once every five to ten seconds—that is, rolling dictation. A complete spelling classroom-based assessment screening would require about two to three minutes to administer. After the dictation, the students' papers are scored for correct spelling, namely, correct letter positions and sequences. Students whose performances indicate a poor phonetic spelling base or a very high number of misspelled words are referred for more detailed and formal assessments.

In math, computation problems appropriate for the students' age and grade can be taken from the curriculum in proportions that approximate the frequency with which they appear in the instructional materials. To use time efficiently, the measure can be multi-operational; that is, it can include two different problem types. For example, in second grade, the problems can include both addition and subtraction, whereas fourth grade would include both multiplication and division. To ensure the measure is biased in favor of minimal skills, the problem types can sample slightly larger proportions of facts and early, prerequisite procedures (for example, borrowing and carrying). Administration again can be as short as two to three minutes. Students are asked to complete as many problems as possible. For each problem, the number of digits that have been positioned in the correct place value are counted. If the student displays few basic skills (math facts) or misapplies basic algorithms, further assessments should be conducted.

Finally, to screen for written expression, the teacher presents a story starter and directs the students to read the starter and write a continuation of the story without editing or revising. First, compositions are scored qualitatively; they are sorted into five piles: extremely competent, above average, average, below average, and incompetent. Judgments are based on writing dimensions, such as organization-cohesion, conventions-mechanics, and basic communication competence. The compositions of those students who fall in the lowest two categories should also be scored for the number of words spelled correctly and in correct sequence.

To conduct a comprehensive classroom-based assessment screening of reading, math, spelling, and written expression requires about an hour for the oral reading fluency measure and an additional 15 minutes for the spelling, math, and writing measures. All measures (except reading) can be group administered. When using classroom-based assessment as a screener, scoring may take the most time. Thus, it may be more efficient to use subjective ratings or judgments in sorting students' performances and quantitative scoring of those students whose performance falls in the lowest two ratings; that is, provide a numerical summary of the student's performance. For example, the following procedures can be used:

1. Sort the students' protocols into five piles using a normal distribution; that is, a few students should be placed in the extremely high and extremely low pile, more students should be placed in the somewhat high and somewhat low piles, and most students should be placed in the middle pile.
2. For those students who fall into the two lowest groups, apply quantitative analysis to their work.

These procedures work particularly well for reading and written expression, where the scoring is done concurrently with administration or is too involved for all students' performance to be scored.

Ranking students on achievement and classroom conduct.   In this second screening procedure, rather than assessing all students to identify those discrepant in academic skills, students are ranked from highest to lowest based on the teacher's judgment of achievement and classroom conduct. Thus, only those students performing in the lower half are examined; that is, those exhibiting the lowest achievement and poorest classroom conduct. After these students have been identified, the classroom-based assessment screening procedures described earlier are used to assess individual performance.

This procedural variation is more encompassing than the Request for Assistance, which is based on an individual student, and less involved than screening the entire school. Without a systematic screening procedure, teachers may overlook students who need additional instructional assistance. However, a systematic rank-ordering strategy would probably identify these students, because it is unlikely that they would be placed in the upper half of the class. Other researchers have found that teacher rankings of child academic achievement are accurate and predict status on specific criterion measures, especially at the extremes of the distributions (Greenwood et al., 1979; Walker & Fabre, 1987).

Summary.   Regardless of which classroom-based assessment procedures used (whole class or class ranking), the objective is to assume a proactive, preventive position in which low-performing students can be identified *before* their performance places them at significant risk for school failure. Early screening gives teachers the opportunity to develop and present remedial instruction so more intensive specialized attention and services are not required.

Classroom-based assessment procedures take advantage of the teacher's classroom experience and knowledge and emphasize the curriculum found in the teacher's daily instructional planning. Although teachers may effectively apply these academic screening procedures in their individual classrooms, we recommend that teachers within grade levels (for example, all third-grade teachers or all math teachers of eighth-grade students) cooperate to develop valid pictures or criteria of what constitutes minimum competency in a given academic area—especially in reading, math, spelling, and written expression. It is important that teachers realize that interpretations of their students' performance are closely related to an analysis of the curriculum or instructional expectations for their classes.

Systematic Screening of Social Behaviors

Generally, the systematic assessment of social behaviors is rarely conducted at the systems level. School systems are usually operated in a manner that allows student social behavior problems to reach a point where the teacher or building administrator is forced to respond because previous intervention attempts have been unsuccessful and resources or standard alternatives have been exceeded. Marlin's situation is a good example of this mode of operation. Two examples of procedures used to screen systematically for social behavior are described in this section.

Hill Walker and his associates at the University of Oregon have developed an instrument and procedure that illustrates how teachers can screen for social behavior problems in a systematic and comprehensive manner (Walker, Severson, & Haring, 1985; Walker, Severson, Haring, & Williams, 1986). The Systematic Screening for Behavior Disorders (SSBD) consists of three screens or "gates" that provide a precise, methodical way to identify students at-risk for social behavior failure.

The SSBD screens for both "externalizing" and "internalizing" behavior problems. Externalizing problems include behaviors typically labeled as aggressive, noncompliant, argumentative, hyperactive, or impulsive. Teachers are less willing to tolerate these behaviors and are more likely to respond to them at full strength. A unique feature of the SSBD screening procedure is a forced examination of behaviors that are usually overlooked or tolerated, but are equally important. These internalizing problems or behaviors are tagged as shy, avoiding, withdrawn, or depressed.

The basic SSBD procedure consists of three "stages," which are illustrated in Figure 2.4. For a detailed description of the procedures, refer to Walker, Severson, and Haring (1985). At Stage 1, teachers are asked to rank order (from highest to lowest) the ten students in the classroom whose characteristic behavior is best described as *externalizing*. Teachers make a similar list for students whose behaviors are best characterized as *internalizing*.

At Stage 2, teachers examine the specific kinds of behaviors displayed by the three students who rank highest on the externalizing list and the three who rank highest on the internalizing list. Three simple rating instruments—critical events, adaptive behavior, and maladaptive student behavior—are used. At Stage 3, those students whose behavior ratings exceed the normative criteria at Stage 2 are directly observed in the classroom (the amount of academic engaged time) and during recess (peer adjustment). Students who exceed Stage 3 age and sex normative criteria are referred for further evaluation and possible referral for specialized services.

A district-level screening procedure incorporating features similar to the SSBD was developed in a large metropolitan area of Western Australia to identify students with high-risk academic and social behaviors at the classroom, building, and district levels (Sugai & Evans, 1991). Three-hundred-and-two elementary teachers completed a screening instrument called the Screening for Students with High-Risk Behaviour (SSHRB); see the sample in Figure 2.5. Using a list of the students on their class roll, preschool, kindergarten, and first- through seventh-grade teachers were asked in Step 1 to identify one student who was "about average" in each of three academic areas (reading, math, and language arts), three social behavior areas (with peers, with adults, and with self), and one physical/sensory area; and in Step 2 to make judgments (+ for above average, 0 for average, − for below average, = for significantly below average) about each student on their class roll based on the curriculum being used, the average student identified in Step 1, and the behaviors/performance of the larger peer group. The use of teacher judgments and ratings on the behavior of their students has been shown to be accurate and

FIGURE 2.4

Multiple-gating assessment procedure for identifying behavior-disordered students

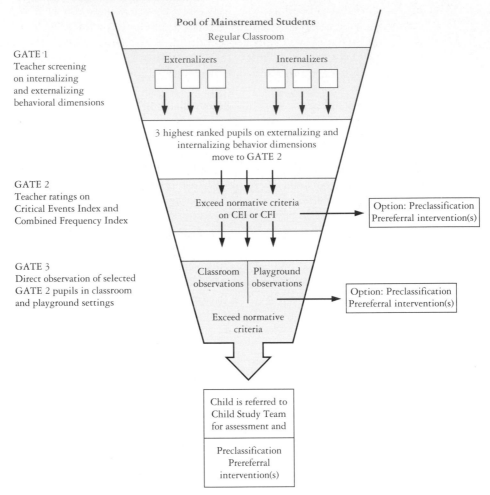

Pool of Mainstreamed Students
Regular Classroom

GATE 1
Teacher screening
on internalizing
and externalizing
behavioral dimensions

Externalizers   Internalizers

3 highest ranked pupils on externalizing and
internalizing behavior dimensions
move to GATE 2

GATE 2
Teacher ratings on
Critical Events Index and
Combined Frequency Index

Exceed normative criteria
on CEI or CFI

Option: Preclassification
Prereferral intervention(s)

GATE 3
Direct observation of selected
GATE 2 pupils in classroom
and playground settings

Classroom   Playground
observations   observations

Option: Preclassification
Prereferral intervention(s)

Exceed normative
criteria

Child is referred to
Child Study Team
for assessment and

Preclassification
Prereferral
intervention(s)

Reprinted by permission from Walker, H. M., Severson, H. (1990). Systematic Screening and Identification of Behavior Disorders. Longmont, CO: Sopris West.

reliable (Gresham & Elliott, 1987; Gresham, Elliott, & Black, 1987; Walker et al., 1988).

Results from this project were found to be reliable and valid and to provide individual teachers with an estimate of which students were most at-risk in three academic, three social behavior, and one physical/sensory areas (Sugai & Evans, 1991). In addition, building administrators obtained an estimate of the percentage of students within and across grade levels who were judged as having high-risk characteristics. District administrators, in turn, were able to identify school buildings and geographic areas with specific high-risk student patterns. Based on

FIGURE 2.5

**Sample worksheet from the Screening for Students
with High-Risk Behavior**

SCREENING WORKSHEET

Teacher coding: _____   Grade: _____

Date: _____

Coding: + Above average, doing great (above curriculum/peers)

0 Average, doing fine (same as curriculum/peers)

− Below average, okay but struggling (slightly behind curriculum/peers)

= Significantly below average (>2 years below curriculum/peers)

_____ Number of students on class roll

Student No.	Academic			Social			Physical/Sensory
	Reading	Math	Language	With Peers	With Adults	With Self	
1							
2							
3							
4							
5							
6							
7							
8							
9							
10							
11							
12							
13							
14							
15							
16							
17							
18							
19							
20							

these outcomes, prevention and intervention programs could be developed at the student, classroom, building, and district levels. On average, each teacher took about 15 minutes to complete the screening instrument, giving evidence to the efficiency and utility of the SSHRB procedure.

Screening procedures, like the SSBD and the SSHRB, that screen for academic and social behavior problems in a comprehensive and systematic manner increase opportunities for early identification and intervention. Problematic behaviors can be flagged before they increase in intensity and frequency. Consultants should consider using such systems-level screening procedures in order to develop a more proactive perspective and to use the Request for Assistance more efficiently and appropriately.

Risk Factor Tracking

Although less comprehensive and accurate than classroom-based assessment and systematic screening of behavior disorder procedures, risk factor tracking provides another approach to systems-level screening. Risk factor tracking takes advantage of indicators of student performance that are routinely available in public school buildings; examples include the number of office referrals, grade point average, number of failed classes or subjects, days of absenteeism, number of tardies, and number of grade retentions. These factors are commonly used to characterize students who are high risk for academic and/or social behavior failure. Typically, examination of these data occurs at the end of major grading intervals like the end of a semester or academic year.

We suggest that classrooms and school buildings develop mechanisms that provide for immediate, ongoing collection *and* evaluation of risk factors, so that remedial programs can be developed and implemented before a problem intensifies and more expensive interventions are required. The first step in the development and implementation of a risk factor–tracking procedure consists of identifying classroom and school-related risk factors (such as absenteeism, office referrals, or subject/class failure) that typically characterize students who are at-risk for or experience school failure. Because of cultural differences, resources, grade level, and so on, the actual factors selected by an individual school might vary. A review of the performance profiles of students who have experienced school difficulties or failure or who have needed specialized assistance can help make the factor selection process more systematic and relevant.

The next step is to develop a continuous, systematic method of collecting and managing data on each identified risk factor. Attempts should be made to incorporate existing data collection procedures. For example, daily attendance data are generally collected early in the morning, office referrals are usually filled out immediately after an incident occurs, and grades are recorded in grade books on an ongoing basis. With the advent of computer-managed school offices and classrooms, management of these data can be narrowed to data entry and output. An office or student assistant can oversee the input of most attendance and tardy data, once a simple data management or spreadsheet program has been established.

Once the data collection and management system is implemented, a specific set of data decision rules should be generated. The development of these rules is essential to the efficient operation of a risk factor–tracking procedure because it provides a structure for continuous evaluation and identification. Without data decision rules, judgments are delayed and become haphazard and qualitative. A data decision rule is a simple but specific guide for making a judgment about a student's performance (White & Haring, 1980). Data decision rules work like the setting on a furnace thermostat. After a desired temperature is set (for example, 72° F—the data decision rule), the furnace turns itself on if the temperature drops below the setting and off if the temperature reaches the setting. Without the thermostat, the furnace would operate in an unregulated manner until the temperature becomes so uncomfortable that a remedial response is required.

Like thermostat settings, data decision rules help determine when a student's performance has reached some minimum acceptable criterion. For example, a school might use a three-day absenteeism rule or a two-office referral rule. The instant any student is absent from school for three days or has two office referrals, his or her name is "flagged" and overall school performance is reviewed. The actual numerical values used for rules should be individualized for the school or classroom in which they are being applied; however, we recommend relatively conservative values (for example, two or three days or incidents). It is better to be overly cautious than too late. Data decision rules provide immediate, systematic opportunities to review student performance and develop early interventions.

Empirically based data decision rules can be easily established using existing school data. For example, in a recent district program evaluation, six types of risk data were examined: tardiness, absences, attendance, office visits, disruptions, and suspensions (Tindal, 1990). Then, the data on four groups of students—special education, Chapter I, low-achieving regular education, and regular education—were compared. Significant differences were found in tardiness, absences, attendance, and office visits. Special education and Chapter I students were tardy twice as much as regular education students (over three days versus just over one day). They were also absent nearly ten days versus six days for regular education students. Those students in specialized programs had ten fewer days of attendance and were sent to the office an average of three times, whereas regular education students were sent only once; likewise, special education students, on average, displayed disruptive behavior twice as often as regular education students who averaged only one disruptive episode. The evaluation found that the averages generated by the performance of regular education students provided an excellent data base for risk factor tracking (Tindal, 1990).

To review, developing empirical data decision rules for a risk factor–tracking system requires the completion of two important steps. First, the general education population needs to be analyzed and compared with groups receiving specialized programs. If significant differences are present, data from the different groups should not be collapsed; instead, separate averages should be maintained. Second, an average to use as a standard for flagging students who are at-risk needs to be established. Typically, this average is represented by the lowest functioning yet successful regular education group. Thus, the standard is based on a local group of students, who presumably are not at-risk. When students reach a level of performance that exceeds this value, they are, de facto, at-risk.

After data decision rules are established, a systems-level structure or procedure for evaluating a student behavior problem should be installed. As discussed earlier, a team of teachers (namely, the teacher assistance team) can be used; however, a consultant or other combination of professionals also might be utilized. The primary function of this team or individual would be to evaluate the data for any student whose performance breaks the data decision rule and to make a recommendation about further action; for example, continue monitoring the student's performance, collect more data, review records, meet with the student's teacher, suggest a formal Request for Assistance, or recommend an intervention.

Risk factor tracking is a relatively simple procedure of schoolwide screening that employs available performance data to pinpoint students who are at-risk for academic or social behavior failure. However, because risk factor tracking is still a broadly based method of screening, we strongly recommend that schools move toward classroom-based assessment and systematic screening of social behavior procedures. These screening methods are more comprehensive and sensitive.

Regardless of the systems-level screening procedure employed, the goal is to identify students whose performance is problematic and to develop remedies that decrease the probability that more intensive interventions, including a formal Request for Assistance, will be required.

SUMMARY

In this chapter, we presented a specific model for enabling teachers to request assistance, specifically at the building level. We have focused on a system that is overt, systematic, organized, and founded on a systems-level perspective. Procedures for screening students with high-risk academic and social behavior problems were also described. A list of the chapter's key features follows:

1. The purpose of this chapter was to describe a systems-level approach for managing the Request for Assistance.

2. A Request for Assistance is a formal, written solicitation made by any staff person to a formally established person or body.

3. All members of a school building should be able to seek assistance for any persistent problem.

4. A model for any Request for Assistance system must avoid the problems noted in research on the special education referral process and follow prevailing legal mandates that demand a fair and unbiased process in which due process safeguards are observed.

5. A Request for Assistance procedure can only be as effective and efficient as the system or structure that supports it.

6. Development of a systems-level procedure for requesting assistance requires four steps: (a) select a format, (b) operationalize the essential

elements of the format, (c) develop supporting material and resources, and (d) train personnel on the format.

7. Any Request for Assistance is premised on the assumptions that problem behaviors (a) are learned, (b) are influenced by situational variables of the setting or context, and (c) can be changed by teaching more appropriate responses and manipulating situational variables.

8. The Request for Assistance should be initiated in a form that asks the teacher to provide a general, objective description of the presenting problem and the context in which it occurs.

9. To standardize the process, one person should be designated to process all requests.

10. When a Request for Assistance is submitted, completeness and accuracy should be checked. Determining the appropriateness of the Request for Assistance should occur after sufficient information is collected and analyzed.

11. A Request for Assistance should emphasize a situation-centered approach in which attention is focused on the observable characteristics of the problem behavior and the conditions under which occurs, rather than a person-centered approach in which the problem is said to reside within the student or teacher.

12. Systems-level screening for classroom-based problems identifies potential problem situations before they reach a level requiring more intensive interventions. Three screening procedures were illustrated: (a) classroom-based assessment, (b) systematic screening of social behaviors, and (c) risk factor tracking.

REFERENCES

CARTER, J., & SUGAI, G. (1989). Survey on prereferral practices: Responses from state departments of education. *Exceptional Children, 55,* 298–302.

CHALFANT, J. C., PYSH, M. V., & MOULTRIE, R. (1979). Teacher assistance teams: A model for within-building problem solving. *Learning Disability Quarterly, 2,* 85–96.

DENO, S. L., MIRKIN, P. K., & SHINN, M. (1979). *Behavioral perspectives on the assessment of learning disabled children.* (Monograph No. 12). Minneapolis: University of Minnesota, Institute for Research on Learning Disabilities.

EGNER, A. N., & LATES, B. J. (1975). The Vermont Consulting Teacher Program: A case presentation. In C. Parker (Ed.), *Psychological consultation: Helping teachers meet special needs* (pp. 31–53). Reston, VA: Council for Exceptional Children.

FUCHS, D., & FUCHS, L. S. (1989). Exploring effective and efficient prereferral interventions: A component analysis of behavioral consultation. *School Psychology Review, 18,* 260283.

FUCHS, D., & FUCHS, L. S. (1990). Mainstream assistance teams: A scientific basis for the art of consultation. *Exceptional Children, 57,* 128–139.

GRADEN, J. L., CASEY, A., & BONSTROM, O. (1985). Implementing a prereferral intervention system: Part II. The data. *Exceptional Children, 51,* 487–496.

GRADEN, J. L., CASEY, A., & CHRISTENSON, S. L. (1985). Implementing a prereferral intervention system: Part I. The model. *Exceptional Children, 51,* 377–387.

GREENWOOD, C., HOPS, H., WALKER, H. M., GUILD, J., STOKES, J., & YOUNG R. (1979). Standardized classroom management program: Social validation and replication studies in Utah and Oregon. *Journal of Applied Behavior Analysis, 12,* 235–254.

GRESHAM, F., & ELLIOTT, S. (1987). The relationship between adaptive behavior and social skills: Issues in definition and assessment. *Journal of Special Education, 21,* 167–181.

GRESHAM, F., ELLIOTT, S., & BLACK, F. (1987). Teacher-rated social skills of mainstreamed mildly handicapped and nonhandicapped children. *School Psychology Review, 16,* 78–88.

HELLER, K. A., HOLTZMAN, W. A., & MESSICK, S. (1982). *Placing children in special education: A strategy for equity.* Washington, D.C.: National Academy Press.

IDOL, L. (1983). *Special educator's consultation handbook.* Austin: PRO-ED.

IDOL, L. (1989). The resource consulting teacher: An integrated model of service delivery. *Remedial and Special Education, 10*(6), 38–48.

IDOL-MAESTAS, L. (1981). A teacher training model: The resource/consulting teacher. *Behavioral Disorders, 6,* 108–121.

IDOL-MAESTAS, L., & RITTER, S. (1985). A follow-up study of resource/consulting teachers: Factors that facilitate and inhibit teacher consultation. *Teacher Education and Special Education, 8,* 121–131.

MCKENZIE, H. (1972). Special education and consulting teachers. In F. Clark, D. Evans, & L. Hamerlynck (Eds.), *Implementing behavioral programs for schools* (pp. 103–125). Champaign, IL: Research Press.

MCKENZIE, H., EGNER, A. N., KNIGHT, M. F., PERELMAN, P. F., SCHNEIDER, B. M., & GARVIN, J. S. (1970). Training consulting teachers to assist elementary teachers in the management and education of handicapped children. *Exceptional Children, 37,* 137–143.

MEYERS, J. (1973). A consultation model for school psychological services. *Journal of School Psychology, 11*(1), 5–15.

SHINN, M. S. (1989). *Curriculum-based measurement: Assessing special children.* New York: Guilford Press.

SUGAI, G., & EVANS, D. (1991). *Using teacher perceptions to screen for primary students with high risk behaviours.* Unpublished manuscript. Mount Lawley (Australia): Edith Cowan University.

THURLOW, M., CHRISTENSON, S., & YSSELDYKE, J. (1984). Referral research: An integrative summary of findings. Research Report No. 141. Minneapolis: University of Minnesota Institute for Research on Learning Disabilities.

TINDAL, G. (1990). *Evaluation report of MERGE: Maximizing educational remediation within general education.* Unpublished report. Eugene: University of Oregon.

TINDAL, G., & MARSTON, D. (1990). *Classroom-based assessment: Evaluating instructional programs.* Columbus, OH: Charles Merrill.

TUCKER, J., STEVENS, L., & YSSELDYKE, J. (1983). Learning disabilities: The experts speak out. *Journal of Learning Disabilities, 16,* 6–14.

WALKER, H. M., & FABRE, T. R. (1987). Assessment of behavior problems in the school setting: Issues, problems, and strategies revisited. In N. G. Haring (Ed.), *Assessing and managing behavior disabilities.* Seattle: University of Washington Press.

WALKER, H.M., & SEVERSON, H. H. (1990). *Systematic screening and identification of behavior disorders.* Longmont, CO: Sopris West.

WALKER, H. M., SEVERSON, H., & HARING, N. G. (1985). *Standardized screening and identification of behavior disordered (SSBD) pupils in the elementary age range: Rationale, procedures and guidelines.* Eugene: University of Oregon, Center on Human Development, Clinical Services Building.

WALKER, H. M., SEVERSON, H., HARING, N., & WILLIAMS, G. (1986). Standardized screening of behavior disordered (SSBD) pupils in the elementary age range. *ADI News, 5*(3), 15–18.

WALKER, H. M., SEVERSON, H. J., STILLER, B., WILLIAMS, G., HARING, N. G., SHINN, M., & TODIS, B. (1988). Systematic screening of pupils in the elementary age range at risk for behavior disorders: Development and trial testing of a multiple gating model. *Remedial and Special Education, 9*(3), 8–14.

WEST, J. F. (1989). Prereferral consultation teams found in violation of section 504 regulations. *The Consulting Edge, 1*(2), 1–2.

WHITE, O. R., & HARING, N. G. (1980). *Exceptional teaching* (2nd ed.). Columbus, OH: Charles Merrill.

PART II

SOCIAL BEHAVIOR PROBLEMS

CHAPTER THREE

Problem Identification and Information Collection

Mr. Prine, a fifth-grade teacher at Beattle Elementary School, has tried all his "best tricks" to motivate Abbey. However, after repeated failures to change her behaviors and performance in class, Mr. Prine completes a Request for Assistance and sends it to Ms. White, the district educational consultant. On receipt of the request, Ms. White calls Mr. Prine and arranges a meeting to review the request, clarify the problem, and schedule classroom observations.

Ms. White and Mr. Prine are at the Problem Identification and Information Collection stage of the consultation process. After receiving a Request for Assistance and deciding that further consultation action is appropriate, consultants collect information that will enable them to conduct an organized analysis of the problem and develop an intervention that has a high probability of success. Without this information, the selection and development of a useful intervention becomes a trial-and-error enterprise that can squander time and resources and unnecessarily frustrate participants.

In this chapter, we emphasize the assessment and analysis of critical elements of the instructional setting or context, teacher's instructional behaviors, and student social behaviors. We examine academic assessment and analysis procedures in Chapter 8. However, we consider both academic and social behaviors as closely related and not easily separated in the applied setting. From this perspective, we also believe that best instructional practices must be in effect before considering comprehensive social behavior interventions.

In this chapter, we also discuss information collection and data analysis principles and procedures for social behavior. Two major sections are covered: a review of assessment points of focus, terminology, and definitions; and strategies for conducting a problem identification interview.

FOCAL POINTS, TERMINOLOGY, AND DEFINITIONS

Whenever we measure something—whether it is academic performance, a permanent product, or a social behavior—we engage in assessment. To be effective and efficient, this information-gathering process must be conducted in a systematic, objective manner. Assessment information is used for a variety of purposes. First, it can be used to describe a student's current level of functioning. For example, a consultant reports to members of a building Teacher Assistance Team that Candy takes items that belong to other children at an average rate of six items a day, or one per hour. Second, assessment information can also help identify factors that might be affecting or influencing a student's performance. For example, after conducting a classroom observation, the consultant observes that Rodrigo says "no" to his teachers more often when Pierre and Luis are his neighbors. Third, a consultant can use assessment information to determine a student's direction of progress (that is, improving, deteriorating, staying the same). For example, after four consecutive observations in the lunchroom, Ms. Sims notes that Gladys is spending more and more time sitting alone, while her friends play outside.

Fourth, teachers can use assessment information to help evaluate the effectiveness of an intervention. Ms. Phillips noted that Randall used to arrive to class three to four minutes late each day, but after five days on a special contract, he has not been late to a single group lesson. Finally, assessment information can be used to communicate effectively with others. For example, Ms. Phillips also uses her assessment information to let Randall's father know that his son's school performance is improving and to tell the principal that Randall deserves special recognition for his punctuality.

Before considering techniques to achieve these outcomes, we are going to discuss some definitions and points of focus that are the foundation for the assessment and analysis practices of an analytic approach to consultation. For assessment and evaluation to be effective, we must focus on the following:

1. Observable and discrete behaviors
2. Direct and formative observation procedures
3. Assessment of immediate setting factors and their relationship to behavior
4. An ecological assessment perspective

Focus #1: Observable and Discrete Behaviors

We recommend that teachers and consultants focus on observable, discrete behaviors. A discrete behavior has a clear beginning and end that allows the observer to discern the extent to which it has occurred. It also has measurable dimensions that can be used to communicate information about the behaviors to others (Wolery, Bailey, & Sugai, 1988). An observable behavior can be described using one or more of six dimensions: rate, duration, latency, locus, topography, and intensity. Definitions and examples for each dimension are given in Box 3.1.

When dimensions are used to define a behavior in observable terms, the result is an *operational definition*. Using operational definitions helps make communications between consultants and teachers objective and informative, minimize indi-

BOX 3.1
Definitions and examples of dimensions of behavior

DIMENSION	DEFINITION	EXAMPLE
Rate	Frequency or number of responses	Maggie whispers with her neighbors seven times in a 30-minute reading group.
Duration	Length or elapsed time of behavior	Glenda argues with her teacher for 3.5 minutes on the average.
Latency	Elapsed time between an antecedent and beginning of a response	Terrance takes 5 minutes, on the aveage, to begin complying with teacher directions.
Locus	Location or place where a response is observed	Most of the time, Roger is on the bus when he gets into verbal arguments with his peers.
Topography	Shape, contour, or appearance of a response	When Bobby hits other children, he strikes them with his index and middle fingers with an open palm.
Intensity	Force, strength or magnitude of a response	When Heloise talks out, students and teachers in neighboring classrooms can hear her voice.

vidual bias and opinion, and redirect blame for the problem away from the student: attention is focused on the behavior and setting in which the behavior is observed.

In addition, greater accountability can be established by focusing on observable behaviors. For example, Roslind and her teacher are discussing the conditions of a new behavior contract. Roslind says she is very sorry for repeatedly forgetting her homework, but promises to bring in her next homework assignment finished and on time. As she "crosses her heart and hopes to die," she tells her teacher that "it's as good as done." Roslind's teacher says she appreciates her verbal promises, but the bottom line is seeing the homework assignment (the dimensions are topography and latency)! Another common scenario is Max who verbally promises to "never swear or talk out in class again." Ultimately, what is important is that he raises his hand more and talks out less (the dimensions are frequency and topography).

Focus #2: Direct and Formative Observation Procedures

Although many types of data collection procedures are available to the consultant, we emphasize observation procedures that are direct and formative. In a "direct" observation procedure, the consultant or teacher observes actions, behaviors, and interactions *firsthand*. This is in contrast to indirect methods, in which information is collected from archival records (such as confidential files or cumulative records), interviews and self-reports, or traditional standardized test formats. For example, Mr. Garcia makes a Request for Assistance, meets with a consultant, and indicates that Celeste disrupts his lessons and is socially withdrawn (indirect information based on verbal report and interview). After reviewing Celeste's psychological file, the consultant reads that other teachers have reported similar problems (indirect information based on archival records). When visiting Mr. Garcia's classroom and reading group, the consultant watches Celeste leave the group three times during a 30-minute lesson (direct observation). The consultant notes that Celeste leaves each time Mr. Garcia asks her to give an oral response in front of her peers (direct observation).

Although directly collecting information can sometimes be time consuming and intrusive, it lets the consultant observe the problem context objectively—that is, free of secondhand interpretation or individual subjectivity. Of course, a consultant's own observation analysis is affected by his or her individual interpretation and criteria, but it is at least one step closer to the actual problem context. By observing the situation directly, the consultant avoids having to reinterpret another's analysis and speculate about the reliability or validity of another's report. Strategies for increasing the soundness of direct observation procedures are discussed in detail in Chapter 4.

When information is collected on a frequent or ongoing basis, a "formative" procedure is being used; that is, the information is used on a regular basis to evaluate performance and intervention effectiveness. Information collected summatively—that is, at the beginning and end of major intervals—may not highlight performance patterns, therefore causing a teacher to miss opportunities for more timely decision making. If performance is not monitored regularly, students (or teachers) can practice errors without corrective feedback, lose interest in maintaining accurate or fluent patterns of performance, or engage in other attention-getting behaviors (such as talking out).

Data displayed in Figure 3.1 were taken from assessments conducted at the beginning and end of a six-week period (summatively), in which six students received daily social skills instruction. Cal, Virginia, and Minnie appear to have achieved the desired level or criteria for mastery. Tex, Washington, and Georgia appear to have been slow or low in their achievement. However, studying information collected on a daily or near-daily basis (see Figure 3.2) reveals data patterns and trends that provide different conclusions about the students' progress. Cal immediately demonstrated mastery and maintained it until the posttest was administered. In contrast, Tex also achieved immediate mastery but failed to maintain his performance. Both Virginia and Washington had erratic, highly variable performance. On the day of the posttest, Virginia was observed on a "good" day and Washington on a "bad" day. Minnie and Georgia never really improved their performance through most of the six weeks; however, Minnie performed above criteria on the day of the posttest.

Direct, formative observation procedures help teachers and consultants make more efficient and timely intervention decisions. Procedures used to indirectly collect information about a problem may help frame a problem history and context, determine the impact the problem has on the perceptions and expectations of

FIGURE 3.1

Display of six-week summative data for six students

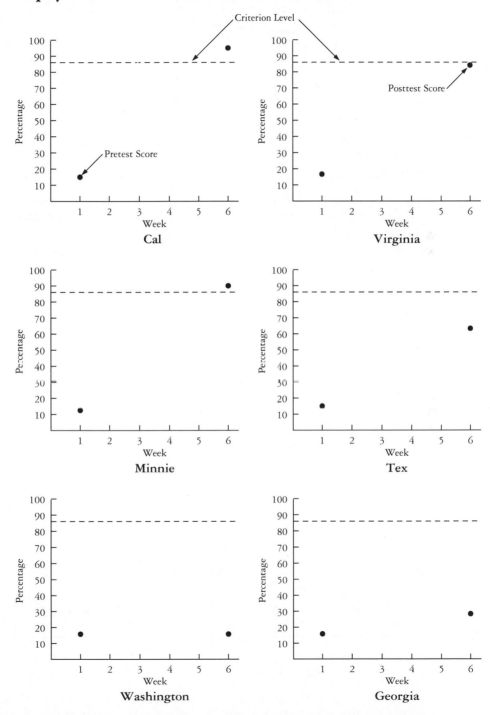

FIGURE 3.2

Display of six-week formative data for six students

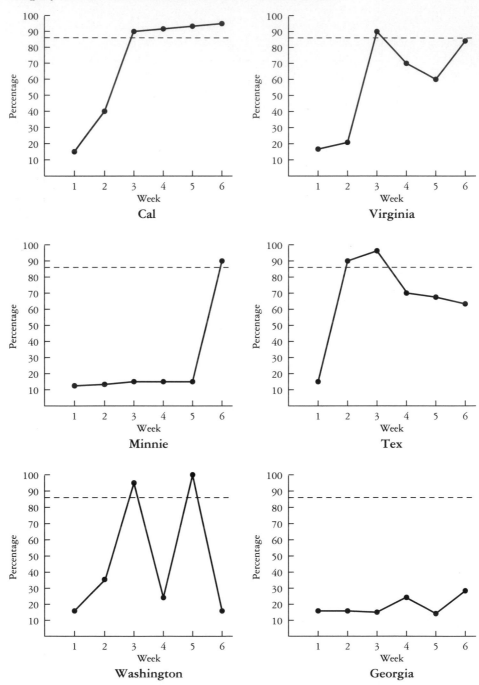

relevant social agents, and give the consultant a place to start. However, these procedures do not often provide an accurate picture of the current status of the problem. Similarly, traditional one-shot or pre-/postassessments often fail to provide a precise profile of the problem over time—that is, its trends or its variability or stability.

Teachers regularly collect academic performance data on a daily, direct, routine or formative basis. For example, they monitor the percentage of words spelled correctly on weekly tests, the number of math computation problems correct on homework assignments, the number of main ideas identified and developed in written compositions, the number and kinds of evidence used to justify a position, and a variety of other academic pinpoints. When recorded accurately, summarized appropriately, and used systematically, these data can help assess learning progress and evaluate instructional effectiveness. In general, teachers do not collect formative data on social behaviors. They rely on "memory" to recall social behavior events or make brief notes of a particular incident or occurrence. We strongly believe that formative assessment strategies for social behaviors should be incorporated into a teacher's daily instructional routines (see Chapter 4 for classroom strategies). In addition, these data should be used at the program and building level to evaluate the effectiveness of classroom and building-level management systems.

Focus #3: Assessment of Immediate Setting Factors and Their Relationship to Behavior

It is difficult for classroom teachers to manipulate predisposing factors, such as a bus citation or disruption at home, that affect how a student is likely to respond to classroom events. However, an assessment approach that informs teachers of what the student does when predisposed and the setting variables that trigger and maintain behaviors provides a useful tool for intervention planning.

In an analytic approach to consultation, we focus on the assessment of immediate setting factors. By concentrating on what immediately precedes and follows a response, a consultant can develop specific strategies for the teacher to use in the classroom (Sugai & Colvin, 1989; Wolery, Bailey, & Sugai, 1988). It is in the classroom or school environment where the teacher has the most control and expertise. For example, Ms. Black, Don's teacher, has observed that when Don is "anxious" (his behavioral state is characterized by tense shoulders, single word or no responses to questions, verbal noncompliance, and frequent academic errors), her requests or demands to redo a problem or make corrections are followed by an escalation of inappropriate behaviors. When his behaviors escalate (that is, become more intense and frequent), his peers tell him to "keep it down." The result is further escalation to threats and aggressive behavior. The relationship between Don's behaviors and setting variables is illustrated in Box 3.2.

Given this assessment information about the immediate factors that appear to be affecting Don's behaviors, a consultant can develop specific interventions. For example, when Don displays "anxious" behaviors, Ms. Black might change her initial interaction to emphasize what he has done correctly on his assignment, and after illustrating the correction on the chalkboard to the whole class, she might tell

BOX 3.2

Relationship between Don's behaviors and immediate setting events

ANTECEDENTS	DON'S BEHAVIORS	CONSEQUENCES
Ms. Black: "How are you today, Don?"	"OK"	Ms. Black steps closer.
"Just okay?"	"Yeah"	"Here's your assignment from yesterday."
c*	"So?"	"I want you to do this page over again because . . ."
c	(Interrupts) "Just give me the grade. I don't give a damn."	Ms. Black steps closer. "What did you say?"
c	"You heard me!" (louder)	Gladys and Tony: "Hey, keep it down. Some of us want to read."
"You two mind your own business."	"Yeah, why don't you stick it where . . ."	"Don, that's enough."

*c indicates that previous consequence also functions as an antecedent for the next behavior.

them to correct their errors. This redirection increases the probability that the escalated disruption will not occur. By highlighting those factors that trigger or maintain a behavior in the immediate setting, specific intervention manipulations can be developed. Often these strategies are preventive and teaching oriented, rather than reactive.

Focus #4: Ecological Assessment Perspective

In the preceding section, we emphasized the importance of examining the relationship between behaviors and immediate environmental events—that is, antecedents and consequences). In an expansion of this last assumption, the analytic approach to consultation emphasizes an ecological analysis of the relationship between behavior and environment. An ecological analysis broadens the assessment process to include measures of response covariation, desirable and undesirable intervention "side effects," and setting events (Martens & Witt, 1989; Vyse, Mulick, & Thayer, 1984).

Response covariation is used to describe the situation in which behaviors or responses appear to be functionally related to one another. For example, when Marrietta calls someone a name, she also glares, shakes her fist, and stomps her feet. Vyse, Mulick, and Thayer (1984) indicate that "when individuals share a common environment, such as a special education classroom, it follows that they will be confronted with many common stimuli. The manner in which they respond to these stimuli may be very different, but some behavioral covariation is to be expected" (p. 398).

Response covariation also refers to observed changes in nontargeted behaviors (desirable and undesirable) when targeted behaviors are the focus of an intervention. For example, when an intervention for Marrietta's name-calling is implemented, her glares, fist shaking, and feet stomping decrease, and cooperative play and on-task academic performance increase. Traditionally, these changes in nontargeted behaviors are referred to as *side effects.*

Setting events (Wahler, 1969; Wahler & Fox, 1981; Wahler & Graves, 1983) are factors that occur outside the immediate antecedent-response-consequence context but appear to be functionally related to the occurrence of a behavior. They are "environmental events temporally distant from the child's behaviors and their stimulus contingencies appear to exert control over these stimulus-response interactions" (Wahler & Graves, 1983, p. 19). For example, on a typical day, Barry's bus ride to school is uneventful. When he enters the room, his teacher can give him a variety of directions and tasks, which he begins without protest. However, on the bus one day Barry has a fight with a friend. When he enters the classroom, he is still very angry because his friend said he hated him and the bus driver gave Barry a bus citation. Now, when his teacher approaches him with a usually simple direction, like "Don't forget to hang up your coat," Barry has a fervent verbal outburst in which he protests the cruelty of the world and his adamant dislike for school. A variety of other setting events—such as being hungry, tired, frustrated, or bored—can also increase the probability that a student will respond in an atypical manner.

An ecological approach to assessment increases the consultant's opportunities to describe the range of influencing factors, develop effective treatments, and measure the full impact of the treatment. Martens and Witt (1988) refer to this focus as a systems approach to behavioral consultation. A systems approach enables the consultant to determine the (a) quality and frequency of instructional arrangements across individuals or groups of students, (b) conditional probabilities of academic responding under different instructional arrangements (for example, task, structure, teacher position, teacher behavior), and (c) differences in conditional probabilities across the individuals or groups of students (Greenwood, et al., 1985). This approach has also been described as *behavioral ecology* (Willems, 1974), *ecological behavior analysis* (Martens & Witt, 1989; Rogers-Warren & Warren, 1977), *ecobehavioral interaction analysis* (Greenwood, et al., 1985), and *ecobehavioral assessment* (Vyse, Mulick, & Thayer, 1984).

For example, Ms. Perth makes a Request for Assistance for a problem she is having with Sol, one of her fifth-grade students. She indicates that during math group Sol puts his head down on his desk. When the consultant conducts a series of direct observations during math group, she fails to uncover any immediate contributing antecedent or consequent events. However, when she expands to a more ecologically based assessment by examining other related behaviors and the physical and instructional contexts in which the behaviors are emitted, she discovers that Sol's putting his head down is part of a larger class of responses that includes whining, verbal protests, high rates of math errors, long response latencies to questions, and failure to respond in unison with other students. She also finds that these behaviors occur during other academic lessons. The consultant notes that when these behaviors occur, Ms. Perth tends to interact less often with Sol, slow the lesson down, give Sol answers, and ask him to do fewer problems. She also modifies her instruction to accommodate his behaviors, tends to give other students more praise for correct behaviors, and invites more instructional engagements with Sol's peers. The frequency of problematic behaviors is higher just after lunch and before going home.

Martens and Witt (1989) indicate that the ecological or systems approach has practical implications for consultants at the Problem Identification and Information Collection phases. First, they suggest applying a molar (broad, multiple) focus to problem assessment and information collection. A molecular or single behavior–only focus fails to uncover how changes in one classroom or behavioral factor affect other factors and how, in turn, the homeostasis, or functioning level, of the system, or classroom, is affected.

Second, to operationalize this molar focus, Martens and Witt recommend conducting comprehensive functional analyses in which a variety of behavioral measures are applied across multiple situations and from proximal (close) and distal (distant) reference points. This type of analysis provides information about behavior frequencies, immediate antecedent and consequent events, setting events, response chains and classes, and interactive contingencies.

Third, they recommend preplanning assessment procedures to enable the consultant to analyze intervention outcomes, in particular, how responding is "redistributed" as a result of intervention. This information can be used to plan and assess for multiple treatment effects—that is, primary and secondary effects and side effects.

Last, Martens and Witt suggest basing intervention development on information obtained from comprehensive assessments and cautiously implementing interventions. They warn of the possible cumulative effects of treatments over time, which can result because the effects of an intervention cannot be withdrawn. For example, numerous interventions have been tried to improve Carol Sue's in-class behaviors. The following sequence of strategies was tried: ignoring, verbal reminders, self-recording, a peer tutor, a token economy, token economy plus response cost, time-outs. In this example, the effectiveness of one intervention is affected by the student's experience with the previous intervention(s).

These assumptions form the foundation for Problem Identification and Information Collection in this chapter and for the direct observation procedures described in Chapter 4. However, before we discuss strategies for collecting direct observation data, we must clarify the problem that has been presented through the Request for Assistance. The Problem Identification Interview is a mechanism for bridging this gap.

CONDUCTING A PROBLEM IDENTIFICATION INTERVIEW

After receiving a Request for Assistance, the consultant must decide if consultation is required, and if so, what level should be provided—that is, direct versus indirect, and client, consultee, or system. Interviewing the teacher (consultee) and directly observing the problem context provide necessary input for making these decisions.

However, before engaging in direct observation procedures, begin by collecting preliminary information that provides a general picture of the presenting problem—namely, the relationship between student and teacher behaviors and the educational contexts in which they are observed. Some of this information can be collected from archival records, such as pertinent family history, past academic achievement, social behavior history, and teacher perceptions and expectations. However, an excellent source for initial information about the student's *current* status is the teacher who has made the request. In this section, we consider strategies for conducting a problem identification and information collecting interview. We also review some general comments about interviewing and use a specific format called the *Problem Identification Interview* to illustrate key strategies.

General Comments About Interview Assessment Procedures

Interviewing strategies are indirect assessment methods of collecting data based on retrospective reporting. Typically, the interviewer directs a verbal exchange then notes responses from the interviewee. Several outcomes are associated with interviews: definition and elaboration of the problem, classification or diagnosis of the problem, establishment of treatment goals, validation of target behavior selection, and identification of possible interventions. In addition, interviews serve as a vehicle for building a working relationship between the consultant and the teacher and establishing a direction or focus for intervention.

Traditionally, interview information has been used to help diagnose and classify or label a problem type, including conduct disorders, affective disorders, schizophrenia, depression, and the attention deficit hyperactive disorder. Although useful for research and clinical contexts, information collected from these diagnostic interviews, typically, do not provide details sufficient for thorough intervention development (Sugai, Maheady, & Skouge, 1989; Walker & Fabre, 1987). For the consultant in educational settings, the function of the interview is to clarify the problem so more efficient information collection and intervention development can occur. Behavioral interviews have become popular ways to accomplish this end (Bergan & Kratochwill, 1990; Morrison, 1988; Shapiro, 1987) because the consultant can determine how the teacher (a) characterizes or describes the problem, (b) is affected by the problem, (c) perceives the severity of the problem, and (d) describes his or her relationship to the problem.

Behavioral interviews, however, are characterized by many of the disadvantages associated with other indirect assessment procedures. First, reported information is based on the interviewee's perceptions and interpretations. How an individual describes what he or she sees is influenced by a variety of factors, such as learning history, culture, values, and emotional status (like frustrated, angry, or sad). For example, although Mr. Valvano regards Willie's talkouts as appropriate expressions of assertiveness, Mr. Green considers them as unacceptable aggressiveness.

Second, a behavioral interview can produce large amounts of information that are difficult to analyze or are unrelated to problem identification. For example, Mr.

Green describes how his standard strategies have worked with other students, but he sees Willie as a very different kind of student. He also indicates that Willie was an above-average student in second grade, he has been diagnosed as having an attention deficit disorder, and his sister, Wilma, was a model student when she was in the fifth grade. Although this information is associated with Willie, some of it is historical, some of it is not observable, and some of it is indirectly related to the prevailing talkout problem.

Third, interview information can be difficult to quantify. In Willie's situation, it is very difficult to measure "attention deficit disorders," "aggressiveness," and "assertiveness." Fourth, a skilled interviewer is required to help the teacher describe the problem and translate the information into measurable terms. The interviewer must be able to indicate his or her concern and willingness to assist the teacher while also focusing the teacher on the immediate problem and helping him or her clearly define it. For example, the consultant might make the following kinds of statements:

> "I hear what you're saying about his sister, but what does he do that makes him different?"
>
> "I've sensed the same problem when I'm with Willie. What do you see him doing that causes us to react that way?"
>
> "When he talks out, it sure sounds disruptive. Is he more likely to talk out at the beginning or end of a lesson?"

Fifth, the interviewer's theoretical and personal biases can affect the types of questions that are asked, the kinds of responses the teacher provides, what information is deemed important, and how the information is interpreted and reported. The interviewee's professional status and training, race, gender, theoretical perspective, and personal biases are characteristics that affect the outcomes of a behavioral interview (Morganstern, 1988). For example, one consultant was a regular classroom teacher before being trained to be a consultant. His co-worker was previously a school counselor who led values clarification groups and provided small group therapy. Both will view Willie's behaviors from slightly different perspectives because of their professional experiences and training.

These disadvantages are more characteristic of and more conspicuous with less structured or open-ended behavioral interviews. Bergan and Kratochwill (1990) have developed procedures for conducting more objective consultation interviews. They also propose a set of indexes that provide a relative measure of interview effectiveness and comprehensive computation and conversion procedures. A brief summary of their indexes is as follows:

1. *Index of Content Relevance* is the "extent to which consultant verbalizations represent a balanced coverage of appropriate interview content" (p. 437). Depending on the phase of consultation (problem identification, problem analysis, or problem evaluation), high effectiveness is associated with balanced use of relevant content subcategories (that is, behavior, behavior-setting, observation, or plan).

2. *Index of Process Effectiveness* is the "extent to which the consultant uses process subcategories appropriately in the achievement of consultation

goals'' (p. 438). Depending on the phase of consultation, high effectiveness is associated with a balanced use of different types of utterances, such as specifications, summarizations, validations, or inferences.

3. *Index of Interview Control* is the ''extent to which elicitors are used in an interview'' (p. 443). High effectiveness is associated with a greater number of consultant elicitors than emitters.

4. *Index of Content Focus* is the ''extent to which interview content shifts from one topic to another'' (p. 443). High effectiveness is associated with the ability to stay on one topic of conversation.

Like the Bergan and Kratochwill model, the analytic approach to consultation provides a highly structured format to minimize disadvantages, makes efficient use of the time available for consultation, and increases the efficiency of subsequent problem identification and intervention development activities.

The Problem Identification Interview

A practical, highly structured format for collecting information and conducting behavioral interviews at the Problem Identification and Information Collection phases is the Problem Identification Interview (PII) (Sugai & Carter, 1989). This format shares features from a structured problem-solving strategy developed by Sprick (1987). These characteristics—(a) timed activities, (b) prepared forms, (c) specific content areas, and (d) consultant directed—enable the consultant and teacher to focus on the problem behavior and the context in which it has been observed. The consultant acquires preliminary information that will oper-ate as background for subsequent information collection activities like direct observations.

The Problem Identification Interview has four major sections (see Figure 3.3), which the consultant completes with information provided by the teacher. The first section is for describing general, identifying information about the teacher and the student (name, date, room, age and sex). Frequently, this information is available from the Request for Assistance before the interview is conducted. The second section contains a set of specific items designed to define the specific characteristics of the problem. A suggested time limit is indicated after each item so the consultant can keep the interview focused and the pace brisk. Each item in this section is defined and illustrated with an example as follows:

1. *Describe the problem:* Description of the problem behavior in observable/measurable terms (that is, frequency, duration, intensity, locus, topography, and latency).

    EXAMPLE: ''Phillip talks out—e.g., makes animal noises, calls the teacher name, answers—over ten times within a 40-minute period without permission and raising his hand.''

2. *Describe other behaviors that seem to be related to the problem behavior:* Observable descriptions of other appropriate and inappropriate behaviors that are concurrently observed with, just prior to, or just following the targeted problem behavior.

FIGURE 3.3

Problem Indentification Interview Form

PROBLEM IDENTIFICATION INTERVIEW FORM	Page 1 of 3

Consultant _____ Teacher _____

Date ___/___/___ School _____

Student Information: Name _____ Room ____

Grade _____ Age _____ Sex: M F IEP: Y N

Describe the <u>problem</u> behavior. (5 minutes)

Describe <u>other behaviors</u> that seem to be related to the problem behavior.
(3 minutes)

Describe the conditions under which the problem behavior is <u>most likely</u> to occur.
(2 minutes)

When: _____

Where: _____

With Whom: _____

FIGURE 3.3   (*continued*)

PROBLEM IDENTIFICATION INTERVIEW FORM	Page 2 of 3

Describe what usually happens <u>after</u> the problem behavior occurs. (2 minutes)

Describe what usually happens immediately <u>before</u> the problem behavior occurs. (2 minutes)

Describe what <u>you</u> usually do when the behavior occurs. (2 minutes)

Describe what <u>other students</u> do when the behavior occurs. (2 minutes)

FIGURE 3.3 (*continued*)

PROBLEM IDENTIFICATION INTERVIEW FORM	Page 3 of 3

Describe what you would like the student to do <u>instead</u> of the problem behavior. (2 minutes)

List or describe <u>other interventions</u> that have been tried. (3 minutes)

Make an appointment to conduct an observation and debriefing. (1 minute)

Date ___/___/___ Time ___:___ to ___:___ Place/Classroom _____

Other information/notes

EXAMPLE: "When Phillip talks out, he also stands up, glares, and shakes his fists. Just before talking out, he raises his hand and says that he hates school and the work is too hard. After he talks out, he pounds his fists on the desk, stomps his feet, and says he'll try to do his work if someone will help him."

3. *Describe when, where, and with whom the behavior is most likely to occur:* Description of specific contexts or conditions in which the problem behavior is most frequently observed.

EXAMPLE: *When*—"Teacher asks the class a question about the reading assignment, and sitting next to Rasha and Hwang"
Where—"During science and social studies lessons"
With whom—"Mr. Green, science teacher, and Mrs. Revere, social studies"

4. *Describe what usually happens immediately after the behavior occurs:* Description of observable events (not planned intervention) that immediately follow the occurrence of the target behavior.

EXAMPLE: "Teachers ask Phillip if he remembers the rule for answering questions during class and then ask him for his answer, and Rasha and Hwang tell him not to interrupt while others are trying to answer."

5. *Describe what usually happens immediately before the behavior occurs:* Description of observable events that immediately precede the observation of the target behavior.

EXAMPLE: "Teachers ask open-ended questions to the whole class and scan the room for students who have their hands raised."

6. *Describe what you usually do when the behavior occurs:* Description of what planned intervention is used when the target behavior occurs.

EXAMPLE: "Teachers give Phillip a warning of possible negative consequences if interruptions continue. If the target behavior continues, Phillip is sent immediately to in-school suspension where the vice-principal discusses the problem with him."

7. *Describe what other students usually do when the behavior occurs:* Description of what peers do at the occurrence of the target behavior.

EXAMPLE: "Rasha and Hwang tell Phillip to shut up and complain to the teacher. Other students ignore Phillip's talkouts."

8. *Describe what you would like the student to do instead of the problem behavior:* Description of observable, more appropriate (acceptable) replacement behavior for problem behavior.

EXAMPLE: "Raise hand and wait quietly until acknowledged by teacher. If teacher does not call on Phillip after 15 seconds, put hand down and wait for better opportunity."

9. *List or describe other interventions that have been tried:* Brief listing or descriptions of interventions that have previously been tried to correct the problem behavior.

> EXAMPLE: "Talks with the vice-principal and principal, removal from the classroom, ignoring, parent conferences, special contracts."

The third section provides an appointment prompt for bringing closure to the interview, making arrangements for direct observations, and debriefing the interview session. The last section is for recording any additional information about the problem behavior, such as notes about events or conditions outside the immediate context or setting in which the target behavior is observed, ideas for possible interventions, or potential roadblocks to the consultation process. To facilitate the use of the PII, guidelines have been identified and framed as a self-checklist (see Box 3.3). Four sets of guidelines for completing the Problem Identification Interview are included: (a) planning the interview, (b) before beginning the actual interview, (c) during the interview, and (d) at the end of the interview.

The purpose of the behavioral interview is to clarify the problem and set the occasion for further interactions and activities. Attention is focused on the student's immediate behaviors and the ecology of that context. The Problem Identification Interview format is designed to make achievement of these ends efficient, objective, and productive. Figure 3.4 is an example of a completed Problem Identification Interview form.

After conducting the Problem Identification Interview, the consultant should review the information obtained. In general, to be most functional, this information should be succinct, objective, and observable. All descriptions should be based on the immediate context in which the problem is most frequently observed. In particular, the behaviors of the target student and relevant others, such as peers and teachers, and features of the problem context should be described in observable terms. To assist in determining if the replacement behavior is reasonable and functionally related to the problem behavior, the consultant should have obtained an observable description of what the teacher expects or wants the student to do instead of the problem behavior. Finally, to increase accountability, a specific date and time should have been set for follow-up observations and meetings.

The questions in Box 3.4 can be used to evaluate the outcomes from the interview. Guidelines for six major areas are addressed: (a) general accuracy and completeness, (b) behaviors, (c) events and stimuli, (d) expectations, (e) previous intervention attempts, and other. If the consultant finds any deficiencies or ambiguous descriptions, he or she should seek clarification and revise the Problem Identification Interview information sheets. If the outcomes from the Problem Identification Interview are incomplete or not succinct, the consultant should rewrite those aspects of the interview that were inadequately described or seek additional information from the teacher. This kind of revision will help facilitate a more objective and efficient evaluation of the Request for Assistance.

EVALUATING THE REQUEST FOR ASSISTANCE

After the initiating problem has been discussed through the Problem Identification Interview, the teacher and consultant must determine if the process should be continued to the next formal step, which involves collecting additional information

BOX 3.3

Checklist of guidelines for facilitating the Problem Identification Interview

---

PROBLEM IDENTIFICATION INTERVIEW CHECKLIST

1. Planning for the interview:
   - ___ Review any relevant archival information.
   - ___ Review the purpose or goal of the PII.
   - ___ Review the components and structure of the PII form.
   - ___ Provide the teacher with copy of the PII form to prepare for the actual interview.

2. Before beginning the actual interview:
   - ___ Indicate that the structured components of the interview will take approximately 25 minutes.
   - ___ Indicate that supplemental information or elaborations can be discussed at the end of the structured part of the PII.
   - ___ Indicate that one of the consultant's primary tasks is to keep the interview process on task and to promote objective information collection.
   - ___ Indicate that the major outcomes of the interview include a completed PII form, a clear description of the problem behavior, and information about the context in which the problem behavior occurs.

3. During the interview:
   - ___ Use the PII form as an agenda to structure the interview.
   - ___ Complete the PII form collaboratively with the teacher.
   - ___ Use a watch to keep track of the recommended time limits.
   - ___ Give a signal when 30 seconds remain in the recommended time limit.
   - ___ Refer all off-task discussions back to the PII item being addressed.
   - ___ Use effective communication strategies (see Chapter 11 on Working with Others).
   - ___ Make notes in the Other Information Section of the PII of unrelated information and indicate that it will be discussed at end of meeting.

4. At the end of the interview:
   - ___ Review the purpose of the PII.
   - ___ Briefly review what has been written down.
   - ___ Clarify any items that are unclear or confusing.
   - ___ Set a date and time for follow-up observations or meetings.
   - ___ If possible, leave a copy of the completed PII.
   - ___ Thank the teacher.

---

and carefully analyzing the problem. In this next phase, the emphasis shifts from indirect assessment toward direct observation procedures.

We prefer, however, to assume that a problem does exist if a teacher submits a completed formal Request for Assistance. We assume that this teacher has tried to remedy the problem to the best of his or her ability and available resources. However, because the Problem Identification Interview provides a highly structured, complete, and systematic analysis of the problem, the teacher may determine that the consultation sequence can be discontinued or modified—that is, conducted in a more informal manner. For example, Ms. Davidson discovers that Lila's wetting and soiling accidents occur immediately after lunch and just before math group. Seeing this pattern, Ms. Davidson indicates that she would like to try

FIGURE 3.4
Completed Problem Identification Interview form

PROBLEM IDENTIFICATION INTERVIEW FORM	Page 1 of 3

Consultant __Maloney__   Teacher __Robertsen__
Date __12/17/90__   School __Main Street Elementary__

Student Information: Name __Kevin__   Room __7a__
Grade __6__   Age __12__   Sex: (M) F   IEP: Y (N)

Describe the problem behavior. (5 minutes)

Kevin leaves the classroom without permission and disrupts other classrooms by banging on doors and shouting obscenities.

Describe other behaviors that seem to be related to the problem behavior. (3 minutes)

- not following teacher directions
- failure to complete in-class assignments
- late to class from recess and lunch

Describe the conditions under which the problem behavior is most likely to occur. (2 minutes)

When: __Just before math and science classes__
Where: __Hallways outside his classroom__
With Whom: __Robertsen and vice-principal__

FIGURE 3.4   *(continued)*

PROBLEM IDENTIFICATION INTERVIEW FORM   Page 2 of 3

Describe what usually happens <u>after</u> the problem behavior occurs. (2 minutes)

Other classroom teachers tell him to go to office, or Robertsen tries to convince him to return to his classroom. Other students back away from him.

Describe what usually happens immediately <u>before</u> the problem behavior occurs. (2 minutes)

Directions are given to class to get math or science notebooks out of desks and to turn in homework.

Describe what <u>you</u> usually do when the behavior occurs. (2 minutes)

Try to keep him from leaving room by using verbal reasoning and/or threats of in-school suspension.

Describe what <u>other students</u> do when the behavior occurs. (2 minutes)

Move away from him. Look away from him. Some students giggle and smile at him.

FIGURE 3.4 (*continued*)

PROBLEM IDENTIFICATION INTERVIEW FORM   Page 3 of 3

Describe what you would like the student to do <u>instead</u> of the problem behavior. (2 minutes)

- Stay in seat and classroom.
- Follow directions.
- Ask for help by raising his hand.

List or describe <u>other interventions</u> that have been tried. (3 minutes)

- In-school suspensions
- Ignoring him
- parent conference
- Complete work assignments after school

Make an appointment to conduct an observation and debriefing. (1 minute)

12:00 to 1:00

Date 12/21/90   Time 9:30 to 10:30 Place/Classroom ___Room 7a___

Other information/notes

- Occurs once every two or three days
- Parents report no difficulties with his behaviors at home
- Has been given "easier" homework and in-class assignments

BOX 3.4.

Checklist for evaluating the outcomes of the Problem Identification Interview

1. *General*
   ___ Do descriptions emphasize the *immediate problem context?*
   ___ Are descriptions written in *observable/measurable* terms?
   ___ Are descriptions *complete?*
   ___ Are descriptions stated in *objective* terms?
   ___ Are descriptions *succinct?*

2. *Behaviors*
   ___ Are behaviors described in *observable/measurable* terms?
   ___ Is emphasis placed on behaviors observed in *immediate problem context?*
   ___ Are behaviors of *relevant others* (namely, peers or teacher) provided?

3. *Events and Stimuli*
   ___ Are problem context stimuli—such as behaviors of others and setting specific factors (like instruction, curriculum, setting arrangement)—described in *observable/measurable* terms?
   ___ Is emphasis placed on *immediate* problem context stimuli?
   ___ Are *relevant settings, times, and persons* described?
   ___ Are the *teacher's behaviors* clearly described?

4. *Expectations*
   ___ Is a *replacement* behavior indicated?
   ___ Is the replacement response *reasonable and functional* relative to the problem behavior and the problem context?
   ___ Is the replacement behavior described in *observable/measurable* terms?

5. *Previous Intervention Attempts*
   ___ Are previous intervention attempts described in *identifiable* terms?
   ___ Is the list of previous intervention attempts *complete?*

6. *Other*
   ___ If appropriate, was a *date and time set* for follow-up observations or meetings?

another intervention before continuing to the next, more formal step in the consultation process (for example, Teacher Assistance Team and Information collection). Ms. Davidson says she would like to try meeting Lila at the classroom door immediately after lunch and reminding her to go to the bathroom before sitting down at the math group table.

Consultants may also discover that the teacher has overlooked a simple solution. Trying the new strategy might bypass more involved interventions and consultation activities. For example, Mr. Harlow has concentrated so much on "making" Sally do her assignments that he has overlooked the possibility that Sally does not know how to do the work. When the consultant brings this to his attention during the Problem Identification Interview, Mr. Harlow realizes that he has "overlooked the obvious" in searching for a more complicated solution to a simple problem.

Regardless of the decision to try something differently or to continue with the consultation process, the consultant should assess the situation carefully to ensure that a sound decision has been made. A good rule is to make the most conservative choice in order to increase the probability of developing a sound solution. If the teacher discontinues the formal process, the consultant should honor the decision but schedule an opportunity in two weeks to check the status of the problem. If at this later time, the problem is still unchanged *and* the teacher renews his or her Request for Assistance, the consultation process can be continued by updating the Problem Identification Interview or moving on to the next step in the process.

SUMMARY

When a teacher makes a Request for Assistance, the consultant must collect information that will enable him or her to determine the extent and nature of the problem. In this chapter, we discussed strategies and procedures for Problem Identification and Information Collection. With a focus on social behavior problems (academic problems are addressed in Chapters 8 and 9), we reviewed some basic assessment assumptions, terminology, and definitions; procedures for conducting a Problem Identification Interview; and suggestions for evaluating the Request for Assistance. We emphasized a systems and ecological/behavioral approach. The flow chart in Figure 3.5 provides a systematic, and visual portrayal of the Problem Identification and Information Collection phase of the consultation process.

The chapter's key features are as follows:

1. Assessment is measurement.

2. Assessment information is used to describe, communicate, evaluate, and identify.

3. Behavioral assessment emphasizes (a) observable and discrete behaviors, (b) direct and formative observation procedures, (c) assessment of immediate setting factors and their relationship to behavior, and (d) an ecological assessment perspective.

4. Behavioral interviews are useful tools for collecting preliminary and general information about the problem presented in the Request for Assistance.

5. The Problem Identification Interview provides a highly structured format for conducting interviews at the Problem Identification and Information Collection phases of consultation.

6. When conducting Problem Identification Interviews, consultants should avoid statements of nonobservable events.

7. Because of its systematic and comprehensive structure, the Problem Identification Interview can help teachers develop solutions for their problem situations.

8. The consultant should conduct careful assessments of the information provided by the teacher during the Problem Identification Interview in order to ensure a successful outcome for the student and the teacher.

FIGURE 3.5

Flow chart of the Problem Identification and Information collection phase of consultation

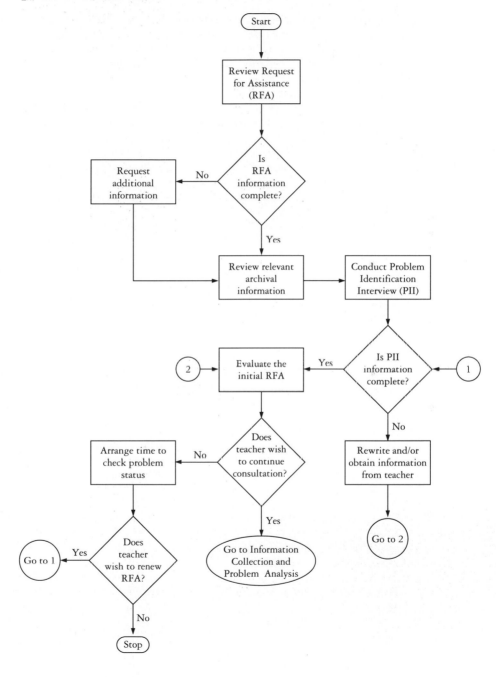

REFERENCES

BERGAN, J. R., & KRATOCHWILL, T. R. (1990). *Behavioral consultation and therapy*. New York: Plenum.

GREENWOOD, C. R., DELQUADRI, J. C., STANLEY, S. O., TERRY, B., & HALL, R. V. (1985). Assessment of eco-behavioral interaction in school settings. *Behavior Assessment, 7*, 331–347.

MARTENS, B. K., & WITT, J. C. (1988). Expanding the scope of behavioral consultation: A systems approach to classroom behavior change. *Professional School Psychology, 3*(4), 271–281.

MARTENS, B. K., & WITT, J. C. (1989). Ecological behavior analysis. In M. Hersen, R. M. Eisler, & P. M. Miller (Eds.), *Progress in behavior modification* (Vol. 22). Beverly Hills: Sage.

MORGANSTERN, K. P. (1988). Behavioral interviewing. In A. S. Bellack & M. Hersen (Eds.), *Behavioral assessment: A practical handbook* (3rd ed.) (pp. 86–118). New York: Pergamon Press.

MORRISON, R. L. (1988). Structured interviews and rating scales. In A. S. Bellack & M. Hersen (Eds.), *Behavioral assessment: A practical handbook* (3rd ed.) (pp. 252–277). New York: Pergamon Press.

ROGERS-WARREN, A., & WARREN, S. F. (1977). *Ecological perspective in behavior analysis*. Baltimore: University Park Press.

SHAPIRO, E. S. (1987). *Behavioral assessment in school psychology*. Hillsdale, NJ: Erlbaum.

SPRICK, R. (1987). *Solving behavior problems: Twenty minute planning process*. Eugene, OR: Teaching Strategies.

SUGAI, G., & CARTER, J. (1989). A prescriptive case consultation approach. Unpublished manuscript. Eugene: University of Oregon.

SUGAI, G., & COLVIN, G. (1989). *Environmental explanations of behavior: Conducting a functional analysis* (2nd ed.). Eugene, OR: Behavior Associates.

SUGAI, G., MAHEADY, L., & SKOUGE, J. (1989). White paper on best assessment practices for students with behavioral disorders: Accommodation to cultural diversity and individual differences. *Behavioral Disorders, 14*, 263–278.

VYSE, S., MULICK, J. A., & THAYER, B. M. (1984). An ecobehavioral assessment of a special education classroom. *Applied Research in Mental Retardation, 5*, 395–408.

WAHLER, R. G. (1969). Setting generality: Some specific and general effects of child behavior therapy. *Journal of Applied Behavior Analysis, 2*, 239–246.

WAHLER, R. G., & FOX, J. J. (1981). Setting events in applied behavior analysis: Toward a conceptual and methodological expansion. *Journal of Applied Behavior Analysis, 14*, 327–338.

WAHLER, R. G., & GRAVES, M. G. (1983). Setting events in social networks: Ally or enemy in child behavior therapy? *Behavior Therapy, 14*, 19–36.

WALKER, H. M., & FABRE, T. R. (1987). Assessment of behavior disorders in the school setting: Issues, problems, and strategies revisited. In N. Haring (Ed.), *Assessing and managing behavior disorders* (pp. 198–234). Seattle: University of Washington Press.

WILLEMS, E. P. (1974). Behavioral technology and behavioral ecology. *Journal of Applied Behavior Analysis, 7*, 151–165.

WOLERY, M. R., BAILEY, D. B., JR., & SUGAI, G. (1988). *Effective teaching: Principles and procedures of applied behavior analysis for exceptional students*. Boston: Allyn & Bacon.

Direct Observation Procedures and Problem Analysis

Kane is a very quiet first-grader who has not said a single word at school. His parents indicate that he talks fluently and frequently at home with them, his two sisters, and three or four neighborhood friends. After three months of unsuccessful attempts to coax Kane to participate in school activities, Ms. Davidson submits a written Request for Assistance (see Figure 4.1).

After reviewing the Request for Assistance and conducting a Problem Identification Interview (see Figure 4.2), Ms. Stillman, the district teacher consultant, and Ms. Davidson determine that the problem requires closer examination. They decide to observe Kane's behaviors directly in the two or three settings—opening group, reading group, and science period—in which the problem is particularly troublesome. They then use the information obtained from these observations to determine the context factors that are influencing Kane's behaviors, obtain an estimate of how often the problem behaviors are being displayed, and identify possible components of an intervention.

In Chapter 3, we focused on information collection strategies designed to clarify the problem presented in the Request for Assistance. These strategies were *indirect* in that the teacher supplied information about the student, primarily during a systematic interview, known as the Problem Identification Interview. In this chapter, we discuss *direct* information collection strategies that help the consultant and teacher analyze the critical features of the problem behaviors within the context of the setting in which they are observed. Specifically, we describe procedural steps for conducting a functional analysis and performing other direct observation methods. Details from these assessments are used to build the prevention and intervention strategies discussed in Chapter 5. Analogous discussions about direct assessment procedures and data analysis guidelines for academic behaviors are covered in Chapters 8, 9, and 10.

FIGURE 4.1

Ms. Davidson's Request for Assistance

REQUEST FOR ASSISTANCE FORM	Referring Person Ms. Davidson
	Title Teacher Date 12/3/90
	Student Kane
	Grade 1 DOB 10/6/84 Sex: (M) F IEP: Y (N)

Check Type of Problem Behavior

Academic: ___Reading ___Math ___Spelling ___Writing ___Study Skills ___Other _____

Social: ___Aggressive ___Noncompliant ___Truant ___Tardy ✓Withdrawn ___Disruptive ___Social Skills ___Self-Management ___Other_____

Communication: ___Language ✓Fluency ___Articulation ___Voice ✓Other speech

Self-Help: ___Dressing ___Hygiene ___Other_____

Health: ___Vision ___Hearing ___Physical ___Other_____

Provide Specific and Observable Description of Problem

Will not speak at school

Provide Specific Description of Problem Context

Where: Opening group. Reading period. Science period.

When: Everyday

With Whom: Adults and peers

Other: _____

Provide List of Previous Remediation Attempts

1. Coaxing with hints   4. Easy tasks

2. Withholding recess

3. Reinforcing peers

FIGURE 4.2
Ms. Davidson's Problem Identification Interview

PROBLEM IDENTIFICATION INTERVIEW FORM	Page 1 of 3

Consultant ___Stillman___   Teacher ___Davidson___
Date _12_/_18_/_90_   School ___Citizen Elem.___

Student Information: Name ___Kane___   Room _7_
Grade _1_   Age _6_   Sex: (M) F   IEP: Y (N)

Describe the problem behavior. (5 minutes)

Will not speak to adults or peers.
Will gesture with hands or turn away.

Describe other behaviors that seem to be related to the problem behavior.
(3 minutes)

Uses gestures to communicate. Walks away when
forced to talk. Sometimes cries when pressed
to speak in front of peers.

Describe the conditions under which the problem behavior is most likely to occur.
(2 minutes)

When: ___When asked to answer orally, especially in front of peers.___
Where: ___Opening group. Reading and Science groups.___
With Whom: ___All adults and students.___

F I G U R E 4.2 (*continued*)

PROBLEM IDENTIFICATION INTERVIEW FORM	Page 2 of 3

Describe what usually happens <u>after</u> the problem behavior occurs. (2 minutes)

1. adults stop interacting with him.
2. peers answer for him.
3. peers walk away.

Describe what usually happens immediately <u>before</u> the problem behavior occurs. (2 minutes)

Teacher or peers make oral request directly to Kane.

Describe what <u>you</u> usually do when the behavior occurs. (2 minutes)

Teacher accepts whatever gesture Kane gives, and moves to next student. Also accepts answers from peers who answer for Kane.

Describe what <u>other students</u> do when the behavior occurs. (2 minutes)

Leave Kane alone or defend Kane when he is pressured by others.

F I G U R E   4.2   (*continued*)

PROBLEM IDENTIFICATION INTERVIEW FORM	Page 3 of 3

Describe what you would like the student to do <u>instead</u> of the problem behavior. (2 minutes)

Answer in one- or two-word sentences in conversational tone, volume, and intensity.

List or describe <u>other interventions</u> that have been tried. (3 minutes)

Give easier work.
Praise his peers who answer with appropriate speech.

Make an appointment to conduct an observation and debriefing. (1 minute)

Date 12/21/90 Time 8:30 to 10:30 Place/Classroom Room 7

Other information/notes

Father reports that Kane speaks at home w/siblings and a few close friends. He was speaking on a limited basis in kindergarten. Hearing and speech skills normal.

CONDUCTING A FUNCTIONAL ANALYSIS

There are many direct observation methods, such as event recording or time sampling; however, few provide information that enables the consultant and the teacher to analyze the relationship between the behavior and immediate setting events. One direct observation procedure, called *functional analysis,* is a mainstay of behavioral assessment and applied behavior analysis (Baer, Wolf, & Risley, 1968; Gelfand & Hartmann, 1984; Skinner, 1953; Sugai & Colvin, 1989; Vargas, 1977; Wolery, Bailey, & Sugai, 1988). A functional analysis is defined as a temporally based direct observation procedure designed to examine the relationship between behavior and setting variables, and is one of the most useful, fundamental direct observation procedures available to the analytic consultant. It enables the consultant and the teacher to clarify the problem behavior, determine the relative effect of immediate setting factors; that is, antecedents and consequences, and initiate the development of effective interventions. This information, in turn, can be used to construct interventions that take into consideration relevant setting factors, including instructional design, curriculum, presentation of instruction and curriculum, and social influences such as peers and teachers. In this section, we describe the outcomes, procedural steps, and guidelines for a functional analysis.

Outcomes from a Functional Analysis

When a functional analysis is conducted, information that characterizes the instructional context—physical and social arrangements and conditions, instructional design, curriculum, presentation of instruction and curriculum—is obtained. In addition, the analysis results in three other outcomes: a sample of behaviors and events, behavior chains, and testable explanations.

A sample of behaviors and events.   One fundamental outcome is a sample of the kinds of behaviors displayed by the student, what these behaviors look like (their dimensions), and an approximation of the number of times each behavior occurs. For example, within a 30-minute observation, Ms. Fernandez finds that Aria correctly and appropriately answers five out of seven questions asked by her teacher, Mr. Romano, talks out without raising her hand seven out of eight times, and has her head down on her desk for a total of 20 minutes.

A functional analysis can also yield a sample of the kinds and frequencies of behaviors and events displayed by adults and other students in that setting. For example, Mr. Romano responds to Aria's handraises once out of every five times, Bruce interrupts Aria each time she tries to provide an answer to a teacher's question, and Julio teases her by raising his hand whenever she does. This information can further be classified into antecedents and/or consequent events. For example, Mr. Romano's questions and Bruce's interruptions are antecedent events. The teacher's response and Julio's teasing are events that follow Aria's handraises—that is, consequences.

Behavior chains.   A functional analysis also helps identify chains or sequences of related responses. These chains are characterized by a series of behaviors that are functionally related to one another; that is, when one behavior occurs, there is a high probability that a specific behavior will follow. For example, after Jason rips up his paper, he throws it on the floor and stomps it with his feet. After he stomps, he verbally complains that the work is too hard. He then says he hates math, sits down at his desk, and glares at the teacher. This sequence of behaviors typically follows the presentation of practice worksheets on new math problems.

Information about these chains facilitates the development of prevention strategies so that interventions can be implemented early in a behavioral sequence. Two kinds of chains are commonly observed. The first involves a sequence of behaviors during which antecedent or consequent events are not observed; that is, antecedent and/or consequent events are seen only at the very beginning or end of the series of behaviors. For example, when Mr. Romano asks the class a question (antecedent), Aria raises her hand, looks at Mr. Romano, waves her hand at him, calls out his name, slaps her hand on the desk, and talks to Julio; then, Mr. Romano asks Aria for the answer (consequence) (Box 4.1).

The second type of chain consists of observable events (antecedents and consequences) that links the behaviors displayed by the student. When Mr. Romano asks the group a question (antecedent), Aria raises her hand, Julio raises his hand and looks at Aria (consequence and antecedent), Aria waves at Mr. Romano, Julio waves harder (consequence and antecedent), Aria calls out Mr. Romano's name, and Mr. Romano tells Aria not to talk out (consequence). In this example, each event that followed one of Aria's behaviors also served as an antecedent for her next behavior (Box. 4.2).

Testable explanations.   The last and possibly most important outcome is a testable explanation or "best guess" about the factors contributing to the occurrence of the student's behaviors. A complete testable explanation consists of two components: an observable behavior displayed by the target student and an event that is observed in temporal proximity to the behavior being explained—that

BOX 4.1

Chain of student behaviors without observable antecedents or consequences

ANTECEDENT EVENT	BEHAVIOR	CONSEQUENT EVENT
Mr. Romano asks the class a question.	Aria raises her hand.	
	Aria looks at Mr. Romano.	
	Aria waves her hand at him.	
	Aria calls out Mr. Romano's name.	
	Aria slaps her hand on the desk.	
	Aria talks to Julio.	Mr. Romano asks Aria for the answer.

BOX 4.2

Chain of student behaviors with observable antecedent and consequent events

ANTECEDENT EVENT	BEHAVIOR	CONSEQUENT EVENT
Mr. Romano asks the class a question.	Aria raises her hand.	Julio raises his hand and looks at Aria.
$c*$	Aria waves her hand at Mr. Romano.	Julio waves harder.
c	Aria calls Mr. Romano's name out.	Mr. Romano tells Aria not to talk out.

*c indicates that the previous consequent event is an antecedent event for subsequent behavior.

is, just before and/or after the behavior is observed. The following sample of testable explanations describes Aria's behaviors:

1. Aria talks out when she raises her hand and has to wait longer than approximately 20 seconds for Mr. Romano to call on her.
2. When Julio sits next to Aria and mimics her behaviors, she raises her hand inappropriately (waves her arm).
3. When Aria talks out without raising her hand, Mr. Romano immediately corrects her and then asks her for the answer.

Each of these examples illustrates two important characteristics of an intact testable explanation. First, the behaviors and events are described in operational terms (that is, by dimensions). For example, Aria's "handraising" is described as "waving her arm." Second, events described as contributors or influential factors associated with the occurrence of the problem behavior can be manipulated. In the third explanation, Mr. Romano could be asked not to correct Aria immediately and ask her for the answer, when she talks out without raising her hand.

When attempting to formulate testable explanations, consultants and teachers must be careful to avoid developing "explanatory fictions" (Vargas, 1977), which are accounts that are (a) simple restatements of the problem behavior (Aria talks out when she has something to say), (b) nonobservable descriptions of behaviors or events (When the teacher takes longer than 20 seconds to call on her, Aria gets *excited and disrupts* the lesson), or (c) broadly defined constructs (Aria talks out in class because she is *conduct disordered*). Consultants must strive to develop testable explanations, discourage explanatory fictions, and use precise communications strategies to help teachers restate explanatory fictions into testable explanations (see Chapter 11). Box 4.3 provides examples of other testable explanations, explanatory fictions, and restatements of explanatory fictions.

A testable explanation is useful for consultants and teachers because it serves as a statement of a possible "functional relationship" between two events. A statement that describes a high probability association between two events is called a functional relationship. By manipulating the antecedent or consequent event, one can determine if a testable explanation can be used to delineate a functional relationship. For example, to test the first testable explanation, Mr. Romano would try responding to Aria's handraises in less than 20 seconds. If a change in her talkouts occurs predictably as a result of this manipulation, the testable explanation describes a functional relationship. If a predictable change is not observed, a new testable explanation needs to be developed. For another example, see Box 4.4.

BOX 4.3

Illustrations of testable explanations, explanatory fictions, and restatements of explanatory fictions

1. Gordon volunteers answers when the group size is smaller than five students. (*Testable Explanation*)

2. When she is frustrated, Sally puts her head down on her desk and does not respond to her teacher's directions. (*Explanatory Fiction*)

   Restatement: When she gets more than half of her math problems incorrect, Sally puts her head on her desk and does not respond to her teacher's directions.

3. Tomoko interrupts games—takes equipment or disrupts play—being played by other children when these children tell her that she can't play with them. (*Testable Explanation*)

4. Brian uses profanity and strikes other children with his fists because he is emotionally disturbed. (*Explanatory Fiction*)

   Restatement: Brian uses profanity and strikes other children with his fists when they tell him to shut up or do not comply with his demands.

5. Monti wanders around the room because he has been diagnosed as having attention deficit disorder. (*Explanatory Fiction*)

   Restatement: Monti walks around the room when the teacher does not give him a series of specific and understandable tasks to do.

6. When other children make verbal comments about her glasses, Barbara sits under her desk with her coat over her head. (*Testable Explanation*)

BOX 4.4

Manipulation sequence

Testable Explanation:	Kirsten (target student) talks, when she sits next to Henry.
Manipulation:	The teacher tests this explanation by moving Henry and placing Mac in Henry's desk.
Observation:	Kirsten talks with Mac. In this case, the testable explanation is not a functional relationship and a new explanation is needed.
Revised Testable Explanation:	Kirsten talks when she sits next to boys.
Manipulation:	The teacher tests this revised explanation by having a girl, Amy, sit next to Kirsten.
Observation:	Kirsten does not talk to her neighbor.

Once a functional relationship is identified and confirmed, the development of an intervention becomes much more focused. For example, without environmentally based explanations, a consultant might propose an intervention consisting of an aversive consequence; for example, writing Kirsten's name on the board, sending her to the office, keeping her in during recess). With information about influential factors, more proactive interventions are possible; for instance, providing Kirsten with an opportunity to talk with boys when it is appropriate, or teaching her when and how it is appropriate to talk with boys.

Conducting a Functional Analysis: Ten Basic Steps

Although conducting a functional analysis is relatively simple, practice is required to build fluency at recording behavioral events that may occur at high rates or in conjunction with many other events. The instrument used to record functional analysis observations (see Figure 4.3) has space to note the identifying and setting information used to demarcate one observation session from another and four simple columns to note events (antecedents, behaviors, consequences) and the approximate time at which they are observed.

Conducting a functional analysis consists of ten basic steps.

Step 1: Collect preliminary information.   The teacher, consultant, or observer collects preliminary information to afford a context for conducting the actual functional analysis. Although a portion of these data can be obtained from archival records and test results, preliminary information should be obtained through behavioral interviews like the Problem Identification Interview, which are conducted directly with the teacher who usually has had the most direct and frequent interactions with the student and who has been affected most directly by the problem. The consultant attempts to gather information that enables him or her to anticipate what behaviors the student will most likely display in the future. For example, Ms. Fernandez conducts a Problem Identification Interview with Mr. Romano and discusses the problem he has had with Aria. The outcome of this interview is displayed in Figure 4.4.

Step 2: Note all identifying information.   After developing a general picture of the problem, the consultant schedules an observation during a time and setting when the problem is most severe or noticeable. Before beginning the actual observation, he or she notes all identifying information, including the date, time of day, classroom/grade, teacher's name, student's name, observer's name, and so on. This identifying information serves as a context for describing the observation results to others or for repeating the observation on another day. An example of identifying information is given in Figure 4.5.

Step 3: Describe the setting conditions in which the observation will be taking place.   The consultant also describes relevant features of the immediate observation setting, as well as the specific stimulus conditions under which the student is being observed and is responding. For example, he or she may note instructional requirements, curriculum, seating arrangement, and student response

FIGURE 4.3
Functional Analysis Observation Form

FUNCTIONAL ANALYSIS OBSERVATION FORM	Date ___/___/___ Time ___:___ Observer _____ Student _____ Teacher _____ Classroom/School _____

Setting Description:

Time	Antecedents	Behaviors	Consequences

FIGURE 4.4

Ms. Fernandez's Problem Identification Interview

PROBLEM IDENTIFICATION INTERVIEW FORM   Page 1 of 3

Consultant __Fernandez__   Teacher __Romano__

Date __8/17/90__   School __Fifth Street School__

Student Information: Name __Aria__   Room __17__

Grade __5__   Age __11__   Sex: M (F)   IEP: Y (N)

Describe the <u>problem</u> behavior. (5 minutes)

Talking out in class without raising hand.
Interrupting others who are speaking.

**Describe <u>other behaviors</u> that seem to be related to the problem behavior.
(3 minutes)**

Name calling
Giving wrong answers
Talking back to teacher

**Describe the conditions under which the problem behavior is <u>most likely</u> to occur.
(2 minutes)**

When: __During lectures and question/answer sessions with large group.__

Where: __Science and social studies classes.__

With Whom: __Teacher and peers.__

FIGURE 4.4   (*continued*)

PROBLEM IDENTIFICATION INTERVIEW FORM	Page 2 of 3

Describe what usually happens <u>after</u> the problem behavior occurs. (2 minutes)

She is ignored or someone tells her to be quiet and follow the classroom rules.

Describe what usually happens immediately <u>before</u> the problem behavior occurs. (2 minutes)

An open-ended question is given to the group to answer, or someone else is answering.

Describe what <u>you</u> usually do when the behavior occurs. (2 minutes)

Try to distract Aria and keep the lesson going. Remind her of the rules.

Describe what <u>other students</u> do when the behavior occurs. (2 minutes)

Get angry that she gets away with misbehaving. Protest to the teacher.

F I G U R E 4.4 (*continued*)

PROBLEM IDENTIFICATION INTERVIEW FORM	Page 3 of 3

Describe what you would like the student to do <u>instead</u> of the problem behavior. (2 minutes)

Raise hand until called on, and wait until others have finished talking.

List or describe <u>other interventions</u> that have been tried. (3 minutes)

Sent to office for disrupting class
Parent conference

Make an appointment to conduct an observation and debriefing. (1 minute)

Date <u>9 / 2 / 90</u> Time <u>9</u> : <u>00</u> to <u>10</u> : <u>30</u> Place/Classroom <u>17</u>

Other information/notes

Does well with written tests.
Parents report similar problems at home.

FIGURE 4.5
Functional Analysis Observation Form

FUNCTIONAL ANALYSIS OBSERVATION FORM	Date 9 / 2 / 90 Time 9 : 20 Observer _Fernandez_ Student _Aria_ Teacher _Romano_ Classroom/School _Room 17/ Fifth Street School_

Setting Description:

Science lesson on insects. Teacher (R= Romano) is lecturing from the back of the room. Teacher shows slide on screen and asks class questions. Students are expected to raise their hand if they want to answer. Students have worksheets with pictures of insects that need to be identified. Aria sitting in first seat in middle row. Julio (J) sits in another row to her left. Brian (B) is behind her, and Candy (C) is on her right.

Time	Antecedents	Behaviors	Consequences
9:23	R shows slide of spider and asks, "Is this an example of an insect?"	A raises her hand.	B raises his hand. R calls on B.
	C *	A: "What gives here? My hand was up first."	R: "Just wait your turn." B: "Yeah, I know the answer."
	R: "Well, let's see if Aria knows the answer."	A: "It's not an insect, it's a bug."	J: "You're stupid; it's a spider."
9:24	C	A: "Well, you're stupid too..... just like B."	— —
	R moves to the next slide of a praying mantis, and asks, "Is this an insect?"	A: "Wow, that's a cool bug."	B: "Hey, you didn't raise your hand or wait your turn."

* C indicates that the previous consequence also functions as an antecedent for the next behavior.

requirements. The example in Figure 4.5 gives information about the lesson and seating arrangements.

Step 4: When the observation begins, record the starting time in the Time column.   The consultant records the time a critical behavior occurs or every four or five minutes. This information is used to determine the relative distribution of a behavior within the observation session. For example, a consultant might find that most of the problem behaviors occur at the beginning or end of an academic period, or that a response class of problem behaviors is distributed equally but does not occur in any predictable temporal order.

Step 5: Record the behaviors displayed by the target student in the Behavior column.   When conducting a functional analysis, the consultant records behaviors displayed by the student in the temporal order in which they are observed. He or she should record multiple appropriate and inappropriate behaviors so possible covariation or competition among responses or behavioral chains can be analyzed. Since it may not be possible to describe everything, only the essential information should be written down. It helps to use abbreviations or shorthand notes, and then go back later to fill in additional information.

Step 6: Record any events in the Antecedent column that immediately precede the Recorded Behavior of the Target Student.   The consultant briefly notes any events that are observed just before the behavior occurs. When developing the testable explanations, he or she assesses the antecedent information as being possible triggering events (that is, discriminative stimuli). In response chains, the prior consequent events may function as the antecedent for the next behavior. When this interaction sequence is observed, the observer places a checkmark ($\checkmark$) or c in the antecedent column (see Figure 4.5).

Step 7: Record any events in the Consequence column that immediately follow the recorded behavior.   The consultant notes any observable events that occur just after the behavior occurs. The objective is to identify those consequent events that may be functionally related to the behaviors displayed. Then he or she analyzes the consequent events for their possible response strengthening (reinforcement) or weakening (punishment) functions.

Step 8: Analyze the observation data and develop testable explanations. We generally recommend conducting two or more functional analyses in a target setting until sufficient occurrences of the target behaviors have been recorded and patterns between behaviors and environmental events (antecedents and consequences) can be discerned. Although time and resources may be limited, we also suggest conducting functional analyses across target settings to examine the pervasiveness of the problem and the range of controlling variables. After conducting the functional analysis observations (that is, obtaining a representative sample of behavior), the consultant analyzes the data and constructs testable explanations, emphasizing those behaviors and antecedent and consequent events noted during the observation.

Step 9: Test the testable explanations.   The consultant should test each testable explanation to determine if a possible functional relationship exists. Manipulations can be conducted in a variety of ways: (a) manipulate antecedent or consequent events in the target setting, (b) observe the student in settings that are slightly different than the target environment, or (c) conduct a series of daily observations to establish a baseline of regular behavior patterns. The goal is to conduct a test with the most direct manipulation possible, so the testable explanation can be confirmed or not shown to be a sound description of observed behavioral episodes.

Step 10: Develop an intervention.   After establishing a functional relationship, the consultant must decide whether to intercede. If appropriate, he or she can construct an intervention, using the setting, antecedent, behavior, and consequence information from the functional analysis.

A functional analysis is a useful tool for (a) identifying chains of predictable behaviors, (b) constructing testable explanations, and (c) shaping the specifics of an intervention. Although it also provides an estimate of how often a problem behavior might be occurring, other methods are more appropriate for establishing an accurate approximation of the student's current level of functioning over time. In the next section, we review some other direct observation procedures.

REVIEW OF OTHER DIRECT OBSERVATION DATA COLLECTION PROCEDURES

The Problem Identification Interview is designed to provide information about the nature of the problem. The functional analysis enables the consultant to observe the problem behavior directly within typical instructional contexts and to determine what other behaviors the student displays, what immediate and consequent factors are associated with those behaviors, and how the interactions between behavior and setting affect the classroom ecology. After this information has been collected, the consultant can begin selecting and developing an intervention (see Chapters 5 and 6). However, before implementing the intervention, he or she must develop a systematic method of collecting data on the behaviors of concern. Baseline information is important to establish a reliable estimate of the student's current level of functioning, which, in turn, can be used as a basis for evaluating the effectiveness of an intervention.

In the following section, we describe guidelines for establishing direct observation procedures, characteristics and examples of common direct observation procedures, and suggestions for reporting and presenting data.

Guidelines for Establishing Direct Observation Procedures

When developing data collection procedures, the objective is to (a) maximize the reliability (consistency or accuracy) and validity (soundness) of the data collected, (b) minimize interference to normal, ongoing instructional activities, (c) increase

ease of use, especially, if possible, by the teacher, and (d) increase the utility of the data produced and summarized. When establishing an observation procedure that will produce these kinds of outcomes, we suggest the following guidelines.

1. *Develop measurable and operational definitions of the behaviors to be recorded.* With clear definitions, the process of identifying and classifying student and teacher behavior is facilitated and greater confidence can be placed on the resulting data. Use one of the six dimensions—frequency, latency, locus, intensity, topography, or duration—to define the behavior.

2. *Develop as many (multiple) measures as is practical.* This is done to assess the full range of behaviors and evaluate the extent to which intervention effects and side effects are produced. Attention should be given to the response classes of both desirable and undesirable behaviors.

3. *Develop a "well-calibrated" measurement system* (Wolery, Bailey, & Sugai, 1988) in which (a) "each repetition of the behavior must represent essentially the same amount of behavior," (b) "the counting system must be directly related to instructional objectives," (c) "it must be possible to assess the behavior easily," and (d) "the counting system must be sensitive to changes in behavior" (p. 74).

4. *Identify specific times and settings to collect the data.* Select as many (multiple) settings as practical. When establishing baseline performance and determining the initial effects of intervention, observations should be conducted as consistently and frequently as practical.

5. *Develop observation systems that are as direct and formative as possible.* Less direct methods lack sensitivity and accuracy, and more summative methods do not expose response patterns, such as trends, variability, level changes, and do not provide ongoing opportunities for decision making.

6. *Practice using the observation procedure.* Practice increases familiarity, fluency, and accuracy with an observation procedure. Practice also assists in evaluating the usefulness and efficiency of a procedure or its instruments, so modifications can be made if necessary.

Characteristics and Examples of Common Direct Observation Procedures

There are many methods for collecting direct observation data; however, three basic categories exist: permanent product recording, event-based recording, and time-based recording. Each of the approaches are briefly described and examples are provided.

Permanent product recording.   If a student's or teacher's behaviors produce a lasting outcome or product, we can obtain an estimate of the behavior's occurrence by counting the outcomes or products (for example, the number of worksheets completed) or some smaller aspect within each product (such as the number of items completed per worksheet). Although permanent product recording is not technically a direct observation procedure, we include it because it is a relatively simple and commonly used procedure. It can be a direct observation procedure, if the observer watches the student engage in the behavior that produces the outcome. For example, the teacher counts the number of papers on the floor as Chuck throws them down.

Permanent product recording is used whenever a response is associated with a durable product or outcome. It is used most commonly in measuring academic performance: for example, the number of words written and spelled accurately; the pages, worksheets, homework assignments, books, or lessons completed; or the math problems computed correctly. Many nonacademic behaviors also produce permanent products or effects that can be counted: for example, the number of discipline, referral, or timeout slips; items disturbed, destroyed, stolen, or missing; pieces of paper on the floor; pencil or pen marks on desktops.

Using permanent product recording is a simple process consisting of the following steps:

STEP 1: Clearly define the behavior(s) and the outcome(s).

STEP 2: Define the setting in which the outcomes will be counted (for example, Room 17, free play area, playground).

STEP 3: Define the time interval within which the outcomes will be produced (for example, the whole school day, math period, first 15 minutes of the day).

STEP 4: Count the number of outcomes.

STEP 5: Summarize the data. Determine the total number of outcomes per session, and calculate the percentage, if the opportunities are known, and/or the rate, if the time interval is known.

A typical recording instrument will include identifying information, setting information, time interval, and outcome information. A generic form is illustrated in Figure 4.6.

Permanent-product recording systems are appealing because they do not interfere with instruction, the teacher or observer does not have to watch the behaviors directly, and they are simple to use. However, permanent-product recording systems have a number of disadvantages. First, unless the observer records the outcomes as they are being produced, it is possible that other students may have furnished some or all of the outcomes. Second, the observer does not have the opportunity to "see" how the student responds; this information would be useful for analyzing errors or response definitions. These disadvantages can be minimized by recording the outcomes as they are being produced. Then the observer would have the opportunity to see who made the product and analyze the response and the conditions—that is, antecedent and consequent events under which it is emitted. A final disadvantage is that there must be a reliable, valid permanent product or outcome. Many student social behaviors do not produce a lasting effect. When establishing a permanent-product recording procedure, it is also important to arrange for equal "size" products so individual counts will be comparable or calibrated.

Event-based recording systems.   Event-based recording systems are similar to permanent product methods in that a simple recording of the behavior is taken. They differ in that the observer directly records some dimension or characteristic

FIGURE 4.6

Permanent Product Recording Form

PERMANENT PRODUCT RECORDING FORM	Observer _____ Student _____ Teacher _____ Classroom/School _____

Opportunity Definition

Outcome Definition

Setting Description

Date	Start Time	End Time	Number of Opportunities	Number of Outcomes	Percentage	Rate (No./min.)

of the behavior as it is being emitted. Event recording requires a discrete behavior that has a clearly defined beginning and end.

A variety of event-based systems can be used: They include tally, duration recording, latency recording, controlled presentations, and trials to criterion. To engage in any of these methods, the following steps should be completed:

STEP 1: Clearly define what the behavior(s) looks like, especially, when it begins and ends.

STEP 2: Define the setting in which the behavior will be recorded.

STEP 3: Define the time interval or session within which the observation will occur.

STEP 4: Record the behavior.

STEP 5: Summarize the data.

A general example of a recording form and a brief description of how recording and summarizing varies for each event-based method follows:

I. **Tally.** Direct observation method in which each occurrence of the targeted behavior(s) is counted—for example, talking out, hits, hand-raises, conversation interruptions, out of seat, sharing episodes, answers given correctly (see generic form in Figure 4.7).

A. *Recording method*
   1. Divide the observation session into smaller intervals (for example, 3–5 minutes).
   2. Observe the student directly and tally the behaviors as they occur within the appropriate interval.

B. *Data summary*
   1. Count the number of tally marks to determine the total number of behaviors (for example, 24 behaviors).
   2. To determine the rate, divide the total by the amount of time observed, usually minutes (for example, 24 behaviors/48-minute observation period = 0.5 behaviors per minute, or one behavior every 2 minutes).
   3. Analyze the distribution of tally marks across session intervals for possible response patterns (for example, the teacher and consultant note that two-thirds of the behaviors occur equally in the first two intervals and last two intervals of the observation session).
   4. Report the data as the number of events per observation session (for example, 24 behaviors in 48 minutes) and/or number of events per minute (for example, 0.5 behaviors per minute).

II. **Duration Recording.** Direct observation methods in which the duration or length of the behavior is of concern—for example, fingersucking, independent or cooperative play, temper tantrum (see the generic form in Figure 4.8).

A. *Recording method*
   1. Mark the time or start a stopwatch when the behavior begins.
   2. Mark the time or stop the stopwatch when the behavior ends.
   3. Record the duration of the behavioral event.

FIGURE 4.7
Event Recording Instrument

EVENT RECORDING FORM	Observer _____ Student _____ Teacher _____ Classroom/School _____

Behavior(s) Definition (Give code if more than one behavior observed.)

Setting Description

Date	Start Time:	Interval #1	#2	#3	#4	#5
	End Time:	#6	#7	#8	#9	#10

	Total Number of Behaviors:	Total Number of Minutes:	Rate:			

Date	Start Time:	Interval #1	#2	#3	#4	#5
	End Time:	#6	#7	#8	#9	#10

	Total Number of Behaviors:	Total Number of Minutes:	Rate:			

FIGURE 4.8
Duration Recording Instrument

DURATION RECORDING FORM	Observer _____ Student _____ Teacher _____ Classroom/School _____				
Behavior(s) Definition					
Setting Description					

Date	Session Start Time:	Event #1	#2	#3	#4	#5
	Session End Time:	#6	#7	#8	#9	#10
	Total Number of Session Minutes:	Total Response Duration:	Percentage of Total Session Time:	Number of Events:	Average Duration per Event:	

Date	Session Start Time:	Event #1	#2	#3	#4	#5
	Session End Time:	#6	#7	#8	#9	#10
	Total Number of Session Minutes:	Total Response Duration:	Percentage of Total Session Time:	Number of Events:	Average Duration per Event:	

B. *Data summary*

1. To determine the cumulative duration, sum the total amount of time the behavior was recorded (for example, 3 min. + 5 min. + 2 min. + 3 min. + 2 min. = 15 min.).

2. To determine the percentage of time, divide the cumulative duration by the total session observation time and multiply by 100 [for example, (15 min./30 min.) × 100 = 50% of session or time].

3. To determine the average duration per response occurrence, divide the cumulative duration by the number of response occurrences (for example, 15 min./5 occurrences = 3 min. per occurrence).

4. Report data as the total duration per session (15 min. in 30-min. session), the percentage of time per session (for example, 50% of 30-min. session), and/or the average duration per response occurrence (for example, 3 min. per occurrence).

III. **Latency Recording.** Direct observation methods in which the time taken between some antecedent event and the beginning of the targeted behavior is recorded—for example, following directions, answering questions, getting into seat, starting work. A clear definition of the antecedent event and the beginning of the behavior(s) is required (see the generic form in Figure 4.9).

A. *Recording method*

1. Define the antecedent events (for example, when the teacher gives an academic task in related direction, like "Put your finger on the first word of the first sentence.").

2. Determine the number of events to be presented or recorded per observation session. This step can be omitted if the number of opportunities is a variable (for example, teacher presents 12 task-related directions in 30-min. reading activity).

3. Present the antecedent event and record the time or start a stopwatch.

4. When the behavior begins, record the end time or stop the stopwatch.

5. Record the latency of each behavioral event (for example, 3 sec., 120 sec., 4 min.).

B. *Data summary*

1. Calculate the average latency per event by summing the total amount of latency and dividing it by the number of events during the observation session [for example, (2 sec. + 3 sec. + 2 sec. + 3 sec.)/4 events = 2.5 sec. per event].

2. Report the data as an average latency per event (for example, 2.5 sec. per event).

IV. **Controlled Presentations.** Specialized form of tally recording in which a preset number of response opportunities or trials are provided. The observer records the presence or absence of a targeted response when the opportunity is available—for example, on time to each of seven class periods, correct responses to 10 teacher questions or directions (see the generic form in Figure 4.10).

FIGURE 4.9
Latency Recording Instrument

LATENCY RECORDING FORM	Observer _____ Student _____ Teacher_____ Classroom/School _____

Behavior(s) Definition

Antecedent Event Definition

Setting Description

Date	Event #1	#2	#3	#4	#5	#6
	#7	#8	#9	#10	#11	#12

	Total Number of Minutes Latency:	Total Number of Antecedent Events:	Average Latency per Event:			

Date	Event #1	#2	#3	#4	#5	#6
	#7	#8	#9	#10	#11	#12

	Total Number of Minutes Latency:	Total Number of Antecedent Events:	Average Latency per Event:			

FIGURE 4.10

Controlled-Presentation Recording Instrument

CONTROLLED-PRESENTATION RECORDING FORM	Observer _____ Student _____ Teacher _____ Classroom/School _____

Behavior(s) Definition

Definition of Trial

Setting Description

Date	Trial #1 + −	#2 + −	#3 + −	#4 + −	#5 + −	#6 + −
	#7 + −	#8 + −	#9 + −	#10 + −	#11 + −	#12 + −

Total Number of + Trials:	Total Number of Trials:	Percentage of Trials:			

Date	Trial #1 + −	#2 + −	#3 + −	#4 + −	#5 + −	#6 + −
	#7 + −	#8 + −	#9 + −	#10 + −	#11 + −	#12 + −

Total Number of + Trials:	Total Number of Trials:	Percentage of Trials:			

A. *Recording method*
 1. Define what constitutes a trial or opportunity (for example, when the teacher asks a question that is directed toward all students in the group or classroom).
 2. Establish the number of trials to be presented within a designated time interval or session (for example, first 15 questions per academic period).
 3. Set the length of the time interval or session within which the trials are provided (for example, two consecutive 40-min. academic periods).
 4. Present trials.
 5. Record the presence or absence of targeted behaviors (for example, handraise observed " + " or not observed " − ").
B. *Data summary*
 1. Divide the total number of targeted behaviors by the total number of trials and multiply by 100 [(10 handraises/15 questions) × 100 = 83% of trials or opportunities].
 2. Report the data as a percentage of trials or opportunities.
V. Trials to Criterion. Specialized form of tally and controlled-presentation methods in which the focus is on the number of trials or attempts required by the student to reach criterion for mastery—for example, the number of trials to complete an assignment, to get to class on time and be prepared (see the generic form in Figure 4.11).
A. *Recording method*
 1. Define what constitutes a trial or opportunity (for example, the teacher gives an academic task in related direction, such as "Turn the page," or "Place your finger on the first word in the sentence.").
 2. Determine the criterion for acceptable trial performance (for example, an accurate response within 2 sec. with no more than one repeat request by the teacher).
 3. Determine the criterion for the number of trials required for mastery (for example, three consecutive appropriate trials in a 45-min. academic period).
 4. Present the trial.
 5. Record the presence or absence of criterion-level performance.
 6. Discontinue the trial presentations when the number of trials required for mastery is met.
B. *Data summary*
 1. Determine the number of trials at criterion level required to meet mastery criterion (for example, three consecutive trials with no more than one teacher restatement of direction must be achieved within seven trial presentations).
 2. Report as number of trials required to meet criterion (for example, four trials to criterion, seven trials to criterion).

Event-based recording methods are simple to implement; however, they require practice and careful planning to minimize any instructional interference. Tallying events can be difficult to accomplish with extremely high rate behaviors,

F I G U R E 4.11

Trials-to-Criterion Recording Instrument

TRIALS-TO-CRITERION RECORDING FORM	Observer _____ Student _____ Teacher _____ Classroom/School _____

Behavior(s) Definition

Definition of Trial

Setting Description

Date	Mastery Criterion	Number of Correct Trials	Number of Incorrect Trials	Total Number of Trials to Criterion

such as rapid talkouts, or with highly variable duration behaviors, such as jumping in and out of the seat or cooperative play. If clear definitions are developed and efficient implementation strategies are planned, event-based methods have the advantage of providing *direct* estimates of response occurrences; that is, the observer sees the individual emit the behavior being recorded.

Time-based recording methods.   When it is difficult or impossible to use event-based recording because of multiple students, multiple targeted behaviors, high rate behaviors, highly variable duration responses, or high instructional interference, time-based recording methods are useful. Time-based methods *estimate* the level or rate of occurrence of a behavior. Three time-based recording variations are commonly used: (a) partial interval, (b) whole interval, and (c) momentary interval. All three methods use the following implementation steps:

STEP 1: Clearly define what the behavior(s) looks like, especially when it begins and ends.

STEP 2: Define the setting in which the behavior will be recorded.

STEP 3: Define the time interval or session within which the observation will occur.

STEP 4: Divide the observation session into smaller intervals (5 sec. to 5 to 10 min.).

STEP 5: Record the presence or absence of the targeted behavior by interval.

STEP 6: Summarize the data.

The recording form for all three time-based observation systems is basically the same. What varies is the number of students observed, the number of behaviors recorded, the size and number of intervals, and when a " + " interval is marked. The example in Figure 4.12 is for a single student and multiple behaviors, but it can also be used for partial, whole, or momentary recording. A brief description of how recording and summarizing data varies for each time-based method follows:

   I. Partial-Interval Recording. A time-sampling procedure in which the presence or absence of some prespecified amount of behavior during an interval is recorded.

     A. *Recording method*

       1. Define the interval size.

       2. Define the amount of behavior required to meet the criterion for presence or absence of the behavior (for example, any amount of behavior, at least 10 sec. in duration).

       3. Observe the specified interval length.

       4. At the end of the interval, record (+) if the criterion-level behavior was observed during the given interval, or (−) if the criterion-level behavior is not observed.

       5. Observe the next interval.

     B. *Data summary*

       1. Divide the number of intervals in which criterion-level performance (+) was observed by the total number of intervals observed and

F I G U R E 4.12
Time-Based Recording Instrument

TIME-BASED RECORDING FORM	Observer _____ Student _____ Teacher _____ Classroom/School _____

Size of Interval:	Type of Recording System:	___ Partial Interval ___ Whole Interval ___ Momentary Interval

Behavior(s) Definitions

Setting Description

Date	Behavior	Interval (+ = observed, − = not observed)									
		1	2	3	4	5	6	7	8	9	10
	1. _____										
	2. _____										
	3. _____										
	4. _____										

Behavior	Number of +'s	Total Number of Intervals	Percentage of Intervals
1.			
2.			
3.			
4.			

multiply by 100 [for example, (12 + intervals/20 intervals) × 100 = 60% of intervals].

  2. Report as a percentage of intervals (for example, cooperative play behaviors occurred in 83% of 15-sec. intervals).

II. Whole-Interval Recording. A variation of partial-interval recording in which the presence or absence of some targeted behavior(s) must be observed during the entire observation interval.

  A. *Recording method*
    1. Define the interval size.
    2. Observe for the specified interval length.
    3. At the end of the interval, record (+) if the targeted behavior is observed during the entire interval, or (−) if the behavior is observed less than the whole interval.
    4. Observe the next interval.

  B. *Data summary*
    1. Divide the number of intervals in which the whole interval criterion (+) is observed by the total number of intervals observed and multiply by 100.
    2. Report as a percentage of intervals (for example, out of seat 33% of one-min. intervals).

III. Momentary-Interval Recording. A variation of partial-interval recording in which the presence or absence of some targeted behavior(s) is assessed at the end of the observation interval.

  A. *Recording method*
    1. Define the interval size.
    2. Observe for the specified interval length.
    3. At the end of the interval, record (+) if the targeted behavior is present at the end of the interval, or (−) if the behavior is absent.
    4. Observe at the end of the next interval.

  B. *Data summary*
    1. Divide the number of intervals in which the behavior is observed at the end of the interval (+) by the total number of intervals observed and multiply by 100.
    2. Report as a percentage of intervals (for example, talking with other students 45% of possible 2-min. intervals).

Time-based recording systems have the advantage of being relatively easy to implement even when the teacher is engaged in other instructional activities. However, consultants and teachers must remember that the resulting data represent *approximations* of the behavior, not direct accounts behavior. For example, within a given interval, a behavior could occur more than once, yet only one " + " mark is recorded; or a single response could begin at the end of one interval and continue into another, yet no " + " intervals would be marked with a whole-interval recording, one " + " interval would be marked with momentary-interval recording, or two " + " intervals would be marked with partial-interval recording. Careful definition of the behavior and determination of the interval size can increase the representativeness of the resulting data.

Determining which time-based recording method to use should be based on (a) the critical dimensions or features of the target behavior (namely, duration versus frequency), (b) the degree of accuracy (or conservatism) required, and (c) the resources available to conduct the observations (for example, having a second observer). In general, the smaller the interval size, the more behavior can be "captured."

Suggestions for Reporting and Presenting Data

As indicated previously, data serve numerous functions: (a) determining current levels of functioning, (b) communicating information to and with others, and (c) evaluating the effectiveness of interventions and making treatment decisions. Data are only as useful as the consultant's and teacher's ability to use the information in a meaningful fashion. Data can be summarized and presented in an assortment of ways and forms. We describe some simple methods for summarizing and presenting data in the following sections.

Summarizing data. Summarizing data on social behaviors is based on the kind of recording procedures used and how the data are to be utilized. The kinds of data summaries associated with each type of recording method are shown in Box 4.5.

Presenting data. After the data have been summarized, they should be displayed for maximum utility, so teachers can make informed instructional decisions and so students can receive feedback about their performance (Wolery, Bailey, & Sugai, 1988). We recommend that consultants select display formats that are (a) easy to read, (b) simple to maintain, (c) accurate pictures of performance, and (d) easy to integrate into daily instructional routines. Today's advanced computer technologies—such as data base, spreadsheet, and graphics software—can simplify the mechanics of displaying information; however, it is important to remember that someone is needed to prepare the computer to receive, enter, format, and display the data. Teachers, consultants, and students can participate in one or all phases of the data presentation process.

Tables and Graphs are the two basic methods of displaying information. In general, tables are systematic organizations of data in which measures or summaries of performance (for example, frequencies, rates, percentages) are presented. An example of Helena's talkout and handraise data is presented in Figure 4.13.

Although tables are useful for displaying numbers, they do not provide a useful visual display or facilitate the process of interpreting the data. Graphs are practical tools for displaying the data so a picture of the student's performance over time can be illustrated. Bar and line graphs are employed most often. Using Helena's data, each of these types of graphs are illustrated in Figure 4.14.

Line graphs are the most useful for displaying data because (a) data can be added, analyzed, and evaluated on a formative basis, and (b) data trends and variability can be identified. Although equal-interval line graph paper is the most common type used to display data, equal-ratio line graph paper (semi-log or

BOX 4.5

Outcome data summaries by type of observation method

RECORDING METHOD	OUTCOME DATA SUMMARY	EXAMPLE
Permanent product	Number Rate Percentage	15 marks on the table 7 pieces of paper per hour 65% of items missing
Tally	Number Rate Percentage	47 animal noises 0.5 talkouts per minute Handraises in 75% of the opportunities
Duration	Cumulative time Average time Percentage	35 out of 55 min. out of seat 7 min. per tantrum Cooperative play in 35% of the time
Latency	Average time	Compliance 18 sec. on the average after the direction given
Controlled Presentations	Number Percentage	On time to class 5 out of 8 opportunities Role plays 25% of the problem-solving steps correctly
Trials to Criterion	Number	4 trials to criterion (90% accuracy for 3 consecutive trials)
Time Sampling (whole, partial, momentary interval)	Percentage	Talking to neighbor in 66% of the intervals

standard behavior charts) (White & Haring, 1980) is also used (see Figure 4.15) visually to display relative changes in performance.

Regardless of the type of graph paper used, a complete graph should contain sufficient information so minimal explanation is required to read it. When preparing a complete line graph, the following conventions should be observed (see Figure 4.16):

1. Include a descriptive title that provides information about what behavior(s) (dependent variable) is being measured and any interventions (independent variables) being used.
2. Label each axis. Time (for example, days, sessions) is indicated along the horizontal axis or abscissa. The targeted behavior(s) are indicated along the vertical axis or ordinate.
3. If more than one behavior is plotted on a line graph, use different symbols. "•" is often used to denote a behavior that is to be increased or strengthened; "☐" is a standard symbol for a behavior to be decreased or weakened.
4. Use vertical phase lines to indicate when a change (for example, intervention), is made. Label the phases.

FIGURE 4.13
Data Summary Table

| STUDENT DATA TABLE | Student Helena |
| | Teacher Mr. Kelani |

Behavior Definitions:

A talkout (TO) is defined as a verbalization made by the student who is not first recognized by the teacher.

An appropriate handraise (HR) is defined as waiting quietly with hand raised appropriately above head and talking when acknowledged by the teacher.

Date	Number of TOs	Number of HRs	Number of Minutes	Number of TOs/Minute	HRs/Minute
9/5 M	17	2	42	0.40	0.05
9/6 T	23	1	35	0.66	0.03
9/7 W	18	4	38	0.47	0.11
9/8 R			absent		
9/9 F	21	2	34	0.62	0.06
9/10 M	18	3	41	0.44	0.07
9/11 T	2	12	39	0.05	0.31
9/12 W	1	13	29	0.03	0.45
9/13 R	1	19	37	0.03	0.51
9/14 F					
9/17 M					

FIGURE 4.14

Example of line and bar graphs

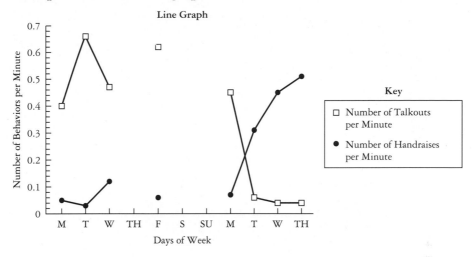

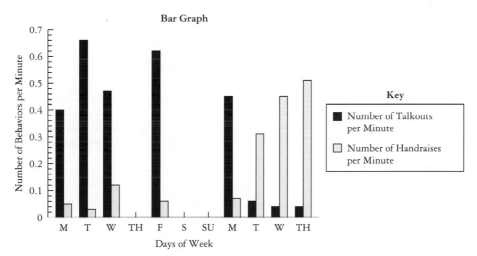

5. Connect consecutive data points. Do not connect across phase lines or when there are no data collected.
6. Plot the data as soon as they become available.

SUMMARY

After indirect information is gathered through the Request for Assistance and the Problem Identification Interview, specific details must be collected to clarify the seriousness of the problem and to establish a baseline of the target behaviors. The purpose of this chapter was to describe information collection procedures that are

FIGURE 4.15

Example of equal-interval and equal-ratio (standard-behavior) graphs

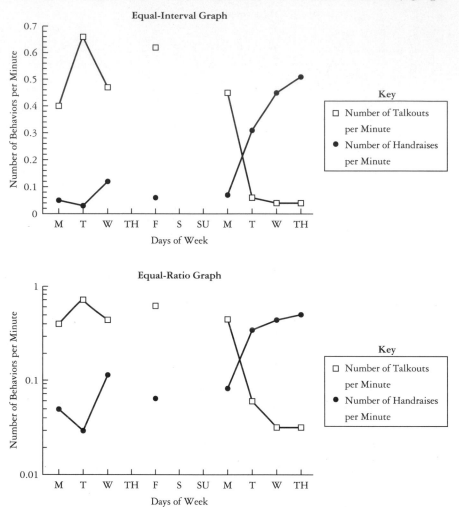

direct and that enable the consultant and the teacher to analyze the critical features of the problem behavior within the context of the setting in which they are observed. The functional analysis is particular useful because it provides a temporally based picture of the behaviors displayed and the immediate antecedent and consequent events associated with those behaviors. With this information, testable explanations and relevant interventions can be developed.

The key features of this chapter are as follows:

1. A functional analysis is a temporally based direct observation procedure designed to examine the relationship between behavior and setting variables—that is, immediate antecedent and consequent events.

FIGURE 4.16
Illustration of graphing conventions

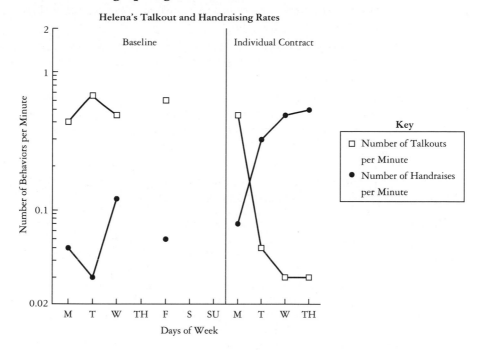

2. A functional analysis can produce three major outcomes: (a) sample of behaviors and events, (b) behavior chains, and (c) testable explanations.

3. Testable explanations are "best guesses" or hypotheses about factors thought to contribute to the behaviors' occurrence. These explanations are called *testable* because their two major components can be observed and manipulated.

4. When a testable explanation provides a reasonable interpretation for a target behavior, it is called a functional relationship because it describes a high probability association between the behavior and a specific antecedent or consequent event.

5. The development of interventions becomes more focused when functional relationships are identified and confirmed; however, practice is required to become fluent at conducting a useful functional analysis.

6. After a functional analysis is conducted, the student's current level of functioning must be estimated in order to determine the effectiveness of an intervention.

7. Direct observation methods should (a) maximize reliability and validity, (b) minimize interference, (c) increase ease of use, and (d) increase the utility of the data.

8. When establishing a direct observation procedure, (a) develop measurable definitions of the behaviors to be recorded, (b) develop as many measures as practical, (c) develop a well-calibrated measurement system, (d) identify specific times and settings to collect the data, (e) develop observation systems that are as direct and formative as possible, and (f) practice using the observation procedures.

9. Three basic categories of direct observation procedures can be used: (a) permanent-product recording, (b) event-based recording, (c) and time-based recording.

10. Data help to (a) determine current levels of functioning, (b) communicate information to others, and (c) evaluate intervention effectiveness; however, data are only as helpful as the observer's ability to meaningfully use the information.

11. Data should be presented so they are (a) easy to read, (b) simple to maintain, (c) accurate pictures of performance, and (d) easy to integrate into daily instructional activities.

REFERENCES

BAER, D. M., WOLF, M. M., & RISLEY, T. R. (1968). Some current dimensions of applied behavior analysis. *Journal of Applied Behavior Analysis, 1,* 91–97.

GELFAND, D. M., & HARTMANN, D. P. (1984). *Child behavior analysis and therapy* (2nd ed.). New York: Pergamon Press.

SKINNER, B. F. (1953). *Science and human behavior.* New York: The Free Press.

SUGAI, G., & COLVIN, G. (1989). *Environmental explanations of behavior: Conducting a functional analysis.* Eugene, OR: Behavior Associates.

VARGAS, J. S. (1977). *Behavioral psychology for teachers.* New York: Harper & Row.

WHITE, O. R., & HARING, N. G. (1980). *Exceptional teaching* (2nd ed.). Columbus, OH: Merrill.

WOLERY, M. R., BAILEY, D. B., JR., & SUGAI, G. (1988). *Effective teaching: Principles and procedures of applied behavior analysis with exceptional students.* Boston: Allyn & Bacon.

C H A P T E R   F I V E

Intervention Selection and Development

INTRODUCTION

In her 17 years as a third-grade teacher, Miss Phillips has never encountered a student with behaviors anything like those displayed by Eduardo. He has been one of her greatest challenges. Ever since September, Eduardo has been on the go. Miss Phillips has chased him all over the school grounds; he has been on the roof, in the furnace room, in and on top of the principal's car, and under the school bus. On those rare occasions when he is in the classroom, he spends most of his time visiting other students, touching their things, and talking about martial arts turtles. Miss Phillips has endured more than five weeks of parent conferences, school suspensions, special contracts, and extra assistance from the school counselor; all have been unsuccessful and extremely frustrating.

Finally, Miss Phillips completed a Request for Assistance (Figure 5.1). The school psychologist, Ms. Kalgoorlie, who also is the teacher consultant for three elementary schools in the district, has collected information about how Miss Phillips sees the problem (Problem Identification Interview, Figure 5.2) and completed two 45-minute observations of Phillips' behaviors (functional analysis, Figure 5.3). Having completed these tasks, Miss Phillips and Ms. Kalgoorlie have determined that Eduardo's behaviors pose a serious problem and warrant further attention.

At this point in the consultation process, the consultant and the teacher must work together to develop an intervention plan. The purpose of this chapter is to describe how the consultant can structure the process of intervention selection and development. Our prescriptive approach focuses on the activities and structures the consultant uses to increase the efficiency of the process and the probability of intervention success.

This chapter is divided into two major sections: an interventionist perspective on behavior change and intervention selection and development. We offer guidelines for the consultant to consider during the intervention selection and

119

FIGURE 5.1

Miss Phillips's completed Request for Assistance

REQUEST FOR ASSISTANCE FORM	Referring Person Ms. Phillips

Title   Teacher   Date 12 / 12/ 91

Student   Eduardo V.

Grade   3   DOB 5 / 21/ 84   Sex: (M) F   IEP: Y (N)

Check Type of Problem Behavior

Academic: ___Reading ___Math ___Spelling ___Writing ___Study Skills ___Other _____

Social: ___Aggressive ✓Noncompliant ✓Truant ___Tardy ___Withdrawn ✓Disruptive
___Social Skills ___Self-Management ___Other_____

Communication: ___Language ___Fluency ___Articulation ___Voice ___Other _____

Self-Help: ___Dressing ___Hygiene ___Other_____

Health: ___Vision ___Hearing ___Physical ___Other _____

Provide Specific and Observable Description of Problem

Disrupts lessons and bothers other students.
Runs from the classroom.

Provide Specific Description of Problem Context

Where: Classroom

When: Afternoons

With Whom: Teacher

Other:

Provide List of Previous Remediation Attempts

1. Suspended

2. Parent Conferences

3. Special Contracts with school counselor

FIGURE 5.2

Miss Phillips's completed Problem Identification Interview form

---

PROBLEM IDENTIFICATION INTERVIEW FORM	Page 1 of 3

Consultant __Kalgoorlie__   Teacher __Phillips__

Date __1 / 5/ 92__ School __Broome Elem.__

Student Information: Name __Eduardo__   Room __4A__

Grade __3__   Age __7__   Sex: (M) F   IEP: Y(N)

Describe the problem behavior. (5 minutes)

Visiting with other students, touching their things, talking about martial arts turtles. When told to return to task, runs from the classroom.

**Describe other behaviors that seem to be related to the problem behavior.
(3 minutes)**

Talking out, losing desk supplies, reading comic books.

**Describe the conditions under which the problem behavior is most likely to occur.
(2 minutes)**

When: __In afternoon during reading and math lessons__

Where: __In classroom__

With Whom: __Classroom teacher and assistant__

FIGURE 5.2 (*continued*)

PROBLEM IDENTIFICATION INTERVIEW FORM	Page 2 of 3

Describe what usually happens <u>after</u> the problem behavior occurs. (2 minutes)

Instructions for task are given out or other students are reading, answering questions, or following teacher directions.

Describe what usually happens immediately <u>before</u> the problem behavior occurs. (2 minutes)

Lesson stops

Describe what <u>you</u> usually do when the behavior occurs. (2 minutes)

- Tell E. to return to seat, keep hands to self, and pay attention.

- Remind E. of classroom rules.

Describe what <u>other students</u> do when the behavior occurs. (2 minutes)

Complain to teacher about E's behavior or attempt to ignore him.

F I G U R E 5.2 (*continued*)

PROBLEM IDENTIFICATION INTERVIEW FORM	Page 3 of 3

Describe what you would like the student to do <u>instead</u> of the problem behavior.
(2 minutes)

— Stay on task when other students are working.

— Keep hands on his own property.

— Follow teacher's directions the first time.

List or describe <u>other interventions</u> that have been tried. (3 minutes)

— 3-day suspensions.

— 2 conferences with E.'s father, who grounded E. for two weeks each time.

— school counselor wrote special contracts for trips to Mickey's Pizza Shop.

Make an appointment to conduct an observation and debriefing. (1 minute)

Date 1 / 6 / 92 Time 1 :30 to 3 : 00 Place/Classroom 4A

Other information/notes

— Can do the work given to him.

— Enjoys playing with peers, especially computer games.

— Parents unable to assist with home program.

— Can stay at-task up to 10 minutes. Longer if at computer.

FIGURE 5.3
Ms. Kalgoorlie's completed Functional Analysis Observation form

FUNCTIONAL ANALYSIS OBSERVATION FORM	Date 1 / 6 / 92 Time 1 : 30 Observer Kalgoorlie Student Eduardo (E) Teacher Phillips (P) Classroom/School 4A / Broome Elem.

Setting Description: Reading group. Students take turns reading 1 sentence from story. Nonreading students follow along. 15 students in group. 10 other students doing seatwork or at computer. P sitting at desk in front of group. E in front row.

Time	Antecedents	Behaviors	Consequences
1:37	P: "Laurie, your turn to read."	E: "Hey, what page are we on?"	P: "Page 77... don't bother, laurie" L: "Yeah"
	✓	E: Takes L page marker and waves it at Trish.	T: "Stop that!" P: "E, stop that!" walks toward E.
1:39	✓	E: Puts it on his head & says he's a samurai turtle.	P: "Okay, everyone, let's start over and behave like big people."
	✓	E: Throws it at T & gets up from desk.	P: "Oh no, you don't... sit yourself down." Puts her hands on E's shoulders.
	✓	E: Pushes hands away	

development phases and also introduce the Intervention Planning form, which has been designed to increase the efficiency of the interaction between the consultant and the teacher.

AN INTERVENTIONIST PERSPECTIVE

In education, there are a multitude of approaches to problem solving and behavior change. At one end of the continuum are "noninterventionist" approaches; here, the teacher is a relatively passive participant in the change process and a highly trained, outside change agent, such as a psychologist or counselor, is usually involved. The student or individual displaying the troublesome behaviors is seen as primarily responsible for the problem and its improvement. Intervention attempts are indirect with respect to the behavior and focus on the underlying, usually internal, causes that are seen as the result of early developmental events. Nondirective therapies—such as psychoanalysis, play therapy, art and music therapy, and other psychoeducational approaches—are examples of the noninterventionist approach.

In the middle of the continuum are numerous "interactionist" approaches, in which teachers are mediators who provide students with social feedback about their behaviors. The source of a problem is viewed as a closely woven interaction between students and their social environments or milieu. Typically, these students have learned misrules about how to interact in a more appropriate manner or have goals that are inconsistent or incompatible with those of the larger social community (that is, the school, county, or state). The result is conflict between student values and cultural practices. Interventions based on consequences focus on helping students shape more desirable societal rules, values, and goals. Social agents provide students with interpretations of their behavior and the specific, real outcomes of their actions. A change in behavior is said to result from a change in goals and values. Teachers are relatively passive, in that they avoid directly teaching or telling the student what is desired, instead they interpret the student's behaviors and the associated effects their behaviors have on the social community. Thus, change agents and students share the responsibility for behavior change. Typical examples of interactionist models of behavior change include Reality Therapy (Glasser, 1965, 1969, 1985, 1990) and Logical and Natural Consequences (Dreikurs, 1968; Dreikurs & Cassel, 1972; Dreikurs, Grunwald, & Pepper, 1982; Gordon, 1974, 1989).

"Interventionist" approaches are at the other end of the continuum. Unlike the non-interventionist and interactionist approaches, emphasis is placed on the environment. Internal influences are seen as difficult to access and relatively incidental, instead interventions focus on behavior and environment. Maladjusted behavior is described as learned; therefore, this approach emphasizes weakening the problem behavior by removing maintaining outcomes and then strengthening more desirable ways of behaving by increasing opportunities for positive reinforcement. Although teachers assume very active roles, students are relatively passive in the behavior change process. Ownership for the problem and its change is closely tied to the teacher's behaviors. Behavior modification (e.g., Martin & Pear,

1988), applied behavior analysis (e.g., Baer, Wolf, & Risley, 1968; Skinner, 1953), and assertive discipline (Canter & Canter, 1992) are examples of the interventionist approach.

This general characterization of approaches to behavior change highlights the role of the environment, behavior, teacher, and student and their relationship to causation and intervention. Box 5.1 provides an overview of the primary characteristics of the noninterventionist, interactionist, and interventionist approaches. Each approach has its strengths and weaknesses; however, we focus on interventionist strategies for the following reasons:

1. Teachers are "empowered" with behavior change tactics that they can learn and implement in school settings.
2. There is a direct approach to behavior change with a focus on behaviors and the immediate environment in which they are observed.

BOX 5.1

A comparison of the major approaches to behavior management

	Noninterventionist	Interactionist	Interventionist
Where did the problem behavior originate?	Early developmental events	Learning of inappropriate rules, values and goals	Learning of inappropriate behavior
Who can change the behavior problem?	Nonteaching specialists	Specially trained teacher	Trained teacher, teaching assistant
Who or what is responsible for change in behavior?	Student	Student and teacher	Teacher and environment
What is the focus of intervention?	Prior developmental events	Social interpretations of behavior	Environmental antecedents and consequences
What role does behavior play?	Symptom of problem	Indicator of social conflict	Focus of attention
What role does the teacher play?	Relatively passive participant	Mediator/interpreter of behavior	Active manipulator of environmental stimuli
What role does the environment play?	Little direct influence	Social environment is influential	Environment is very influential
What role does the student play?	Active participant with primary responsibility for behavior change	Active developer of more compatible values and goals	Relatively passive

3. Emphasis is placed on student and teacher behaviors that are accessible, observable, and changeable.

4. Blame or responsibility is not placed on the student but on the student's learning history, which has been shaped by environmental events.

5. There is a well-documented, empirically supported data base that emphasizes the most positive, least intrusive or aversive, and least restrictive methodologies.

6. The interventionist approach is compatible with a teaching approach to behavior change that focuses on strengthening those behaviors that enable students to be more successful and to experience positive outcomes for their behaviors.

In the next section, we discuss intervention selection and development. Although it is tempting to discuss all that a consultant needs to know about applied behavior analysis, effective teaching, curriculum selection and modification, that is not the primary purpose of this book. Because we focus on school-based consultation, we assume that readers have a basic understanding and practical experience with the elements of effective teaching and applied behavior analysis. Thus, we are not going to discuss applied behavior analysis principles and procedures except as they relate directly to the consultant's responsibility to help teachers select, develop, and implement them.

With respect to the management of social behaviors, we encourage readers to review strategies discussed in sources such as the following:

ALBERTO, P. A., & TROUTMAN, A. C. (1988). *Applied behavior analysis for teachers* (3rd ed.). Columbus, OH: Merrill.

COOPER, J. O., HERON, T. E., & HEWARD, W. L. (1987). *Applied behavior analysis.* Columbus, OH: Merrill.

KAZDIN, A. E. (1980b). *Behavior modification in applied settings* (rev.). Homewood, IL: Dorsey Press.

KERR, M. M., & NELSON, C. M. (1989). *Strategies for managing behavior problems in the classroom,* (2nd ed.). Columbus, OH: Merrill.

MARTIN, G., & PEAR, J. (1988). *Behavior modification: What it is and how to do it* (3rd ed.). Englewood Cliffs, NJ: Prentice-Hall.

WOLERY, M. R., BAILEY, D. B., JR., & SUGAI, G. (1988). *Effective teaching: Principles and procedures of applied behavior analysis with exceptional students.* Boston: Allyn & Bacon.

INTERVENTION SELECTION AND DEVELOPMENT

When Ms. Kalgoorlie and Miss Phillips approach intervention selection and development, they are confronted by an endless array of choices and considerations. Even though the behavioral or interventionist approaches are more focused, they still offer an assortment of strategies and variations.

In the next section, we discuss some tactics that can facilitate the selection and development of behavioral interventions. Consultants must assist teachers by providing strategies that are effective, are easy to implement, do not require an excessive amount of time, and produce immediate effects. Therefore, we will discuss issues related to treatment acceptability, problem analysis, setting analysis, instructional analysis, and other intervention considerations.

We also advocate a prescriptive approach (Fuchs et al., 1990; Sugai & Carter, 1989) that minimizes teachers' efforts to learn and prepare for the initiation of an intervention and to maintain its implementation. Fuchs and Fuchs (1989) observed that consultation failure—that is, deterioration in student behavior—appeared to be closely associated with interventions that were "poorly designed and/or implemented" (p. 277). Further, they noted that consultation success may be closely related to the degree of "directiveness" or prescriptiveness found in the classroom-based interventions used to work with difficult-to-teach students (Fuchs, 1991). We take a prescriptive, directed approach in discussing intervention selection and development.

Treatment Acceptability

Although we would like all teachers and consultants to make clear, carefully documented, and well-informed decisions based on treatment effectiveness, results of recent treatment acceptability research indicate that many factors influence teachers' judgments about selecting intervention strategies.

> At a very basic level, treatments can be evaluated on two dimensions, acceptability and effectiveness. Ideally, only those treatments with a history of documented effectiveness should be considered; thus the pretreatment discussion would be narrowed to issues of acceptability. At this point, a consultant can begin to assess the teacher's philosophy about treatments (e.g., reinforcement v. punishment; teacher initiated v. psychologist or parent initiated; individual v. group), his or her treatment knowledge and skills, time and material resources, and his or her past experiences with treatments. [Elliott, 1988, p. 78]

If the probability of implementing successful interventions is to improve, consultants should consider the teachers' perceptions of what constitutes acceptable treatment (Kazdin, 1981; Witt, Martens, & Elliott, 1984). Martens, Witt, Elliott, and Darveaux (1985) indicate that "acceptability refers to perceptions of whether treatment is fair, reasonable, or intrusive, appropriate for a given problem and consistent with notions of what treatment should be" (p. 191). We find that teacher acceptance of classroom-based interventions is a complex process affected by the interaction of consultant, teacher, and student variables (Elliott, 1988).

In general, teachers tend to view positive interventions as more acceptable than reductive treatments and to be more accepting of treatments with perceived greater effectiveness (Elliott, 1988; Kazdin, 1980a; Witt, Elliott, & Martens, 1984). Other major research findings include the following:

1. Interventions requiring large amounts of time were less acceptable than those requiring little or moderate amounts (Martens et al., 1985; Witt, Martens, & Elliott, 1984).
2. Interventions that can be implemented directly by teachers were more acceptable, even if they required additional time (Algozzine et al., 1982; Martens et al., 1985).

3. The greater the severity of the behavior problem, the more the practicing teachers accepted the interventions (Kazdin, 1980a, 1981; Martens et al., 1985).

4. The more positive (less aversive) the interventions, the more teachers accepted them (Witt & Elliott, 1985).

5. The less experienced the teachers, the more they accepted interventions (Witt & Elliott, 1985).

These relationships suggest that consultants cannot ignore the effects of the amount of time required, the direct involvement of the teacher, and the severity of the problem when selecting and developing interventions. Although individual teacher differences may exist, consultants should be guided by the following rules: Teachers are more accepting of interventions that (a) require less of their time, (b) they implement directly, (c) are selected to solve severe behavior problems, and (d) are more positive. By selecting and developing interventions that are more acceptable to teachers, consultants can increase the probability that treatments will be accurately implemented and maintained. An overview of influential variables is presented in Box 5.2.

We recommend that consultants attempt to increase intervention acceptability by (a) focusing on positive interventions, (b) limiting their use of jargon, (c) promoting teacher ownership of intervention-related decisions, and (d) giving careful consideration to the time and effort associated with an intervention. We

B O X 5.2

Variables affecting the acceptability of intervention treatment

---

Relative to the Consultant
1. Theoretical versus pragmatic jargon
2. Direct versus indirect involvement
3. Interventionist philosophy

Relative to the Teacher
1. Years of experience
2. Knowledge of behavioral principles
3. Type of training
4. Classroom management techniques being used
5. Implementation competence

Relative to the Intervention
1. Time required
2. Type of intervention
3. Reported effectiveness
4. Expense
5. Effort required
6. Adverse side effects
7. Resources available

Relative to the Student
1. Severity of problem behavior
2. Type of problem
3. Perceived benefit

have developed the prescriptive approach and guidelines presented in this chapter with these considerations in mind.

Problem Analysis

At times, it is possible to select and develop an intervention based on the information collected through the Request for Assistance, the Problem Identification Interview, and the functional analysis. Because of the precision with which this information is solicited, teachers sometimes "discover" solutions to their problems. For example, after completing the Problem Identification Interview, Mr. Evans sees that he has been focusing on Nicky's aggressive verbal statements and not attending to Nicky when he is playing cooperatively. Mr. Evans recognizes that he might try giving Nicky more attention when he is behaving appropriately.

However, in most cases, the teacher seeks assistance because he or she has been unable to find a simple solution, even after the Request for Assistance and Information Collection stages have been completed. We believe that intervention selection and development can be facilitated if the consultant can help the teacher systematically, objectively analyze the problem. The purpose of this section is to highlight some analysis considerations.

In selecting and developing an intervention for a consultation problem, three major areas should be considered: problem behavior, replacement behavior, and problem type. In Box 5.3, brief explanations are given for each area.

Consultants and teachers will probably not assess and evaluate their problems against each of these areas of analysis; however, we believe that they must be capable of using them fluently and effectively. We also advise consultants to examine other comprehensive decision models for reducing the occurrence of inappropriate behaviors; these models can be found in the professional literature (see, for example, Evans & Meyer, 1985; Gaylord-Ross, 1980; Lynch, McGuigan, & Shoemaker, 1983; Wolery, Bailey, & Sugai, 1988).

Problem behavior considerations.   Before an intervention can be developed, the problem behavior must be described in simple terms, for example, talking out, out of the seat, noncompliant. Remember that these descriptions, which give information about dimensions, response class, and function, help focus the process of selecting and developing interventions.

In Chapter 3, we indicated that behaviors can be defined using one or more of six dimensions (frequency, duration, latency, locus, topography, and intensity). Knowing the essential features of a problem behavior can direct the selection and development of the intervention. For example, if talkouts occur at a rate of five times per minute, a self-recording and token economy strategy that requires the student to record periods of talkouts at the end of each school day would not be as effective if the same self-recording were to occur at the end of each 5- or 10-minute interval. Similarly, a strategy selected for reducing the duration of sucking on a finger may not be effective for decreasing the number of episodes of the same behavior.

When considering a problem behavior from an ecological perspective, it is important to examine whether the behavior (a) is a member of a large or small

BOX 5.3

Problem analysis considerations for facilitating intervention selection and development

Problem Behavior Considerations
1. Has the problem behavior been defined in observable terms?
2. Does the definition of problem behavior contain the essential dimensions?
3. Has the response class in which the behavior belongs been defined and described?
4. Have testable explanations been tested or manipulated?
5. Have the communicative or critical function characteristics been determined?

Replacement Response Considerations
1. Has the replacement response been defined in observable terms?
2. Are the essential dimensions of the replacement response similar to the problem behavior and are they provided in the definition?
3. Does the replacement behavior come from the same response class as the problem behavior?
4. Has the replacement response ever been displayed accurately and fluently?
5. Does the replacement response have the same communicative or critical function characteristics as the problem behavior?

Problem Type Considerations
1. Has the desired replacement response ever been displayed at greater than 90% accuracy (acquisition problem)?
2. Has the desired replacement response ever been displayed at greater than 90% accuracy at the appropriate rate (fluency problem)?
3. Has the desired replacement behavior ever been observed when instructional assistance (antecedent or consequence) is not available (maintenance problem)?
4. Has the desired replacement response been observed in some setting conditions but not in others (generalization problem)?
5. Has a limited range of replacement response variations been observed when setting conditions are different or modified (adaptation problem)?

response class of behaviors, (b) has higher, lower, or equal chances of occurring as other behaviors in that response class, or (c) is a member of more than one response class and is therefore associated with more than one type of outcome. A *response class* is a set of behaviors that are related along one or more features, frequently topography (dimension) or function (effect) (Kerr & Nelson, 1989). This information can determine how comprehensive an intervention must be, whether the most important target behavior has been selected, and what consequence and setting variables might need to be manipulated. For example, when Kirsten expresses her anger, she screams, paces, pushes furniture and other students out of her way, and uses profanity. Each episode lasts about three minutes. In contrast, when Amy is angry she curses once or twice and then returns to her task. Both students have behaviors that they display when they are angry; however, these behaviors differ in topography, intensity, duration, and frequency.

Generating valid testable explanations and systematically testing them helps consultants narrow the communicative (Donnellan et al., 1984) or critical function (White, 1980) associated with the problem behavior. Two primary functions are generally related to the occurrence of a behavior: the behavior is displayed either to get or obtain something or to avoid or escape something. Knowing the function assists in stipulating the kinds of planned consequences used to follow the behavior's occurrence. For example, a consultant would select different interventions for Alyce who disrupts class to avoid difficult math work than for Allan who disrupts class to get peer approval.

Replacement response considerations.   A replacement response is also called a *fair-pair* (White & Haring, 1980), or the behavior we would like the student to display in place of the problem behavior. Many of the variables discussed for problem behaviors are similar for the replacement response. The dimensions of the replacement response must be identified and described clearly, and the number of required replacement responses (response class) should be determined. In addition, the consultant and the teacher must ascertain if the student needs to be taught the fair-pair, or if it needs to be strengthened. For example, Ms. Summers selects "asking for help" to replace Laurie's classroom disruptions. Because Laurie has never demonstrated this behavior, Ms. Summers will need to teach him how to raise his hand and say, "I need help on . . . ."

Finally, the replacement response should be developed to have the same communicative function as the problem behavior. Ideally, a fair-pair behavior should be (a) in the behavioral repertoire of the student (it does not need to be taught), (b) incompatible with the problem behavior (it is physically impossible to engage in both the problem behavior and the fair-pair simultaneously), (c) adaptive (it is useful to the student, requiring less effort to display than the problem behavior and resulting in appropriate positive reinforcement), and (d) of equal power (it results in at least as much positive reinforcement as the problem behavior).

Problem type considerations.   A final consideration that involves both the problem behavior and its replacement response is the type of problem being presented. We have taken White and Haring's (1980) model of the phases of learning to structure five problem types: (a) acquisition, (b) fluency, (c) maintenance, (d) generalization, and (e) adaptation. Identifying the problem type enables the consultant and the teacher to select an appropriate approach to intervention. A definition, an example, and an intervention emphasis are described for each problem type:

1. *Acquisition Problem:* Characterized by a response accuracy of less than 90%, or the absence of the desired behavior from the student's behavioral repertoire (learning history).

    EXAMPLE: Trish hits other students when they tease her. When asked, she fails to describe or show other ways of "expressing anger," such as walking away, telling the person you are angry, talking with someone. In addition, no one has ever seen her display a more desirable response.

    INTERVENTION FOCUS: The focus is on directly teaching the replacement response to high levels of accuracy. Emphasis is placed on the systematic manipulation of instructional antecedents.

For example, Trish's teacher might set up lessons in which she can (a) see a correct display of the replacement response, (b) practice the skill while receiving encouragement and corrective feedback from the teacher, and (c) use the newly acquired skill in a natural context.

2. *Fluency Problem:* Characterized by accurate use of the skill (over 90%) but the skill is not smooth, automatic, natural, or spontaneous.

   EXAMPLE: Trish can say, "It makes me mad when you tease me, so I can't play with you now," but she screams some of the words and says other words too quickly.

   INTERVENTION FOCUS: Intervention consists of (a) requiring regular and frequent practice with specific feedback about errors and (b) increasing the motivation or reinforcement value for being accurate and fluent. Emphasis is placed on manipulation of instructional consequences.

   For example, as Trish practices "expressing her anger," the teacher (a) gives her immediate feedback when she is correct, (b) reminds her to maintain a normal tone of voice before she says the words, and (c) provides strong reinforcement for each fluent display of the desired skill.

3. *Maintenance Problem:* Characterized by an accurate, fluent response that fails to recur after the instruction or intervention has been halted or removed.

   EXAMPLE: Trish expresses her anger accurately and fluently when the teacher reminds her what to do in the morning and provides large amounts of reinforcement at the end of each day. However, whenever her teacher completely removes the reminder or the reinforcement, Trish fails to display the expected behavior.

   INTERVENTION FOCUS: Intervention involves systematic manipulation (fading or removal) of the instructional antecedent and consequent events. Emphasis is placed on the gradual thinning of the schedule of reinforcement.

   For example, instead of removing all the reminders and reinforcement, Trish's teacher fades the reminder to a wink in the morning and provides reinforcement on an every-other-day schedule.

4. *Generalization Problem:* Present when a behavior learned or displayed under one set of conditions fails to occur under a different but similar set of conditions.

   EXAMPLE: Trish is accurate and fluent at using her new way of expressing anger in the classroom, on the bus, and during morning recess. However, she uses her aggressive behavior when she gets angry during lunch and afternoon recess.

   INTERVENTION FOCUS: The instructional focus is on teaching the student to discriminate between the essential and nonessential features of the conditions under which the desired response is required. This is accomplished by teaching with multiple exemplars and in multiple settings and by highlighting their critical features. A general case response (one that can be used in a variety of conditions) is stressed, and emphasis is placed on the systematic manipulation of instructional antecedents.

For example, Trish's teacher would use role-play examples that cover the range of possible situations in which she would and would not need to express her anger appropriately. These practice sessions are conducted during recess and lunch.

5. *Adaptation Problem:* Characterized by failure to make minor changes in the desired response to accommodate variations in the setting conditions.

EXAMPLE: Trish can express her anger correctly with peers in play situations by saying "It makes me mad when you tease me. I can't play with you any more." However, in nonplay situations (during reading group or walking in the hallway to the library), she fails to modify the skill to accommodate the new context.

INTERVENTION FOCUS: The intervention consists of teaching a range of appropriate response variations (for example, "It makes me mad when you ——. I can't ——.") and the essential features of the conditions that help discriminate when a particular response variation should be used. Although one is difficult to determine, a single response that can be applied successfully across the widest range of conditions is most desirable. The focus is on the systematic manipulation of the desired response and its instructional antecedents.

For example, Trish's teacher would model and coach her in different ways to express anger and the conditions under which each would be required such as walk away, talk about it, ask an adult to help.

Analysis of the problem type helps narrow the intervention focus to manipulate instructional antecedents, response variations, and instructional consequences. Regardless of the problem type, we emphasize using a teaching perspective.

Setting Analysis

While analysis of the replacement response and the problem behavior and type is important, consultants and teachers should not ignore the physical characteristics of the learning environment in which students and teachers interact. Wolery, Bailey, and Sugai (1988) indicate that student learning is maximized in environments that are "comfortable, conducive to teaching and learning, adequately sized and equipped, and, for handicapped students, the least restrictive but effective" (p. 189). They operationalize these attributes in the following manner:

1. *Comfortable:* Adequate lighting, comfortable temperature, fresh air, pleasing colors, sufficient furnishings
2. *Conducive to teaching and learning:* Clearly defined learning areas, smooth traffic patterns, minimal distractions, easily monitored and supervised
3. *Adequate space and materials:* Minimal crowding, comfortable seating arrangements, adequate materials

4. *Least restrictive environment* (Edgar, 1977): High expectations and a challenging learning environment, appropriate and inclusive educational opportunities, participation in normal educational experiences, a high degree of freedom for physical movement and independence, close proximity to nonhandicapped peers, opportunities for interactions with nonhandicapped peers

Although we would like all students to learn how to function effectively under the worst physical classroom conditions, we believe that many students find it difficult to function effectively when instructional settings are uncomfortable, are not conducive to teaching and learning, are not adequately supplied with space and materials, and do not provide a challenging, normal experience. These students may require an adjustment of the physical environment that is derived from a thorough setting analysis.

Instructional Analysis

Although many teachers are threatened by an analysis of their teaching skills, consultants must still give careful consideration to the events, routines, and teaching behaviors that occur within classroom and instructional contexts. They may find that intervention selection and development centers on what is being provided students on a daily, hourly, or even, continuous basis. For example, it is not unusual to find students who display inappropriate social behaviors when instruction is poorly designed, the curriculum is inappropriate, or the presentation of instruction and curriculum is awkward or inefficient. We believe that the design of the instruction and the curriculum and their presentation must be intact and appropriate before major behavior management manipulations are selected. Consultants must consider instructional factors as they assist teachers in intervention selection and development.

> Learning is an individual process that is shaped in the classroom. On a daily basis, teachers and students work together to extend and refine each learner's set of concepts and skills. Thoroughly planned lessons, focused instruction, regular assessment, and positive classroom management increase the probability of success. [Northwest Regional Educational Laboratory, 1990, p. 7]

In Box 5.4 and Box 5.5, we review those classroom and school characteristics associated with effective teachers (Northwest Regional Educational Laboratory, 1990). When these characteristics are in place, we find that maximum student learning occurs with minimum classroom and behavior management difficulties. Although we do not describe this subject in greater detail, consultants must be familiar with these characteristics and practices (see also Chapter 9). For an in-depth review, we recommend the following sources:

BROPHY, J., & GOOD, T. (1986). Teacher behavior and student achievement. In M. C. Wittrock (Ed.), *Handbook of Research on Teaching.* New York: Macmillan.
GOOD, T. L., & BROPHY, J. E. (1987). *Looking in classrooms* (4th ed.). New York: Harper & Row.

BOX 5.4

Classroom characteristics and practices associated with effective teaching and student learning

1. Instruction is guided by a preplanned curriculum.
2. Instructional groups formed in the classroom fit students' academic and affective needs.
3. Classroom learning time is used efficiently.
4. There are smooth, efficient classroom routines.
5. Standards for classroom behavior are explicit and are consistently and equitably applied.
6. Students are carefully oriented to lessons.
7. Instruction is clear and focused.
8. Effective questioning techniques are used to build basic and higher-level skills.
9. Students routinely receive feedback and reinforcement regarding their learning progress.
10. Review and reteaching are carried out as necessary to help all students master learning material.
11. There are high expectations for student learning.
12. Incentives and rewards for students are used to promote excellence.
13. Personal interactions between teachers and students are positive.
14. Learning progress is monitored closely.
15. Students at risk of school failure are given the extra time and help they need to succeed.

SOURCE: Northwest Regional Educational Laboratory, *Effective Schooling Practices: A Research Synthesis (1990 Update)* (Portland, OR: Author, 1990).

BOX 5.5

School characteristics and practices associated with effective teaching and student learning

1. Everyone emphasizes the importance of learning.
2. The curriculum is based on clear goals and objectives.
3. Students are grouped to promote effective instruction.
4. School time is used for learning.
5. Discipline is firm and consistent.
6. There are pleasant conditions for teaching and learning.
7. Strong leadership guides the instructional program.
8. Administrators and teachers continually strive to improve instructional effectiveness.
9. Staff engage in ongoing professional development and collegial learning activities.
10. There are high expectations for quality instruction.
11. Incentives and rewards are used to build strong student and staff motivation.
12. Learning progress is monitored closely.
13. Students at risk of school failure are provided programs to help them succeed.
14. Parents and community members are invited to become involved.

SOURCE: Northwest Regional Educational Laboratory, *Effective Schooling Practices: A Research Synthesis (1990 Update)* (Portland, OR: Author, 1990).

KAMEENUI, E. J., & SIMMONS, D. C. (1990). *Designing instructional strategies: The prevention of academic learning problems.* Columbus, OH: Merrill.
NORTHWEST REGIONAL EDUCATIONAL LABORATORY (1990). *Effective schooling practices: A research synthesis 1990 update.* Portland, OR: Author.
WITTROCK, M. (1986). *Third handbook of research on teaching.* Chicago: Rand McNally.

If consultants narrow their analysis to the lesson or instructional interaction between the teacher and the student, an additional set of effective teaching practices will surface. Years of research have identified exactly what effective teachers do to maximize student learning and minimize opportunities for inappropriate behavior. We have generated a simple tool for observing lessons and assessing the quality of the teaching behaviors displayed by teachers (Sugai, 1990; see Figure 5.4).

Teachers using these practices tend to have students who are more engaged and display fewer behavior problems. These teachers maximize (a) the amount of time allocated for learning to occur (allocated time), (b) the portions of allocated time scheduled for instruction (academic learning time), and (c) the amount of this academic learning time used to involve students in successful instructional activities (academic engaged time). It is clear that the opportunity to learn and academic engaged time are essential to successful student learning (Greenwood, Delquadri, & Hall, 1984; Hall et al., 1982; Walberg, 1988).

To reiterate, the purpose of a prescriptive approach to consultation is to focus the problem-solving process on discrete activities that have manageable outcomes for the teacher. The challenge for the consultant is to evaluate the array of response, setting, and instructional variables and to help teachers build sensible, functional interventions that do not encumber or discourage them. We will discuss strategies to facilitate this process in Chapter 11. However, in the next section, we review other intervention selection and development considerations.

Intervention Selection and Development Considerations

As we indicated earlier, teachers and consultants are confronted by an assortment of intervention choices and variations. In general, we recommend stressing easy-to-implement, effective, positive interventions. However, to accomplish this, consultants must be familiar with a broad range of interventions. Here, we discuss three consideration areas that can facilitate the consultant's activities in intervention selection and development: (a) levels of intervention, (b) basic intervention manipulations, and (c) accountability, protection of human rights, and confidentiality.

Levels of intervention.   A convenient way to bring order to the many types of interventions that can be applied in classrooms is to categorize them according to where the intervention manipulation is focused. Four general management levels can be described: (a) setting or environment, (b) adult/teacher, (c) peer, or (d) self. This type of organizational scheme enables the consultant to match or fit a consultation problem to a general approach to intervention. Generally speaking, with persistent and severe problems, consultants and teachers should emphasize environmental or teacher-directed management tactics. Self-management-based strategies should be considered for milder problems with students who display longer repertoires of desirable behavior.

FIGURE 5.4
Teaching behaviors of effective teachers

EFFECTIVE TEACHING PROFILE

Place an "X" on the scale to indicate the extent to which the teacher displayed the best teaching practices? Connect each "X" to display a teaching profile.

YES-------------NO   1.   Brisk pacing

YES-------------NO   2.   Specific explanations and instructions for new concepts

YES-------------NO   3.   Allocated time for guided practice

YES-------------NO   4.   Cumulative review of skills being taught

YES-------------NO   5.   Regular and varied assessments of
learning of new concepts

YES-------------NO   6.   Regular and active interactions with individual students

YES-------------NO   7.   Frequent and detailed feedback

YES-------------NO   8.   Varied forms of positive reinforcement

YES-------------NO   9.   Positive, predictable, and orderly learning environment

YES-------------NO   10.   Maintenance of student attention within and across
instructional activities and materials

YES-------------NO   11.   Reinforcement for task completion

YES-------------NO   12.   Appropriate selection of examples and nonexamples

YES-------------NO   13.   Consistent application of contingencies for rules and
expectations

YES-------------NO   14.   Appropriate use of model/demonstrations

YES-------------NO   15.   Appropriate use of behavioral rehearsal (role plays)

YES-------------NO   16.   Smooth transition within and between lessons

YES-------------NO   17.   High rates of correct student responding

Environment-based interventions are effective for solving many classroom behavior problems. These interventions have two purposes: to limit opportunities for the problem to occur and to enable the presentation of interventions that could not otherwise be provided. Changing traffic patterns, seating arrangements, group composition, daily schedules, furniture, classroom rules, teaching assignments, and educational placements, for example, are common and useful manipulations. For instance, with severe social behavior or academic problems, students may be moved to more restrictive educational settings, where more intensive interventions can be provided.

However, it is easy to be misled by positive short-term effects and to believe that an environment-based intervention has been successful, when in fact no real growth in student behavior has been achieved. For example, Tom and Jerry are in the same fifth-grade classroom and frequently have fistfights when they are mad at each other. A simple solution would be to place one of them in another classroom. With no opportunities to interact, the fighting would easily be eliminated, and the problem "solved." Unfortunately, whenever Tom and Jerry attend the same assembly, sit at the same lunchroom table, or ride the same bus, they have a fistfight. The intervention has fallen short because neither student has been taught how to interact—to manage anger—appropriately across contexts.

Environment-based management strategies provide opportunities for using other kinds of interventions (such as adult-, peer-, or self-managed interventions), that would not otherwise be possible. For example, Tom and Jerry should be separated if teachers find it impossible to teach them a more appropriate way to interact when they are together. After they achieve reasonable gains, they can gradually be brought back together.

Environment-based strategies can also establish classic negative reinforcement paradigms; that is, teachers often continue to use a strategy because it temporally removes an aversive stimulus from their classroom. The classic illustration is the teacher who sends a student to the office for the "rest of the period" because he or she displays troublesome classroom behaviors. The teacher quickly learns that instruction is easier when the student is absent, so in the future the teacher is more likely to send the student to the office when he or she displays disruptive behaviors. The same effect may be produced when a student is sent to weekly counseling sessions, the resource room on a daily basis, or an alternative program.

If an environment-based management strategy is selected, consultants and teachers must plan to teach the student how to be successful if or when the previous conditions are reinstated. For example, Tom and Jerry must learn how to manage their anger without hitting each another; Trish must learn how to ask for help when the handraising rule is in effect; Laurie must be taught how to get assistance when he returns to his regular science class; Eduardo must learn how to attend properly when he is asked to participate in a "sit-and-watch" lesson. Thus, it is essential that environment-based management strategies be paired with one of the other levels of management.

Teacher-based management strategies are antecedent and/or consequence manipulations made by teachers in direct response to student behavior. Giving Vicki a reminder about expected behavior, telling Linda that she has earned (or lost) a privilege, discussing a problem situation with Lansing, modeling for Amy the correct way to ask for help, and verbally reprimanding Zeus when he has been uncooperative are examples of teacher-based management interventions. The common thread here is the teacher's direct manipulation of the antecedent and/or consequent events that are directly related to strengthening the replacement response and weakening the problem behavior.

Teacher-directed strategies provide students with specific information about their behavior. From a prevention perspective, we provide social skills instruction, give examples of what is appropriate and inappropriate, and describe what might happen if the student engages in a particular behavior. For example, before Roland "forgets" to hang up his coat and walk to his desk, the teacher meets him at the classroom door and verbally cues him to the expectations for coming into the classroom. When teacher-based interventions are used reactively, the student receives feedback after the response has occurred. If Roland runs to his desk, his teacher tells him to walk back to the door, repeat the rule for coming into the classroom, and walk to his desk. When he does it correctly, she praises him and gives him a "high-five."

Of course, consultants and teachers hope that students will become independent; however, one of the biggest oversights is assuming that independence (that is, response maintenance and generalized and adaptive responding) will occur by itself. Like environment-based approaches, teacher-based strategies frequently produce a temporary change in behavior. Then because they are satisfied with or reinforced for their success, teachers make one of two mistakes. They either keep the strategy in place for an extended period to "make sure that they have control" over the behavior, or they prematurely remove the intervention thinking that it has been successful. In the former case, they create a situation where the change in behavior depends on the presence of the intervention and becomes difficult to remove later. In the latter case, the undesirable behavior quickly returns, and they are forced to reinstate the intervention, sometimes at a stronger level.

The solution is for consultants and teachers to develop plans for systematically fading the teacher's involvement and moving toward peer- and/or self-directed interventions where more "natural" contingencies can acquire controlling characteristics. Later, we emphasize the importance of data collection and describe how specific data decision rules can be used to assist in the fading process.

Teacher-directed interventions are designed to provide specific assistance (antecedents and consequence manipulations) so more desirable student responses are shaped and undesirable behaviors are weakened. As soon as a desired level of responding is achieved, assistance must be faded to promote independent functioning. So, when Roland successfully enters the room on three consecutive days with only a reminder and praise, his teacher removes the reminder to every other day and gives him praise once every three days; next, the reminder and the praise will be removed completely.

Another way to teach Roland about entering the classroom appropriately involves Lizzie and Eagle Feather, two of Roland's friends who consistently enter the room appropriately. The teacher instructs Lizzie, Roland, and Eagle Feather about the proper way to enter the classroom. In addition, Lizzie is taught to remind Roland about walking into the classroom as soon as they get off the bus, and Eagle Feather is told to give Roland a "high-five" if he is appropriate. This example illustrates a *peer-directed intervention* in which the teacher initially directs the management of the problem and then turns it over to peers who provide the student with assistance.

Peer-directed management strategies are desirable because peers are an important component of a student's social community and are often more influential change agents than adults. Peers can be used as coaches, tutors, monitors, feedback agents, observers, and data recorders; the literature is replete with examples (Carden-Smith & Fowler, 1984; Dougherty, Fowler, & Paine, 1985; Greenwood et al., 1984; Heward et al., 1986; Strain, 1981). Peer group contingencies, in which the performance of the individual, small group, or whole group affects the outcomes for group members, also take advantage of peer-based interventions (Barrish, Saunders, & Wolf, 1969; Delquadri, et al., 1986; Litow & Pumroy, 1975).

Consultants and teachers should consider the following general guidelines when using peer-direct interventions: (a) select competent peers, (b) initially, teach the target student and peers directly, (c) closely monitor peer implementation of the strategies, and (d) develop a plan for fading peer-directed strategies.

The last management level consists of *self-directed strategies,* in which the student is taught specific behaviors that enable him or her to function "independently"—that is, relatively free of direct adult or peer assistance—in natural contexts. These strategies include self-recording, self-graphing, self-reinforcement, and self-instruction. For example, Mac's teacher has taught him to whisper to himself "hands in pockets" as he is walking down a crowded hallway (self-instruction) and to give himself a check on his chart if he walks to the room without touching someone (self-recording and self-reinforcement).

Self-directed management strategies are advantageous for a number of reasons. First, they can be used to facilitate the maintenance and generalization of student behaviors. For example, Mac can learn to use his self-instruction and self-reinforcement strategies when he is walking in a variety of settings. Second, the teacher does not need to monitor the student's behaviors as closely except to ensure proper implementation of the self-instruction and self-reinforcement strategies and to provide occasional reinforcement when Mac walks properly in the halls. Third, the student assumes the appearance of an individual who has "self-control" and can function independent of adult supervision.

Consultants and teachers should select and develop interventions that move students toward self-management, which is the ultimate goal any management program. If a student had effective self-management skills, he or she would not be the focus of our attention. However, many students must be taught how to engage in self-directed behaviors. We recommend developing intervention plans that help teachers set up and implement self-directed interventions in an efficient, straightforward manner—in other words, a prescriptive approach. In a component analysis study of behavioral consultation, Fuchs and Fuchs (1989) observed that teachers rated highly scripted and prepared self-management strategies as the most effective and acceptable. A sample of their self-directed strategy is illustrated in Figure 5.5 (Fuchs et al., 1989b).

Consultants and teachers should follow these guidelines when selecting and developing self-directed intervention plans: (a) teach the desired skills using

FIGURE 5.5

Sample of self-directed strategy used by Fuchs et al. (1989b) in their perscriptive approach to behavioral consultation.

STUDENT MONITORING SHEET: PHASE 1

Student Name: _____ Goal: _____ Date _____

Part A: Recording

#1	2	3	4	5
6	7	8	9	10
11	12	13	14	15
16	17	18	19	20

1. Total number of plus (+) signs   = _____

2. Total number of plus (+) and   = _____
   minus (−) signs

3. Step 1 + Step 2 (This is a   = _____
   percentage of target behavior.)

Part B: Charting

Chart percentage of behavior

100%
90%
80%
70%
60%
50%
40%
30%
20%
10%

Part C: Global Rating

1 = Needs big improvement
2 = Needs some improvement
3 = Met goal
4 = Better than goal

Student Rating (circle)

(1)   2   3   4

Chart

4	
3	
2	
1	

Teacher Rating (circle)

(1)   2   3   4

Part D: Self-Talk

Question: _____
_____
_____
_____
_____
_____
_____

Answer: _____
_____
_____
_____
_____
_____
_____

teacher- and/or peer-directed interventions, (b) teach the self-directed strategies to students focusing on response maintenance and generalized responding, (c) fade teacher-directed assistance in a systematic fashion, (d) monitor student use of self-directed strategies, and (e) reinforce the appropriate use of self-directed interventions.

Ultimately, we would prefer all students to be independent learners who can respond accurately and fluently to the many nuances of their environment. However, when consultants and teachers select and develop interventions, they must remember that there are a variety of choices that range from environment-based at one end of the continuum to self-directed at the other. Regardless of the choice, we recommend a teaching approach that emphasizes the systematic fading of external assistance, such as environment-, teacher-, or peer-based interventions, and the achievement of self-directed response maintenance and generalization.

Basic intervention manipulations.   The range of available interventions can also be categorized according to the kind of manipulation. There are three basic intervention manipulations: (a) setting, (b) antecedent, and (c) consequence. For example, in those situations where there is high probability that Nickie will engage in verbal aggression, Mr. Evans gives him a simple task to do, such as return a book to the shelf or write his name on the paper (antecedent manipulation). If he must talk to Nickie about a previous verbal aggression and he predicts another outburst, Mr. Evans moves him to the back of the room (setting manipulation). If Nickie manages his anger in the right way (replacement response), Mr. Evans gives him a "thumbs up" (consequence manipulation). These three types of manipulations can be made within each of the management levels described previously.

Setting manipulations are relatively easy to conduct; they vary from simple, small rearrangements of the immediate environment to moving the student to a more restrictive setting. Teachers can add, delete, or modify setting aspects to increase or decrease the probability that a particular behavior will occur or that an intervention can be implemented successfully. Similarly, students can be taught to make a change in their environment to facilitate a change in behavior (self-directed level). For example, Pam's teacher taught her to walk to science class through the north hallway rather than the south hallway when she is angry at her friends.

When consultants and teachers are confronted with acquisition and generalization problems, they focus on *antecedent manipulations.* These consist of a wide range of artificial and natural stimulus manipulations. An artificial stimulus controls a more desirable response (for example, when the teacher models a response) and is used to bring the behavior under the control of a more natural stimulus (that is, one that was not controlling but was more commonly found or used). For example, Palmer's handraising (desired behavior) does not occur when the teacher asks the group a question (noncontrolling natural antecedent stimulus). So Palmer's teacher raises her hand (artificial controlling stimulus) at the same time she asks the group a question because it's an easy way to model the desired response. Over time she hopes that Palmer will learn to raise his hand when the question is presented without needing her model.

Antecedent manipulations can consist of a wide range of objects, events, or activities (for example, directions, instructional models, hints, cues, examples and nonexamples, rules, facial expressions, or gestures). They include anything that precedes and sets the occasion for a desirable response. Manipulations can be additions, deletions, or withholdings, and are designed to help the student make the response more accurately (acquisition) or over a broader range of contexts (generalization).

Consequence manipulations are used when the goal is to increase response fluency or maintenance (for example, academic or social engagement or accurate academic performance) or to decrease the occurrences of inappropriate behavior (such as talking out, noncompliance, touching others). These manipulations consist of adding, deleting, or withholding objects, events, or activities that follow the occurrence of a response. Both reinforcers (things individuals like) and aversives (things individuals do not like) can be manipulated. Typically, students will increase a behavior when it is followed by the presentation of a reinforcer (positive reinforcement) *or* the removal or withholding of an aversive (negative reinforcement), and will decrease behavior when it is followed by the presentation of an aversive or the removal or withholding of reinforcer (response cost, timeout). Box 5.6 provides an illustration of the relationship between the manipulation, the kind of stimulus, and the effect on behavior.

Accountability, protection of human rights, and confidentiality.   Most of us recognize the importance of protecting the rights of the student; however, it is easy to "overlook" the student's interests when one is immersed in a problem situation on a daily basis. Consultants must protect student, family, and teacher rights during the selection, development and implementation of intervention programs. In special education, PL 94-142, Education for All Handicapped Children Act (Individuals with Disabilities Education Act, PL 101-476, 1990), specifies rights, guarantees, and due process procedures. Similar school-based guidelines can be found at the building, district, and state levels, and in many community service agencies, such as mental health or juvenile corrections. We strongly advise consultants to become familiar with local, state, and federal regulations.

The processes of selecting, developing, and implementing interventions must be guided by the intent to protect the student's basic and constitutional rights. All individuals have the right to free speech, life, liberty, assembly, and so on. In appraising these rights, careful consideration must be given to the rights of others, the degree to which the behaviors are discrepant from societal or community standards, and the extent to which the student's rights are being violated. The biggest challenge, however, will be determining when the student (or teach-

BOX 5.6

The relationship between intervention manipulation, stimulus, and behavior

	Aversive Stimulus	**Reinforcing Stimulus**
Removal or Withholding	Increase in behavior	Decrease in behavior
Presenting	Decrease in behavior	Increase in behavior

er's) behaviors are maladaptive, rather than merely expressions of their freedoms.

Obviously, one of the best ways to ensure the protection of everyone's rights is to engage in best teaching and schooling practices. The following list of guidelines highlights some of the more important strategies:

1. *Foster active and involved participation.* Although consultants are frequently placed in an "expert" or "assisting" role, they should actively foster teacher, student, and parent participation. When ownership is understood in the problem-solving process, there is greater likelihood of proper adherence to intervention implementation. Similarly, active participation increases opportunities for informed decision making. Specific strategies are described in Chapter 11.

2. *Maintain strict confidentiality.* Students, parents, teachers, and others involved in a consultation have the right to privacy. Consultation activities should not become part of a public arena. All participants in a consultation should do the following:

   a. Restrict discussions to topics and content relating specifically to the problem behaviors. Avoid discussing irrelevant personal matters. Use the prescriptive approach with its directed interviews and formats to keep participants on task.

   b. Conduct all meetings and case-related discussions in private locations. Teacher lounges, hallways, and public places in the community (the grocery store, restaurant, or social gatherings) are unacceptable. In addition, discussions should not occur in the presence of students or teachers who are not directly involved. Designate a specific, private location for conducting all meetings.

   c. Maintain all written records in a private, preferably locked, place. Avoid leaving materials in places where teachers or students have free access. Make only enough copies of those materials that are absolutely needed. Restrict access to case-related materials to those individuals with direct involvement in the consultation.

   d. Limit discussion about the consultation to participants who are directly involved. Although it is tempting to discuss cases with curious or supportive co-workers or acquaintances, all it takes is "someone who knows someone . . ." to violate confidentiality and privacy. Almost everyone in a school building has some knowledge about or association with a student or teacher who is having serious classroom problems, especially if the problem extends into the community. So, even using pseudonyms (Jane Doe or Mr. Smith's third-grade classroom) does not guarantee individual protection and privacy.

3. *Ensure that all decision making and consent is informed.* Whenever individuals have to make decisions or give approvals, they must be given enough detail to make an informed decision. The prescriptive, behavioral approach increases the structure and opportunity for informed decision making, but the final responsibility rests with the consultant and teacher to secure and clearly communicate the required information. Informed decision making and consent can be maximized by:

a. Completing all information collection and problem analyses before decisions are made.
b. Communicating information in a systematic, jargon-free form. Although written documents are extremely informative, a brief explanation and review of each may be needed for those who are unfamiliar with the procedures and their function.
c. Making written information available to appropriate individuals. Be sure that all case-related information is physically organized so specific pieces of material can be found easily and quickly.
d. Communicating with others on a regular basis. A brief telephone call or a short memo can be extremely informative and appreciated.
e. Involving all participants equally in decision making, in particular parents, teaching assistants, and other support staff.

4. *Be sure that all assessment procedures and data are accurate and complete.* Intervention selection and development are more efficient and comprehensive when assessment information is complete and accurate. Use structured forms and procedures—such as the Request for Assistance, Problem Identification Interview, or functional analysis—for collecting information.

5. *Develop clearly stated, specific, functional goals and objectives.* If information collection is adequate, consultants and teachers will have an estimate of where they are. To write a change plan, they also must know where they want to go. Therefore, it is important to specify goals and objectives that have the following characteristics (see also Chapter 6):
a. They are based on the assessment information that has been collected.
b. They are written in observable and understandable terms.
c. They focus on the positive replacement ("fair-pair") response.
d. They include a measurable criterion for determining when they have been achieved.
e. They focus on achievable levels of performance. Criteria of acceptable performance can be determined by evaluating baseline levels, performance of comparable peers, community (adult) expectations, or task/situation requirements.
f. They are shaped and acceptable or approved by relevant members of the student's social community (parents, teachers, peers, other adults) and/or the student (Kazdin, 1980a; Wolf, 1978).
g. They are based on successful functioning in the least restrictive environment.

6. *Select the most effective, least intrusive and restrictive interventions.* Although there has been much debate on what is an aversive procedure, what procedures should have restricted applications, and whether and when aversive strategies should be used, students and teachers have the right to procedures that have been shown to be the most effective, are the most parsimonious, do not limit the student's basic freedoms, and are free of the potential for physical, social, or emotional injury (a detailed discussion of this perspective can be found in Wolery, Bailey, & Sugai, 1988). These considerations are not limited to procedures used to reduce

behaviors. For example, simple reinforcement strategies can also have negative side effects—for example, the production of "docile and quiet" students (Winnet & Winkler, 1972); the promotion of illegal behaviors such as lying, cheating, and stealing (Balsam & Bondy, 1983); the use of reinforcers to coerce or bribe (Balsam & Bondy, 1983); and the overuse of teacher praise that is nonspecific and elicited by students (Brophy, 1981; Kerr & Nelson, 1989; Worrall, Worrall, & Meldrum, 1983). In addition, interventions should be selected that have the following characteristics:

a. They are socially valid, that is, they have been discussed and approved by relevant members of the social community (Kazdin, 1980a; Wolf, 1978).

b. They are generally acceptable to the teacher (see the section on treatment acceptability in this chapter).

c. They give maximum consideration to the hypothesis about possible maintaining variables and communicative or critical function from functional analysis findings (that is, testable explanations).

7. *Develop a detailed implementation plan* before *actually implementing an intervention.* Wolery, Bailey, and Sugai (1988) indicate that "this plan should include what will be done, who will do it, how it will be done, when it will be done, when it will be reviewed, who will review the effects, and what will happen if potential negative side effects occur" (p. 375). They also indicate that this plan is important because it specifies exactly what will be done, provides program predictability, and functions as a basis for measuring treatment success. The Intervention Planning Form and procedure discussed in the next section focuses on the development of a comprehensive implementation plan.

8. *Monitor critical events and intervention effectiveness on a continuous basis.* Overseeing the progress of a case is an essential responsibility for consultants and teachers. Data are needed to monitor student progress, assess treatment fidelity, evaluate program success, communicate with others, and ensure accountability. Information monitoring procedures should include the following:

a. Development and implementation of a formative observation procedure (see Chapter 3) that examines behaviors to be decreased and increased, settings in which they are being observed, and treatment conditions under which the data are collected.

b. A mechanism for tracking critical program events. Having this kind of record increases accountability and program integrity. A blank form and completed examples of critical events recording forms are illustrated in Figures 5.6 and 5.7, respectively. A simple coding system is used to label the kind of event (M = meeting, O = observation, T = telephone call: i = in, o = out), date and time are noted, and a brief description of the event is described. All events are recorded immediately after they are observed or occur.

c. A schedule and procedures for evaluating program progress. Two aspects should be considered. The first aspect is designation and use of data decision rules that enable the formative evaluation of the

FIGURE 5.6

Blank Critical Events form

CRITICAL EVENTS LOG	Student Initial _____		Page ___ of ___
Legend: (O) = Observation (M) = Meeting ( ) = _____		(T) = Telephone (N) = Note ( ) = _____	
Date	Code	Initial	Description

FIGURE 5.7
Completed Critical Events form

CRITICAL EVENTS LOG		Student Initial __EV__	Page __1__ of ___

Legend:	(O) = Observation (M) = Meeting ( ) = _____	(T) = Telephone (N) = Note ( ) = _____	

Date	Code	Initial	Description
12/12/91	N	KK	RFA received
12/13/91	T	KK	Called Phillips to confirm receipt of RFA
12/15/91	T	KK	Called Phillips to set up PII meeting
12/15/91	N	KK	EV not sp. ed.
12/16/91	N	MN	Blank copies of PII placed in folder.
1/5/92	M	KK	PII meeting completed.
1/6/92	O	KK	Functional analysis 1:30 – 3:00
1/8/92	O	KK	" " "
1/10/92	M	KK	IPF meeting w/ Phillips

student's progress. For example, a simple three-consecutive-day data decision rule ("If three consecutive days below the minimum line of progress occur, consider a change in the intervention") allows daily evaluation of the student's progress. The criteria specified in behavioral objectives also provide a basis for formative evaluation.

The second consideration is a schedule for regular program review meetings in which the consultant, teacher, and other involved parties (such as the parents, counselor, and student) meet to consider the overall progress of the intervention program. At these times, observation data and critical events are reviewed.

d. A plan for achieving generalized responding. As we indicated earlier, one of the most challenging behavior change tasks is to achieve functional responding across different contexts or environments. A "train-and-hope" approach is clearly ineffective (Stokes & Baer, 1977); therefore, a plan and schedule for achieving generalized responding is essential. This plan should focus on the student's return to the least restrictive environment.

Intervention Planning Form and Procedures

One of the many useful features of the prescriptive consultation approach is an emphasis on purposeful, structured interactions between the consultant and teacher. At the intervention selection and development phase, we have described a wide range of factors and considerations that must be pondered. We strongly recommend that consultants develop a prescribed format for directing the intervention selection and development interaction with the teacher. In this section, we provide an example of a form and describe a procedure (Intervention Planning Form) for intervention planning.

Intervention Planning Form.   Without a structure, intervention planning can be inefficient and incomplete, resulting in extra meetings or poorly constructed interventions. The consultant and the teacher must be efficient and comprehensive in their intervention planning activities. Therefore, we suggest that consultants consider a structure like the Intervention Planning Form (Sugai & Carter, 1989).

The Intervention Planning Form (IPF) is a relatively simple two-page form designed to guide the interaction between the consultant and the teacher after both the Request for Assistance and Problem Identification Interview have been completed. A blank form is illustrated in Figure 5.8, and a completed version is shown in Figure 5.9. There are two major sections: a review of information and an identification and description of interventions. Time limits are provided to keep the consultant and the teacher on task. To assist in this process, the consultant and the teacher should focus on filling in the form.

The procedure for intervention planning.   The goal of this interaction is to delineate the major features of the intervention. For example, planning the details and constructing the required materials should be conducted immediately after this planning sheet has been completed. A copy of the completed form should be left with the teacher. Each component of the IPF is described as follows:

FIGURE 5.8

The Intervention Planning form

INTERVENTION PLANNING FORM	Teacher _____ Date ___/___/___ Consultant _____ School _____

Student Information:
  Name _____ DOB ___/___/___ Sex: M F
  Grade _____ Age _____ Room _____ IEP: Y N

Review of Case Information. (4 minutes) (Check each area that has been reviewed.)

  ___ Problem Behavior   ___ Current Level of Functioning
  ___ Replacement Response   ___ Required Level of Functioning
  ___ Problem Context/Setting   ___ Long-Term Objective
  ___ Testable Explanations

List four or five positive strategies to improve student performance. (4 minutes)

1.   4.

2.   5.

3.

Circle strategy (or strategies) to be implemented. (1 minute)

Name one strategy for managing unacceptable behavior. (2 minutes)

F I G U R E 5.8 (*continued*)

Identify what is needed/available to insure implementation. (2 minutes)

Specify the steps for implementation of intervention. (6 minutes)

1.

2.

3.

4.

5.

6.

Describe how student progress will be monitored and evaluated. (3 minutes)

Date for Starting Intervention ___/___/___

Next Meeting Date ___/___/___ and Time _____

Next Observation ___/___/___ and Time _____

Attach Additional Notes

F I G U R E 5.9
A completed Intervention Planning form

INTERVENTION PLANNING FORM	Teacher _Phillips_ ___ Date _1/10/92_ Consultant _Kalgoorlie_ School _Broome Elem._

Student Information:
Name _Eduardo_ _____ DOB _5/21/84_ Sex (M) F
Grade _3_ Age _7_ Room _4A_ IEP: Y (N)

Review of Case Information. (4 minutes) (Check each area that has been reviewed.)

✔ Problem Behavior   ✔ Current Level of Functioning
✔ Replacement Response   ✔ Required Level of Functioning
✔ Problem Context/Setting   ✔ Long-Term Objective
✔ Testable Explanations

List four or five positive strategies to improve student performance. (4 minutes)

1. Contract for martial arts turtle coloring book.
2. Self-recording card.
(3.) Arrangement of hourly visits with friends
4. Work with Ms. Simms, P.E. teacher; as special assist.
5. Computer games

Circle strategy (or strategies) to be implemented. (1 minute)

Name one strategy for managing unacceptable behavior. (2 minutes)

— Sit at desk with head down for each minute out of classroom.

— Lose 1 minute with friends for each disruption.

F I G U R E 5.9 (*continued*)

Identify what is needed/available to insure implementation. (2 minutes)

— stopwatch

— area for playing with friends

— new computer games

— assistance from school counselor to monitor program

Specify the steps for implementation of intervention. (6 minutes)

1. Meet w/ E and present new classroom rules

2. Give 2 minutes free for each ½ hour playing appropriately with friends

3. Give 1 minute for every 5 minutes on task and subtract 1 minute for each 5 minute interval off task

4. or out of classroom.

5. At end of each ½ hour, ask E to pick a friend to play with

6.

Describe how student progress will be monitored and evaluated. (3 minutes)

— Record # minutes earned and lost each ½ hour.

— Evaluate plan if average # of minutes earned is less than 1 per ½ hour.

Date for Starting Intervention __1/14/92__

Next Meeting Date __1/21/92__ and Time __12:15__

Next Observation __1/17/92__ and Time __1:30__

Attach Additional Notes

— see over —

FIGURE 5.9   (*continued*)

NOTES:

— Need to make data recording form.

— Buy new computer game (or borrow from computer lab).

— Call and inform father of new program and get permission to implement.

— Borrow stopwatch from Ms. Simms.

1. *Review case information.* Quickly review information that was previously collected in the Request for Assistance, the Problem Identification Interview, and other observations like the functional analyses. Limit descriptions to the key features. Refrain from elaborating or giving detailed explanations. The major purpose is to confirm the problem and remind the teacher of the specifics. Focus attention on the replacement response. Check each area that has been described.

2. *List positive strategies.* Ask the teacher to identify ("brainstorm") four or five positive strategies that might be used to teach, strengthen, or improve the student's performance—for example, the replacement or fair-pair response. Write a brief, two- to three-word, description for each strategy. Elaborations should be reserved for subsequent meetings. Prepare a list of possible interventions in case suggestions need to be made.

3. *Circle the positive strategy (or strategies) that will be implemented.* Ask the teacher to quickly reread the suggested positive strategies and select one or more strategies from the list. Focus on those strategies that have a high probability of being implemented (see the guidelines and considerations discussed earlier), especially those that are acceptable to the teacher, cause the least disruption, and are the most positive.

4. *Name one strategy for managing unacceptable behavior.* Ask the teacher to identify one behavior-reduction strategy. It might be advisable to use a regular discipline procedure or to have an alternative suggestion. Avoid

spending too much time on strategies for unacceptable behaviors; focus on strengthening the replacement response.

5. *Identify what is needed or available to ensure correct implementation.* Based on the selected strategy, make a list of what materials, training, and/or assistance will be needed to ensure accurate, fluent implementation. Again avoid discussions about rationale or details.

6. *Specify the major steps for implementation of the strategy.* Describe the major steps involved in implementing the strategy. Focus on actual teacher behaviors (for example, writing a contract the student, giving positive verbal feedback once every five minutes if the student is working, walking by the student at least once every five minutes). These steps will serve as the basic procedural or action components for which detailed activities will be developed and described. Consultants may find it easier to display the procedure in the form of a task analysis or flow chart (Sugai & Fabre, in press).

7. *Describe how the student's progress will be monitored and evaluated.* Describe how and when the teacher will assess and record the progress being made by the student. Focus on simple descriptions, such as event recording for 30 minutes after lunch or recording permanent product at the end of the day; elaborate later. Specify simple decision rules for when to make a change or discontinue the strategy.

8. *Dates.* Specify when the strategy will actually be initiated and when the consultant and the teacher will meet to review the implementation and progress of the intervention. Also specify future dates and times for the consultant to conduct observations.

Consultants should remember that the IPF is an example of a structured (prescriptive) approach to intervention selection and development. It is useful to provide teachers with an advanced organizer statement so they can anticipate what the purpose of the IPF is and what activities will occur. For example:

> Today, we're meeting to select and develop a strategy for helping Eduardo stay at task and in the classroom for longer periods. To help us use our time efficiently, I'd like to use a format called the Intervention Planning form.
>
> You'll notice that we have specific pieces of information to identify and some recommended time limits for completing each section. The times are just guidelines, but I'll try to keep us close to them.
>
> If we need to look at anything in greater detail, I suggest that we discuss it after we've completed the Intervention Planning form, on which I'll focus our attention. Do you have any questions?

Finally, we have found that the following tips can facilitate the intervention development process and completion of the IPF:

1. Before the meeting, review all case information and develop alternative strategies in case teachers have difficulty developing them on their own.

2. Model the use of language that is jargon-free and that provides clear, measurable, observable descriptions of behaviors and strategies.

3. Paraphrase and restate what the teacher says to reinforce participation, clarify explanations, and confirm understanding.

4. Quickly review each step or component as it is completed, and focus on moving on to the next one.

5. During brainstorming sessions or while developing lists, avoid making judgements about teacher suggestions; focus on generating a list of as many possibilities or alternatives as possible. Write down a few descriptors for each idea and prompt the teacher for the next suggestion.

6. When the IPF is completed, quickly review what has been completed without elaborating on the details, check for accuracy, and then provide time for elaboration and explanation.

SUMMARY

The purpose of this chapter was to describe how the consultant and teacher can structure the process of intervention selection and development. Our intent was to review intervention aspects that would increase the efficiency of intervention planning between the consultant and the teacher. The following key points were addressed:

1. We took an interventionist approach to intervention selection and development because of its compatibility with prescriptive consultation, and especially, a teaching approach to behavior change.

2. When considering the selection and development of behavioral-based interventions, consultants and teachers should keep in mind factors relating to treatment acceptability, setting features, problem characteristics, and instructional practices.

3. Consultants must consider the effects of time required, problem severity, and direct involvement by the teacher when assisting teachers to make treatment selections.

4. A thorough analysis of the consultation problem can facilitate intervention selection and development, especially aspects of the problem behavior, replacement response, and problem type.

5. Knowing about the type of problem behavior can direct the selection of interventions.

6. Features of the instructional environment—that is, classroom events and routines and teaching behaviors—must be considered when selecting interventions.

7. Teachers who engage in effective teaching practices tend to have students who are more engaged and display fewer behavior problems.

8. Environments that promote learning and appropriate social behaviors are comfortable and conducive to teaching and learning, have adequate space and materials, and are focused on the least restrictive environment.

9. Consultants and teachers should focus on selecting interventions that are easy to implement and are effective and positively focused.

10. Interventions planning generally should be sequenced in the following order: environment-based, teacher-based, peer-based, and self-based.

11. Instructional assistance should be manipulated and faded in a planned, systematic manner to ensure adequate levels of independent student functioning—that is, response maintenance and generalized responding.

12. Three basic types of intervention manipulations should be considered: setting, antecedent, and consequence.

13. Give careful consideration to the rights and interests of the student and the teacher when helping teachers select and develop interventions: confidentiality, informed consent, valid goals and interventions, continuous program monitoring.

14. Prescribed formats, like the Intervention Planning Form, can help keep consultant and teacher interactions purposeful, structured, and efficient.

REFERENCES

ALBERTO, P. A., & TROUTMAN, A. C. (1988). *Applied behavior analysis for teachers* (3rd ed.). Columbus, OH: Merrill.

ALGOZZINE, B., YSSELDYKE, J., CHRISTENSON, S., & THURLOW, M. (1982). *Teachers' intervention choices for children exhibiting different behaviors in school* (Research Report No. 76). Minneapolis: University of Minnesota, Institute for Research on Learning Disabilities.

BAER, D. M., WOLF, M. M., & RISLEY, T. R. (1968). Some current dimensions of applied behavior analysis. *Journal of Applied Behavior Analsyis, 1,* 91–97.

BALSAM, P. D., & BONDY, A. A. (1983). The negative side effects of reward. *Journal of Applied Behavior Analysis, 16,* 283–296.

BARRISH, H., SAUNDERS, M., & WOLF, M. M. (1969). Good behavior game: Effects of individual contingencies for group consequences on disruptive behavior in the classroom. *Journal of Applied Behavior Analysis, 2,* 119–124.

BROPHY, J. (1981). Teacher praise: A functional analysis. *Review of Educational Research, 51,* 5–32.

BROPHY, J., & GOOD, T. (1986). Teacher behavior and student achievement. In M. C. Wittrock (Ed.), *Handbook of Research on Teaching.* New York: Macmillan.

CANTER, L., & CANTER, M. (1992). *Assertive discipline: A take-charge approach for today's educator.* Santa Monica: Lee Canter Associates.

CARDEN-SMITH, L. K., & FOWLER, S. A. (1984). Positive peer pressure: The effects of peer monitoring on children's disruptive behavior. *Journal of Applied Behavior Analysis, 17,* 213–227.

COOPER, J. O., HERON, T. E., & HEWARD, W. L. (1987). *Applied behavior analysis.* Columbus, OH: Merrill.

DELQUADRI, J., GREENWOOD, C. R., WHORTON, D., CARTA, J. J., & HALL, R. V. (1986). Classwide peer tutoring. *Exceptional Children, 52,* 535–542.

DONNELLAN, A. M., MIRENDA, P. L., MESAROS, R. A., & FASSBENDER, L. L. (1984). Analyzing the communicative functions of aberrant behavior. *Journal of the Association for Persons with Severe Handicaps, 9,* 201–212.

DOUGHERTY, B. S., FOWLER, S. A., & PAINE, S. C. (1985). The use of peer monitors to reduce aggressive behavior during recess. *Journal of Applied Behavior Analysis, 18,* 141–153.

DREIKURS, R. (1968). *Psychology in the classroom* (2nd ed.). New York: Harper & Row.

DREIKURS, R., & CASSEL, P. (1972). *Discipline without tears.* New York: Hawthorn.

DREIKURS, R., GRUNWALD, B., & PEPPER, F. (1982). *Maintaining sanity in the classroom.* New York: Harper & Row.

EDGAR, E. (1977). *Least restrictive educational alternatives for the severely/profoundly handicapped.* Unpublished paper, University of Washington, Seattle.

ELLIOTT, S. N. (1988). Acceptability of behavioral treatments: Review of variables that influence treatment selection. *Professional Psychology: Research and Practice, 19,* 68–80.

EVANS, I., & MEYER, L. (1985). *An educative approach to behavior problems: A practical decision model for interventions with severely handicapped learners.* Baltimore: Paul Brookes.

FUCHS, D. (1991). Mainstream assistance teams: A prereferral intervention system for difficult-to-teach students. In G. Stoner, M. Shinn, & H. Walker (Eds.), *Interventions for achievement and behavior problems* (pp. 241–268). Washington, D.C.: National Association of School Psychologists.

FUCHS, D., & FUCHS, L. S. (1989). Exploring effective and efficient prereferral interventions: A a component analysis of behavioral consultation. *School Psychology Review, 18,* 260–283.

FUCHS, D., FUCHS, L. S., BAHR, M. W., FERNSTROM, P., & STECKER, P. M. (1990). Prereferral intervention: A prescriptive approach. *Exceptional Children, 56,* 493–513.

FUCHS, D., FUCHS, L., GILMAN, S., REEDER, P., BAHR, M., FERNSTROM, P., & ROBERTS, H. (1989a). Prereferral intervention through teacher consultation: Mainstream assistance teams. *Academic Therapy, 25,* 263–276.

FUCH, D., FUCHS, L., REEDER, P., GILMAN, S., FERNSTROM, P., & MOORE, P. (1989b). *Mainstream assistance teams: A handbook on prereferral interventions.* Nashville, TN: Department of Special Education, Peabody College, Vanderbilt University.

GAYLORD-ROSS, R. (1980). A decision model for the treatment of aberrant behavior in applied settings. In W. Sailor, B. Wilcox, & L. Brown (Eds.), *Methods of instruction for severely handicapped students* (pp. 135–158). Baltimore: Paul Brookes.

GLASSER, W. (1965). *Reality therapy: A new approach to psychiatry.* New York: Harper & Row.

GLASSER, W. (1969). *Schools without failure.* New York: Harper & Row.

GLASSER, W. (1985). *Control theory in the classroom.* New York: Perennial Library.

GLASSER, W. (1990). *The quality school: Managing students without coercion.* New York: Harper & Row.

GOOD, T. L., & BROPHY, J. E. (1987). *Looking in classrooms,* (4th ed.). New York: Harper & Row.

GORDON, T. (1974). *Teacher effectiveness training.* New York: Wyden.

GORDON, T. (1989). *Teaching children self-discipline—At home and at school.* New York: Times Books.

GREENWOOD, C. R., DINWIDDIE, G., TERRY, B., WADE, L., STANLEY, S. O., THIBADEAU, S., & DELQUADRI, J. C. (1984). Teacher- versus peer-mediated instruction: An ecobehavioral analysis of achievement outcomes. *Journal of Applied Behavior Analysis, 17,* 521–538.

GREENWOOD, D., DELQUADRI, J., & HALL, R. (1984). *Opportunity to respond and student academic performance.* In W. L. Heward, T. E. Heron, D. S. Hill, & J. Trap-Porter (Eds.), *Focus on behavior analysis in education* (pp. 58–88). Columbus, OH: Merrill.

HALL, R. V., DELQUADRI, J., GREENWOOD, C. R., & THURSTON, L. (1982). The importance of opportunity to respond in children's academic success. In E. B. Edgar, N. G. Haring, J. R. Jenkins, & C. G. Pious (Eds.), *Mentally handicapped children: Education and training* (pp. 107–149). Baltimore: University Park Press.

HEWARD, W. L., HERON, T. E., ELLIS, D. E., & COOKE, N. L. (1986). Teaching first grade peer tutors to use verbal praise on an intermittent schedule. *Education and Treatment of Exceptional Children, 9,* 5–15.

KAMEENUI, E. J., & SIMMONS, D. C. (1990). *Designing instructional strategies: The prevention of academic learning problems.* Columbus, OH: Merrill.

KAZDIN, A. E. (1980a). Acceptability of alternative treatments for deviant child behaviors. *Journal of Applied Behavior Analysis, 13,* 259–273.

KAZDIN, A. E (1980b). *Behavior modification in applied settings* (rev.). Homewood, IL: Dorsey Press.

KAZDIN, A. E. (1981). Acceptability of child treatment techniques: The influence of treatment efficacy and adverse side effects. *Behavior Therapy, 12,* 493–506.

KERR, M. M., & NELSON, C. M. (1989). *Strategies for managing behavior problems in the classroom.* Columbus, OH: Merrill.

LITOW, L., & PUMROY, D. K. (1975). A brief review of classroom group-oriented contingencies. *Journal of Applied Behavior Analysis, 8,* 341–347.

LYNCH, C., MCGUIGAN, C., & SHOEMAKER, S. (1983). An introduction to systematic instruction. *British Columbia Journal of Special Education, 7,* 1–13.

MARTENS, B. K., WITT, J. C., ELLIOTT, S. N., & DARVEAUX, D. X. (1985). Teacher judgments concerning the acceptability of school-based interventions. *Professional Psychology: Research and Practice, 16,* 191–198.

MARTIN, G., & PEAR, J. (1988). *Behavior modification: What it is and how to do it* (3rd ed.). Englewood Cliffs, NJ: Prentice-Hall.

NORTHWEST REGIONAL EDUCATIONAL LABORATORY (1990). *Effective schooling practices: A research synthesis 1990 update.* Portland, OR: Author.

SKINNER, B. F. (1953). *Science and human behavior.* New York: Knopf.

STOKES, T. F., & BAER, D. M. (1977). An implicit technology of generalization. *Journal of Applied Behavior Analysis, 10,* 349–367.

STRAIN, P. S. (1981). *The utilization of classroom peers as behavior change agents.* New York: Plenum Press.

SUGAI, G. (1990). Effective teaching profile. Unpublished manuscript. University of Oregon, Eugene.

SUGAI, G., & CARTER, J. F. (1989). Prescriptive case consultation. Unpublished manuscript. University of Oregon, Eugene.

SUGAI, G., & FABRE, T. (In press). Using flowcharts to display behavior teaching plans. *Teaching Exceptional Children.*

WALBERG, H. J. (1988). Synthesis of research on time and learning. *Educational Leadership, 45,* 76–86.

WHITE, O. R. (1980). Adaptive performance objectives: Form versus function. In W. Sailor, B. Wilcox, & L. Brown (Eds.), *Methods of instruction for severely handicapped students.* (pp. 47–70). Baltimore: Paul Brookes.

WHITE, O. R., & HARING, N. G. (1980). *Exceptional teaching* (2nd ed.). Columbus, OH: Merrill.

WINNET, R. A., & WINKLER, R. C. (1972). Current behavior modification in the classroom: Be still, be quiet, be docile. *Journal of Applied Behavior Analysis, 5,* 499–504.

WITT, J. C., & ELLIOTT, S. N. (1985). Acceptability of classroom management strategies. In T. R. Kratochwill (Ed.), *Advances in school psychology* (Vol. 4, pp. 251–288). Hillsdale, NJ: Erlbaum.

WITT, J. C., ELLIOTT, S. N., & MARTENS, B. K. (1984). Acceptability of behavioral interventions used in classrooms: The influence of amount of teacher time, severity of behavior problem, and type of intervention., *Behavioral Disorders, 9,* 95–104.

WITT, J. C., MARTENS, B. K., & ELLIOTT, S. M. (1984). Factors affecting teachers' judgments of the acceptability of behavioral interventions: Time involvement, behavior problem severity and type of intervention. *Behavior Therapy, 15,* 204–209.

WITTROCK, M. (1986). *Third handbook of research on teaching.* Chicago: Rand McNally.

WOLERY, M. R., BAILEY, D. B., JR., & SUGAI, G. (1988). *Effective teaching: Principles and procedures of applied behavior analysis with exceptional students.* Boston: Allyn & Bacon.

WOLF, M. M. (1978). Social validity: The case for subjective measurement or how applied behavior analysis is finding its heart. *Journal of Applied Behavior Analysis, 11,* 203–214.

WORRALL, C., WORRALL, N., & MELDRUM, C. (1983). The consequences of verbal praise and criticism. *Educational Psychologist, 3,* 127–136.

Programming Strategies

Having completed a Request for Assistance, Problem Identification Interview, and functional analysis, consultants and teachers must now build intervention programs to help students decrease undesirable behaviors, strengthen more appropriate behaviors, and function more successfully and independently (that is, be better self-managers). Although a structure like the Intervention Planning Sheet guides the intervention process, teachers and consultants must still choose from an extensive range of strategies, learn how to implement the strategy, and then carry it out accurately and fluently. Achieving these outcomes is not easy.

One of the major challenges facing the consultant and the teacher is the search for an intervention that will bring about meaningful change in the student's behavior *and* be easy to implement. However, given the hundreds of behavior and classroom management strategies available, choosing one can be difficult. In addition, teachers' skill and knowledge levels are quite varied. Therefore, consultants must be well versed in the (a) range of available intervention strategies, (b) the variations of the chosen intervention, (c) the circumstances under which the intervention may be effective, and (d) the strengths and weaknesses of the intervention.

In this chapter, we discuss the relevant features of interventions that consultants and teachers might select, develop, and implement. Our intent is to familiarize consultants with the essential features of classroom-based interventions that teachers can use to solve important social behavior problems. As in the previous chapter, we believe that this content on programming strategies is essential. Although teachers and consultants may not be able to engage in all the skills described, we strongly believe that they should try to acquire as many as possible.

To begin this discussion, we review the necessary characteristics of a complete, systematic intervention program. Our subsequent presentation of programming strategies is organized into four sections: teaching new social behaviors, strengthening existing behaviors, weakening or eliminating existing problem behaviors, and implementing contingency contracting and self-management strategies.

PREREQUISITE KNOWLEDGE AND SKILLS
FOR SYSTEMATIC INTERVENTION PROGRAMS

Consultation and intervention success is often a function of the degree to which an intervention strategy is complete, usable, organized, and understandable. In this section, we highlight the characteristics of a systematic approach to intervention planning and development. For additional information about systematic approaches to program development and management, see the following readings:

LYNCH, V., MCGUIGAN, C., & SHOEMAKER, S. (1983). An introduction to systematic instruction. *B.C. Journal of Special Education, 7,* 1–13.

SUGAI, G., & FABRE, T. (1987). The behavior teaching plan: A model for developing and implementing behavior change programs. *Education and Treatment of Children, 10,* 279–290.

WOLERY, M. R., BAILEY, D. B., JR., & SUGAI, G. (1988). *Effective teaching: Principles and procedures of applied behavior analysis with exceptional students.* Boston: Allyn & Bacon.

To begin, we recommend that consultants use some type of systematic structure to organize the development and presentation of an intervention selection. The Intervention Planning form and procedure discussed in Chapter 5 initiates the process by identifying the general aspects of the selected intervention but does not stipulate which tasks are done and when. The consultant and the teacher must describe these particulars, regardless of which intervention is selected. Each of the following tasks must be addressed:

1. Gather the necessary materials.
2. Establish clear definitions for the undesirable behavior and its replacement response (fair-pair).
3. Develop possible testable explanations or hypotheses for the problem behavior.
4. Set a goal or behavioral objective.
5. Establish a way to collect and display formative student performance data.
6. Sequence and display all intervention steps for decreasing the undesirable behavior and increasing the replacement response.
7. Establish a schedule for regular program review.

Guidelines and implementation suggestions for each task are discussed in the following section.

Gather Necessary Materials

Program development and implementation can be hindered if the necessary materials are not available or require extra time and effort to construct. Although teachers may have some materials on hand, consultants should work under the assumption that resources will not be available to teachers and should attempt to minimize the amount of effort and time required to gather and/or construct other materials. The following strategies can help the consultant respond effectively when intervention materials need to be developed.

1. *Collect samples of intervention programs.* Consultants should use their intervention experiences as the basis for developing new programs and building a collection of intervention alternatives. Mr. Dianella, for example, was a teacher before he became a consultant, so he gathered samples of forms and other intervention-related materials from his classroom.

Consultants should also collect examples of successful interventions from teachers and other consultants. These strategies might have a greater likelihood of succeeding and being accepted by the teacher if taken from successful applications.

2. *Generate generic forms for high-frequency procedures.* To avoid recreating a form or procedural sequence, standardized materials should be developed for widespread application. Generic observation forms were illustrated in Chapter 4, and sample self-recording and contingency contract forms are shown later in this chapter. Ms. Fernandez, for example, finds that she frequently uses contingency contracting and self-recording, so, she uses a contract form that has blanks for inputting key information. This contract form is also kept on her computer where she can simply edit new and old information before printing a copy.

3. *Develop a filing system that will allow easy sorting and searching for intervention strategies.* As examples of interventions, forms, and other materials begin to accumulate, finding a particular piece of information can be frustrating. We suggest that consultants establish a simple filing strategy to organize frequently used materials. For example, Mr. Dianella sorts his social behavior–intervention materials into the following categories: (a) strategies for teaching social skills, (b) strategies (such as reinforcer menus and surveys, token economies, behavioral contracts) for strengthening behaviors, (c) strategies (such as time-out, response cost, behavioral contracts) for eliminating undesirable behaviors, (d) behavioral contract forms, (e) behavior-recording forms and procedures, and (f) self-management forms and procedures. Each category is in a separate file folder or box.

In contrast, Ms. Fernandez organizes her intervention materials around frequently encountered consultation problems: (a) noncompliance, (b) talking and acting out and aggressive behaviors, (c) shyness and withdrawn behaviors, (d) study skills (homework, preparedness), (e) attendance and truancy, and (f) antisocial behaviors (substance abuse, delinquent behaviors). Although she maintains a filing system like Mr. Dianella, Ms. Fernandez also keeps records of frequently used programs in a small notebook that she takes with her when meeting teachers. The notebook contains blank contract forms, student self-recording sheets, data collection samples, and intervention task analyses.

Establish Clear Definitions for the Behavior and Its Replacement Response (Fair-Pair)

We have discussed how behaviors can be described and written in observable ways, by using dimensions and focusing on discrete behaviors. Clear definitions increase the probability that consultants, teachers, and students can respond accurately and consistently. In addition, highlighting the definition of a replacement response emphasizes its importance and communicative function. The following response definition guidelines can increase the completeness of an intervention:

1. *Write definitions of the undesirable behavior and its replacement response in observable/measurable terms.* Clear definitions help describe which behaviors are being targeted for change and what type of observation procedure is needed.
2. *Discuss examples and nonexamples of the targeted behaviors.* Identifying positive and negative examples of the behavior helps identify the behavior's boundaries.

Develop Possible Testable Explanations or Hypotheses for the Problem Behavior

Replacement responses that have or can have similar communicative or critical functions as the target behavior should be selected. The success of the intervention may be hindered, if a more desirable replacement response cannot be developed that is as useful to the student as the targeted undesirable response.

1. *If possible, conduct at least two functional analyses in the problem context.* One reason to conduct a functional analysis is to determine predictable relationships between the student's behavior and events in the immediate environment. Once a number of samples of student behaviors and antecedent and consequent events have been obtained, useful testable explanations can be developed. (See Chapter 3 for elaboration.)
2. *Develop testable explanations that help identify communicative or critical function.* Identifying the function of a problem behavior can facilitate the development of an effective intervention. Mr. Dianella, for example, discovered that most of George's disruptive behaviors function to gain adult social attention in Ms. Morley's classroom. This information enables them to develop a behavioral contract that strengthens a replacement response for gaining adult social attention.

Set a Goal or Behavioral Objective

Establishing an intervention goal or aim is important for numerous reasons. First, its functions as an end point or goal for the student and teacher. Second, a behavioral objective can serve as a gauge to evaluate intervention success or student progress. Finally, it can function as a convenient, informative way to communicate with others about a program. Following these four guidelines can increase the usefulness of behavioral objectives in intervention programming:

1. *Write complete behavioral objectives.* All behavioral objectives should include four components: the learner, the condition or where the behavior needs to be emitted, the behavior or what the student must emit, and the criteria or to what accuracy or level the behavior must be emitted. Without

these pieces of information, it is impossible to evaluate student progress. Mr. Dianella and Ms. Morley wrote the following long-term objective:

> Given an eight-class-period day, George will be in the classroom and in his seat before the bell rings in seven out of eight class periods for five consecutive days.

2. *Focus on the replacement response.* Emphasizing the replacement response in the behavioral objective creates a positive approach to the problem and highlights the importance of the response and the procedure used to strengthen it.

3. *Describe all components of the behavioral objective in observable/ measurable terms.* Intervention development, implementation, and evaluation can be more accurate and understandable if the condition, behavior, and criterion of an objective are written in terms that are easily identifiable and replicable (repeatable).

4. *Write the criterion based on an appropriate standard or normative base.* To be meaningful and enable accurate evaluation of intervention progress, the criterion in the objective should be based on a clearly stated and relevant standard—for example, (a) the student's previous baseline performance, (b) the standard displayed by the student's peer group, (c) the expectations from relevant individuals from the student's home, school, or community, or (d) the developmental norms for same-age students. The chosen standard should reflect the minimum performance level that would enable the student to be successful and independent in the observed problem context; that is, in the least restrictive environment, such as the school, home, or community.

Establish a Way to Collect and Display Formative Student Performance Data

Although teachers and consultants resist collecting data, some mechanism must be established for assessing student performance and evaluating progress toward the behavioral objective. The following guidelines are intended to supplement the general data collection issues, fundamentals, and procedures described in Chapter 3.

1. *Use a data collection system that is compatible with classroom routines and activities.* If a data collection procedure interferes with classroom routines and practices, the teacher will abandon it or it will result in unreliable information. Mr. Dianella helped Ms. Morley develop a simple event-recording procedure in which she keeps eight paper clips (one for each class period) in the left-hand pocket of her skirt or slacks. Whenever George is on-time to class, she moves a paper clip to her right-hand pocket. At the end of the day, she counts the number of paper clips, (or the number of classes on-time).

2. *Observe long enough during the problem context to obtain a valid sample of the student's behavior.* A determination of how long and where data should be collected is frequently obtained from the functional analysis,

where patterns can be evaluated within a temporal context. Observations should be conducted in the setting where the problem behaviors are most troublesome and should continue until changes in behavior can be observed.

3. *Use available resources to collect data.* Although we tend to first think of using teachers as resources, teaching assistants, competent peers, student assistants from higher grade levels, parent volunteers, and practicum students from neighboring teacher-training programs can all be used to collect performance data. In addition, even though reactivity to a procedure and accuracy can be a problem, the target student can also be taught to self-record behaviors or record them with the teacher's help. Whatever methods are selected, the consultant and teacher should conduct regular, independent probes to ensure high levels of agreement with the student. To minimize observation inconsistencies, the same person should record throughout the consultation.

4. *Conduct sample probes.* The consultant (if the teacher is collecting the data) or the teacher (if someone else is observing) should conduct regular probes to obtain a sample of the student's performance. This information can be used to (a) assess the observer's reliability (consistency or accuracy), (b) determine the accuracy with which an intervention is implemented, (c) evaluate if the student's behavior is changing (the intervention is effective), and (d) confirm old or establish new testable explanations about the problem behavior.

5. *Establish clear criteria for evaluating student performance and intervention effectiveness.* Formative recording procedures give the teacher and the consultant an opportunity to evaluate intervention progress on a continuous basis. To structure this evaluation, simple data decision rules should be stated. It is against these rules that systematic intervention decisions—such as to continue, discontinue, or modify the intervention—can be made. A more detailed discussion of formative evaluation and data decision rules is found in Chapter 7.

6. *Establish a formative and visual display of performance data.* To increase the ease and probability of ongoing program evaluation, we strongly encourage the consultant and the teacher to develop a means of visually displaying collected data. The procedure should be easy to use and should facilitate daily decision making. A number of graphing procedures were discussed in Chapter 3. Additional evaluation and graphing strategies are discussed in Chapter 7.

Sequence and Display All Intervention Steps for Decreasing the Undesirable Behavior and Increasing the Replacement Response

As indicated previously, the Intervention Planning form does not provide information about what teachers should do; at best, it labels the intervention strategy. To increase accurate implementation and the probability of success, consultants and teachers must delineate the particulars of the intervention. The following guidelines are based on the assumption that the consultant is knowledgeable, has access to the necessary materials and resources, and is required to sequence and display the intervention. We also assume that the teacher is generally accepting of the intervention and does not have the expertise or experience to sequence and display the intervention.

1. *Task-analyze the intervention into its main procedural steps.* One of the first steps in preparing a procedural display of an intervention is to identify its principal components. All setting, antecedent, and consequence manipulations should be considered. Conducting a temporal (beginning to end) task analysis can facilitate this task. One type of analysis would describe the overall steps of the program, for example:

   a. Obtain parent approval for contracting.
   b. Gather and prepare materials.
   c. Meet with student and develop contract.
   d. Train student what appropriate and inappropriate behaviors look like.
   e. Train student to use the self-recording sheet.
   f. Implement intervention in the classroom.
   g. Evaluate the intervention's effectiveness.

   A second task analysis focuses on the actual implementation of an intervention, for example:

   a. Before the class period bell rings, remind the student to self-record on the monitoring sheet what he or she is doing immediately after the bell rings.
   b. When the class period bell rings, observe the student's behavior.
   c. If the student is in his or her seat and behaving appropriately, give verbal praise with specific feedback and a reminder to self-record behavior.
   d. If the student is out of his or her seat and/or behaving inappropriately, give a reminder to mark the self-recording sheet.
   e. At the end of the day, review the student's self-recording sheet. If more than six periods are checked with a " + ", provide specific verbal praise and place a " + " on the calendar for that day. If six or fewer " + " marked, encourage the student to try harder the next day and place a " − " on the calendar.
   f. Evaluate student performance relative to the data decision rules and behavioral objective.

2. *Identify the major decisions that will need to be considered in the implementation of an intervention.* Most intervention programs consist of more than a static series of steps. The student's actions dictate what the teacher does. Typically, teachers must consider a number of decisions and corresponding actions in situations such as the following:

   a. Immediately when the desired replacement response occurs.
   b. Immediately when the undesirable problem behavior occurs.
   c. Immediately when the problem or replacement responses occur repeatedly.
   d. When more than one type of reinforcer is possible.
   e. When more than one type of consequence is possible for problem behaviors.

F I G U R E   6.3
Implementation flow chart

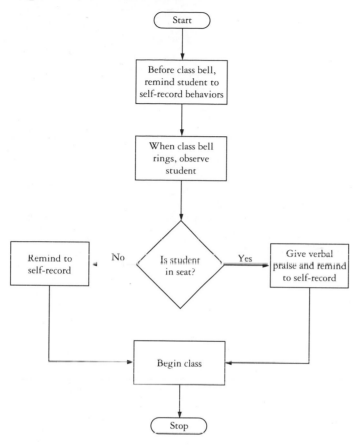

minimum requirements. When any programming strategy is considered, this kind of systematic approach should be applied.

TEACHING NEW SOCIAL BEHAVIORS

One of the major themes of this book is the identification and strengthening of a replacement or fair-pair response when problematic behaviors need to be weakened or eliminated. Many students already have the necessary replacement response in their learning history; it merely needs to be strengthened and made more functional or useful. However, for other behaviors and students, the replacement response does not exist in the students' learning repertoire, and a new behavior must be taught directly—that is, in a structured teacher-directed format that includes multiple examples, demonstrations, practice, and informative feedback. These students are at the acquisition phase of learning, and the teacher

f. When different levels or intensities of problem or replacement responses are observed.

g. When the daily criterion is met or not met.

Stipulating these types of major decisions and associated actions in advance reduces the probability of inconsistent program implementation. In particular, teachers can be ready with specific responses when the "unexpected" occurs—for example, a student runs away, refuses to go to a time-out location, or fails to respond after a third restatement of the rule.

3. *Develop a visual display of the intervention procedure.* When implementing a new academic program, teachers rely on the curriculum guide or manual to highlight precisely what is done. A similar strategy should be applied to behavior change procedures. A visual display should be precise, easy to follow, and complete. Depending on what is being illustrated, a variety of display formats, such as lesson plans, checklists, or flow charts, are possible. Task analysis information is used to develop these displays. An example of a checklist for a contingency-contracting task analysis is illustrated in Figure 6.1.

Flow charts are another way to visually display the major actions and implementation decisions of an intervention program. As symbolic communication tools, they help logically portray linear processes (Sugai & Fabre, in press). Three types of flow charts can be used: descriptive, implementation, and evaluation. A more detailed discussion of flow charting can be found in Sugai and Fabre (in press). In Figure 6.2, a descriptive flow chart is used to illustrate the procedural steps of the contingency-contracting program. This linear portrayal does not describe what is done if more than one action is possible. The program's major implementation actions and decisions to increase on-time to class are shown in the flow chart in Figure 6.3. This type of flow chart shows what the teacher should do if the student is in or out of his or her seat when the class bell rings. Finally, the evaluation pinpoints for the same program are depicted in the flow chart in Figure 6.4. In this example, the student's daily performance is used to determine the consequences and the plan for the next day.

Establish a Schedule for Regular Program Review

A complete intervention program provides scheduled opportunities for program review. Two levels of review are needed. The first level is an evaluation of daily performance and the degree to which the student's progress will enable the student to achieve his or her long-term objective or goal. The major point of interest is whether the intervention program should be adjusted; that is, determining if the student's progress is acceptable or unacceptable.

The second level of review focuses on overall program evaluation, that is, the degree to which the interventions have been successful in achieving the program's long-term goals and objectives. This review occurs at the end of longer time periods, such as the calendar month, the academic quarter or semester, or after the review of individualized education plans. Success is assessed against a variety of criteria: (a) how much confidence the observers have in the intervention's contribution to

FIGURE 6.1

Checklist for the implementation steps of a contingency contracting program

---

CONTINGENCY CONTRACTING PROGRAM CHECKLIST

Date completed:

___/___/___ 1.   Obtain parent approval for use of contracting program.

___/___/___ 2.   Gather and prepare materials.

        ___   Behavior definitions
        ___   Contract forms
        ___   Reinforcers
        ___   Observation instruments

___/___/___ 3.   Meet with student and develop contract.

        ___   Define behaviors
        ___   Identify data collection procedure
        ___   Identify reinforcers and schedule of reinforcement
        ___   Identify responsibilities
        ___   Specify timelines
        ___   Obtain signatures

___/___/___ 4.   Train student what appropriate and inappropriate behaviors look like.

___/___/___ 5.   Train student to use data collection procedure.

___/___/___ 6.   Implement intervention in classroom.

---

the observed effects (empirical or internal validity), (b) how generalizable the treatment effects are to other settings or students (external validity), (c) how large the treatment effects are relative to pretreatment levels and school or classroom standards (educational validity), (d) how the intervention effects compare to the functioning levels of similar peers (social validity), and (e) how intervention effects are evaluated by relevant adults (social validity). A more detailed, applied discussion about evaluation strategies and procedures is found in Chapter 7.

In summary, the ease of the consultant's job and the teacher's success at program implementation can be influenced by the degree of preparedness, organization, systematicity, and completeness associated with an intervention program. We advocate a systematic approach to program development and presentation in which the seven components discussed in this section are the

FIGURE 6.2

Descriptive flow chart

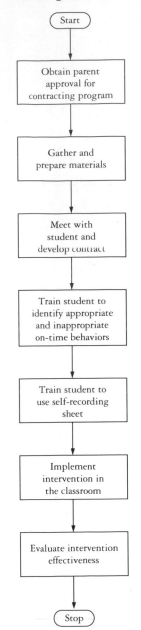

FIGURE 6.2

Descriptive flow chart

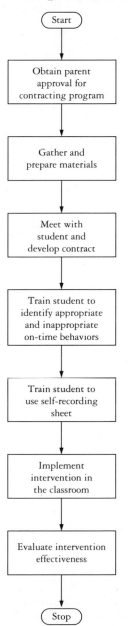

FIGURE 6.3

Implementation flow chart

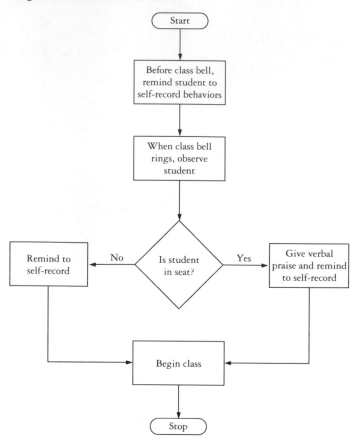

minimum requirements. When any programming strategy is considered, this kind of systematic approach should be applied.

TEACHING NEW SOCIAL BEHAVIORS

One of the major themes of this book is the identification and strengthening of a replacement or fair-pair response when problematic behaviors need to be weakened or eliminated. Many students already have the necessary replacement response in their learning history; it merely needs to be strengthened and made more functional or useful. However, for other behaviors and students, the replacement response does not exist in the students' learning repertoire, and a new behavior must be taught directly—that is, in a structured teacher-directed format that includes multiple examples, demonstrations, practice, and informative feedback. These students are at the acquisition phase of learning, and the teacher

FIGURE 6.4
Evaluation flow chart

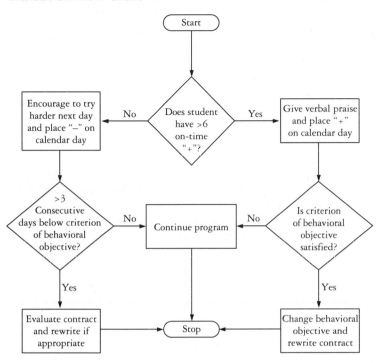

focuses on showing and telling them how to do the skill, with a strong emphasis on antecedent manipulations (such as prompts, models, and examples) and on the differential reinforcement of correct and incorrect responses.

In this section, we emphasize the teaching of new social behaviors and describe some of the critical features of the strategies used. Again, the focus is on skills we believe consultants should be fluent in and able to assist teachers to implement. We present our assumptions about the consultant's role in teaching new behaviors and about issues that must be considered before, during, and after implementing the instruction. For more information on acquisition training and designing effective instructional sequences, we recommend *Designing Instructional Strategies: The Prevention of Academic Learning Problems,* by E. J. Kameenui, and D. C. Simmons (especially, Chapter 4, ''Principles of Designing Instruction'').

Assumptions About the Consultant's Role

Although the teaching of new social behaviors is very important, it is often overlooked because teachers tend to focus on the teaching or remediation of academic skills or the elimination of problematic social behaviors. We believe that consultants should recognize the importance of teaching social skills and attend to that need. The following assumptions serve as the foundation for our position.

Social behaviors are taught in the same way as academic behaviors.   To teach a new academic response or skill, the teacher begins with a verbal or visual presentation to help the student observe what the skill looks like and when it should be used. For example, to teach Esta that Canberra is the capital of Australia, Ms. Ramwood first models or tells her the answer in the presence of the question "What is the capital city of Australia? The capital city of Australia is Canberra." Next, she presents her with an assisted opportunity to give the correct response (lead), using some kind of teacher prompt (a flashcard or simultaneous oration) to ensure a correct response. Finally, Ms. Ramwood asks her to give the answer when the assists or prompts are removed (test). At each point in the instruction, she provides reinforcement for correct responses and a correction or no reinforcement for errors.

When teaching Esta how to get adult attention the right way (social behavior), Ms. Ramwood applies the same instructional sequence and strategies. First, either Ms. Ramwood or a competent peer models the correct social skill so Esta can see what it looks like (model). Ms. Ramwood highlights the critical features of the modeled display and asks Esta to provide a verbal description of these features. Then, Esta practices how to get adult attention in a role-play situation, which contains assists and prompts to ensure accurate responding (lead). Finally, Ms. Ramwood presents a new role play but without any assistance (test). She gives reinforcement and corrective feedback throughout the model and lead portions of the instruction. Effective social skills instruction is associated with the application of the same effective teaching skills used to teach academic skills—that is, brisk pacing, smooth transitions, clear explanations, and high academic engagement.

Social skills instruction must be systematic and ongoing.   For this instruction to be effective, it must be a planned, scheduled, and ongoing component of the instructional day. If it is haphazard and unstructured, student learning will probably be haphazard and inefficient as well. Opportunities for social behavior instruction should be scheduled with the same regularity as daily reading and math instruction.

As soon as a skill has been acquired, the teacher can move to more intermittent, less predictable instructional strategies that focus on response maintenance and generalization. But first, he or she must be sure that the student can perform the skill accurately and fluently.

Social skills instruction should focus on the natural context and generalized responding.   To help students acquire useful social behaviors, the instruction must emphasize real examples or situations that approximate those found in the context where the behavior must be displayed. Since research has not produced a technology that enables us to easily achieve generalized responding (Stokes & Baer, 1977), it is important to teach social behaviors in the actual setting in which they are required. For example, Mr. Evans was trying to teach Sallee and her friends appropriate bus-riding skills. Lessons consisted of lining up classroom chairs in rows to approximate the seats in a bus, but actual bus-riding behaviors did not change until Mr. Evans arranged to have the lessons taught on an actual school bus.

Consultants may need to teach teachers how to teach social behaviors.
Teachers who are ineffective in teaching social skills may need to be taught how
to teach them. Although academic instructional strategies and basic classroom and
behavior management strategies are included in most teacher-training programs,
trainees typically receive little systematic training in how to teach social behaviors. Consultants may need to provide planned in-service training opportunities
that also include a discussion of what social skills are and a strong rationale for
teaching them. The topic of training and motivating others is covered in-depth in
Chapter 11.

Considerations Before Implementation of Instruction

Like teaching any new reading, math, or physical education skill, the more prepared
the teacher, the smoother the lesson, the more effective the instruction, and the
greater the student's learning. In assisting teachers to prepare for a social behavior
lesson, consultants should consider the following:

1. Select and prepare an appropriate curriculum. Some useful published social
   skills curricula include:
   > *Skillstreaming the Adolescent: A Structured Learning Approach to Teaching
   > Prosocial Skills* (Goldstein, Sprafkin, Gershaw, & Klein, 1980).
   > *Getting Along with Others: Teaching Social Effectiveness to Children* (Jackson,
   > Jackson, & Monroe, 1983).
   > *Skillstreaming the Elementary School Child: A Guide for Teaching Prosocial
   > Skills* (McGinnis, Goldstein, Sprafkin, & Gershaw, 1984).
   > *The Walker Social Skills Curriculum: The ACCEPTS Program* (Walker,
   > McConnell, Holmes, Todis, Walker, & Golden, 1983).
   > *The Walker Social Skills Curriculum: The ACCESS Program* (Walker, Todis,
   > Holmes, & Horton, 1983).
2. Select appropriate examples and nonexamples.
3. Sequence examples appropriately.
4. Prepare, sequence, and schedule instructional activities (for example,
   practice, seatwork, teacher-engaged work, role play).
5. Identify appropriate instructional prompts and assists to increase correct
   responding and decrease errors.
6. Select appropriate reinforcers.
7. Select an appropriate error correction procedure.
8. Practice instructional sequences for teaching difficult skills.
9. Develop a procedure for recording student performance data.

Considerations During the Implementation of Instruction

Assuming that the preinstructional activities are complete, consultants must be able
to assist teachers in the actual implementation of social behavior instructions. While
achieving all of the following pinpoints may not be realistic, consultants should try
to help teachers consider as many of them as possible:

1. Review, teach, and reinforce rules and expectations.
2. Review, teach, and reinforce task requirements.
3. Distribute material efficiently.
4. Secure and maintain student attention.
5. Present instructions or directions in a clear manner.
6. Present instruction at a brisk pace.
7. Continuously monitor and give feedback about student performance and behavior.
8. Use clear, consistent signals for group and individual responses.
9. Continuously reinforce correct responses.
10. Present a correction procedure when errors occur.
11. Continuously check or assess student understanding.
12. Review the skills being taught.

Considerations After the Implementation of Instruction

After completing a social behavior lesson, teachers should provide appropriate follow-up activities and evaluate student performance and the effectiveness of the instruction. Consultants should consider the following points when assisting teachers in their postinstruction activities:

1. Evaluate student performance against the behavioral objective.
2. Present homework or other practice activities based on student performance and the instructional lesson.
3. Modify behavioral objective, instruction, and/or curriculum based on performance. Additional evaluation factors and strategies are discussed in Chapter 7.

STRENGTHENING EXISTING BEHAVIORS

After a social behavior has been acquired, the teacher's focus shifts to strengthening the student's ability to use fluently and successfully what he or she has already learned in a variety of contexts (that is, generalization and adaptation). Instructional activities center on (a) maintaining or enhancing performance motivation (that is, the manipulation of consequent events such as reinforcers and schedules of reinforcement), (b) providing numerous opportunities to practice the skills, and (c) highlighting the critical features of the antecedent and setting conditions under which the desired skill would be required.

In this section, we discuss strategies associated with strengthening existing or acquired responses—that is, achieving proficient (fluency), lasting (maintenance), and generalized (generalization) responding. We believe that consultants must make the identification and effective use of positive reinforcement their highest priority in helping teachers develop and implement behavior change programs. Without a careful manipulation of reinforcers, behaviors will not be strengthened, long-lasting, or useful across settings. Thus, we discuss the following areas:

(a) identifying useful reinforcers, (b) developing effective reinforcers, (c) scheduling reinforcement, and (d) administering reinforcement.

Identifying Useful Reinforcers

One of the most important aspects of any behavior teaching or change program is the use of informative and functional feedback, in particular, feedback for and about appropriate responses. Through feedback, students obtain information about the accuracy of their performance or receive incentives for changing their behaviors. Teachers and consultants must be able to identify useful feedback forms, especially positive reinforcers.

Definitions.   Although different foods are often used as reinforcers, consultants must dispel myths that reinforcers are limited to edibles (candy, peanuts, and apple slices) or to tokens (stickers, points, and marbles). It is more important to strengthen the idea that just about anything is or can become a reinforcer for a given student. Some items, such as money or candy, may be reinforcers for a large number of students. However, reinforcers should be seen as individually determined and defined. Using a functional definition, a *reinforcer* is any object, event, or activity that, when presented contingently as a consequence to a behavior, is associated with an increased probability that the behavior will be observed in the future.

Similarly, *positive reinforcement* is "the contingent presentation of a stimulus following a response that results in an increase in the future occurrence of the response" (Wolery, Bailey, & Sugai, 1988, p. 235). Thus, deciding whether something is a reinforcer is determined by (a) the individual's learning history or past experience and (b) whether the behavior increases when the reinforcer is presented contingently as a consequence. For example, Mr. Evans thought that verbal praise statements were effective reinforcers for Sallee; however, he observed a decrease in Sallee's cooperative play after he gave verbal praise. This is not to say that positive reinforcement does not work, or that verbal praise cannot become a more reinforcing consequence, but it does suggest that a more effective reinforcer needed to be developed or identified for this student.

Characteristics of effective reinforcers.   Many different objects or events can be reinforcers. The consultant's and teacher's challenge is to find reinforcers that are also effective. Effective and useful reinforcers have the following characteristics: (a) easy to obtain and store, (b) inexpensive, (c) easily transportable, (d) under the teacher's control, (e) appropriate in the least-restrictive environment, (f) administrable in small amounts, (g) not disruptive or distracting, (h) delay satiation, and (i) bridge the gap between behavior and a later reinforcing event.

A common teacher complaint is that a student has "no reinforcers." For example, one teacher makes the following comment:

> Hidalgo is one of the most unmotivated students I've ever seen. He comes to class everyday, but instead of working he's talking with his friends and finding ways to distract me from the day's planned activities. I spend all my time nagging at him

to get busy. I've tried extra free time, library passes, independent time on the computer, sitting out in the hallway . . . all kinds of unsuccessful incentives. I don't understand why he just doesn't stay home!

From a functional perspective, it is inaccurate to say that Hidalgo has no reinforcers; in fact, numerous possible reinforcers are maintaining his behaviors: attention from peers, nagging from the teacher, and avoidance of planned activities. All are effective reinforcers for behaviors that the teacher finds unacceptable; nevertheless, they are still reinforcers. Therefore, it may be more accurate to say that for Hidalgo, there are no effective and *appropriate* reinforcers being applied contingently for completing work.

The task of finding effective reinforcers can be more productive if the consultant and the teacher use one or more of the following strategies:

1. Ask the student to indicate what kinds of things or activities are interesting, challenging, and/or pleasurable.
2. Observe the student in variety of contexts and settings and note high interest and frequency activities; that is, those where the most time is spent and the highest engagement rates are observed.
3. Ask teachers, parents, employers, or peers who are familiar with the student to identify reinforcers that they have used and found to be effective.
4. Review the archival records and determine what has been effective in the past.
5. Try reinforcers that have been effective with similar students.
6. Pair (and then fade) a less desirable but more effective reinforcer with another reinforcer that is less effective but more desirable.

First, teachers should not assume that a potential reinforcer is effective until they have observed an increase in performance when it is presented as a contingent consequence. Second, a given reinforcer may not maintain its reinforcing qualities and strength over time and may need to be strengthened or replaced with a strong reinforcer. Finally, identification of effective reinforcers should be an ongoing priority. We recommend that consultants maintain lists of potentially useful reinforcers, by type and/or grade level, and add to these lists as they identify other functional reinforcers.

Developing Useful Reinforcers

In some classroom contexts, naturally occurring consequence events that should have reinforcing qualities (such as verbal praise, smiles, social attention, or grades) fail to be effective reinforcers for the behaviors of some students. In these cases, consultants must help the teacher develop these nonreinforcing events into useful reinforcers. Reinforcers can be strengthened in four ways.

One way is to create a condition in which the student does not have enough of the specific reinforcer. For example, Mr. Jarra used a point system (token economy) to let his students know when they were on-task and following classroom rules. When he noticed that his points were losing their reinforcing qualities (that is, on-task and other rule-following behaviors were decreasing), he found that by giving out fewer points during the day, the reinforcing or "motivating" potential of his points increased.

A second method is to systematically pair a strong, effective reinforcer with a weaker, ineffective one. As the reinforcing quality of the weaker one increases, the paired reinforcer is systematically removed. For example, Mr. Jarra found that verbal praise was an ineffective reinforcer for Alice (that is, it was not associated with an increase in her behaviors), and her other teachers frequently used verbal praise. Since Mr. Jarra observed that Alice found earning points to be reinforcing, he paired the points with clear, specific verbal praise. After a short time, he systematically delayed giving the points but continued to give immediate verbal praise. Eventually, he discontinued the presentation of points altogether as verbal praise alone became an effective reinforcer.

A third way is to manipulate the back-up reinforcers for which tokens are traded. For example, Mr. Jarra found that he could increase the reinforcing value of his tokens by regularly adding to and removing the kinds of back-up reinforcers in his classroom token store.

Finally, to facilitate generalized responding, consultants and teachers should select reinforcers that are as effective *and* "natural" as possible. Natural reinforcers are those functional consequences that are experienced in everyday school, home, and community settings (such as in the classroom, at recess, on the playground, in the cafeteria, on the bus). These include most (a) social reinforcers (such as verbal praise, smiles, gentle physical contact, and handshakes), (b) token reinforcers (such as grades, points, and money), (c) tangible reinforcers (such as stickers, happy-face stamps, pencils, certificates, and awards), and (d) activity reinforcers (such as time to play games, use of the computer, and trips to the library).

Unfortunately, with some students, teachers must use artificial reinforcers because they are more effective than those found naturally. These unique reinforcers can include edibles (candy and other snacks), special tokens (marbles), or novel events (off-campus lunch, field trips). Although the use of these atypical reinforcers is appropriate, a systematic plan should be provided for fading out their use and developing more natural consequences as effective reinforcers.

In summary, consultants and teachers must remember that whether some thing or event is a reinforcer is based on how it affects the future occurrences of a behavior. Also one student's reinforcer might be a strong aversive for another student's behaviors. Many reinforcers can be identified on the basis of their effects on student behaviors. Unfortunately, some reinforcers are not appropriate in all settings or are associated with undesirable student behaviors. The teacher's challenge is to identify useful, natural reinforcers that can be used to strengthened setting-appropriate student behaviors.

Scheduling Reinforcement

Ideally, teachers would like desirable student behaviors to last for a long time and undesirable behaviors to be eliminated or extinguished immediately. Achieving these maintenance goals is affected in great part by the kind of schedule used to administer reinforcers (that is, when or how often a reinforcer is provided).

In general, there are three basic schedules of reinforcement. The first is a schedule of no reinforcement, or extinction. Under this schedule, no reinforcers are provided contingent on the emission of a particular behavior. We would like desirable behaviors to maintain under extinction conditions for as long as possible and undesirable behaviors to decrease or weaken as quickly as possible under these same conditions. Unfortunately, problem situations are usually characterized in the opposite way: desirable behaviors do not maintain and undesirable behaviors persist. Accounting for or achieving these response outcomes is related to the kind of schedule of reinforcement controlling the behavior.

The second schedule is a response-based or ratio schedule of reinforcement in which reinforcers are provided contingent on the occurrence of a constant (fixed) or an average (variable) number of targeted behaviors. For example, Mr. Evans remembers to reinforce Sallee for raising her hand and asking for help about once out of every six opportunities (variable ratio 6, FR6).

The third schedule is a time-based or interval schedule of reinforcement in which reinforcers are provided contingent on the passage of a constant (fixed) or an average (variable) amount of time and the concurrent presence of a targeted

BOX 6.1

Similarities and differences in schedules of reinforcement

Interval	**Fixed** FI3 = At the end of every 3 minutes (e.g., 3, 3, 3, 3), give a reinforcer if the target behavior is present. FI17 = At the end of every 17 minutes (e.g., 17, 17, 17, 17, 17, 17, 17), give a reinforcer if the target behavior is present. **Variable** VI20 = On the average of every 20 minutes (e.g., 18, 22, 19, 21, 20), give a reinforcer if the target behavior is present. VI4 = On the average of every 4 minutes (e.g., 3, 4, 5, 4, 3, 5), give a reinforcer if the target behavior is present.
Ratio	**Fixed** FR23 = After every 23rd occurrence of the target behavior (e.g., 23, 23, 23, 23, 23, 23), give a reinforcer. FR7 = After every 7th occurrence of the target behavior (e.g., 7, 7, 7, 7), give a reinforcer. **Variable** VR9 = On the average of every 9th occurrence of the target behavior (e.g., 7, 9, 11, 8, 9, 10), give a reinforcer. VR45 = On the average of every 45th occurrence of the target behavior (e.g., 45, 50, 40, 47, 43), give a reinforcer.

behavior. For example, Ms. Morley sets the timer on her wristwatch to ring once every three minutes. If George is in his seat and working on his assignment when the timer goes off, she gives him a token reinforcer and verbal praise (fixed interval 3 minutes, FI3). The examples provided in Box 6.1 illustrate the similarities and differences among the three schedules.

It is important for consultants to keep schedules of reinforcement in mind when developing intervention programs with teachers. Different plans or schedules produce different kinds of response patterns. Thus, familiarity with the response characteristics of each type provides consultants and teachers with information for selecting and implementing the most appropriate schedule of reinforcement (Box 6.2).

Consultants and teachers must select and manipulate schedules of reinforcement to accommodate the kind of intervention program they are implementing. In general, continuous schedules of reinforcement should be used during the acquisition of a new skill or behavior. More intermittent (that is, more delayed, less predictable, more sporadic) schedules are used when fluency, response maintenance, and generalization become the focus of instruction. The ultimate goal is to leave the behavior under the control of a reinforcement schedule that approximates the schedule found in the natural or least-restrictive environment.

BOX 6.2

Response characteristics of interval and ratio schedules of reinforcement

INTERVAL SCHEDULES OF REINFORCEMENT

1. There is a tendency to produce relatively low rates of responding when the interval size is large and relatively moderate rates of responding when the interval size is small.
2. When the interval size becomes too large for a given individual, responding decreases.
3. There is a tendency to produced "scalloped" patterns of responding in which there is a slight increase in responding just before the end of the interval and a slight decrease immediately after reinforcement has been given.
4. Response maintenance under extinction conditions is longer, with responding controlled by larger, more variable interval schedules of reinforcement.

RATIO SCHEDULES OF REINFORCEMENT

1. There is a tendency to produce moderate (small number of responses) to high (large number of responses) rates of responding.
2. Response deterioration (loss of accuracy or fluency) can occur if the number of responses (ratio) becomes too large.
3. If ratios are too small in number or if the ratio is not increased frequently enough, decreases in responding can occur because too many reinforcers are received (satiation).
4. Response maintenance under extinction conditions is longer with behaviors that are controlled by larger, more variable ratio schedules of reinforcement.

Administering Reinforcement

In addition to the identification of useful, effective reinforcers and the establishment of appropriate schedules of reinforcement, consultants and teachers must also consider how to administer reinforcers to strengthen existing responses. In these cases, consultants and teachers should administer the reinforcers contingently, systematically increase the delay for administering the reinforcers, and move from teacher-directed to student-directed administration of the reinforcers.

Administer reinforcers contingently.   It is not sufficient to only provide reinforcers following the targeted behavior. Consultants and teachers should also administer them contingently—that is, in association with or related to the behavior. Noncontingent use of reinforcement can strengthen undesirable or other behaviors. For example, Ms. Bunbury likes to give verbal praise whenever her students are working independently. In one instance, she notices three students with their eyes on their work and their pencils moving busily over their papers, so she says, "Good job, I like what you are doing." At that moment, Randy is doing the assigned work, Felicity is working on the wrong page, and Trish is eating a candy bar while she does her work. Because Ms. Bunbury's verbal praise is not contingent (specific and associated with the desired response), she could be strengthening Felicity's and Trish's undesirable behaviors. Ms. Bunbury corrects her mistake by making more contingent verbal praise statements the next time: "Randy and Trish, good job at working independently on the page 63 assignment. Felicity, it's nice to see you working. Stop working on that page and switch to page 63. Trish, remember that snacks are eaten at lunch or after school."

Systematically increase the delay for the administration of reinforcers.
When teaching a new behavior or skill (acquisition), teachers should provide reinforcers immediately and on a continuous schedule of reinforcement. Immediate reinforcement maximizes the attention given to correct or appropriate responses and decreases the likelihood of reinforcing superfluous events that might occur between the response and presentation of the reinforcer. However, as soon as a skill has been acquired, the aim is to increase the delay or the amount of time between the response and the reinforcer.

In natural and least-restrictive settings, reinforcers tend not to be delivered immediately following many behaviors. For example, written assignments are returned with evaluations the next day, report cards and grades are distributed at the end of quarters or semesters, tokens are traded for back-up reinforcers at the end of the week, and students must wait with their hands raised until the teacher calls on them. Therefore, consultants and teachers should arrange to increase the size of delays to approximate the delays found in the least-restrictive environment. However, caution should be taken to ensure that the target behavior continues during the delay and to minimize occasions for competing behaviors to occur.

Move from teacher-directed to student-directed administration of reinforcers.   When behaviors and skills are first being learned, provide systematic feedback. Through the differential presentation or withholding of positive reinforcers, students are told what is correct and incorrect about their responses. However, once a behavior has been acquired and fluency is achieved, teachers attempt to decrease the amount of attention they provide so students can learn to function more independently (maintenance) and in settings where the teacher is not present (generalized responding). Students who can move effectively through their environment with little adult supervision are characterized as having good self-control and being "well behaved."

Consultants and teachers, therefore, should develop reinforcement programs that systematically remove the amount of teacher-directed feedback and increase the amount of self-directed reinforcement. To achieve this end, they need to teach students how to self-manage—that is, self-monitor and self-reinforce, when teacher attention is not available. Procedures for instructing students to self-manage are discussed later in this chapter. By enabling students to accurately self-direct their own reinforcement, teachers can fade teacher-directed programs and promote response maintenance and generalized responding.

The strengthening of existing behaviors is an important goal of any behavior change program, and consultants and teachers must give careful consideration to three important areas: finding effective and natural reinforcers, scheduling reinforcement, and administering reinforcement. In Box 6.3, some of the guidelines we have discussed for effectively using reinforcers and reinforcement are presented within the context of the five phases of learning.

BOX 6.3

Guidelines for the effective use of reinforcers and reinforcement

PHASE OF LEARNING	REINFORCEMENT GUIDELINES
Acquisition	Provide *immediate* and *contingent* reinforcement. Use a *continuous schedule of reinforcement*.
Fluency	Provide *contingent* reinforcement for *improved performance* (i.e., proficiency, rate).
Maintenance	Provide *contingent* reinforcement on an increasingly *intermittent schedule of reinforcement*. Provide contingent reinforcement on an increasingly *delayed* basis. Move from teacher-directed to *student-directed* administration of reinforcement.
Generalization	Use *natural reinforcers* that are employed in nontraining settings. Use *natural schedules of reinforcement* that are similar to the schedules found in the natural context. Move from teacher-directed to *student-directed* administration of reinforcement.
Adaptation	Provide *contingent* reinforcement for *variations* of the desired behavior.

BOX 6.4

A procedural checklist for building reinforcement programs

_____ **1.** Operationally define the behavior (and its variations) to be strengthened.

_____ **2.** Describe the setting (training and nontraining) conditions under which the behavior must occur to be reinforced.

_____ **3.** Identify an effective and natural reinforcer.

_____ **4.** Determine the amount of the reinforcer to present.

_____ **5.** Determine when the reinforcer should be presented (immediately or delayed).

_____ **6.** Determine how often the reinforcer should be presented (schedule of reinforcement).

_____ **7.** Develop a procedure for fading the teacher-directed administration of reinforcement and increasing the amount of student-directed reinforcement.

_____ **8.** Establish a data decision rule for evaluating the effectiveness of reinforcement and the level of progress being made.

When consultants and teachers build programs to strengthen existing behaviors, they should address a number of procedural points. Box 6.4 contains a simple checklist that summarizes these points.

WEAKENING OR ELIMINATING EXISTING PROBLEM BEHAVIORS

There is little disagreement that a majority of the Requests for Assistance are for excessive problem behaviors that need to be eliminated. These requests generally describe students who are disruptive, defiant, fail to follow directions, are verbally and physically aggressive toward others, and express themselves with derogatory language. In this section, we describe some critical programmatic factors that consultants and teachers should consider when selecting and developing response-weakening procedures, specifically the role of positive reinforcement, the role of the consultant, and characteristics of behavior-reduction procedures.

The Role of Positive Reinforcement

Every program built to weaken or strengthen an existing behavior _must have, first and foremost,_ a component for teaching and increasing or strengthening a suitable replacement (fair-pair) response. This is important for a number of reasons: (a) reinforcement-based programs tend to be nonaversive, (b) an affirmative and constructive emphasis is established, (c) provisions are made for increased opportunities to receive positive reinforcement, and (d) an opportunity to evaluate the student's level of adaptive functioning is possible. Thus, we firmly believe that consultants and teachers must _first_ consider the procedural points indicated in Figure 6.2, before they build any program designed to weaken or eliminate troublesome behaviors.

The Role of the Consultant

Except for those procedures involving the differential use of positive reinforcement (for example, the differential reinforcement of other behaviors, of incompatible behaviors, or of low rates of behavior), most procedures designed to reduce or eliminate troublesome behaviors have aversive qualities that increase the potential or risk of harm (physical, educational, emotional, behavioral) to the student or teacher. These procedures have aversive characteristics because they involve the removal of reinforcement or the opportunity to access reinforcement, or the presentation of an aversive stimulus (object, event, or activity).

Because consultants play an integral role in assisting teachers, they must assume responsibility for safeguarding the rights and well-being of the student, teacher, and others involved in the consultation, especially when aversive procedures are being considered or implemented. By attending to "the minimally acceptable conditions under which punishment conditions can be considered and employed" (Wolery, Bailey, & Sugai, 1988, p. 339), consultants will be acting in a professional and defensible manner when aversive or controversial interventions are involved. Many of the 11 conditions that need to be considered before using punishment are listed as follows and have been described in other sections of this book:

1. "Systematic use of a decision model" (p. 340) to develop reasonable and defendable answers for questions having legal, ethical, and/or moral implications.
2. "Careful assessment of factors that are maintaining the behavior including its communicative function" (p. 341) in order to develop appropriate interventions based on valid hypotheses.
3. "Use of assessment information when planning interventions" (p. 341) to increase intervention effectiveness.
4. "Deliberate and concentrated attempts to teach and reinforce adaptive behavior including replacement behaviors" (p. 341) to give the student the opportunity to access reinforcement with appropriate forms of behavior.
5. "Reliable measurement of the target behaviors and of treatment implementation" (p. 342) to increase accountability, evaluate treatment effectiveness, and assess student progress.
6. "Periodic monitoring of intervention side effects" (p. 342) to maintain treatment effectiveness and avoid the occurrence of undesirable and maladaptive behaviors.
7. "Attention to maintenance and generalization of adaptive outcomes" (p. 343) because generalized and persistent responding is unlikely without focused training.
8. "Informed consent from parents and administrative authorities" (p. 343) to ensure clear understanding and endorsements by others who are directly involved.
9. "Prior peer review of the intervention plan" (p. 344) in order to benefit from the experience and perspectives of others.
10. "Open implementation of the intervention" (p. 345) to increase accountability and provide opportunities for feedback.

11. "Implementation of aversive procedures by a competent team of professionals" (p. 345) to ensure proper execution of procedures and minimal side effects.

Characteristics and Comparison of Behavior-Reduction Procedures

If proper development and implementation are to be achieved, consultants and teachers must be familiar with how behavior-reduction procedures are characterized. In this section, we describe the essential features of interventions commonly used to decrease or eliminate excess behaviors. Because we have elected to review these procedures, however, readers should not infer that we necessarily support their use. Instead, we believe that consultants should be knowledgeable enough to effectively evaluate a procedure and know its subtleties should its use be required. First and foremost, we advocate a positive reinforcement–based program that focuses on strengthening a competing prosocial replacement response.

In general, behavior-reduction procedures fall into two categories; within each category, there are numerous variations. Both categories are distinguished by the contingent and consequent manipulation or action taken by the teacher and the subsequent effect on future occurrences of the behavior. The first category, called *Type I punishment,* consists of procedures in which the contingent presentation of an aversive stimulus (action) results in a decrease in the occurrence of the target behavior (effect). The second category, called *Type II punishment,* consists of the contingent withdrawal of a reinforcing stimulus (action) that results in a decrease in the target behavior (effect). The two types of punishment procedures are both characterized by a decrease in behavioral occurrences (effect). They differ in that Type I interventions involve the contingent presentation of a stimulus, whereas Type II entails the contingent withdrawal of a stimulus. This functional (effect and manipulation) approach to definition and description is used to characterize the procedural variations and minimal implementation conditions for each category. Additional discussion about Type I and II punishment is presented in later sections.

Although we have stressed the importance of selecting an intervention based on assessment information (that is, functional analysis, testable explanations, communicative and critical function), consultants should also give careful consideration to the degree of intrusiveness associated with a given behavior-reduction intervention. Wolery, Bailey, and Sugai (1988) define intrusiveness as "the extent to which interventions are obtrusive and intrude, impinge, or encroach on students' bodies or personal rights; intrusiveness is associated with pain, discomfort, and/or social stigma" (p. 369). They provide a useful listing of possible reduction interventions by relative degree of intrusiveness (Box 6.5).

When selecting interventions designed to reduce behaviors, consultants should consider the four criteria described by Wolery, Bailey, and Sugai (1988):

1. *The principles of the least-restrictive treatment and the least-intrusive treatment should be considered* (p. 369). We defined intrusive earlier. Restrictiveness refers to the degree to which an intervention inhibits a student's movement yet still produces a change in behavior (Budd & Baer,

BOX 6.5

Possible reduction interventions by relative degree of intrusiveness

TYPE OF INTERVENTION	EXAMPLES
Medical Interventions	Medications Surgery Dietary changes
Curricular/Environmental Modifications	Change social dimension of the environment Change physical arrangement of environment Change schedule of activities Change the amount and type of materials or activities Change instructional methods being used Teach responses that fulfill same communicative function currently performed by aberrant behavior
Manipulation of Reinforcement Contingencies	Differential reinforcement of other behavior (DRO) Differential reinforcement of incompatible behaviors (DRI/A) Differential reinforcement of low rate of behaviors (DRL) Contingency contracting Token economies
Mildly Intrusive Punishment Procedures	Extinction Response cost (II)
Intrusive Punishment Procedures	Time-out (II) Overcorrection (I) Direct, contingent application of aversive stimuli (I)

SOURCE: M. R. Wolery, D. B. Bailey, Jr., and G. M. Sugai (1988). *Effective Teaching: Principles and Procedures of Applied Behavior Analysis With Exceptional Students*. Boston, MA: Allyn & Bacon Publishing Company.

1976). We prefer a simple statement by Gast and Wolery (1987): "Use the simplest, yet effective, intervention when changing behavior" (p. 311).

2. *The principle of the least-dangerous assumption should be considered when selecting intervention strategies* (p. 370). The selected intervention should produce the least amount of harm if it is ineffective (Wolery, Bailey, & Sugai, 1988).

3. *Social validity should be considered when selecting intervention strategies* (p. 370). Consultants should request that experts and relevant consumers review the selected intervention, taking into consideration the acceptability and value of goals, procedures, and projected outcomes (Wolf, 1978).

4. *The hypothesis generated during assessment should be considered when selecting intervention strategies* (p. 371). It is important to consider information obtained (that is, testable explanations) through functional

analyses in order to determine the factors and possible communicative function or effects.

Type I Punishment Procedures

Type I punishment procedures are defined by a contingent presentation of an aversive stimulus (object, activity, or event) and a decrease in the target behavior. Although there is a range of variations, generally speaking, they are considered the most aversive and intrusive of all behavior-reduction procedures and a last resort. As such, consultants should give great care when considering a Type I punishment strategy. The two major kinds of Type I punishment procedures include direct, contingent application of aversive stimuli and overcorrection.

Direct, contingent application of aversive stimuli.   An aversive stimulus is any object, event, or activity that the student finds disagreeable, irritating, or annoying. The student will increase a behavior when there is a contingent removal of an aversive stimulus (negative reinforcement) or decrease a behavior when there is a contingent presentation of an aversive stimulus. In the latter case, many different forms are possible. In relatively mild forms, teachers give verbal reprimands and other admonishments (frowns, finger pointing, stares). In the more severe forms that are used with extremely problematic behaviors (such as self-injury or physical aggressions), the direct, contingent application of aversive stimuli can include more aversive consequences; for example, aversive tasting substances (lemon juice), aversive smelling material (aromatic ammonia), physical discomfort (corporal punishment), and brief episodes of physical restraint.

If less-aversive procedures have been ineffective, if the necessary safeguards have been satisfied, and if the problem behavior is severe, the direct, contingent application of an aversive stimulus might be considered. Wolery, Bailey, and Sugai (1988) provide six guidelines for evaluating the application of procedures involving this type of punishment:

1. Since the aversiveness of a stimulus is individually determined, consultants and teachers must carefully select and evaluate the stimulus that is selected as an aversive for each student.
2. Since the intensity of a stimulus is related to its effectiveness, consultants and teachers must "select the intensity of the aversive stimulus that will be effective, but will not be too harsh" (p. 449).
3. Since side effects may occur, consultants and teachers should plan for, monitor, and, when appropriate, treat both desirable and undesirable side effects.
4. Since maintenance of effects is variable, consultants and teachers "should plan for maintenance and teach and reinforce the occurrence of desirable replacement behaviors" (p. 449).
5. Since the effectiveness of an aversive stimulus is related to how it is used, consultants and teachers should carefully develop and monitor an appropriate implementation plan.

6. Since the use of aversive procedures should be restricted, consultants and teachers should use a decision model that enables the careful evaluation of the conditions under which the use of an aversive stimulus is being considered.

Overcorrection. Overcorrection, the second Type I punishment procedure, is defined by a decrease in behavior (effect) and requiring the student to contingently (manipulation) (a) return the environment to a state better than before the problem behavior occurred (restitutional overcorrection) or (b) engage in more relevant, appropriate, and incompatible forms of the problem behavior (positive practice). Both forms of overcorrection have successfully been used with a wide range of behaviors, including self-injury (Gibbs & Luyben, 1985), stereotypic behavior (Bierly & Billingsley, 1983), spelling errors (Matson, Esveldt-Dawson, & Kazdin, 1982), and incorrect cursive letter formation (Trap et al., 1978).

Consultants and teachers may wish to consider use of an overcorrection procedure to reduce a problem behavior; however, they must remember that it is an aversive consequence that can have negative side effects, such as aggression, escape, or avoidance. As such, overcorrection should be considered only as a last resort and reinforcement-based procedures should be given highest priority. In addition to the guidelines given for the direct, contingent application of an aversive stimulus, users of overcorrection should be sure that:

1. "The behaviors performed during positive practice (overcorrection) should be related conceptually to the target aberrant behavior" (Wolery, Bailey, & Sugai, 1988, p. 457); that is, the practiced response should be topographically similar to the problem behavior.
2. The interval of positive practice or restitution should not exceed three minutes; long enough to be effective without being too intrusive.
3. Positive reinforcement for a functional replacement response is provided.
4. Careful planning and consideration are given to the use of verbal instruction and physical prompts or assists during the overcorrection procedure.
5. Specific strategies are planned and used to increase the likelihood of desirable effects and reduce negative side effects.

Finally, we strongly recommend against overcorrection if excess physical assistance is required to ensure consistent implementation of the procedure or if the probability of negative side effects cannot be minimized.

Type I punishment procedures are generally the most intrusive behavior-reduction procedures. Their selection and implementation must be given careful consideration. If consultants and teachers determine that the direct, contingent application of an aversive stimulus or overcorrection is the most appropriate (that is, least aversive and most effective intervention), we recommend further study and practice of the procedures.

Type II Punishment Procedures

Type II punishment procedures are similar to Type I procedures in that they are defined by a decrease in future occurrences of the behavior (effect); however, they are different in that there is a contingent withdrawal or removal of a stimulus (manipulation). Relatively and generally speaking, Type II punishment procedures are less intrusive.

The most common examples of Type II procedures include extinction, response cost, and time-out. However, before we describe these procedures, we discuss the use of differential reinforcement to reduce behaviors. We discuss definition, procedural guidelines, and implementation considerations in detail because these procedures are commonly used in school settings.

Differential reinforcement.   One of the least-intrusive procedures for reducing the occurrence of existing behaviors is differential reinforcement. We encourage its use because (a) its implementation is based on the use of positive reinforcement, (b) attention is focused on more desirable behaviors, and (c) no aversive or intrusive objects or activities are involved.

The definition of differential reinforcement is based on the use of two procedures: contingent positive reinforcement when the replacement response is observed and extinction when the problem behavior is emitted. Definitions, uses, and implementation guidelines for four variations of differential reinforcement are described as follows.

1. *Differential Reinforcement of Low Rates* (DRL)
   DEFINITION: Contingent positive reinforcement with displays of behavior at or below criterion level, and contingent extinction with performance that exceeds criterion level.
   USES:
   a. Use with behaviors whose rates need to be reduced but not eliminated (such as handraising, pencil sharpening, trips to the water fountain, asking questions).
   b. Use when initial high rates of behavior can be tolerated.
   c. Use when effective competing reinforcement can be provided.
   d. Do not use when immediate behavior reduction is needed.
   IMPLEMENTATION GUIDELINES:
   a. Develop a clear definition of the behavior to be reduced.
   b. Determine the baseline level of functioning.
   c. Determine the criterion level of performance (behavioral objective).
   d. Determine the effective reinforcers.
   e. Determine the size of the criterion change.
   f. Develop data decision rules for determining when to gradually reduce or increase the criterion level.

2. *Differential Reinforcement of Other Behavior* (DRO)
   DEFINITION: Contingent positive reinforcement when absence of a target behavior is observed for a specified time, and contingent extinction when the behavior targeted for reduction is observed.
   USES:
   a. Use when the reinforcer maintaining the target behavior can be identified and removed.

    b. Do not use when the student displays a large number of inappropriate behaviors that cannot be ignored or tolerated by the teacher or others in the classroom environment.

    c. Do not use when reinforcement for occurrences of inappropriate behaviors cannot be controlled.

    d. Do not use when teacher reinforcement is less powerful than the reinforcement that is maintaining inappropriate behaviors.

IMPLEMENTATION GUIDELINES:

    a. Develop a clear definition of behavior.

    b. Collect the functional analysis and baseline data.

    c. Identify the reinforcer maintaining the undesirable target behavior.

    d. Identify the size of the DRO interval (interresponse interval).

    e. Identify the effective reinforcer and schedule of reinforcement.

    f. Determine the criterion level of performance (behavioral objective).

    g. Develop data decision rules for determining when to gradually reduce or increase the interval size.

3. *Differential Reinforcement of Alternative/Incompatible Response* (DRA/I)

DEFINITION: Contingent positive reinforcement on the emission of a specified replacement response (DRA for a functionally similar replacement; DRI for a physically incompatible replacement behavior), and contingent extinction when the undesirable target behavior occurs.

USES:

    a. Use when a suitable replacement response can be identified.

    b. Use when a replacement response is in the student's behavioral repertoire.

    c. Use when occurrences of the undesirable target behavior can be tolerated.

    d. Use when the reinforcer maintaining the undesirable target behavior can be manipulated.

    e. Use when the positive reinforcement for the replacement response is stronger than the reinforcement for the undesirable behavior.

IMPLEMENTATION GUIDELINES:

    a. Develop a clear definition of the undesirable problem behavior.

    b. Conduct a functional analysis and baseline data collection.

    c. Identify and define a functional and an incompatible replacement response.

    d. Identify an effective reinforcer and schedule of reinforcement.

    e. Determine the criterion level of performance (behavioral objective).

    f. Develop data decision rules for determining when to gradually reduce or increase the criterion level of performance.

All three variations of differential reinforcement are positively based approaches for reducing existing inappropriate behaviors. Consultants and teachers should consider these procedures before selecting other, more intrusive procedures.

Extinction. Although extinction is not typically defined by its effect, we find it useful to define it as a procedure associated with the contingent termination of a maintaining reinforcer (manipulation) and the eventual decrease in the occurrence of a behavior (effect). This definition enables the consultant and the teacher to plan systematically for its implementation and evaluate its effectiveness. As one of the least intrusive and aversive Type II procedures, extinction is rarely used in isolation; it is usually used in conjunction with positive reinforcement (that is, with differential reinforcement of other behavior, differential reinforcement of low rates of behavior, or differential reinforcement of alternative or incompatible behavior).

Consultants and teachers will find that extinction is a very useful, effective procedure if they understand and plan for the common response patterns observed when it is put into effect. First, they must evaluate their ability to tolerate an immediate increase in responding before an improvement (decrease) is observed. Teachers and consultants should be certain that "(a) the schedule of reinforcement previously maintaining the behavior is analyzed, (b) extinction is continued during the increase, (c) the social environment can tolerate an increase, and (d) more adaptive behaviors are being strengthened" (Wolery, Bailey, & Sugai, 1988, p. 399).

Second, when extinction is applied, teachers must be extremely consistent in terminating the maintaining reinforcement. Inadvertent presentation of a reinforcer can result in a "spontaneous recovery" of the problem behavior to rates equal to or greater than those observed before extinction was in effect. Teachers must determine if they are capable of sustaining strict control over the availability of maintaining reinforcers.

Finally, a behavior that has been maintained for a long time under thin intermittent schedules of reinforcement may be "resistant to extinction." Teachers may find that extensive time is required before a decrease in the behavior is observed. Consultants and teachers must determine if they and others in the environment can continue the extinction conditions for an extended period.

When planning for the implementation of extinction, one of the most important procedural considerations is the identification of the reinforcers that are maintaining the problem behavior. This is accomplished by conducting a functional analysis and noting what kinds of consequences commonly follow the occurrence of the problem behavior. More than one or two observations may be required if the behavior is being maintained on an intermittent schedule with infrequent reinforcement. How often the reinforcers are provided and how much reinforcement is presented must also be determined. Teachers and consultants should use these data to ascertain if these reinforcers can be terminated and controlled.

Another procedural consideration is the identification of a functional replacement response (fair-pair) and suitable reinforcers, which can be provided when the replacement response is observed. Teachers and consultants should attempt to identify replacement responses and reinforcers that will compete with the undesirable target behavior and its maintaining reinforcers.

To minimize the probability of spontaneous recovery, the size of the extinction burst, and how quickly the behavior is decreased, extinction must be consistently and accurately implemented. A formative data collection and evaluation strategy can facilitate the monitoring of treatment effectiveness.

To summarize, the effective planning and development of extinction requires (a) observable definitions of the problem and replacement behaviors, (b) identification of maintaining reinforcers through functional analyses, (c) determination of effective reinforcers, and (d) planning for possible negative side effects. Extinction can be a useful and effective procedure if teachers can plan for and respond consistently to the predictable patterns of responding observed when extinction conditions are created.

Response cost.   Some teachers find it useful to provide token reinforcement (points, stickers, minutes of reinforcing activity, or tangible objects) when students engage in appropriate academic or social behaviors. To decrease the occurrence of inappropriate behaviors, they remove earned reinforcers contingently when inappropriate behaviors are observed. When reinforcers are withdrawn contingent on the occurrence of a behavior (action) and a decrease is observed in that behavior (effect), response cost has been implemented.

The use of response cost has several appealing advantages. First, it is a procedure that is found in everyday experience (penalties in sports, fines for legal violations, charges for late payments). Second, response cost is relatively easy and convenient to use across a wide range of behaviors and with individuals or groups of students. Third, its reductive effects are more immediate and long-lasting than with extinction and differential reinforcement alone.

If consultants and teachers select response cost, they should attend to a number of implementation considerations. First, a clearly defined procedure for positive reinforcement should be well established before implementing a response-cost procedure. Response cost is difficult to implement if the student is without reinforcers that can be withdrawn. In addition, positive reinforcement programs can be used to strengthen replacement behaviors. When reinforcers are being considered and before artificial reinforcers are selected, teachers should try to determine if naturally occurring reinforcers (minutes of recess or independent free time) are available for contingent removal. This consideration will reduce the effort needed to fade artificial reinforcers.

Second, students must be taught rules for how to earn reinforcers and how reinforcers can be lost. Clear examples and role-play situations should be used to ensure that students understand what is involved in the response-cost procedures, for example, what behaviors result in response cost and how they are defined, how large or small the reinforcer loss is for each behavior, and what happens when there are repeated occurrences of the problem behaviors. Student familiarity with how the response-cost procedure operates will increase the accuracy with which teachers implement a response-cost consequence and the level of compliance behaviors students display.

Third, the implementation of the response-cost procedure should be consistent and closely monitored. There is a possibility of negative side effects (such as noncompliance, aggressions, escape/avoidance, or stealing reinforcers), and strategies to respond to these side effects should be carefully planned. Repeated use, increases in problem behavior, or increasing penalty sizes are indicators that the procedure is not working or being abused and should be evaluated for modification.

Finally, the size of the response-cost consequence should be determined after considering (a) the size, frequency, strength, and amount of positive reinforcement and (b) the student's learning history or experiences with response-cost procedures. We recommend using the smallest effective response-cost consequence.

If monitored closely and implemented consistently and contingently, response cost is a relatively effective reduction procedure that can easily be incorporated into most positive reinforcement programs. Consultants and teachers should consider adding a response-cost consequence if positive reinforcement alone and other less aversive or intrusive procedures are ineffective. Like any other reduction procedure, response cost is defined by an observed decrease in behavior. If an increase or an insignificant decrease is observed, teachers and consultants should immediately evaluate and consider the need for revising the intervention plan.

Time-out.   Time-out is another Type II reduction procedure that, in one form or another, is frequently observed in classroom and school settings. *Time-out* is the removal of the opportunity to receive positive reinforcement contingent on a behavior (action) and a decrease in the occurrence of the behavior (effect). Instead of removing previously acquired reinforcers, as in response cost, time-out is the designation of a time period in which less positive reinforcement is available; both procedures are defined by a decrease in behavior.

Consultants and teachers should be aware that there are many forms of time-out, which can be arranged along a continuum from least intrusive (nonexclusionary time-out) to most intrusive (exclusionary time-out). Nonexclusionary time-out involves the removal of sources of reinforcement (such as teacher attention, instructional materials, or toys). In one-on-one instructional situations, a type of nonexclusionary time-out, called "planned ignoring time-out," is used. It is based on the presumption that teacher attention is a positive reinforcer for a given student. When an inappropriate behavior occurs, the teacher contingently turns and/or moves away from the student for a brief period (less than a minute) (Rutherford & Nelson, 1982). In another variation, instructional materials and teacher attention are removed contingent on the behavior for a specified period. Nonexclusionary time-out procedures are considered intrusive because instruction is interrupted and delayed and students do not receive positive reinforcement.

Exclusionary time-out is another variation that removes the student from reinforcement. In general, exclusionary forms of time-out are more intrusive than nonexclusionary forms because they require students to change their location or place in the classroom. Three forms of exclusionary time-out are commonly used.

The first and least intrusive form, called "contingent observation," entails "a brief period of time where the student, contingent upon an inappropriate behavior, is required to move to another location and is instructed to watch other students behave appropriately" (Wolery, Bailey, & Sugai, 1988, pp. 421–422). The student is moved into a condition where positive reinforcement is removed, and opportunities are provided for the student to see others engaging in more appropriate behaviors and receiving positive reinforcement for those behaviors. Contingent observation is an intrusive procedure because opportunities to receive positive reinforcement are removed and direct instruction with the student is interrupted.

Wolery, Bailey, and Sugai (1988) indicate that most of the research on contingent observation time-out has been used with young children (preschool), so use with older students should be conducted carefully.

A second and relatively more intrusive form is "exclusion time-out," which is defined as any procedure, contingent on a target behavior

> that (a) requires the student to be removed from instructional activities, (b) does not require the student to watch others (as in contingent observation), and (c) does not require the student to enter a specifically designed timeout room (as in isolation/seclusion timeout). [Wolery, Bailey, & Sugai, 1988, p. 422]

Thus, the student sits in a chair or stands in a specially designated location in the classroom. Having a student stand or sit in the hallway is also a variation of exclusion time-out. Generally, exclusion time-out is more intrusive than planned ignoring and contingent observation because the students' instruction is interrupted, they are required to move from one location to another, and they are not able to view or hear what is occurring in the instructional setting.

The most intrusive form of all time-out variations is "isolation/seclusion time-out." It is also the most restrictive because the student must leave the instructional context and move into a special time-out room for a specified and relatively brief time (less than five minutes). It is important for teachers and consultants to distinguish isolation/seclusion time-out from other removal and isolation consequences—such as, in- and out-of-school suspension, expulsion, solitary confinement, jail—that generally involve unspecified or extended durations of removal and might be aligned more closely with the direct, contingent application of an aversive stimulus (Type I punishment).

Because of numerous legal and ethical ramifications, consultants and teachers must give careful and strict consideration to procedural safeguards (for example, informed consent, safety, or supervision/monitoring) when selecting and implementing isolation/seclusion time-out procedures. Of special concern is the level of prohibition or control in the use of isolation/seclusion time-out exerted by courts, local agencies, and other legal or regulatory bodies (Wolery, Bailey, & Sugai, 1988). Generally, we recommend that consultants and teachers not consider the use of isolation/seclusion time-out unless clear and specific procedural safeguards are in place. In addition, specialized consultation may be required.

Regardless of the form or type of time-out, implementation must include a positive reinforcement component that focuses on the teaching and strengthening of a suitable replacement response and, most important, on the existence or development of a highly reinforcing "time-in" environment, such as the classroom or instructional setting. If the time-in environment is less reinforcing than the time-out consequence or if the student can access more positive reinforcement in time-out than in time-in, time-out will be ineffective and there will be a concurrent increase in the problem behavior.

We cannot emphasize enough the importance of creating a reinforcing time-in context in which (a) students receive large amounts of and frequent positive reinforcement for successful academic and social behavior functioning, (b) classroom routines and environments are predictable, safe, and nourishing, (c) the students' individual needs are addressed in a positive and preventive manner, and

(d) instruction and curriculum are appropriate and effectively presented. If the time-in setting has few reinforcing features, it is less likely that a decrease in the target behavior will be observed. In fact, an increase in the target behavior is probable as the student emits behaviors to avoid the nonreinforcing conditions of the time-in setting (negative reinforcement) or to access the more reinforcing qualities of the time-out condition (positive reinforcement).

When consultants and teachers are considering the use of time-out from positive reinforcement to reduce a behavior, they should give careful notice to the following guidelines:*

1. Use a *systematic approach to intervention planning* to evaluate the nature of the problem and assist in the selection of the most appropriate form of time-out (see the first section, "Prerequisite Knowledge and Skills for Systematic Intervention Programs," in this chapter).

2. *Enrich the time-in environment* so that "a meaningful difference exists in the level of reinforcement during timein and timeout" (Wolery, Bailey, & Sugai, 1988, p. 424). An important aspect of enriching the time-in environment is selecting a replacement response that can be reinforced positively.

3. Select a type of time-out based on *whether reinforcing conditions can be removed from the student (nonexclusionary time-out) or whether the student can be removed from reinforcing conditions (exclusionary time-out).*

4. When *verbal explanations* are used to explain the time-out contingencies, they should be *preplanned, scheduled, and presented in a concise, businesslike, and nonjudgmental manner,* for example, "each time a student expresses anger by hitting, swearing, or destroying property the student will earn a two-minute timeout."

5. When a *signal* is used to indicate when time-out is in effect, it should (a) be easily administered, (b) not be distracting to others, (c) not bring about excess attention for the target student, (d) be easily faded once behavioral control is developed, and (e) not set the occasion for other or more disruptive behavior. A signal may consist of a simple verbal instruction ("You have earned a one-minute time-out for getting out of your seat without permission.") or pointing gesture (Mr. Summers nods at the student and raises one finger to indicate that the student must take a one-minute time-out).

6. When *warnings* are used to signal an impending time-out consequence, they should be concise, identify the behavior in question, and be used only once. If a warning does not result in a change in behavior, time-out should immediately be implemented. When early signs (slumping in the seat) of a problematic behavior (out-of-seat) are observed, a warning may be used ("Remember, time-outs are given for out-of-seat. Sit up straight and look at your work.") to reduce the probability that the problematic behavior will be observed. As with signals, warnings should not increase the probability of more disruptive behavior.

7. Students should be required to remain in time-out for the shortest duration that results in significant decreases in the problem behavior. Prior learn-

*Adapted from "Using Timeout from Positive Reinforcement," in M. R. Wolery, D. B. Bailey, & G. M. Sugai, *Effective Teaching: Principles and Procedures of Applied Behavior Analysis with Exceptional Students* (Boston: Allyn & Bacon, 1988, pp. 416–444).

ing experiences with time-out consequences is an important factor affecting the effectiveness of a given time-out duration. For example, when a student has experienced ten-minute time-out consequences, any time-outs less than ten minutes are likely to be ineffective. We recommend not considering time-outs longer than about ten minutes because of (a) increased opportunities for other undesirable behaviors and negative side effects, (b) decreased academic engagement, (c) decreased opportunities to encourage and strengthen appropriate replacement responses, and (d) increased restrictiveness of the procedure. If students have had considerable experience with time-out, especially longer consequences, another intervention strategy should be considered.

8. Preplan a *back-up contingency* for the student who displays noncompliant behavior during the implementation of time-out, such as refusing to go to time-out, attempting to escape from time-out, or displaying aggressive and dangerous behaviors. Students should be taught about specific consequences that will be enforced should noncompliance be observed. For minor disruptive behavior during time-out (noises, talking, standing rather than sitting), the duration can be increased in prespecified amounts or the start of time-out can be delayed temporarily until appropriate time-out-completing behaviors are observed. If a back-up response is required when minor infractions are repeated or major behavioral violations occur, consultants and teachers should immediately evaluate the effectiveness and appropriateness of the time-out program.

9. A specific rule should be stated and taught for *signaling the end of time-out and releasing the student.* Although relative effectiveness research is inconclusive, we suggest a simple teacher-directed verbal ("Your time-out is over, return to your desk.") or gestural (nod and point to desk) signal that informs the students that the time-out is completed *and* they have been given permission to return to the time-in setting or condition. Teachers should specify how long the student must display appropriate "time-out-taking" behavior (sitting quietly with hands on lap and without talking or noises). If verbal or gestural signals set the occasion for more disruptive behaviors, teachers may wish to use a timer to signal the end of the interval. If disruptive behaviors occur, the timer is simply reset without any verbalizations.

10. Establish a *debriefing sequence* with the student after the time-out consequence has been completed. Teachers and students should use debriefing times to review the events leading to time-out and to identify more acceptable behaviors and a plan to prevent the problem behavior from recurring. These meetings should be brief and businesslike to prevent the student from seeing a time-out episode as a prerequisite for a more reinforcing interaction, such as positive reinforcement.

11. Establish a *time-out record-keeping system* to document the following pieces of information: the student's name, the teacher's name, the date and time, the location, the nature of the offense, the time of release, and, if used, the date and time of the debriefing. These data should be reviewed on an ongoing basis to evaluate the effectiveness of the time-out procedure and the need for its modification.

In sum, time-out procedures may take many forms with varying levels of intrusiveness and restrictiveness. Time-out must be used with a planned program for strengthening a suitable replacement response. It can be an effective procedure with careful planning and implementation; however, time-out is intrusive, removing the student's opportunities for positive reinforcement. The selection and use of time-out should be based on the documented ineffectiveness of other less intrusive procedures; similarly, the repeated use of time-out or the failure to weaken a specific problem behavior should be seen as signs that the procedure must be evaluated and modified.

For additional information and research about time-out and its application, consultants and teachers should consult the following references:

NELSON, C. M., & RUTHERFORD, R. B. (1983).Timeout revisited: Guidelines for its use in special education. *Exceptional Education Quarterly,* 4(3), 56–67.

RUTHERFORD, R. B., & NELSON, C. M. (1982).Analysis of the response contingent time-out literature with behaviorally disordered students in classroom settings. In R. B. Rutherford (Ed.), *Monographs in behavior disorders: Severe behavior disorders of children and youth* (Vol. 5) (pp. 79–105). Reston, VA: Council for Children with Behavioral Disorders of the Council for Exceptional Children.

IMPLEMENTATION FEATURES OF CONTINGENCY CONTRACTING AND SELF-MANAGEMENT STRATEGIES

In this section, we describe key features of two commonly applied strategies for managing student behavior: contingency contracting, because it functions as a useful structure for organizing and presenting the details of a social behavior change program, and self-management strategies, because of the emphasis on turning "control" and responsibility of an intervention over to students and reducing the amount of teacher-directed involvement. Without question, many more procedures and strategies—for example, peer-directed strategies, cooperative learning—could be included in this section. We suggest that consultants and teachers refer to the supporting references mentioned throughout this text.

Contingency Contracting

Whenever a teacher and a student engage in and agree on an "if-then" relationship, a contract is formed. This contract can be as simple as a verbal agreement or as formal as a detailed written document. Regardless of its form, *contingency contracting* (also called behavior contracting) is defined as any agreement between two or more individuals that delineates (a) how one or more of the involved persons will behave, (b) to what extent, where, or under what conditions those behaviors must occur, and (c) what consequences are associated with each behavior.

In simple terms, when a stipulated behavior or set of behaviors is observed, a specified consequence follows. Any of the strategies mentioned previously (for example, reinforcer withdrawal, loss of opportunity to access reinforcement, presentation of a reinforcer) can be incorporated into a contract. For example, in Figure 6.5 a contingency contract between Roger and Ms. Santana illustrates the details of a positive reinforcement and response-cost program designed to improve Roger's getting-to-class behavior.

Components.   Contingency contracts may take many forms, depending on the age and skill level of those involved and the degree of accountability required. However, they should be as simple as possible to increase the students' understanding and include five major components (Kazdin, 1975; Wolery, Bailey, & Sugai, 1988): behaviors, rewards and privileges, penalty clauses, bonus clauses, and record-keeping procedures. When developing and implementing these components, we recommend attention to the following guidelines:

1. *Behaviors*
   a. Describe in observable and measurable terms.
   b. Focus on positively stated behaviors.
   c. Indicate conditions and criteria of acceptable behavioral performance.

FIGURE 6.5
A contingency contract

CLASSROOM CONTRACT

I, Roger, agree that each time I get to class on time (in my seat when the bell rings), I will receive a star sticker to put on my notebook calendar. At the end of each day, I may trade each star sticker for 2 minutes of time to play a computer game of my choice. If I am late, I will lose one minute of computer time for each minute I'm late. If I get a perfect day (8 out of 8), I will earn an extra four minutes of computer time. If I get a perfect week (five consecutive school days with 8/8), I may select a friend to play a computer game.

This contract will begin on Tuesday, August 17th, and be reviewed on August 31st.

Signed _____ (Student) Date ___/___/___

Signed _____ (Teacher) Date ___/___/___

    d. Select one or more behaviors that are useful and important to the student and parents, administrators, and so on.

    e. Select behaviors that are easily achievable in first contracts.

2. *Rewards and Privileges*

    a. Include level of accuracy (criterion) required.

    b. Indicate who will deliver them.

    c. Specify how and when they will be delivered.

    d. Indicate how much will be dispensed.

    e. Include the student and relevant others in selection of reinforcers.

    f. Select highly reinforcing rewards and privileges.

    g. Provide them immediately and contingently in initial contracts.

3. *Penalty Clauses*

    a. Include the level of accuracy (criterion) required.

    b. Indicate who will deliver them.

    c. Specify how and when they will be delivered.

    d. Indicate how much will be dispensed.

4. *Bonus Clauses*

    a. Include the level of accuracy (criterion) required.

    b. Indicate who will deliver them.

    c. Specify how and when they will be delivered.

    d. Indicate how much will be dispensed.

5. *Record-Keeping Procedures*

    a. Establish ongoing procedures for data collection and evaluation.

    b. Include student in record-keeping activities, such as self-recording.

Contracts also should include relevant timelines (for example, starting, ending, and review dates) and signatures of involved parties (the student, teacher, peer, and principal). A model illustrating the essential components of a complete contingency contract is given in Figure 6.6.

    When contracts are constructed, they should be designed in an age- and style-appropriate manner. Contracts for older students should emphasize the essential components, as in Figures 6.6 and 6.7. For younger students, it may be more interesting and motivating (reinforcing) if the contract has pictures or cartoonlike features. In Figure 6.7, we illustrate a contract that also functions as a record-keeping tool. The children are allowed to use a crayon to color in a balloon each time they write their name on the paper without being prompted.

Implementation.   When consultants and teachers develop a contingency contract, student involvement should be maximized. The degree of involvement will vary depending on the sophistication of the student's skills and his or her previous experiences with contracting. In general, we suggest introducing students to contracts that the teacher has constructed and predetermined; in this way, the student can focus on the operation of the contract, which increases the likelihood of success. As the student becomes more experienced with contracting and successfully completing contracts, he or she can be given greater responsibility for delineating the contract's components.

FIGURE 6.6
Complete model of a contingency contract

CONTINGENCY CONTRACT

If _____,

    then _____.

If _____,

    then _____.

If _____,

    then _____.

Bonus Clause: _____

_____

Penalty Clause: _____

_____

Starting Date___/___/___   Ending Date___/___/___   Review Date___/___/___

Signature _____   ___/___/___
               (Student)

Signature _____   ___/___/___
               (Teacher)

Signature _____   ___/___/___
               (Witness, other)

For students with little or no experience with contracting, teachers should teach directly to the components of the contract and how they are developed, negotiated, and implemented. Simple role-play arrangements in which contract development and negotiation are practiced can be useful. In addition, these students should begin with contracts that have short implementation durations and work up to longer contract periods (for example, hourly, daily, weekly, monthly contracts). This will allow them more opportunities to practice the contracting process and provide more frequent access to reinforcers for successful contract completion.

As students successfully complete contracts, the behaviors, conditions, and criteria of the contract should become more challenging. Less formal, written

FIGURE 6.7

A high-interest contingency contract for younger students

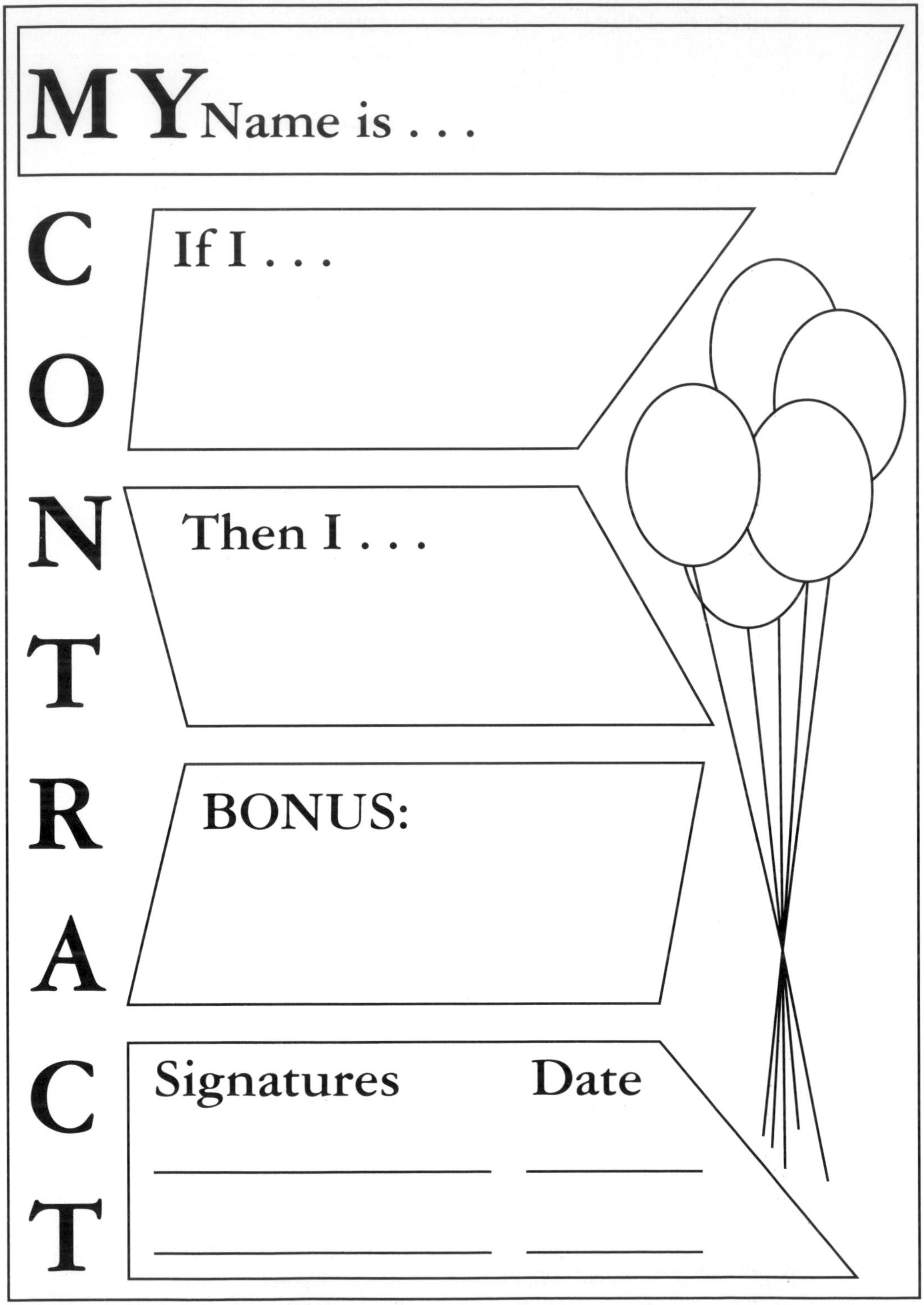

MY **Name is . . .**

C

If I . . .

O

N

Then I . . .

T

R

BONUS:

A

C

Signatures   Date

T

_____   _____

_____   _____

contracts can also be used and verbal agreements can be developed around socially or setting-appropriate reinforcers and consequences. Remember that contracts are used to provide a structure or "behavioral prosthesis" for the systematic delivery of consequences for student behavior (Stuart, 1971). They enhance both teacher and student accountability. The procedure framed within the contract, not the contract itself, is responsible for the change in student behavior.

A checklist of necessary components and implementation guidelines for contract development and implementation is shown in Figure 6.8 (Wolery, Bailey, & Sugai, 1988, p. 476).

Advantages. Contingency contracting is an important tool for consultants and teachers for a number of reasons. First, it entails the active involvement of the student and teacher in the process of programming for behavior change. This involvement allows opportunities for (a) more student investment in the change process through selecting behaviors, rewards, and privileges, (b) clear student and teacher understanding of program particulars, (c) selection of interventions that are more acceptable to the student and teacher, and (d) individualized intervention planning.

Second, contingency contracting provides a structure for developing student self-management skills. As students become more experienced and successful, they can assume greater responsibility for the construction of contracts. The development and implementation of a contract can require a variety of self-management skills, including self-assessment, self-recording, self-instruction, and self-reinforcement.

Third, experiences with contingency contracting provide students with practice in real-life management structures. Contractual agreements structure many relationships inside and outside the school setting, for example, car and house purchases, rental agreements, and work arrangements. As a result, students and teachers learn about accountability and contingency agreements.

Finally, contingency contracts provide teachers with a predictable, standardized format for structuring the development and implementation of behavior change programs. Negotiations between students and teachers can be focused on the components of the contract, implementation can be guided and evaluated against the conditions stipulated in the contract, and written contracts provide a record of a student and teacher agreement.

Self-Management Strategies

When we teach students academic and social behaviors, we hope to enable them to function independently of external or teacher-directed control and interventions. Specifically, we would like students to be successful under conditions in which (a) reinforcement is provided on an intermittent basis, (b) reinforcement is available on a delayed basis, and (c) naturally occurring persons, objects, and setting are present. Students who can function independently under these conditions (a) become more independent across settings, communities, and situations, (b) can extend their learning opportunities or functioning where teachers and other adults are not available, (c) are able to bridge the gap between the behavior and delayed

FIGURE 6.8
Checklist of necessary components of a complete contingency contract

____ 1. A clear statement of the target behavior.

        ____ Defined in operational terms.
        ____ Stated positively.
        ____ Stated in behavioral objective form.

____ 2. Designation of all persons directly involved.

____ 3. Description of a data-collection method.

        ____ Described in reliable and replicable terms.
        ____ Summarized in chart or graph form.

____ 4. Clear identification of all reinforcers to be used.

        ____ Specified schedule of delivery.
        ____ Designation of who will deliver.
        ____ Indication of how much will be delivered.

____ 5. Specification of behaviors, responsibilities, and/or conditions for earning or securing reinforcers.

____ 6. Specification of consequences for failure to meet expectations and responsibilities, or emission of inappropriate behaviors.

        ____ Procedures for renegotiation.

____ 7. Specification of a bonus clause for exceptional performance.

____ 8. Designation of specific timeliness.

        ____ Beginning or start date.
        ____ Deadline for ending contract.
        ____ Review dates for assessing progress.

____ 9. Signatures of all involved and dates of agreement.

Source: M. R. Wolery, D. B. Bailey, Jr., and G. M. Sugai (1988). *Effective Teaching: Principles and Procedures of Applied Behavior Analysis with Exceptional Students.* Boston, MA: Allyn & Bacon Publishing Company.

consequences associated with that behavior (Kazdin, 1974), and (d) acquire a tool that will enable them to access other learning opportunities (Wolery, Bailey, & Sugai, 1988). For these reasons, the use of self-management strategies is a preferred and effective way for consultants to structure behavior change programs (Fuchs & Fuchs, 1989; Fuchs et al., 1989).

We prefer to use a behaviorally oriented description that defines self-management as a set of learned behaviors or skills that enable students to move independently and successfully through the environment and to receive favorable evaluations (Wolery, Bailey, & Sugai, 1988). These behaviors are socially and situationally appropriate and are maintained by stimuli found in the natural environment. In addition, parents, teachers, and peers describe students who display these behaviors as having good self-concepts or self-esteem.

Given this characterization, self-management can be separated into three major types: self-recording, self-reinforcement, and self-instruction.

Self-recording.   Self-recording, one of the most common forms of self-management strategies, is defined as a behavior in which the student objectively records the occurrence of a specific behavior or class of behaviors. Although self-recording usually consists of making a mark with a pencil on a recording form, it can also include moving an object (such as a marble, toothpick, or bead on a string) from one location to another, making a mark on a chalkboard, or some other action to indicate that a behavior has occurred (like tying a knot on a piece of string or making a tear in a piece of paper).

Regardless of the form, the student must be taught or must be able to determine the relevant features or dimensions of the behavior to be recorded and whether the behavior meets the criteria of a recordable behavior. The student also must be able to judge time to determine when, where, and how long they should engage in self-recording.

When teachers have students implement a self-recording strategy, they should select and develop a recording instrument that is easy to use. Event recording, permanent product recording, and momentary time sampling are useful recording procedures. In addition, clear definitions of discrete target behavior should be developed to increase student accuracy and maximize agreement between the student and teacher about what is being recorded. With written self-recording, the instrument should be age/grade appropriate and not interfere with the student's normal academic and social functioning. Two examples of elementary self-recording forms are illustrated in Figures 6.9 and 6.10, and two sample secondary self-recording forms are illustrated in Figures 6.11 and 6.12.

After the instrument is developed and the target behaviors defined, teachers should teach the self-recording procedure to the student; that is, what behavior is recorded, when recording is to occur, and how often recording should happen. A model-lead-test format is suggested. The teaching sequence should involve showing the student how it is done (model), giving the student opportunities for guided practice (lead), and checking on the student's accuracy (testing).

Actual student self-recording should begin with relatively short sessions in which the teacher and student record the behavior. Teachers should provide students with reinforcement when the student displays the appropriate target behavior, self-records accurately, and meets the target behavior criteria. As soon as high levels of teacher and student agreement are demonstrated, teachers should immediately and gradually fade the amount of assistance and checking that they provide.

FIGURE 6.9

Primary-level self-recording form

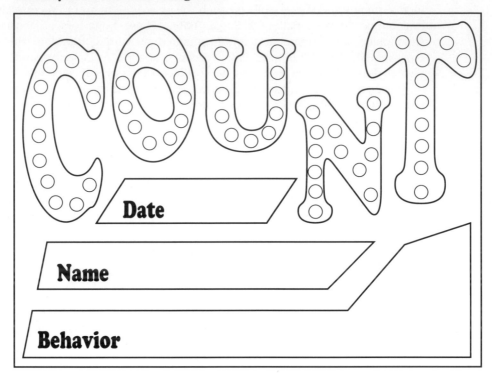

To increase the initial effectiveness of self-recording, students should be encouraged to self-record immediately after the behavior occurs or at the end of the designated time interval. Prompts (such as teacher verbal or gestural cues, recorded tones, or timer alarms) should be used to cue the student (and teacher) when to observe and record. In addition, periodic checks for accuracy should be made, especially at the beginning of the use of self-recording.

Self-reinforcement. When students are fluent at monitoring or recording their own behaviors, they can be taught how to engage in self-reinforcement. In this behavior, students arrange opportunities to reward or reinforce behaviors that they have emitted. They must be involved in the development of the reinforcement contingencies, and reinforcers must be effective.

As in self-monitoring, students may need to be taught how to engage in self-reinforcement. The same model-lead-test approach should be used to teach the student an association (contingency) between a behavior and some reinforcement (for example, "Nice job. I raised my hand, so I earn a point."). Initially, reinforcement should be teacher directed or controlled. As soon as the mastery or performance criteria are met, the administration of reinforcement can be shifted to the student by fading teacher control or participation and teaching the student how to self-reinforce.

FIGURE 6.10

Primary-level self-recording form

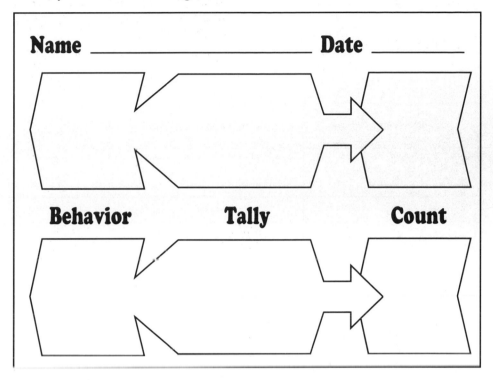

When implementing a self-reinforcement procedure, the fading of teacher control should be done systematically, based on the student's demonstration of fluent performance. In addition, natural reinforcers and schedules of reinforcement should be emphasized to increase the possibility of response maintenance and generalized use of the target behaviors and self-reinforcement. The teacher should periodically check the student's use of self-reinforcement to ensure that it is being applied accurately and contingently.

Self-instruction.   Self-instruction is the third type of self-management. Self-instruction has been described as language directed toward oneself (Kazdin, 1975). We prefer to use a definition that focuses on the student's accurate use of verbal or oral language (overt or covert) to set the occasion for a behavior or set of behaviors. When students say a specific self-statement or "jingle" (such as "Look before you leap" or "Stop, look, and listen.") that leads to successful action and functioning, self-instruction has occurred.

Before being taught to self-instruct, students must be fluent at self-recording (that is, self-assessment and self-monitoring). They must be able to identify the conditions under which the self-statement is required and then engage in the required target behavior. As with self-recording and self-reinforcement, students must be taught clear definitions of the self-instruction statement and the associated target behavior.

FIGURE 6.11

Secondary-level self-recording form

Student_____ Date ___/___/___	Behavior:	
Class Period/Time	**Number of Behaviors**	**Daily Rating** **G**ood **F**air **P**oor
1.	1 2 3 4 5 6 7 8 9 10	G F P
2.	1 2 3 4 5 6 7 8 9 10	G F P
3.	1 2 3 4 5 6 7 8 9 10	G F P
4.	1 2 3 4 5 6 7 8 9 10	G F P
5.	1 2 3 4 5 6 7 8 9 10	G F P
6.	1 2 3 4 5 6 7 8 9 10	G F P
7.	1 2 3 4 5 6 7 8 9 10	G F P
8.	1 2 3 4 5 6 7 8 9 10	G F P

Next, students are taught when and under what conditions self-instruction should occur and how to vocalize the self-statement ("Look before I talk.") before engaging in the target behavior (beginning a conversation with the teacher). Once accurate oral self-instruction is displayed (that is, the self-statement plus the target behavior), the self-statement should gradually be faded by having the student whisper the self-statement and finally, just "thinking about it" (pausing). If fading is successful, teachers should witness successful behavior without indications of the self-statement.

As with the other self-management strategies, students must be taught how to self-instruct, effective reinforcement should be used, controlling aspects of the natural environment should be considered, and teacher involvement and control should be faded systematically and gradually. In addition, teachers should periodically check to determine if the student is still using the self-statement. Self-instruction behaviors should be reinforced.

In sum, all three self-management strategies function as potentially useful strategies for consultants and teachers in the management of problem behaviors. They are advantageous because they provide a structure for fading teacher involvement in program implementation, teach the student how to look more independent and self-reliant, and serve as strategy for increasing generalized responding across settings and response maintenance over time.

FIGURE 6.12

Secondary-level self-recording form

Student				Date ___/___/___	
Behavior:					
DATE	___/___	___/___	___/___	___/___	___/___
TALLY					
DATE	___/___	___/___	___/___	___/___	___/___
TALLY					
DATE	___/___	___/___	___/___	___/___	___/___
TALLY					

The decision to use self-management strategies does not lessen the teacher's responsibility and active participation in the programming of a behavior change program. When self-management strategies are considered, teachers must (a) assess the student's prerequisite skills, (b) provide clear observable response definitions, (b) analyze the conditions under which the problem behavior is observed and its replacement response is required, (c) teach the strategy directly and systematically to the student, (d) collect assessment and evaluation data, (e) use systematic fading procedures to fade teacher control, and (f) monitor the student's accurate, fluent use of the self-management strategy.

SUMMARY

In this chapter, we presented definitions, descriptions, and implementation guidelines and considerations of strategies that can be used to teach new social behaviors or strengthen or weaken existing behaviors. As indicated previously, many useful sources contain in-depth descriptions of these procedures and strategies. Our intent was merely to give consultants and teachers relevant and essential information as classroom-based interventions are selected and developed.

The following is a list of key features from this chapter:

1. The extent to which an intervention strategy is complete, usable, organized, and understandable can affect consultation and intervention success.

2. A clearly organized structure should be used to organize the development and presentation of an intervention plan.

3. When students fail to display accurate, fluent use of a social skill (the acquisition phase of learning), intervention programs must focus on showing and telling the student how to do the skill, having the student practice the skill with informative feedback, and demonstrating the skill under natural, unassisted conditions.

4. Consultants must recognize and attend to the need and importance of teaching social skills and training teachers how to teach social skills.

5. When teaching social skills, teachers and consultants must prepare their lessons carefully, teach their lessons effectively, and evaluate the effectiveness of the instruction systematically and completely to ensure smooth lessons, effective instruction, and greater student learning.

6. Consultants should make the identification and effective use of positive reinforcement their highest priority in helping teachers develop and implement behavior change programs, specifically finding effective and natural reinforcers, scheduling reinforcement appropriately, and systematically administering reinforcement.

7. Every program developed to weaken or strengthen an existing behavior must have, first and foremost, a component for teaching and increasing or strengthening a suitable replacement response.

8. Consultants must assume the responsibility for safeguarding the rights and well-being of the student, the teacher, and others involved in the consultation.

9. When attempting to reduce problematic behaviors, every effort should be made to select reinforcement-based programs.

10. Type I punishment procedures are generally the most intrusive of the behavior-reduction procedures, and, as such, their selection and implementation must be given careful consideration.

11. Type I punishment procedures include direct, contingent application of aversive stimuli and overcorrection.

12. Type II punishment procedures include extinction, response cost, and time-out.

13. Contingency contracting is based on the ''if-then'' principle and used to structure the intervention programming relationship between the teacher and the student.

14. Students must be taught self-management strategies so they can become more independent of teacher-directed programming.

15. Three basic types of self-management can be considered: self-recording, self-reinforcement, and self-instruction.

REFERENCES

BIERLY, C., & BILLINGSLEY, F. F. (1983). An investigation of the educative effects of overcorrection on the behavior of an autistic child. *Behavioral Disorders, 9,* 11–21.

BUDD, K. S., & BAER, D. M. (1976). Behavior modification and the law: Implications of recent judicial decisions. *Journal of Psychiatry and the Law, 4,* 171–244.

FUCHS, D., & FUCHS, L. S. (1989). Exploring effective and efficient prereferral interventions: A component analysis of behavioral consultation. *School Psychology Review, 18,* 260–283.

FUCHS, D., FUCHS, L., GILMAN, S., REEDER, P., BAHR, M., FERNSTROM, P., & ROBERTS, H. (1989). Prereferral intervention through teacher consultation: Mainstream assistance teams. *Academic Therapy, 25,* 263–276.

GAST, D. L., & WOLERY, M. R. (1987). Severe maladaptive behaviors. In M. E. Snell (Ed.), *Systematic instruction of persons with severe handicaps* (3rd ed.) (pp. 300–332). Columbus, OH: Merrill.

GIBBS, J. W., & LUYBEN, P. D. (1985). Treatment of self-injurious behavior: Contingent versus noncontingent positive practice overcorrection. *Behavior Modification, 9,* 3–21.

GOLDSTEIN, A. P., SPRAFKIN, R. P., GERSHAW, N. J., & KLEIN, P. (1980). *Skillstreaming the adolescent: A structured learning approach to teaching prosocial skills.* Champaign, IL: Research Press.

JACKSON, N. F., JACKSON, D. A., & MONROE, C. (1983). *Getting along with others: Teaching social effectiveness to children.* Champaign, IL: Research Press.

KAMEENUI, E. J., & SIMMONS, D. C. (1990) *Designing instructional strategies: The prevention of academic learning problems.* Columbus, OH: Merrill.

KAZDIN, A. E. (1974). Reactive self-monitoring: The effects of response desirability, goal setting, and feedback. *Journal of Consulting and Clinical Psychology, 42,* 704–714.

KAZDIN, A. E. (1975). *Behavior modification in applied settings.* Homewood, IL: Dorsey Press.

LYNCH, V., MCGUIGAN, C., & SHOEMAKER, S. (1983). An introduction to systematic instruction. *B.C. Journal of Special Education, 7,* 1–13.

MATSON, J. L., ESVELDT-DAWSON, K., & KAZDIN, A. E. (1982). Treatment of spelling deficits in mentally retarded children. *Mental Retardation, 20,* 76–81.

MCGINNIS, E., GOLDSTEIN, A. P., SPRAFKIN, R. P., & GERSHAW, N. J. (1984). *Skillstreaming the elementary school child: A guide for teaching prosocial skills.* Champaign, IL: Research Press.

NELSON, C. M., & RUTHERFORD, R. B. (1983). Timeout revisited: Guidelines for its use in special education. *Exceptional Education Quarterly, 4*(3), 56–67.

RUTHERFORD, R. B., & NELSON, C. M. (1982). Analysis of the response contingent time-out literature with behaviorally disordered students in classroom settings. In R. B. Rutherford (Ed.), *Monographs in behavior disorders: Severe behavior disorders of children and youth* (Vol. 5) (pp. 79–105). Reston, VA: Council for Children with Behavioral Disorders of the Council for Exceptional Children.

STOKES, T. F., & BAER, D. M. (1977). An implicit technology of generalization. *Journal of Applied Behavior Analysis, 10,* 349–367.

STUART, R. B. (1971). Behavioral contracting within the families of delinquents. *Journal of Behavioral Therapy and Experimental Psychiatry, 2,* 1–11.

SUGAI, G., & FABRE, T. (In press). Using flowcharts to display behavior teaching plans. *Teaching Exceptional Children.*

SUGAI, G., & FABRE, T. (1987). The behavior teaching plan: A model for developing and implementing behavior change programs. *Education and Treatment of Children, 10,* 279–290.

TRAP, J. J., MILNER-DAVIS, P., JOSEPH, S., & COOPER, J. O. (1978). The effects of feedback and consequences on transitional cursive letter formation. *Journal of Applied Behavior Analysis, 11,* 381–393.

WALKER, H. M., MCCONNELL, S., HOLMES, D., TODIS, B., WALKER, J., & GOLDEN, N. (1983). *The Walker social skills curriculum: The ACCEPTS program.* Austin: Pro-Ed.

WALKER, H. M., TODIS, B., HOLMES, D., & HORTON, G. (1983). *The Walker social skills curriculum: The ACCESS program.* Austin: Pro-Ed.

WOLERY, M. R., BAILEY, D. B., JR., & SUGAI, G. (1988). *Effective teaching: Principles and procedures of applied behavior analysis with exceptional students.* Boston: Allyn & Bacon.

WOLF, M. M. (1978). Social validity: The case for subjective measurement or how applied behavior analysis is finding its heart. *Journal of Applied Behavior Analysis, 11,* 203–214.

Intervention Implementation, Monitoring, and Evaluation

Mrs. Ayers is the resource consultant at Bushland Senior High School. She has been working with Mr. Burswood on a problem social behavior displayed by Birnie, one of his tenth-grade science students. When engaged in science experiments that involve working with or near others, Birnie touches and handles the lab equipment and property of other students. She does this four or five times a science period, disrupting lessons and angering other students. Mr. Burswood reprimands Birnie and moves her to a different table to work alone. He is frustrated that verbal reprimands and office referrals seem to have little effect.

After completing the Problem Identification Interview and Functional Analysis (see Figures 7.1 and 7.2, respectively), Mrs. Ayers and Mr. Burswood decide to write a home-school contract in which Birnie can earn a new science-fiction magazine for every three consecutive days that she keeps her hands on her own equipment and property. Birnie, her father, and Mr. Burswood also agree that whenever Birnie touches someone else's property, Mr. Burswood will ask her to move to an empty lab table for the remaining class time. The basic elements of this program are shown in the Intervention Planning form in Figure 7.3.

In previous chapters, we described procedures and guidelines for selecting and developing interventions that can be used prescriptively by consultants and teachers to solve social behavior problems. For example, we described what elements should be included in Birnie's contract and how the contract should be implemented (see Figure 7.4). Our intent was to cover material that could (a) facilitate the consultant's role, (b) maximize the teacher's acceptability of and participation in an intervention, and (c) increase the probability of intervention success.

With the details of the interventions determined, the consultant and the teacher concentrate on actually implementing and monitoring the intervention. In

FIGURE 7.1

Mr. Burswood and Mrs. Ayers's completed Problem Identification form

PROBLEM IDENTIFICATION INTERVIEW FORM	Page 1 of 3

Consultant _Mrs. Ayers_   Teacher _Mr. Burswood_
Date _5 / 9 / 91_   School _Bushland Senior H.S._

Student Information: Name _Birnie B_   Room _17_
Grade _10_   Age _15_   Sex: M (F)   IEP: Y (N)

Describe the problem behavior. (5 minutes)

Touching and handling property of others
(e.g., science lab equipment, pens & paper,
books & notebooks)

Describe other behaviors that seem to be related to the problem behavior.
(3 minutes)

Failing to complete assignments
Verbal arguments with peers
Smiling at other students when they are
    irritated

Describe the conditions under which the problem behavior is most likely to occur.
(2 minutes)

When: _Unstructured, independent labwork; working with one or two
     other students. Engaging in expts._
Where: _In science class at lab tables_

With Whom: _One or two neighboring students_

FIGURE 7.1 (*continued*)

PROBLEM IDENTIFICATION INTERVIEW FORM	Page 2 of 3

Describe what usually happens <u>after</u> the problem behavior occurs. (2 minutes)

Teacher has given instructions. Lab equipment distributed and placed on tables. Students setting up for experiments

Describe what usually happens immediately <u>before</u> the problem behavior occurs. (2 minutes)

B & other students go off-task

Describe what <u>you</u> usually do when the behavior occurs. (2 minutes)

Tell B to keep hands to self and get started on expts. Move B to a table where no other students. If she persists or arguments occur with peers, send to office or tell her to come after school to finish assignment.

Describe what <u>other students</u> do when the behavior occurs. (2 minutes)

Complain to student. Tell her to keep hands to self. Argue. Call her names.

F I G U R E   7.1   (*continued*)

PROBLEM IDENTIFICATION INTERVIEW FORM	Page 3 of 3

Describe what you would like the student to do <u>instead</u> of the problem behavior. (2 minutes)

Keep hands on her own property. Ask teacher for help or extra equipment. Ask before touching property of other students. * Obtain peer attention in appropriate manner.

List or describe <u>other interventions</u> that have been tried. (3 minutes)

- Verbal reprimands
- Parent conferences
- Office referrals
- change seating arrangement

Make an appointment to conduct an observation and debriefing. (1 minute)

Date __5/10/91__ Time __10:00__ to __11:00__ Place/Classroom ___Room 17___

Other information/notes

- Has skills to complete tasks
- Does not steal property
- Parents report no difficulties at home
- Similar problems reported by year 9 science teacher

FIGURE 7.2

Mrs. Ayers's completed Functional Analysis Observation form

FUNCTIONAL ANALYSIS OBSERVATION FORM	Date _5 / 10 /91_ Time _10 :00_ Observer _Ayers_ Student _Birnie B._ Teacher _Burswood_ Classroom/School _Bushland Sr. H.S._

Setting Description: Science class
B. sitting w/ 3 other students (#2 = partner)
Task = measure amount of growth in plants.
Plants, rulers, data sheets, pencils, watering cans on table.

Mr. B.
2 3   45
B 1   67
89   12
10 11

Time	Antecedents	Birnie Behaviors	Consequences
10:07	Mr. B.: "Does everyone understand? Good. Get to work."	Looks around. Turns & takes ruler from 8's table.	8: "Hey, get your own." Takes it back.
	✓	Smiles at 8 & 2	Mr. B.: Looks at B. "Everyone get busy."
10:12		Drops pencil. Takes 1's pencil & begins to write	1: Grabs pencil back & moves all things to edge of table.
		smiles, "I was just borrowing it."	1 & 3: "Use your own damn stuff."
	Mr. B.: "3, watch your mouth... what's the problem?"	smiles at Mr. B. and 3.	Mr. B.: "Ok, B.... come here. I want to talk with you."
	✓	smiles...	

FIGURE 7.3

Mr. Burswood and Mrs. Ayers's completed Intervention Planning form

INTERVENTION PLANNING FORM	Teacher __Mr. Burswood__ Date _5/13/91_ Consultant __Mrs. Ayers__ School __Bushland Sr. H.S.__

Student Information:

Name _Birnie_ DOB _2/11/76_ Sex: M (F)

Grade _10_ Age _15_ Room _17_ IEP: Y (N)

Review of Case Information. (4 minutes) (Check each area that has been reviewed.)

✓ Problem Behavior   ✓ Current Level of Functioning

✓ Replacement Response   ✓ Required Level of Functioning

✓ Problem Context/Setting   ✓ Long-Term Objective

✓ Testable Explanations

List four or five positive strategies to improve student performance. (4 minutes)

1. Use best friend as lab partner

(2.) Home – school contract for new sci-fi magazines

(3.) Verbal praise for appropriate behavior

4. Self-recording sheet

5. Reinforce her neighbors

Circle strategy (or strategies) to be implemented. (1 minute)

Name one strategy for managing unacceptable behavior. (2 minutes)

Move to empty lab table to work alone for rest of period.

F I G U R E 7.3   (*continued*)

Identify what is needed/available to insure implementation. (2 minutes)

— contract (Ayers will get examples)

— 2-3 recent sci-fi magazines (Ayers will get from father

— data recording sheet (desk calendar)

— empty lab table

Specify the steps for implementation of intervention. (6 minutes)

1. meet w/ B. & father to write contract

2. Go over contract w/ B.

3. Just before class, remind B of contract

4. Record # of touching episodes

5. Review B's performance daily

6.

Describe how student progress will be monitored and evaluated. (3 minutes)

Burswood will record # of touching episodes on desk calendar. He will evaluate B's progress on daily basis.

Date for Starting Intervention 5/15/91

Next Meeting Date 5/22/91 and Time 3:15

Next Observation 5/17/91 and Time 10:00

Attach Additional Notes

See attached

FIGURE 7.4

Birnie's science class contract

CONTINGENCY CONTRACT

If _Birnie keeps her hands on her own property during a_ ,
45 minute science class

   then _she will receive one credit for purchase_ .
   of a science fiction magazine

If _____ ,

   then _____ .

If _Birnie earns 7 credits_ ,

   then _she can go to bookstore with her dad to_ .
   buy one science fiction magazine

Bonus Clause: _For every 3 consecutive days of "good_

hands," an extra credit is earned.

_____

Penalty Clause: _If B. touches someone else's property_

without their permission, she must forfeit one

credit.

Starting Date _5 / 6 / 91_   Ending Date _5 /30/ 91_   Review Date _5 /20/91_

Signature _Birnie B._   _5/5/91_
         (Student)

Signature _Mr. Burwood_   _5/5/91_
         (Teacher)

Signature _Mrs. Ayers_   _5/5/91_
         (Witness, other)

this chapter, we provide strategies and guidelines for (a) implementing and monitoring a planned intervention program, (b) evaluating intervention effectiveness, and (c) terminating the consultation. We emphasize what consultants and teachers should do after they complete the initial planning and when they should put the intervention into effect. As in previous chapters, we maintain a best-practices approach; that is, strategies that have been shown to be effective and appropriate are emphasized and described. We do not expect consultants to master all the content presented, but we encourage them to always move toward mastery and to refer to this content as they engage in consultation relationships with teachers.

IMPLEMENTING AND MONITORING PLANNED INTERVENTION PROGRAMS

Immediately after the completion of the Intervention Planning Form, in which the general aspects of an intervention are identified, the consultant and the teacher develop the particulars of the procedure, such as the implementation details, and collect required materials and resources. For example, Mr. Burswood and Mrs. Ayers identify precisely (a) what Birnie will be told when she is working on her science experiments appropriately (what kind of verbal praise statements) and when she is observed touching the property of others (how to ignore and provide redirection prompts), (b) what science fiction magazines will be used as reinforcers, (c) how other students will be treated when their property is touched, (d) what level of performance is required for a new contract to be developed, and (e) how Birnie can be taught to obtain peer attention in an appropriate way. This information is displayed in written form—on a lesson plan, checklist, or flow chart—to increase clarity, accountability, and implementation accuracy. These aspects of the intervention were covered in detail in Chapter 6. In addition, it is important to ensure that the teacher is fluent on how to engage in the specific behaviors of the intervention; therefore, it may be necessary for the consultant to train the teacher. This topic is examined in detail in Chapter 11.

The specifics of the intervention program are important for several reasons. First, teachers can be more consistent in their implementation of an intervention. For example, there will be fewer occasions when Mr. Burswood will have to "think" on his feet, and Birnie will know exactly what happens regardless of the behavior she displays. Second, greater specificity reduces the possibility that teachers will inadvertently strengthen the problem behavior by attending to it. For example, like many teachers, Mr. Burswood reactively responds to problem behaviors with verbal reprimands and criticism, which are powerful sources of attention (or positive reinforcement) for some students. As a result, the problem behavior is strengthened. Finally, when the specifics of the program are highlighted, there is a greater probability of attending to and strengthening the desired replacement response.

The extent and accuracy with which an intervention is implemented is affected by a number of variables. For example, after the details of an intervention have been specified, one teacher may delay implementing an intervention because of the amount of effort and time required. Another teacher, using the same strategy, may start the procedure but stop after a week because the student's behavior is not changing rapidly enough.

To increase the extent and accuracy with which an intervention is implemented, consultants must be familiar with the range of factors that can interfere with a teacher's ability to implement an intervention and be able to develop a method of increasing implementation accuracy. To address this concern, we discuss three topics: contributing factors, assessment strategies, and strategies for achieving, improving, and maintaining implementation accuracy.

Contributing Factors

Numerous factors can contribute to or affect the extent and accuracy with which a teacher is able to implement a procedure. These factors are discussed within the context of two basic problems: inadequate implementation or no implementation, and decreased implementation accuracy.

Inadequate implementation or no implementation.   One type of implementation problem consultants might encounter is the teacher who fails to implement an intervention entirely or who implements the strategy inaccurately or inadequately. Several factors might be attributed to this kind of problem. As we discussed in Chapter 5, a teacher may find that an intervention is unacceptable because (a) it involves the use of aversive or intrusive procedures, (b) it requires more effort or costs more than the teacher can give or is willing to give, (c) it has the potential for adverse side effects, (d) it is based on an incompatible theoretical approach, (e) it has an unknown effectiveness or probability of success, or (f) it requires resources and materials that are unavailable to the teacher. For example, Mr. Bunbury hesitates to use an intervention involving generous amounts of token (tickets) reinforcers because he believes that the use of external and material reinforcers is "bribery." Ms. Chang is incomplete in her implementation of a differential reinforcement program because she finds it difficult to keep track of time, observe the student's behavior, and give extra social attention when the student is engaged in appropriate behavior.

Intervention failure also can be affected by poorly defined interventions (Peterson, Homer, & Wonderlich, 1982). If the details of the Intervention Planning form or subsequent definitions of intervention components are deficient or lacking, teachers can find implementation of a strategy difficult and even aversive. For example, Mr. Nelson's plan for giving verbal praise was limited to saying, "I like the way you are _____" more often. The condition "more often," however, does not give Mr. Nelson much information; in fact, he operationalizes it as "once every half hour," which is actually twice as often as he usually provides verbal praise. As a result of this interpretation, the student's behavior does not improve because the schedule of reinforcement is too thin, and Mr. Nelson abandons the program.

A lack of teacher fluency in using an intervention can also influence implementation. This problem can be attributed to a failure to train the teacher sufficiently, especially when the procedure requires the teacher to make a number of implementation decisions. For example, Ms. Kulczycki taught Mr. Gittings about the components of a complete contract and how it should be constructed; however, she did not teach him how to meet with the student and negotiate the specifics of the contract. As a result, the development of the contract was incomplete and a number of loopholes caused the intervention to fail. Similarly, insufficient opportunities to practice before actually implementing a new procedure can result in a failed or incomplete implementation.

A final contributing factor is poor planning. If materials have not been prepared and organized or if the scheduling of intervention opportunities has not been arranged, difficulties can arise. For example, Mrs. Sanchez has developed a strategy designed to decrease the amount of time it takes Petur to begin following a direction. However, she found it difficult to implement her intervention because she did not arrange for ten directions to be given during Petur's 40-minute reading session.

Decreased intervention implementation. A second type of problem that consultants might encounter is exemplified by the teacher who initially implements a strategy accurately and effectively, but whose level of execution decreases over time. In this case, consultants might detect one of four possible explanations. First, the teacher may be using an ineffective procedure. If positive or noticeable changes in the problem behavior are not observed, teachers may decrease their use of an intervention procedure.

Second, there may be a lack of positive reinforcement for the teacher's behaviors. If teachers are not encouraged to sustain their implementation of an intervention, if they do not receive immediate positive reinforcement when they are using a strategy, or if they are not prepared for slow or delayed changes in the student's behavior, they may discontinue or decrease their use of an intervention. For example, Mr. Herlihy expected immediate, dramatic changes in Lori's work completion when a self-recording, goal-setting procedure was initiated. When he observed only slight changes in her work during the first few days, he became less consistent in checking the accuracy of her self-recording and providing verbal praise when she completed her work.

Third, teachers may decrease the accuracy with which they implement a strategy because over time small changes are made in different aspects of a procedure. For example, the definition of the problem or replacement behavior changes, a different form of positive reinforcement is used, setting conditions are modified, or less attention is given to intervention detail (that is, when reinforcement is given, how much reinforcement is given, and where it is given). These situations may be associated with poorly constructed interventions, inadequate training, or a lack of accountability for accurate and complete implementation.

Fourth, there may be a lack of sufficient positive reinforcement for the teacher's implementation of an intervention. If it is to be maintained over time, a teacher's behavior, like any behavior, must receive some level of effective positive reinforcement. Although it can vary for each individual, reinforcement can consist of improvement or progress in student behavior, encouragement and praise from others (such as parents, administrators, consultant, or other teachers), or a decrease in a problematic behavior (that is, negative reinforcement). In all of these instances, a decrease or removal of reinforcement creates an extinction condition, which in turn is associated with a decrease in the teacher's use of a strategy. In one sense, a removal of a strategy or a "loosening" of the contingencies is desirable because it can promote response maintenance and generalized responding; however, when a satisfactory change in behavior is not observed in the intervention setting, teachers and consultants have not succeeded in solving the problem.

In sum, we have described numerous variables that can affect a teacher's ability to initiate and maintain high levels and accuracy of intervention implementation. Knowing that these influences are possible, consultants should watch continually for their presence and interact with teachers in a manner that will prevent or reduce their effects.

Assessment Strategies

To ensure high implementation accuracy and to catch procedural deficiencies, consultants must systematically assess the teacher's intervention implementation. Initial assessments should be conducted immediately to avoid early procedural errors and on a regular schedule thereafter to monitor implementation maintenance. If the accuracy of implementation is decreasing or if a teacher is avoiding implementation, consultants can identify contributing variables quickly through regular assessments.

Although an interview with the teacher may elicit useful information, we recommend direct observation. Two types of direct observation should be considered. The first method, called *procedural reliability,* involves assessing the degree and accuracy with which a teacher follows the intervention plan (Billingsley, White, & Munson, 1980). Typically, the consultant obtains a copy of the procedural checklist, lesson plan, or flow chart. Then he or she observes the teacher, checking off which steps were conducted accurately and inaccurately. The consultant also notes what should be done differently. Finally, the consultant calculates the percentage of the steps completed accurately. If the score falls below 90%, the implementation of the procedure is said to be inaccurate. This type of procedural observation pinpoints precisely where implementation deficiencies exist. Figure 7.5 contains a checklist used to assess the procedural reliability of Ms. McCoy's implementation of a self-recording procedure.

Conducting a functional analysis is a second way of directly observing implementation accuracy. Using the same procedures described in Chapter 4, the consultant notes the conditions under which the intervention is being implemented (that is, the setting description) and all procedurally related behaviors displayed by the teacher. The consultant also notes all student behaviors as antecedent or consequent events and examines testable relationships between the teacher's and students' behaviors. In addition, he or she assesses the accuracy of the teacher's behaviors in response to the student's behaviors, the frequency with which the teacher displays intervention-related behaviors, and the student's response to those behaviors.

If the consultant is unable to conduct a procedural reliability observation directly, he or she should encourage the teacher to make an audio tape or videotape, which can be examined at a later time by the teacher, the consultant, or

FIGURE 7.5

Intervention implementation checklist

Teacher: Ms. McCoy   Date: August 19, 1992
Classroom: Room 4 - Third Grade Observer/Consultant: Mrs. Broome
Student: Lansing   Intervention: self-recording

Intervention Implementation Checklist

(+ = good, − = improvement needed, 0 = not observed, N = not applicable)

_____ Teacher (T) meets student (S) at the door, gives him a self-recording sheet, and reviews previous day's performance.

_____ T asks S to tell her what behaviors he is recording on his sheet.

_____ T tells S to identify what happens if he meets his daily goal <u>and</u> he is 90% in agreement with the teacher.

_____ T sets timer for five-minute intervals.

_____ When bell rings, T looks at student to see what behavior he is displaying and if he is self-recording.

   _____ If no, she gives a brief verbal prompt to record.

   _____ If yes, she gives a brief verbal praise statement on the average of every three intervals.

_____ At end of session, T counts her tally marks and asks S to count his behaviors.

_____ T compares her total with the student's total.

   _____ If >90%, T gives verbal praise and bonus coupon.

   _____ If <90%, T reviews behavior definitions and self-recording procedures with S.

_____ T graphs her data and student's data.

_____ T prepares materials for next day.

both. Then any implementation inconsistencies can be corrected and procedural accuracies can be reinforced.

Regardless of which direct observation procedure is used, the consultant's goal is to determine if the teacher is implementing all aspects of the intervention at high levels of accuracy and proficiency. If procedural reliability is below 90%, the consultant should conduct observations regularly and frequently until high, consistent accuracy is obtained. If reliability is above 90%, the consultant can conduct observations less frequently. In addition, procedural reliability checks should be conducted whenever major adjustments are made in a procedure. For example, a teacher decides to change from one type of differential reinforcement to another (for example, differential reinforcement of other behaviors to differential reinforcement of alternative behaviors). To ensure accurate implementation of the new response-based procedure, she uses a video camera to record her first implementation. After school, she reviews the tape to determine if she is accurate and fluent.

Strategies for Achieving, Improving, and Maintaining Implementation Accuracy

Based on the information collected, consultants can provide feedback that positively recognizes (reinforces) what teachers do correctly and enables them to improve their implementation accuracy. However, to maximize initially high intervention accuracy and avoid early procedural errors, consultants should ensure that teachers are accurate and fluent at a procedure before actually implementing it. Regardless of what teachers say about their ability to execute a procedure, consultants should ask them to tell or show precisely how a procedure will be used.

If a teacher is able to demonstrate accurate (over 90%) and fluent use of a procedure, the consultant can encourage actual implementation and assess the procedural reliability in the actual problem or classroom context. If, however, the teacher is unable to demonstrate high implementation accuracy, the consultant may need to teach the procedure directly (Chapter 11 contains a discussion on using a model-lead-test direct instructional approach to train teachers). Prompts and assists—such as cue cards, checklists, or flow charts—should be considered if the teacher has difficulty learning any part of an intervention.

If a teacher demonstrates high accuracy but has difficulty with fluency, the consultant should provide controlled practice opportunities, including specific coaching with contingent positive feedback.

If high procedural reliability is not maintained after the teacher begins the actual implementation, the consultant should provide both corrective feedback designed to increase accuracy and fluency and positive reinforcement to maintain high accuracy. Once high accuracy and fluency are achieved, assessments of procedural reliability can be conducted on a less regular basis. At this point, the consultant can cut down his or her involvement and provide a schedule of reinforcement that promotes treatment maintenance. In Figure 7.6 the major decisions and actions associated with promoting high intervention implementation accuracy are illustrated in a flow chart.

FIGURE 7.6

Major consultant decisions and actions that promote high intervention implementation accuracy

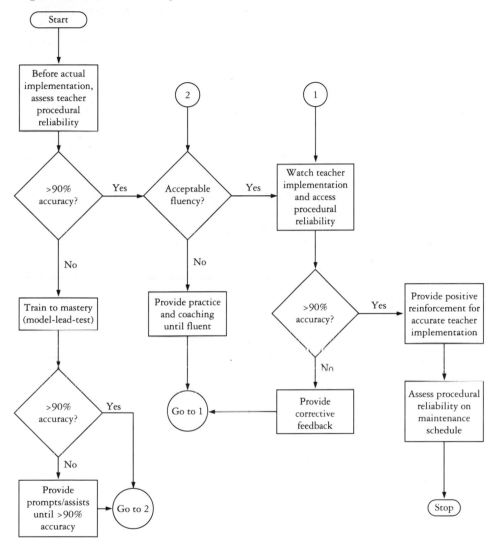

Numerous other strategies might be considered when helping teachers maintain reliable intervention implementation. For example, teachers should be encouraged to implement a new strategy for short intervals and set achievable criteria for success for both the teacher and the student. Many teachers attempt to implement a procedure all morning or the entire day. As a result, they can expend large amounts of energy and time on a procedure that may be ineffective or may even exacerbate the problem. Interventions should be piloted for short periods (during reading class, for example), and, at first, only in the setting or context in which the behavior is most problematic. This will enable the teacher to (a) receive immediate reinforcement if it is successful, (b) avoid expending an exorbitant amount of energy and time on an ineffective procedure, and (c) revise or adjust a procedure to be more effective. In addition, on the initial implementation of a procedure, the teacher may set criteria that are difficult to achieve. To increase the probability of a successful first implementation, the criteria should be attainable. Student participation and continued teacher implementation are more likely if they both achieve success.

In the same way that student behavior can be strengthened through positive reinforcement, teacher behavior also can be increased and maintained through effective positive reinforcement. Although the goal is to develop natural reinforcers (such as positive changes in student behavior and less problematic behavior), consultants may need to provide other forms of positive reinforcement until more natural positive outcomes acquire more reinforcing qualities. We suggest that consultants consider using the following reinforcement tactics:

1. Provide explicit, informative positive feedback about teacher behavior; for example, "You did a nice job of not attending to Roy's off-task verbal behavior. You could really see Roy's on-task behavior change when you gave his neighbors attention for their appropriate behaviors."

2. At the beginning of the implementation, give frequent and immediate positive reinforcement; for example, at the end of the first two days of the token economy procedure, the consultant told the teacher that she had given out tokens accurately and effectively.

3. Give feedback that focuses on improvement in the student's behavior; for example, a consultant tells a teacher, "Calla has shown steady progress over the past four days of intervention. Your implementation of the intervention is working."

The success or failure of an intervention and consultation is frequently associated with how accurately and fluently teachers implement the procedure. Many variables can be identified through direct observation. However, it is most important that consultants treat teacher implementation behavior objectively, realizing that it can be affected by the same principles and forces that affect student behavior.

EVALUATING INTERVENTION EFFECTIVENESS

Once accurate, fluent teacher intervention implementation is achieved and maintained, consultants and teachers must determine whether the intervention is effective and successful. This task is complicated by the many ways in which effectiveness and success can be determined. In this section, we discuss (a) the different perspectives from which success can be determined, (b) methods of evaluating success, and (c) evaluation outcomes and decisions.

Success Perspectives

Success or intervention effectiveness can have different meanings for different individuals and from different perspectives. For example, Ms. Gottlieb reports that she knows that Mac's in-class problem behaviors (verbal interruptions, talking out without raising his hand, using a loud voice) have improved because his behaviors look no different than the behaviors of other students. The consultant who has been working with Ms. Gottlieb has noticed that when the intervention is in effect, Mac's appropriate behaviors increase and his inappropriate behaviors decrease. The principal believes that the intervention has been successful because Mac is now following the school's rules and expectations. Mac's parents think that the intervention has been effective because he is more cooperative at home as well, and because they have not received any office referral or discipline notices for a month. Mac likes his new program because his friends and teachers are paying more attention to him and seem nicer.

In this example, success or intervention effectiveness is based on perspective and expectations and/or the kind of impact the problem has had on others in the environment. In general, we can derive four perspectives from which intervention success or effectiveness can be assessed: (a) empirical, (b) normative, (c) educational, and (d) social.

Empirical.   The empirical perspective focuses on the extent that a functional or predictable relationship can be identified or demonstrated between the intervention (independent variable) and the problem or replacement behavior (dependent variable). All extraneous or outside influences that might be associated with the observed behavior change are noted or dismissed. The stronger the predictable control demonstrated between the intervention and target behaviors, the greater the empirical soundness of the intervention. Presentation and removal of the intervention and systematic replication of effects are used to demonstrate control.

In classroom contexts, the extent of empirical control is usually explored through single-subject designs (such as reversal/withdrawal designs or multiple-baseline designs), where each student serves as his or her own control and the intervention is systematically added or withdrawn. For example, after collecting five days of baseline data, Ms. Gottlieb introduced a self-recording procedure in which Mac records the number of times he raises his hand appropriately, answers questions in the proper voice tone and volume, and waits until others have stopped talking before he speaks. After Mac self-recorded for six days and Ms. Gottlieb observed a clear change in his behaviors, she discontinued the intervention. She returned to baseline to see if the intervention is functionally related to the observed change in behavior. When Mac's inappropriate behaviors began to increase and his appropriate behaviors decreased, Ms. Gottlieb reinstated self-recording. By doing so, she is examining a third demonstration of intervention effects. The data graphed in Figure 7.7 show this classroom application of a single-subject ABAB withdrawal design. The visual changes in the data between phases (that is, baseline to self-recording, self-recording to baseline, and baseline to self-recording) indicate the effects associated with the intervention.

If Ms. Gottlieb had not collected baseline data (B phase only), she would have nothing with which to compare Mac's performance under self-recording conditions. If she did not return to baseline conditions, she would only have one demonstration of the intervention's effect (the AB design: baseline and intervention), and she would not be able to rule out unrelated factors, such as a talk with the principal, a change in class schedule, or a new home contract.

FIGURE 7.7

Classroom application of an ABAB withdrawal design

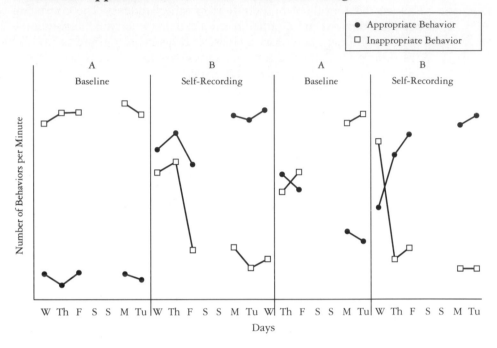

Under some circumstances, it may be inconvenient or inadvisable to return to baseline conditions, for example, when (a) the student's behaviors are severe or extremely disruptive (frequent, loud verbal outbursts or physical aggression), (b) the behavior is difficult to reverse because it comes under the control of natural classroom factors (receiving peer reinforcement by learning to work cooperatively with others, or earning high marks or grades by learning to stay on task or completing work), or (c) the teacher or others cannot tolerate a return to baseline conditions. In these circumstances, empirical validity can be assessed by using a multiple-baseline design. This technique does not require a return to baseline conditions, instead, the teacher identifies three or more conditions (such as behaviors, students, or settings) in which the intervention can be implemented on a staggered basis. For example, Ms. Gottlieb notes that Mac's disruptive behaviors are most problematic during reading, math, and art. To use a multiple-baseline design across settings, she collects baseline data on Mac's behaviors in each class. After five or six days, she implements the self-recording strategy in reading class only. When a stable change in behavior is observed during reading, she has Mac self-record during art class. Similarly, about five or six days later, she initiates self-recording in math class. In the end, self-recording is in effect in all three problem settings, a return to baseline is avoided, and three demonstrations of the functional relationship between the intervention and observed changes in the problem behavior are examined (see Figure 7.8).

A multiple baseline can also be used across behaviors or students. For behaviors, the teacher selects three or more different behaviors. After collecting

FIGURE 7.8

Application of a multiple-baseline design across settings

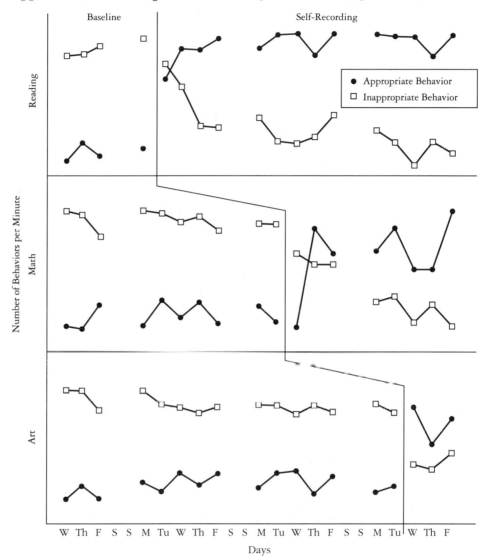

baseline data across all of them, the teacher would implement the intervention on a staggered basis across each behavior. For students, the teacher selects three different students, staggering the initiation of the intervention strategy across each student. In each case, every replication or implementation of the intervention demonstrates the functional relationship between the intervention (independent variable) and the observed change in the target behavior (dependent variable). A return to baseline conditions is not required; however, the behavior, the student, or the setting must be independent so the effect of the intervention on one does not influence the effect on the other.

When investigating intervention success from an empirical perspective, we are attempting to make the strongest, most defensible statement about the relationship between the intervention and the change in the target behaviors. Such statements enable consultants and teachers to attribute the change in student behavior to the intervention and recommend use of the intervention in other situations. Unfortunately, the tests required to examine success from this perspective are often difficult to implement in instructional settings, either a return to baseline conditions is impractical or more immediate implementation of an intervention is required. In addition, although a functional relationship is confirmed, the size of the change in the target behaviors may not be educationally or socially relevant.

Normative.   Assessing success from a normative perspective emphasizes the extent or degree to which new levels of the student's behavior are acceptable in comparison to the levels of behavior displayed by the student's peers. Peer behaviors are used as the standard against which intervention success is evaluated. For example, Mr. Frangia observed that (a) most students in his general science classes raised their hands to ask a question or get teacher help once or twice each 40-minute class period, and (b) about once every two weeks, some students would talk out without raising their hands or waiting to be acknowledged. Karen used to talk out four to five times per class period. Although she raised her hand, she did not wait for the teacher to call on her. Three weeks after establishing a simple differential reinforcement of lower rates program, Karen's talkouts and handraising were occurring at the same levels as her peers. Mr. Frangia was satisfied with the effectiveness of the program because Karen no longer looked different from her peers. In fact, when the vice-principal conducted a classroom observation, she reported that Karen's behaviors seemed more acceptable than some of her peers.

We recommend that teachers and consultants use local standards of student behavior as criteria for evaluating intervention success. Samples or probes of the target student's peers can provide these local standards. We prefer using local norms collected through regular and direct observations, because norms obtained from indirect sources—such as standardized tests, checklists, or other sources—are often based on data from student populations and settings that differ from the setting in which the target student is present.

Direct observation procedures should be used (see Chapter 3 for additional guidelines) at the same time and for the same interval as the target student's behavior and under the same conditions (setting, seating arrangement, instruction) in which the problem behavior is observed and the intervention is to be implemented. If a normative approach is taken, levels of peer performance should be collected on a formative basis—for example, once every four or five days—to assess fluctuations in peer behavior.

Too often, the immediate demands of a student's problem setting cause teachers to overlook the requirements of future environments when they evaluate student progress or intervention effectiveness. To ensure more generalized success, local norms should be collected and established for two settings. The first setting is the existing context; that is, where the student is currently required to function. The second setting is the future context in which the student will be required to function (the least-restrictive environment, the next grade or classroom, or another setting in which the problem behavior is also observed). For example, Juan is in eighth grade. His teachers establish criteria for acceptable social behaviors based on his current middle-school placement. However, in less than two months he will be moving into a high school situation with a different ecology. To ensure more long-term success, Juan's teachers are also examining the expectations and levels of social behavior performance that will be required when he enters high school.

Educational. Assessing success from an educational perspective focuses attention on the criteria established for the behaviors of the general population of the school or institution. These criteria have usually been installed to maintain the smooth operation of the classroom and school, to standardize the implementation of the school's behavior management programs, and to reinforce the expectations of the larger community or society. For example, at Washington School, teachers and students have established four building expectations: (a) they must be respectful to others, (b) cooperate with others, (c) behave in a legal and healthy manner, and (d) manage themselves. The school's discipline handbook is written to reinforce these goals, and schoolwide rules and classroom routines are based on these expectations. Levels of appropriate and inappropriate behaviors are specified. For example, each student is allowed two unexcused tardies each school year before a note is sent home. When five or more unexcused tardies occur, a parent conference is requested. In addition, whenever a student has one, two, and three months of perfect attendance, he or she receives a certificate of recognition, and a letter of commendation is sent to the parents.

Evaluating program success from an educational perspective is important when considering the appropriateness of a current placement or preparing for a student's return to least-restrictive settings. An intervention might be effective empirically, but the level of change might be insufficient from a classroom or school perspective. For example, before an individualized program was initiated, Marcos attended school approximately five out of every ten school days. After the program was in place for a month, Marcos's attendance improved by 50%; that is, he was attending seven out of every ten school days. From an empirical perspective, Miss Stillman considers the attendance program a success; however, from an educational standpoint, Marcos's progress remains below the acceptable criteria established for all students in the school.

Evaluating intervention success from an educational perspective is also related to the extent to which the change in the target behavior is approaching or reaching the criteria specified in the student's behavioral objective. In cases where an individual education plan (IEP) (or learning contract) is written for a student, teachers and consultants have set specifically defined goals to evaluate the size and quality of the change in behavior and the effectiveness of an intervention. For example, Theora's IEP has eight social behavior objectives and goals. Every six weeks, her teacher and a consultant evaluate her total intervention program against the criteria specified in the IEP.

Social. Assessing intervention success from a social perspective focuses on how key elements of an intervention program are evaluated by individuals who are directly affected by the student's problem behaviors (Kazdin, 1977; Wolf, 1978). Teachers, parents, administrators, and peers assess the appropriateness of (a) program goals, (b) the intervention choice, (c) the features of the intervention, and (d) the size and quality of the change in the student's behavior. The worth or acceptability of these intervention aspects can also be considered by the student who is involved in the selection and development of interventions.

Social evaluations of behavioral objectives and intervention procedures enable consultants and teachers to (a) judge what individuals consider acceptable, (b) secure a level of quality control and protection of student/human rights, (c) obtain an indirect endorsement from others, (d) expand the level of participation by relevant others in the student's environment, and (e) provide a subjective baseline against which progress and goal achievement can be assessed.

Although actual changes in the size of the behavior might be empirically or educationally significant, subjective evaluations are required to determine whether individuals consider an intervention program and its effects useful. For example, Tomas's use of swear words during a 15-minute recess has been reduced from five per minute to two per minute; however, adults and children still find two swear words per minute intolerable.

In addition, because of the intrusiveness of their behavior or the development of notorious reputations, some students must achieve levels of behavior that exceed those displayed by their peers (normative perspective) or established by the classroom or school (educational perspective). For example, before a consultant and her teacher developed a special token economy and response-cost program, Myounghee spent nearly 50% of the school day wandering through the hallways and disrupting classroom activities. After a month with the new program, she has learned to stay in her assigned classrooms. Occasionally, she must be in the halls, but she is careful to obtain a hall pass. Despite this improvement in behavior, teachers automatically assume that she does not have a hall pass and that she is engaged in unacceptable behavior. They frequently stop her in the hall, tell her that she should not be without a pass, and warn her not to spend too much time out of class. Even though she meets the school's expectations, Myounghee has learned that she must demonstrate levels of behaviors that exceed those her peers display.

Involving the student in intervention implementation is an important aspect of social validation. Teachers and consultants can discover if useful targets have been selected, if effective reinforcers are being used, and if the student considers the change in behavior as significant. In addition, obtaining social validation data from students can increase their "investment" in the intervention by highlighting relevant features and more important, facilitate the shift from teacher-directed to student-directed interventions through self-assessment and self-reinforcement.

Methods of Evaluating Success

Before a change procedure is initiated, consultants and teachers should determine how they will evaluate intervention effectiveness. At minimum, consultants and teachers should select evaluation methods that enable meaningful (reliable and valid) comparisons and systematic data analyses. To facilitate the evaluation of intervention effectiveness, they can use visual analysis procedures, formative data decision making, and summative evaluation outcomes.

Visual analysis procedures.   Although statistical approaches, such as *t* tests and chi squares, are useful for determining empirical validity, visual analysis procedures are more practical in classroom contexts. Tawney and Gast (1984) indicate that visual analysis procedures are advantageous because they (a) can be used with groups of students as well as individuals, (b) emphasize the use of continuous data collection procedures, (c) permit teachers to make systematic data-based decisions on an ongoing basis, (d) focus attention on behavior patterns rather than qualitative factors (like feelings, emotions, or opinions), (e) facilitate an individualized approach to behavior change and consultation, and (f) provide a basis for analyzing possible functional relationships between the intervention (independent variable) and the target behavior (dependent variable).

For these reasons, we recommend that consultants and teachers be fluent with these procedures. However, to be useful, consultants and teachers must collect and present direct observation data on an ongoing basis whenever possible (see Chapter 4). Visual analysis is possible when a graphic presentation of a student's performance includes (a) labeled phases and axes, (b) a descriptive title (student, dependent and independent variable), and (c) a legend when more than one behavior is displayed.

The visual analysis of graphic data consists of the systematic examination of three data patterns: trend, level, and stability. These patterns are inspected within and between phases. Therefore, the consultant and the teacher look at six different visual analysis inspection points (see Figure 7.9), that is, trend, level, and stability patterns, and changes within and between phases.

Trend refers to the direction or slope of the data series; that is, "the steepness of the data path across time" (Tawney & Gast, 1984, p. 162). It is usually described as increasing, decreasing, or flat; that is, it describes the trend in the student's behavior—about the same, worse, or better. Level refers to the magnitude or quantity of the data and is described in terms of the scaling used on the ordinate

FIGURE 7.9
Visual-analysis inspection points

	Data Pattern		
	Trend	Level	Variability
Within a Phase	1	2	3
Between Phases	4	5	6

or *y* axis. Variability refers to the amount of stability seen in a data series. The more variability, or instability, the more difficult it is to discern trend or level; in turn, it is more difficult to make predictions about future performance and to evaluate the effectiveness of an intervention.

For example, in Figure 7.10, Sydney's peer interactions are displayed under two phases or conditions—that is, six days of baseline and seven days of social skills instruction. In this example, the following *within-phase patterns* are noted: (a) during the baseline, the negative peer interaction trend is increasing, low stability is apparent in positive peer interactions, and no level changes are apparent in negative and positive peer interactions, and (b) during the social skills instruction phase, positive peer interactions initially indicate an increasing trend, then change to a decreasing trend; a level change (low to high) is indicated in the number of negative peer interactions. After the baseline is discontinued and social skills instruction is initiated, the following *between-phase changes* are noted: (a) high-to-low level and increasing-to-flat trend changes in negative peer interactions and (b) high instability to low variability in positive peer interactions. A summary of these data pattern descriptions is given in Figure 7.11.

By engaging in a systematic analysis of data patterns within and between phases or conditions, consultants and teachers can increase the objectivity and accuracy of their evaluations. However, as the variability in a data series increases, it becomes more difficult to discern trend and level changes, and many different interpretations may result. Lines of progress are visual aids that summarize the student's behavioral progress and increase the teacher's and consultant's ability to predict performance. By drawing a trend line through a data series, it is possible to facilitate visual analysis

F I G U R E   7.10

Effect of social skills instruction on Sydney's peer interactions

FIGURE 7.11

Data pattern descriptions for Sydney's social skills instruction program

Data Pattern

	Trend	Level	Variability
Within Baseline Phase	Increasing negative peer interaction	None	High in positive peer interactions
Within Intervention Phase	Increasing positive peer interactions, then decreasing	Low to high in negative peer interactions	None
Between Baseline and Intervention Phases	Increasing to flat in negative peer interactions	High to low in negative peer interactions	High to low in positive peer interactions

of data. To illustrate how trend lines increase analysis information, data series with and without trend lines are shown in Figure 7.12.

A trend line can be drawn through a data series freehand by "eyeballing" the data and estimating what kind of line would best describe the series. Although this method is relatively easy to use, it can produce unreliable outcomes. White and Haring (1980) have developed a method that, with a small amount of practice, can produce a more accurate estimate of data trend. The *split middle line of trend estimation* makes it possible to describe and predict the direction of a student's data. Using the split-middle line, a teacher can tell whether a student is getting worse, better, or staying about the same, and can make a safe estimation of what the student will do in the next few days if similar instruction conditions are maintained.

Split-middle lines of trend estimation are useful for several reasons. First, simply looking at graphed data is an inaccurate means of describing and predicting the direction of the data. Second, the split-middle line will assist in determining when and whether the students will reach a given criterion. Finally, it allows for an immediate prediction of how a student will perform in the next few days, given that instructional conditions do not change.

Drawing the split-middle line is a simple procedure that can be mastered with a little practice. The steps are as follows:

STEP 1: Plot the data (preferably on semilogarithmic graph paper).
STEP 2: Count the number of data points in the series.
STEP 3: Draw a vertical line that divides the number of data points into two equal halves. If there are an odd number of points, the line will be drawn through a data point.
STEP 4: For each equal set of data points (each half) from step 3, calculate the *middate*. Follow directions for step 3.

FIGURE 7.12

Data patterns with and without trend lines

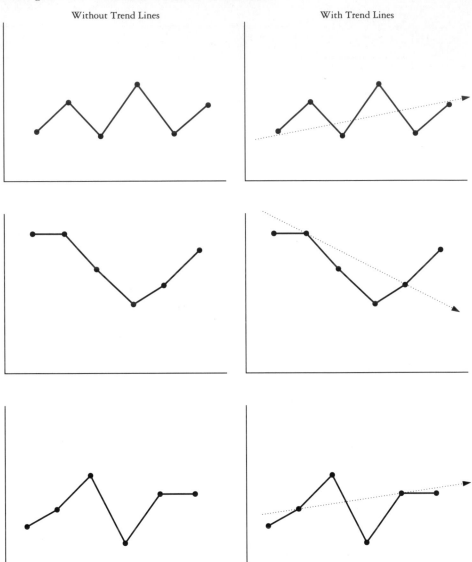

Without Trend Lines   With Trend Lines

STEP 5: For each equal set of data points (each half) from step 3, calculate the *midrate*. Counting from the bottom up, draw a horizontal hash mark through the *middle* point.

STEP 6: Draw a straight line that connects and passes through the two points of intersection between the vertical and horizontal lines for each half.

STEP 7: Draw a line parallel to the line from step 6 that has 50% of the data points on or above it, and 50% of the data points on or below it. This line is the split-middle line of trend estimation.

FIGURE 7.13

Steps for drawing the split-middle line of trend estimation

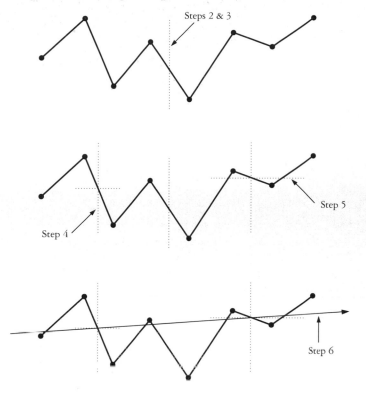

These steps are illustrated in Figure 7.13; completed trend lines are shown in Figure 7.14.

Consultants and teachers can use split-middle trend lines to summarize a student's performance data. They also provide an estimation of the direction of the student's performance if no changes are made in the current conditions. The following guidelines should be followed when using split-middle trend lines:

1. Avoid using less than five data points to draw a split-middle trend line. Ideally, seven or more data points should be used.
2. Predictions about future performance should not be made for more days than the number of data points used to draw the trend line. For example, if six data points are used to draw a trend line, do not predict future performance more than six days ahead.

Formative data decision making. At all stages of the consultation process, we have emphasized the formative collection of data. Although it is extremely important, having the data is only a small aspect of evaluating intervention effectiveness. In addition to data collection, teachers and consultants must have a systematic, accountable way of using the data as they are being collected and after

FIGURE 7.14

Completed trend lines

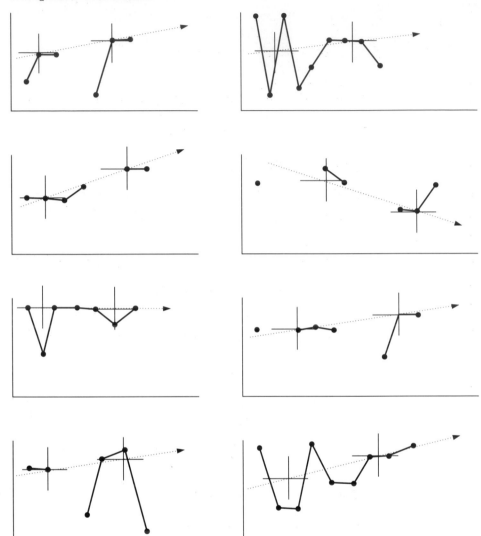

they have been graphed. Once a structured decision-making model is in place, intervention modifications and program adjustments can be identified.

A useful method of structuring the decision-making process, as student performance data are being collected, involves the use of "minimum celeration lines" (White & Haring, 1980). Minimum celeration lines are also called *aim lines* and consist of a start mark and an aim star. The "start mark" is a point that summarizes the student's current level of performance and serves as the beginning of the aim line. The "aim star" is a point that represents the expected or required level of performance. It is composed of two criteria: the level of expected performance (such as 90% of opportunities, 150 words per minute, 5 handraises per hour) and the interval of time within which the expected level of performance must be achieved. An aim line is drawn by connecting the start mark and the aim star. Aim lines are similar to trend lines in that they provide a visual picture; however, aim lines are used as a line of comparison for evaluating student performance and for predicting the likelihood of the student reaching the criterion specified in a behavioral objective (or classroom or school rules). Aim lines are used in combination with trend lines; that is, actual student progress or performance (trend line) is evaluated against desired progress rates (aim lines).

Like split-middle lines of trend estimation, aim lines are easy to draw in four basic steps:

STEP 1: Plot the data (preferably on semilogarithmic graph paper).

STEP 2: Draw a *start mark*.
  a. Use the last three data days (or collect and plot three consecutive data days).
  b. Draw a vertical line at the *middate* of these three data days.
  c. Draw horizontal line at the *midrate* of these three data days.

STEP 3: Draw an *aim star*.
  a. Determine the target behavior aim rate from the criterion of the behavioral objective (or other comparison source).
  b. Determine the target behavior aim date (that is, when the behavior objective should be reached).
  c. Draw an aim star at the intersection of the aim rate and aim date. Use it for the target behaviors to be increased and the deceleration target behaviors.

STEP 4: Draw the *aim line* by connecting the aim star to the start mark with a straight line.

The above steps are illustrated in Figure 7.15; completed aim lines are shown in Figure 7.16.

When using aim lines, data decision rules must be specified (White & Haring, 1980). Decision rules are specifically defined "procedures by which users sequentially apply specific information to select a solution to a particular problem" (Liberty & Haring, 1990, p. 32). These rules give guidelines for making instructional decisions. A useful rule of thumb is, "If student performance fails to meet a minimum celeration (that is, criterion) for three consecutive data days, the intervention procedures should be evaluated and, if appropriate, modified." When the data decision rule is broken, the teacher or consultant should draw a trend through the data series to determine if the student's performance will reach the aim star within the time remaining. In Figure 7.17, two illustrations are provided. Example A shows an intervention data pattern in which the data decision rule has not been broken. In this case, the intervention should be continued as planned. In Example B, the three-consecutive-data-day decision rule has been broken; that is, there are three consecutive days below the aim line for an acceleration aim star. The teacher should draw a split-middle line to determine if the aim star is achievable in the remaining number of days. If it is, the intervention should be continued with close, daily monitoring. If it is not, an error analysis should be conducted and the intervention modified. In Example B, the data decision rule has been broken, and

FIGURE 7.15

Steps for drawing aim lines

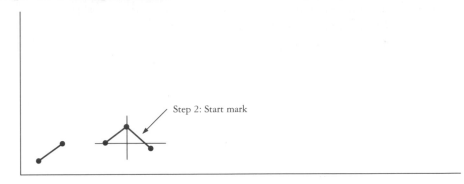

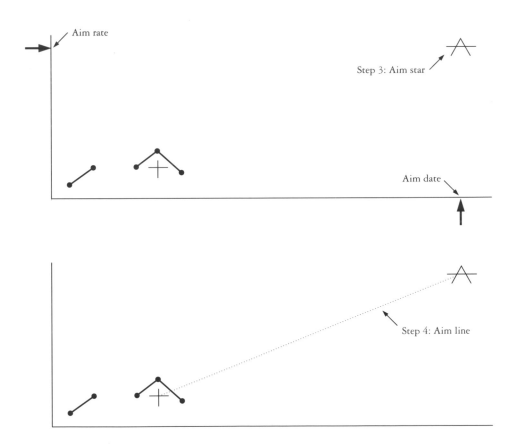

the trend line shows that the student will not meet the aim star within the time available.

When a data decision rule is broken and an intervention change is needed, teachers and consultants may consider two main types of modifications. First, they could change some operating feature of the intervention program, such as using

FIGURE 7.16

Completed aim lines

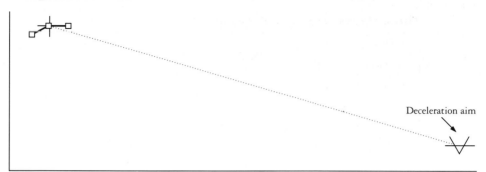

Deceleration aim

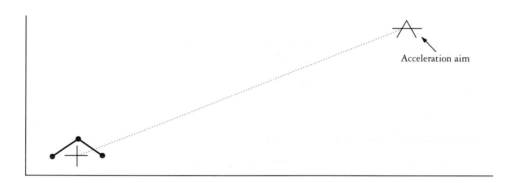

Acceleration aim

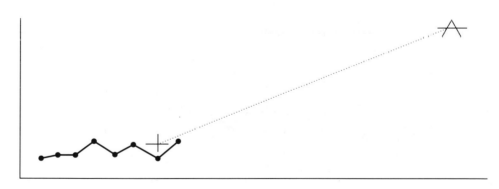

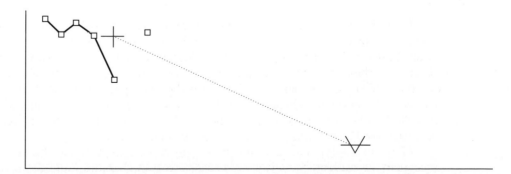

F I G U R E   7.17

Three consecutive data decision rules

Example A

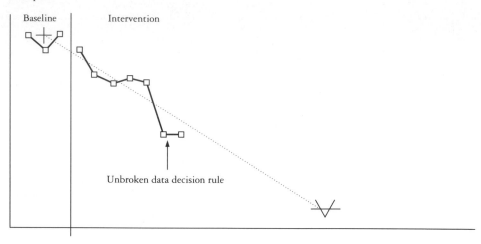

Example B

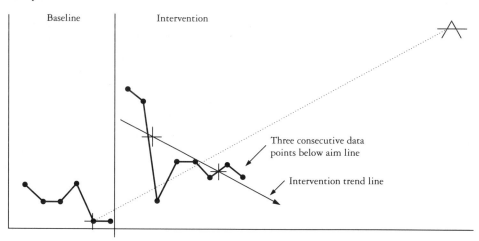

a different reinforcer, adding a response cost contingency, spending more time in social skills instruction, or incorporating a different peer manager. Second, they could adjust the criteria for acceptable performance; that is, they could move the position of the aim star by adding more time or setting a more achievable rate or level of performance. Regardless of the decision, a new phase line should be drawn to show the program change. Both the intervention and the aim star can be modified. In Figure 7.18, Example A shows a decision to change the intervention, and Example B illustrates a change in the aim star.

All the examples described thus far require a program modification because a change in the student's behavior was unsatisfactory. A change should also be made

FIGURE 7.18

Broken data decision rules and adjustment in the intervention (Example A) and in the aim star (Example B)

Example A

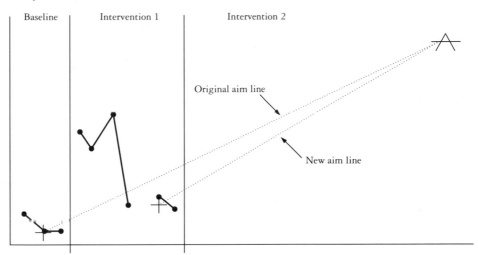

Example B

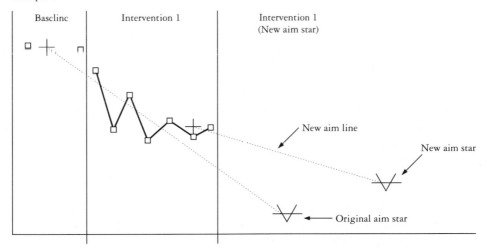

when the student achieves the criterion from the behavior objective. For example, Sammy Kay's behavior objective is stated, "Given a peer or adult conflict situation between 9:00 and 10:00 a.m., Sammy Kay will solve the problem appropriately in 80% of the opportunities for three consecutive days." Figure 7.19 shows that Sammy Kay has achieved the criterion specified in his behavioral objective before the aim star date. His teacher changes the intervention to a maintenance program; that is, to a more intermittent schedule of reminders and positive reinforcement. She draws a phase line to show the program change, and maintains the aim line.

FIGURE 7.19

Change in the intervention program after the aim star has reached

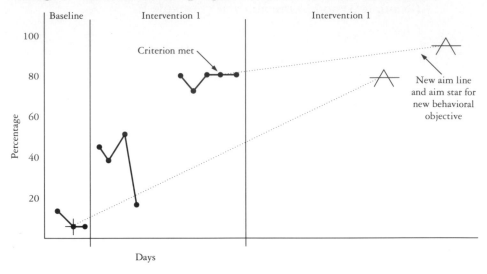

Days

Trend lines, data decision rules, aim stars, and aim lines are useful tools that help teachers and consultants monitor their student's performance on a formative basis and systematically evaluate the effectiveness of their intervention programs. The flow chart in Figure 7.20 summarizes the major decisions and outcomes associated with this data-based approach to program evaluation.

Summative evaluation outcomes. Thus far, we have discussed methods and guidelines for assessing the student's progress on a formative basis—that is, on an ongoing or continuous basis. We emphasized the modification of a program if progress toward the student's behavioral objective is unsatisfactory or if the student achieves the level of performance stipulated in the objective. Next we consider two summative outcomes: to continue the current educational placement or to request specialized assistance.

Teachers and consultants may choose to continue a student's educational placement for several reasons. The first reason is if the behavioral objective still has not been achieved but progress is adequate (current data patterns indicate that the aim star will be reached in the time allocated). For example, Candi is learning how to initiate and maintain appropriate conversations with her peers. Although she has not met her long-term objective of 80% of the conversation opportunities, an assessment of her performance (trend line) suggests that she will achieve her criterion on or before the date set for her aim star. Her teacher decides to maintain her placement in the regular third-grade classroom.

Second, if students achieve their behavioral objectives, teachers and consultants can decide to set new behavioral objectives that will allow them to be more successful in their current placement and prepare them for transitions to new settings. For example, Mario met his long-term objective well before his aim star date. Using a self-recording card, he learned to arrive to his classes on time and be

FIGURE 7.20

Major decisions and outcomes associated with data-based approach to program evaluation

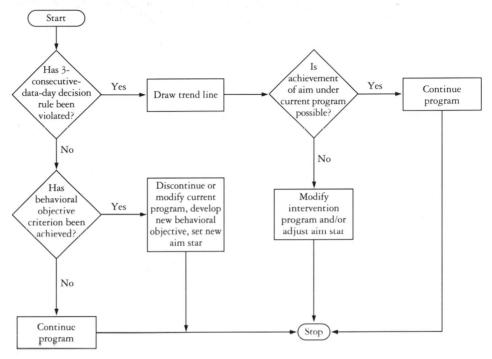

prepared with the schoolwork he needs for a given period. His teacher, however, decides that he should continue with his combined regular and special education placement until he can function successfully without a self-recording card; therefore, she writes a new behavioral objective to reflect his performance without prompts or intervention.

Finally, if the student's performance breaks the data decision rule (there is inadequate progress), consultants and teachers can decide to change the behavioral objective, aim star, or intervention. For example, using a three-consecutive-day rule, Mr. Tilly discovers that Carmelita's progress toward her behavioral objective is inadequate and that she will not reach it in the time allocated. Since only one intervention has been tried, Mr. Tilly decides to select an alternative intervention and determine if he can improve Carmelita's progress toward her behavioral objective before requesting specialized assistance or a change in educational placement. The school district requires Mr. Tilly to document at least two unsuccessful intervention attempts before requesting a change of placement or specialized assistance.

Teachers and consultants might ask for a change in specialized assistance for a number of reasons. First, if the student has met his or her objective, they may decide to reduce the amount of specialized assistance. For example, the student might be moved to less restrictive settings, individualized intervention programs might be removed, or consultation might be reduced or discontinued. Second, specialized assistance might be enhanced if the student's progress is unacceptable. For instance, the schedule might be changed, a referral for special education might be initiated, a more intrusive intervention might be developed, or a more restrictive setting might be scheduled. Whatever the reason for a change in specialized assistance, consultants should carefully assess the student's behaviors, the environment in which the behaviors are observed, and significant antecedent and consequent events to determine the specific kind and extent of change required.

These changes are the result of a summative evaluation of a student's progress and the teacher and the consultant's intervention plan. Summative decision making usually takes place at significant points in the academic or calendar year. For example, Ms. Monticello is a district consultant who conducts summative program reviews with each of the teachers in her caseload. These reviews occur at the middle and the end of each semester. Ms. Monticello works with each teacher to answer the following kinds of questions: (a) Are the current goals appropriate? (b) Are the intervention strategies acceptable and are they producing the desired effects? (c) Are the sizes of treatment effects sufficient? (d) Are interactions between the target student and his or her peers and adults more appropriate? and (e) Are additional assessments required? Answers to these summative-type questions help the teacher and the consultant determine if the current educational placement is appropriate, needs to be modified, or should be changed.

TERMINATING THE CONSULTATION

One of the most satisfying, and reinforcing, outcomes of a consultation activity is solving an educational problem and achieving a behavioral objective; that is, when the student's performance reaches the desired rate (aim star) by the desired date. This accomplishment is especially significant when educationally *and* socially important changes are observed in *both* the student's and the teacher's behaviors. When this occurs, consultants and teachers can set a new behavioral objective or change some aspect of the intervention program and begin developing a plan to terminate the program. Teachers and consultants must determine if students have achieved a level of functioning that causes them to appear and function like their peers or to levels expected by relevant adults.

As soon as the student's progress or rate of change is acceptable and the teacher begins to function successfully and independently, the consultant should immediately begin to reduce the consultation relationship. To assist the consultant in the termination process, we discuss two guideline topics: when to terminate consultation relationships and procedures for terminating the relationships.

When to Terminate Consultation

Determining when to end a successful consultation relationship is a challenge for many consultants. They must determine whether the teachers can maintain the new or improved skills over time, under changing conditions, and with different students. Unfortunately, consultants' decisions to terminate their working relationships with teachers are often based on indirect, subjective criteria, such as what the teachers tell the consultants, their own increased caseload, indications of improvement in the student's behaviors, or a successful implementation of a specific teacher-student intervention. These indicators may not be dependable if they do not focus on the conditions under which the newly acquired or mastered skills are being maintained or supported. When trying to determine the opportune time or conditions to terminate these relationships, consultants must consider factors that affect the occurrence and maintenance of the teacher's behaviors.

In addition, teachers must learn to respond to similar problem situations or to new ones without the consultant's support or assistance. For the consultant, this problem is exactly the same as the one teachers face when they remove an intervention after a student acquires a new skill. The difference is that consultants must concern themselves with the teacher's behavior, not the student's. If we analyze this situation carefully, we see that the problem is how to maintain teacher behavior under extinction (that is, nonreinforcement) or even under aversive conditions.

A teacher-student example and a teacher-consultant example illustrate this situation. By using behavioral contracts and self-recording sheets, Mr. Martinez is successful in reducing Alexis's physical aggression and increasing her cooperative play with peers. However, whenever he attempts to discontinue the use of the contracts and self-recording sheets, Alexis's behaviors worsen. In other words, when the interventions are withdrawn (when extinction conditions are created), the achieved behavior changes do not maintain. A similar set of circumstances are observed in the teacher-consultant example. Ms. Stillman has been using the Intervention Planning Sheets and biweekly meetings to help Mr. Tao improve the bus-riding behaviors of five boys on his morning route. Mr. Tao is very conscientious about calling Ms. Stillman every Thursday morning to give a report on the effectiveness of the program they have developed, and Ms. Stillman is careful to praise Mr. Tao positively and explicitly. Unfortunately, whenever she withdraws her weekly consultation assistance and intervention debriefing meetings, Mr. Tao fails to implement his interventions accurately and fluently. Again, when the consultant's assistance is withdrawn (when extinction conditions are created), the achieved skills do not maintain. Both Mr. Martinez and Ms. Stillman are unable to terminate their involvement because the recipients of their services do not maintain the gains they have achieved.

Successful consultation termination and follow-up are a problem of how to achieve successful response compliance or maintenance. Thus, when consultants plan to terminate a consultation relationship with a teacher, they should assess several possible testable explanations that might account for response maintenance failure. Each of these explanations can serve as the basis for building a termination plan or strategy.

First, artificial reinforcers are maintaining the teacher's behaviors. In our example, Ms. Stillman was providing the reinforcers (regular meetings, verbal praise, positive conversations) that were maintaining Mr. Tao's teaching behaviors. "Natural" reinforcers were not available, strong enough, or learned to maintain his behaviors. Examples of natural reinforcers that must become conditioned (learned) reinforcers for the teacher's behaviors include (a) positive or desirable changes in the student's behaviors, (b) successful achievement of a behavioral objective, (c) social validation from relevant others (such as teaching peers, administrators, parents), and (d) successful and generalized use of a new strategy.

Second, the schedule of reinforcement provided by the consultant or the natural environment fails to approximate a more intermittent schedule found in the natural environment. Like student behavior, teacher behavior that has been learned under a rich or relatively continuous schedule of reinforcement will not maintain when reinforcement is removed; that is, the behavior is not under the control of a schedule of reinforcement or feedback that approximates the schedule found in the natural environment. In our illustration, Ms. Stillman provides Mr. Tao with feedback on a regular weekly schedule. Most teachers in Mr. Tao's building receive feedback about their teaching behaviors on a highly intermittent, infrequent basis (about once every three months). The discrepancy between the two feedback schedules is extremely large.

Finally, the teacher's new skills or strategies require more effort, energy, and time than is possible in the normal classroom context. Mr. Tao is not likely to continue an intervention that requires continuous data collection, hourly student progress checks, the provision of high rates of positive reinforcement to students, and daily monitoring and evaluation of student progress reports. Similarly, a teacher is not likely to maintain an intervention program that is not usable across a variety of student behaviors and settings.

These explanations for unsuccessful attempts to terminate consultation relationships serve as the basis for determining when there is a greater likelihood of a productive termination. Consultants should consider the following questions when judging whether to terminate the relationship:

1. Are the teacher's behaviors being maintained by natural reinforcers, such as student progress or goal acquisition, positive feedback from relevant others, or successful generalized use of a strategy?
2. Are the teacher's behaviors being maintained by an intermittent schedule of reinforcement that approximates the frequency of feedback observed in the natural environment?
3. Are the teacher's behaviors easily implemented within the natural instructional environment?

Another useful way of structuring the consultation termination determination is by phrasing questions that are based on phases of learning (White & Haring, 1980) and focused on the teacher's behaviors or skills: Has the teacher demonstrated the following:

1. High levels of accuracy (acquisition)?
2. Accurate and proficient rates of performance (fluency)?
3. Accurate and fluent rates of desired behavior over time when the intervention contingencies have been completely removed (maintenance)?
4. Accurate and fluent rates of desired behavior across settings that are independent of intervention assistance where and when appropriate (generalization)?

5. Appropriate, accurate, and fluent variations of the desired behavior when setting conditions or contexts are varied (adaptation)?

Predicting successful termination of the consultation focuses on the assessment of teacher compliance and noncompliance. Consultants must answer the question, "Will the teacher's behaviors or skills maintain and generalize when consultation is removed?" To answer this question, it is helpful to determine what useful and interfering behaviors are displayed by the teacher and what is maintaining (reinforcing) and punishing these behaviors? Therefore, by looking at the actual behaviors displayed by teachers and the conditions under which the behaviors are observed, and by developing termination strategies based on answers to these questions, consultants may increase the probability that teacher skills and student gains will be maintained after they terminate their working relationships with teachers.

Procedures for Terminating Consultation

After carefully assessing the conditions under which teacher behaviors are being maintained, consultants can develop procedures for terminating the consultation relationships. Many of these procedures parallel the strategies teachers used to achieve response maintenance and generalized responding from students. We discuss two sets of guidelines: teacher/classroom-level strategies and systems-level strategies.

Teacher/classroom-level strategies. The following teacher/classroom-level strategies focus on what the consultant can do with the teacher to facilitate the successful termination of a consultation relationship:

1. Transfer assessment and intervention skills directly to the teacher. By putting themselves into a position in which they implement all or part of an intervention, consultants strengthen their direct association with successful student gains and remove opportunities for teachers to enhance their own skill levels. Consultants should work toward increasing the teacher's skills so they can prevent and/or respond more effectively to similar student problems in the future (Gutkin & Curtis, 1982).
2. Rather than intervening directly, use remedial problem-solving services to help teachers solve presenting problems. Consultants should strive to provide working relationships that enable teachers to assess and solve their own problems.
3. Initially, to ensure skill acquisition and fluency, reinforce teacher implementation behaviors immediately and continuously. Teachers must demonstrate high accuracy in the implementation of a newly acquired skill to minimize the probability of failure and to maximize access to natural reinforcers (that is, a positive change in student performance).
4. As soon as teacher skill implementation is accurate and fluent (for example, when a specific data decision rule is achieved), systematically make feedback more delayed and intermittent. Try to approximate the existing

natural positive feedback schedules. In addition, consultants can decrease the predictability of their contacts with teachers.

5. Arrange for the use of natural reinforcers when the teacher demonstrates accurate, fluent skill implementation. Consultants directly should pair social reinforcers, like verbal praise, and professional recognition with natural consequences associated with successful skill implementation, such as improved student performance or peer approval. Consultants may also need to inform teaching peers and administrators of the teachers' intervention successes to enhance the likelihood of positive peer feedback and administrator attention. Teachers can also be asked to describe ways they can share their teaching successes.

6. Reinforce skill maintenance and generalization. Initially, natural positive consequences may not be immediate or strong enough, so consultants should provide specific, meaningful positive reinforcement when they observe the teacher's maintained and generalized use of a newly acquired skill.

7. When teaching a new intervention strategy, provide multiple examples of intervention variations (that is, teach the general case). Like students, if teachers can acquire a general case use of an intervention, the probability of generalized use of the skill across students, settings, or problem contexts can be increased.

8. Teach teachers how to self-manage their use, evaluation, and modification of intervention strategies. The more successful teachers can be in solving new problem situations independently, the greater the probability of a successfully terminating the consultation.

9. Develop a systematic plan for reducing consultation engagement. Like student behavior interventions, a "train and hope" approach is not likely to succeed. A specific plan for consultation termination should include specific termination goals and objectives, data decision rules for structured evaluations, and a clearly specified timeline for fading engagements.

Systems-level strategies.   In the previous section, we focused on what the consultant can do directly with the teacher to increase the probability of successful termination of a consultation relationship. At the systems (program, school, district) level, consultants can enhance their effectiveness by engaging in practices that increase accountability and leave consultation participants with histories of positive consultation experiences:

1. Leave a "paper trail." Maintain and leave a copy of everything that was produced or became part of a consultation. Complete records increase accountability, give teachers someplace to look for answers rather than contacting the consultant, and function as effective communication devices with others.

2. Provide teachers with specific conditions under which they should contact the consultant. Leave them with alternative problem-solving strategies, such as referral to previous paperwork or talking with a peer.

3. Before engaging in a consultation, inform teachers and building administrators of the procedures for terminating a consultation relationship.

4. Provide positive feedback or reinforcement for teachers, especially through their supervisors.

5. Establish an increasing intermittent schedule for follow-up meetings and telephone calls.

SUMMARY

The purpose of this chapter was to discuss strategies for (a) implementing and monitoring intervention plans, (b) assessing and evaluating consultation success, and (c) discontinuing a consultation relationship. The following points were emphasized:

1. Inadequate intervention implementation or no implementation and decreased implementation accuracy are the two basic problems facing consultants when monitoring teacher implementation of intervention plans.

2. Initial assessments must be conducted immediately to avoid early procedural errors and on a regular schedule thereafter to monitor teacher implementation of an intervention plan.

3. Whenever possible, consultants should conduct direct observations to identify variables that contribute to implementation errors or failures.

4. An analysis of the degree and accuracy with which the teacher is following an intervention plan is called procedural reliability. High levels (over 90%) are desirable.

5. Conducting a functional analysis is a useful way of directly observing how teachers implement the intervention plan.

6. To maximize initially high intervention accuracy and avoid early procedural errors, consultants should ensure that teachers are accurate and fluent at using a procedure before they implement it.

7. Specific prompting, coaching, practice, and reinforcement strategies should be used to assist teacher implementation of intervention plans.

8. Success or intervention effectiveness can be assessed from a variety of perspectives: (a) empirical, (b) normative, (c) educational, and (d) social.

9. Single-subject designs provide useful structures for determining empirical effectiveness.

10. Social validity focuses on how teachers, parents, administrators, and peers view the key elements of an intervention plan.

11. Educational validity refers to the criteria established for the behaviors of the general population of the school or institution.

12. At minimum, consultants and teachers should select evaluation methods that will enable meaningful (reliable and valid) comparisons and systematic data analyses.

13. Useful methods of evaluating intervention success include visual analysis procedures, formative data decision making, and summative evaluation outcomes.

14. To terminate a consultation relationship with teachers, consultants must assess the conditions under which discontinuing a consultation will be successful and use strategies that increase teacher maintenance and generalization of acquired skills.

REFERENCES

BILLINGSLEY, F. F., WHITE, O. R., & MUNSON, R. (1980). Procedural reliability: A rationale and an example. *Behavioral Assessment, 2,* 229–241.

GUTKIN, T. B. & CURTIS, M. J. (1982). School based consultation: Theory and techniques. In C. R. Reynolds & T. B. Gutkin (eds.), *The handbook of school psychology* (pp. 796–828). New York: Wiley.

KAZDIN, A. W. (1977). Assessing the clinical or applied significance of behavior change through social validation. *Behavior Modification, 1,* 427–452.

LIBERTY, K. A., & HARING, N. G. (1990). Introduction to decision rule systems. *Remedial and Special Education, 11*(1), 32–41.

PETERSON, L., HOMER, A. L., & WONDERLICH, S. A. (1982). The integrity of independent variables in behavior analysis. *Journal of Applied Behavior Analysis, 15,* 477–492.

TAWNEY, J. W., & GAST, D. L. (1984). *Single subject research in special education.* Columbus, OH: Merrill.

WHITE, O., & HARING, N. G. (1980). *Exceptional teaching* (2nd ed.). Columbus, OH: Merrill.

WOLF, M. M. (1978). Social validity: The case for subjective measurement or how applied behavior analysis is finding its heart. *Journal of Applied Behavior Analysis, 11,* 203–214.

PART III

ANALYSIS OF INSTRUCTION

CHAPTER EIGHT

What to Teach

Mr. Hagerty teaches seventh-grade social studies and is experiencing difficulty in managing the academic and social behaviors of his students. He reports that one of his students, Mike, is "rowdy and boisterous." Mike talks to others during lectures, his homework is incomplete and incorrect, he rarely stays focused on the appropriate topic during class discussions, and he shows little interest in learning anything new. After five weeks, Mr. Hagerty is frustrated because he has run out of solutions. As a last resort, he contacts Ms. Kimo, the building resource consultant, and completes a Request for Assistance (see Figure 8.1).

After reviewing the Request for Assistance, Ms. Kimo visits Mr. Hagerty to collect information in order to define the problem more clearly (see Figure 8.2 for the completed Problem Identification Interview form). When she asks about his curriculum, Mr. Hagerty shows her a social studies lesson and text about "North Africa Today" (Patton, Rengert, Saveland, Cooper, & Caro, 1985, pp. 259–260), part of a larger unit on "Countries on the Mediterranean." The written text is the main source of the students' information. Mr. Hagerty has his pupils read the paragraphs individually and out loud, then asks individual students questions about what they have read. Near the end of the period, they complete worksheets. About every other week when the class completes a unit, Mr. Hagerty schedules a special event. For example, after the unit on Greece, a friend of one of his students' parents was invited to talk to the class about living in Athens. The class also used the library for a special five-day display of Grecian history, artifacts, and books.

However, after looking more closely at the content of the unit and Mr. Hagerty's teaching activities and behaviors, Ms. Kimo noticed several serious instructional limitations that could explain the students' misbehavior. For example, she noticed that the lessons consisted mainly of facts that Mr. Hagerty presented in an uninteresting manner. He used few concepts and principles to bring order to the multitude of facts, and factual relationships and generalizations were missing as well. Box 8.1 contains the text of the curriculum. Notice the density of information,

FIGURE 8.1

Mr. Hagerty's Request for Assistance

REQUEST FOR ASSISTANCE FORM	Referring Person Mr. Hagerty Title Soc. Studies teacher Date 6/12/91 Student Mike Rhiman Grade 7 DOB 7/24/79 Sex: (M) F IEP: (Y) N

Check Type of Problem Behavior

Academic: ___Reading ___Math ___Spelling ___Writing ___Study Skills ✓Other social studies

Social: ___Aggressive ✓Noncompliant ___Truant ___Tardy ___Withdrawn ___Disruptive
               ___Social Skills ✓Self-Management ___Other_____

Communication: ___Language ___Fluency ___Articulation ___Voice ___Other _____

Self-Help: ___Dressing ___Hygiene ___Other_____

Health: ___Vision ___Hearing ___Physical ___Other_____

Provide Specific and Observable Description of Problem

Mike fails to participate in class and does not complete assignments.

Provide Specific Description of Problem Context

Where: Social Studies classroom

When: 9:30 – 10:17 M-F / 2nd trimester

With Whom: Mr. Hagerty – teacher

Other: _____

Provide List of Previous Remediation Attempts

1. Name on board after 3 warnings
2. Move desk
3. Threaten to flunk

FIGURE 8.2
Mr. Hagerty's Problem Identification form

PROBLEM IDENTIFICATION INTERVIEW FORM	Page 1 of 3

Consultant _Ms. Kimo_   Teacher _Mr. Hagerty_
Date _6/17/91_ School _Lower Lake Middle_

Student Information: Name _Mike Rhiman_   Room _107_
Grade _7_   Age _12_   Sex: (M) F   IEP: (Y) N

Describe the problem behavior. (5 minutes)

— In-class worksheets are incomplete; questions are left unanswered; about ½ of questions are wrong

— No participation: No working with other students, no question-answering.

Describe other behaviors that seem to be related to the problem behavior. (3 minutes)

— Engages other students inappropriately (e.g., teases, talks about sports and other school events.) when working independently

— Draws on the back of handouts and assignments

Describe the conditions under which the problem behavior is most likely to occur. (2 minutes)

When: _During seatwork (indiv. or group) and when teacher is lecturing._
Where: _Social Studies class_
With Whom: _Teachers and peers_

FIGURE 8.2 *(continued)*

PROBLEM IDENTIFICATION INTERVIEW FORM Page 2 of 3

Describe what usually happens after the problem behavior occurs. (2 minutes)

Teacher is either lecturing on content or working at his desk with individual students who are having problems with the assignment.

Describe what usually happens immediately before the problem behavior occurs. (2 minutes)

Teacher generally reminds Mike what expectations are for whole class. If Mike doesn't respond or shows inappropriate behavior, Mike is told he must stay after school to finish work.

Describe what you usually do when the behavior occurs. (2 minutes)

Repeat directions and expectations

Describe what other students do when the behavior occurs. (2 minutes)

Most ignore him, except those he engages.

FIGURE 8.2   (*continued*)

PROBLEM IDENTIFICATION INTERVIEW FORM   Page 3 of 3

Describe what you would like the student to do <u>instead</u> of the problem behavior.
(2 minutes)

Work on assignments silently. Listen to lectures and take notes, complete all questions on assignments, look up information when stuck.

List or describe <u>other interventions</u> that have been tried. (3 minutes)

Putting name on board
Moving his desk
Keeping him after school
Threatening to flunk him.

Make an appointment to conduct an observation and debriefing. (1 minute)

Date 6/14/91 Time 9:30 to 10:17 Place/Classroom _____

Other information/notes

Is earning a D; barely passing end-of-unit tests

Parents report he seldom works at home (they assume he gets his work done during study hall)

Mike is doing well in Earth Science and Health class (getting "B's" and "C's")

BOX 8.1

Mr. Hagerty's geography text

NORTH AFRICA TODAY

┌─ **VOCABULARY** ────────────────────┐
Maghreb
phosphate
└─────────────────────────────────────┘

Neighboring countries   Egypt and Libya are neighboring countries that share several traits. Both countries lie mostly in the Sahara. Arabic is the language and Islam is the religion of each country. The majority of Egyptians and Libyans are farmers. Both countries were Turkish colonies for centuries before being ruled by Europeans. The differences between the two nations, however, are much more important than these similarities.

Egypt   Egypt has more people than any other Arab nation. It has 14 times as many people as Libya, even though it is only half as large. Most of the people live on a narrow strip of land along the Nile River and its delta. Cairo, the capital of Egypt and the most populated city in Africa, is located on the Nile. Alexandria, the second most populated city in Egypt, is located on the edge of the Nile Delta.
The Nile Valley has rich soil. Most of Egypt's farmland lies along the course of the river. Cotton is Egypt's most important crop. Egypt is one of the world's leading producers of cotton. Other important crops include oranges, beans, corn, sugarcane, and wheat. Farming is Egypt's main source of income. The Nile River is Egypt's chief natural resource.
Egypt has tried to modernize, but it has many problems. There are some deposits of oil and other minerals, but these resources are not very great for a country of 46 million people. Although Egypt is an agricultural country, it has to import food. Egypt's growing cities and industries have taken over land once used for farming. It is now against the law in Egypt to put an industrial building on land that can be used for crops. Egypt imports machinery, motor vehicles, and other industrial goods, but it exports few manufactured goods. The result is that Egypt spends much more on imports than it receives from exports. The country has to borrow money to make up most of the difference.

SOURCE: C. P. Patton, A. C. Rengert, R. N. Saveland, K. S. Cooper, and P. T. Caro (1985). *The World and Its People: A World View.* Morristown, NJ: Silver Burdett Ginn.

the "dry" writing style, and the lack of integration between ideas. Also, Mr. Hagerty's manner of presenting the material (addressed in Chapter 9) lacks systematicity and does not promote active learning. Occasionally, Mr. Hagerty would tell students to "Remember that" after they read some of the text, or ask them to underline that word and say "That's important." Clearly the text dominated instruction, a practice that is not uncommon.

In contrast to previous chapters when we emphasized the role of the consultant in managing social behaviors, we now focus on how consultants can work effectively with teachers who have students with academic problems. More specifically, we focus on "what to teach." In the next chapter, we cover "how to teach." In keeping with the best-practices theme of this book, we present what we believe to be the most important knowledge and strategies for consultants to be effective in working with academic instruction problems. The consultant's challenge is to generalize the concepts, principles, and guidelines presented in this chapter to the problems they will face in their jobs.

In covering what to teach, we discuss two major topics: focusing and modifying what to teach so that low-achieving students can succeed, and teaching study skills to ensure transfer of instruction from the teacher to the students. In the first topic, six steps provide a structure for organizing the content of information. First, we emphasize instruction of basic skills, then the next four steps accent teaching structure and relationships, with the curriculum content serving as a medium for teaching that structure. In the last step, we include the topic of study skills, so students can self-manage their learning.

FOCUSING OR MODIFYING WHAT TO TEACH

Few educators would argue that the content of instruction can have a significant effect on how students learn and how they interact with the teacher and their peers. Teachers must be sure that what they teach maximizes student learning, provides a stimulating learning context, and reduces academic errors and social behavior problems. Consultants must be familiar with strategies that enable them to systematically analyze and modify any curriculum materials or instructional content.

Six steps are used to help consultants and teachers look at what is being taught. Although they are presented sequentially and described separately, consultants should view them as interrelated. They may not be equally applicable to all situations or problems and some steps may be stressed more than others, but all six steps should be considered. Finally, our discussion assumes that the consultant has been working with the teacher from the beginning of a lesson. However, consultants may be asked to provide assistance after a lesson has been initiated, thus making it difficult to complete all the steps. Or they may find it necessary to modify what is being taught and reteach from the beginning of the lesson.

The six steps are as follows:

1. Determine if students are proficient in basic skills, or "tool movements" (White & Haring, 1980), so content can be taught.
2. Determine if students are "motivated" to learn and if they have adequate background information to integrate new information.
3. Identify the major structural characteristics—story main ideas, concepts, and principles—of the materials being taught.
4. Identify the organizing principles that encompass most of the structural elements.
5. Determine if all elements—e.g., concepts and principles—are present in order to develop or support the organizing concepts and principle(s).
6. Determine if students have the requisite skills to extend learning and convey what they have learned.

In the first step, we emphasize instruction of basic skills or tool movements (Tindal & Marston, 1991) before instruction in content areas. These skills consist of basic reading, writing (including spelling), and math skills, and are considered tool movements because they function as indicators of what students are capable of doing. Generally, students must be able to execute tool movements correctly, fluently, and automatically to be successful in working with new content. We discuss the characteristics of these basic skills in Chapter 10.

In the middle four steps, we focus on expository and narrative materials in our examples, although any instructional materials can be used in either elementary or secondary settings. In Chapter 10, we distinguish between basic skills (reading, writing, spelling, and math computation), content knowledge, and procedural knowledge. Content and procedural knowledge (that is, concepts and principles) are emphasized in this chapter.

With the narrative materials, we focus on story grammar—the structural elements that appear consistently in most stories, including information descriptive of settings, time, characters, events, problems, actions, and resolutions. Whether they are fables or popular fiction, most stories have these elements.

When we cover expository material, this structure is not pertinent; rather, information takes on specific knowledge forms (that is, facts, concepts, principles, and procedures). Facts are one-to-one correspondences between events, dates, locations, names, and so on. Concepts are defined as clusters of attributes, characteristics of names, or constructs. They may be "thought of as a category of experience having a rule which defines the relevant category, a set of positive instances or exemplars with attributes and a name (although this latter element is sometimes missing)" (Martorella, 1972, p. 7). In this definition, rules provide the formulas for organizing concept attributes, which, in turn, provide the criteria for distinguishing exemplars from nonexemplars. Principles are defined as if-then or cause-effect relationships. They reflect relationships between and among different concepts or facts. Principles often reflect a dimension of time or space, in which different concepts interact in predictable ways. Finally, procedural knowledge is defined as concepts and principles that are arranged in several steps and form a hierarchy, in which prerequisite knowledge is incorporated into a problem solution, and rules are used to organize and sequence these concepts and principles. To provide continuity across the six steps, we use one primary example and several secondary examples. Although math and language arts examples could have been used, our primary examples come from reading and content areas such as science that permeate most classroom instruction.

Finally, we address a range of study skills or learning strategies that students can use to extend their amount of learning, or engaged, time. These skills focus on organization and how students work with material—for example, selecting, highlighting, sorting, and organizing data. These skills are generally applicable across content areas and help students structure information.

DETERMINING STUDENTS' BASIC SKILLS

Before content can be taught, students must have some minimum proficiency in the basic skills—reading, writing, and mathematics—that are the focus of early elementary grades. However, in middle and high school, basic skill instruction is inappropriate because of the student's age and the "developmental inappropriateness" of primary grade basals and other basic skill curricula. Although middle and high school students must become increasingly knowledgeable in content areas, direct instruction in basic skills cannot be ignored if they have not achieved reading and writing proficiency.

The following sections provide a brief analysis of the basic skills for instruction. Consultants must consider these skills when working with teachers who have students with academic problems.

Reading

Although the debate over phonics or code-based versus meaning-based programs has continued unabated for the last 30 years, no one can argue with the need for students to be skilled at decoding and breaking words into syllables (Adams, 1990). The question is how such instruction should proceed. "The ability to read does not emerge spontaneously, but through regular and active engagement with print" (Adams, 1990, p. 71). Students must learn reading building blocks (letter names, letter sounds, blends, digraphs, consonants, vowels) and how to orchestrate these building blocks smoothly and efficiently. Adams (1990) makes the following instructional recommendations:

1. Reading aloud to children regularly and interactively is probably the single most important activity for building the requisite knowledge and skills.
2. Print awareness can be accomplished easily through language experience activities.
3. Instruction in individual letter names and sounds needs to occur directly and cannot just happen accidentally through encounters with environmental print.
4. Phonemic awareness also needs to be taught directly and explicitly.
5. Printing and writing are useful activities for developing awareness of the concept of *word*.
6. Instruction should include a blend of "systematic code instruction along with the reading of meaningful connected text" (p. 125).
7. The text that children read is an important influence on their achievement.
8. Explicit instruction on blending is useful in developing the skills needed to analyze the phonemic structure of words.
9. Practice in reading is important; texts with which students are accurate (90% to 95%) need to be used for independent practice.

If consultants are working with teachers who have students with reading difficulties, the issues raised in Adam's recommendations may provide information for analyzing the problem and identifying potential solutions. Intact and proficient basic reading skills are needed for students to obtain information in content instruction. Because so much instruction is anchored to curriculum, any deficits in basic skills are likely to be compounded if the student's reading skills are inadequate as well. Content instruction must supplement, not supplant, basic reading instruction.

Writing

In many ways, writing is like reading. First, it is a complex compilation of skills that includes discrete, well-defined behaviors that can be orchestrated in a variety of ways. Second, writing has building blocks, such as letters, words, sentences, and paragraphs; yet, it results in an outcome, a composition, that is greater than any of its individual parts. Third, writing instruction can be skills and/or process oriented. We believe that consultants need to work with teachers to ensure that both aspects are present. If writing skills or behaviors are being emphasized, then instruction must also include the type of discourse (persuasive, narrative, expository, or autobiographical writing) and coherence and cohesion across the composition. If a process-oriented approach to writing instruction is taken, the mechanics of writing (letter formation, spelling, sentence structure, syntax, and grammar) must be taught directly. Finally, writing must be practiced to achieve fluency.

Math

Of the three basic skill areas, mathematics has the most discrete and hierarchically arranged set of skill components. Elementary, middle, and high school educators, as well as academicians, have defined 12 basic skill areas in math (Denmark & Kepner, 1980):

1. *Elementary computation:* Skills normally introduced in grades 1–6.
2. *Advanced computation:* Skills normally introduced in grades 5–8.
3. *Applications:* The use of mathematics in problem solving.
4. *Estimation:* Giving "ball-park" answers.
5. *Measurement:* Using English and metric systems, perimeters, areas, or volume.
6. *Algebra:* Applying formulas, solving equations, simplifying expressions.
7. *Understanding:* Describing rationale and logic for solutions or procedures.
8. *Geometry:* Construct shapes, prove theorems.
9. *Probability and statistics:* Interpret charts and graphs, make predictions.
10. *New math:* Apply set language, read/write nonbase 10 numerals.
11. *Calculator use:* To solve computational problems.
12. *Mathematics appreciations:* Incorporate math into a larger social context.

According to the National Institute of Education, the following basic math skills are also needed: (a) making linkages between mathematical ideas and physical situations, (b) drawing inferences from functions and rates of change, and (c) using computers.

Tindal and Marston (1991) note that mathematics is generally hierarchical and that students learn (a) sets (properties, notation, and operation), (b) numbers and notation, (c) operations and symbols (basic math facts), (d) properties (such as associative and distribute properties), (e) four basic operational algorithms (addition, subtraction, multiplication, and division) applied in multistep computational problems, (f) sentence solving, and (g) problem solving. Students must be accurate and fluent at any prerequisite step before moving to the next step. If consultants are working with teachers who have students with math performance difficulties, they should determine where on the hierarchy the student is functioning on an automatic (mastery) level and develop support materials and strategies for instruction on the next step.

In beginning our discussion about steps for defining what to teach, we analyzed basic skills. In elementary grade settings, consultants and teachers face many student problems that require a focus on basic skills. In middle and high school settings, basic skills instruction is often required before many students can benefit from content instruction. We believe that students must be fluent in basic skills in order to engage successfully in content area instruction. The next four steps assume that the consultant is either addressing basic skills independently or as part of a requisite supplement to content area instruction.

DETERMINING STUDENTS' MOTIVATIONS AND LEVELS OF BACKGROUND KNOWLEDGE

A major task of consulting is to conduct functional analyses and make informed judgments about controlling events (that is, reinforcers and punishers that appear to be operating in the environment). Such functional analyses need not be limited to social behavior environments; they can also be conducted within instructional environments. We can observe teachers and students interacting in academic contexts to determine what events influence interest and motivation (that is, reinforcers and aversives). We can also ascertain what information is familiar and novel.

We define student interest in terms of the amount of time spent and the kind of performance displayed when a student interacts with academic subject content. Consultants and teachers must determine if there are preferred content area activities or media and if students engage in these activities differentially. For example, if students are given free time in the library, what books do they select and how much time do they spend reading them? If they are allowed to watch different educational films, which topics do they select and how long do they watch them? Implied in these questions is an analysis of the reinforcers presented when students are engaged.

Background knowledge is more difficult to operationalize. In part, it is a function of how teachers define opportunities for students to present previously learned information; students do not tend to exhibit what they know spontaneously. Furthermore, student background knowledge can be complete, incomplete, or lacking. Opportunities to present their knowledge may not allow them to assess complete information. For example, a student can answer multiple-choice items correctly, but for all the wrong reasons.

Motivation and background knowledge are intertwined and interrelated. If the basic skills are poor, content learning may suffer. For example, if an intermediate elementary student has poorly developed reading skills and is not a fluent reader, (reading 20 to 30 words per minute), reading is probably not a highly motivating or reinforcing activity. Students' lack of fluency can affect the sources from which they access information. For example, instead of using books and printed media to gain information, a student may be more likely to listen to others or watch films and tapes. Skill levels also affect the amount and types of interactions students have with content information. Poorly developed skills are highly related to poorly developed information bases in content areas. Consultants must formally assess for and confirm relationships, rather than assume or infer their existence. Systematically assessing background information can help consultants and teachers determine high interest and motivation areas as well as the adequacy of the student's knowledge base for learning new material.

In summary, when considering student interest, we are referring to the (a) kinds of topics and activities that are reinforcing (watching films, reading articles and books, listening to others speak), and (b) the amount of engagement they exhibit. In contrast, background knowledge focuses on the student's verbal repertoire; that is, what information does the student use proficiently. In the end, student interest and background knowledge are interrelated and difficult to isolate and manipulate separately.

In assessing these two areas, we emphasize direct observation, interviews, and paper-pencil tasks. Observations help determine the existence of specific behaviors and their associated antecedents and consequent events, interviews provide access to information about environments that are less observable, and paper-and-pencil assessments document how students structure and organize information. One of the consultant's major efforts is to help teachers focus what they are teaching so that low-achieving students can learn; that is, so what they teach is reinforcing and familiar. Several assessment systems are described in the next section to help consultants define this content.

Assessing Interest

Although a number of interest inventories are commercially available, the most powerful information can be collected by conducting a functional analysis and student interview. As covered in Chapter 3, assessments should focus on observable, discrete behaviors and immediate settings and their relationships to behavior. In conducting interviews, we emphasized a structured format in which teachers report objective, descriptive information. In this section, we discuss strategies and guidelines—direct observation, interview strategies, and the assessment of background knowledge—for assessing student interest within academic contexts.

Observing academic behaviors related to interest.   In 1963, Carroll developed a model of learning that included two variables: the time spent learning and the time needed to learn. Since then, scores of studies have been conducted on time under a number of terms such as *academic learning time, engaged time, instructional time,* and others. Outcomes from these studies clearly show that the use of time is an important marker variable, highly correlated with other variables (such as the degree or amount of learning) and a powerful predictor of learning outcomes.

We also use time as an important marker variable in our definition of *motivation* or *interest*. Because interest (how much a student likes or enjoys something) is difficult to measure, we prefer the term *perseverance-in-learning-to-criterion* (PLC), which can be objectively measured. PLC refers to the amount of time a student is actively engaged in learning specific tasks or information to some criterion level. Although PLC may be affected by other influences (like "other-pleasing" behavior, contingencies of grades, or rebukes from significant others), more time engaged reflects more motivation and more learning. The most direct way to measure PLC involves determining the average duration per occurrence. This measure is calculated by starting a stopwatch when the student begins working on an instructional activity. After a prespecified minimum interval (such as two seconds), when the student disengages from the activity, the watch is stopped. This cycle is repeated until the student moves to another activity or setting. Data from such an observation system can be used to determine the (a) frequency of initiations, (b) the range and average engagement per occurrence, and (c) the total engaged time on the instructional task or activity.

We can list many examples of PLC. On some tasks, students spend hours engaged in learning to some level of criterion proficiency—for example, Nintendo and other computer games, video arcade games and pinball machines, or shooting "buckets" on a street basketball court. On other tasks, students spend as little time as possible and required—for example, drilling and practicing math facts or spelling words from lists, or diagramming sentences. Interestingly, all these tasks are similar in the repetitive nature of the required behavior, yet they differ drastically in their reinforcing value and the degree to which students are motivated to spend the time to learn.

To assess motivation, the best and simplest observation system would be to measure how long the student remains engaged in learning a task at some level of proficiency. Students who remain engaged are motivated and likely to become more proficient. For example, in a free-writing task like journal writing, students who remain engaged also tend to find writing to be more reinforcing and to be motivated to learn more about writing.

The assessment of motivation can also incorporate a functional analysis to analyze antecedent, behavior, and consequent events associated with the activity. In the writing example, when students ask questions, they may interact with teachers, assistants, or other students. Potentially effective controlling stimuli and/or reinforcers can be identified. In Ms. Kimo's functional analysis, she collected considerable information showing that Mike was not interested in the content of his social studies class (Figure 8.3).

Based on this functional analysis, the consultant sees that (a) the unit begins with a task that appears easy for all students except Mike, (b) the teacher fails to bring Mike into the lecture content, and (c) threats finally produce short-lived effects. Mike's motivation and interest to learn about the countries on the Mediterranean Sea are low. Unless salience of learning this content is increased, later efforts to ensure that learning is maintained or extended are likely to fail and/or to require considerable external supports, such as more monitoring by the teacher.

FIGURE 8.3

Functional Analysis Observation

FUNCTIONAL ANALYSIS OBSERVATION FORM	Date _6_/_14_/_91_ Time _9_:_45_ Observer __Kimo__ Student __Mike__ Teacher __Hagerty__ Classroom/School __107 / Lower Lake Middle.__

Setting Description:

Whole-class lecture on "countries of the Mediterranean."

Independent seatwork on mapping the countries

Time	Antecedents	Behaviors Mike	Consequences
9:45	T:"Today we begin studying about 'C. of the M.,' their histories, societies, and government."	M: Talking with student behind him — hands him a piece of paper	T:"Clear your desks and face the front of the room."
	T:"On this map (overhead), you can see outlines of all the countries."	M: Turns around to get another piece of paper	T:"M, I want you to pay attention today, so you can complete the assignment."
	T:"Can anyone name some of the countries we will be studying?"	M: "Canada"	Students behind M laugh and name other countries (Japan & Mexico)
	T:"Come on - get serious."	M: "Egypt" "Greece"	
	T:"OK, I want you to name the countries, major religions, & language... Use the encyclopedia..."	M: starts coloring in countries and connecting them with doodles.	T:"Here's a new map that you can come in after school to finish. It's due tomorrow."

Interviewing students to document historically relevant variables.   Unlike other interview formats that emphasize "understanding" student perceptions, we believe interviews should be used to gain information that is not observable but may be helpful in explaining current behaviors or identifying relevant and immediate settings to conduct observations. Consultants must concentrate on eliciting information about observable behaviors and relevant settings. We suggest that consultants ask teachers and students structured questions to (a) narrow behavioral definitions, (b) obtain setting descriptions, and (c) obtain estimates of behavioral occurrences. The following questions can be used directly with students or reworded for teachers:

1. "What do you do when you complete math assignments at home?" Follow-up questions may focus on the working setting, the presence of other stimuli (radios, televisions, people), and work habits.
2. "What do you do when you cannot answer a question on your social studies worksheet?" Follow-up questions may probe how they ask questions or what they do when no one is available to answer the question.
3. "How much time do you spend studying in each of your subjects and how are you doing?" Follow-up questions may focus on the kind of work expected in each subject area or on descriptions of grading systems or course expectations.

These questions may help explain student "motivation" or identify relevant settings for conducting observations. For example, low motivation may be indicated if students identify a specific subject area in which they are receiving marginally passing grades and the course assignments are frequent and difficult requiring many hours of homework. To confirm this report, the consultant should observe the class and a contrast setting in which course expectations are high, engagement is frequent and extended, and consequences are positive. By observing the differences in these two settings, testable explanations can be developed about student motivation and interest.

Assessing background knowledge.   To understand academic content information, students must be fluent with and have background knowledge of the vocabulary or words associated with that content. Every field of study has specific terms that have meaning only in that field. Unless students are familiar with these vocabulary words, they are unlikely to understand, interpret, and learn the content information. For example, in a recent newspaper account, politicians who took "hawkish" positions, were given a *nom de guerre* like Hussein, Arafat, and Gaddafei. Understanding this information requires knowing and linking two specific terms: *hawkish* (a reference to birds of prey) and *nom de guerre* (a reference to names of warriors). Numerous formats can be used to assess background knowledge; however, consultants should become proficient with those that can be done within classroom, applied to any content area (either expository or narrative text), and used with everyone in the class. We focus on assessing background knowledge because it is important to obtain information about the students' vocabulary knowledge and topic familiarity. We describe formats for collecting this information.

For example, which words are the most important to understanding the content and are central to the main idea? Which words can be put together or viewed as synonyms? An example of a useful tool for assessing student vocabulary knowledge is the "bull's-eye" chart (see Figure 8.4) developed by Valencia, Stallman, Commeyras, Pearson, and Hartman (1991).

The bull's-eye chart provides a structure for relating the student's vocabulary knowledge with the essential features of a concept or rule. After defining the concept or rule, unique vocabulary words (examples and nonexamples) are identified. These words are written in the columns on either side of the bull's-eye. Students are then asked to circle the number of each vocabulary word in the ring that they believe best describes the relevance of the word to the central concept or rule; if the word is unrelated, they are asked not to circle any number. Based on a given student's overall response pattern, the teacher and the consultant can determine whether the student's background vocabulary knowledge is adequate. In turn, they can develop an appropriate intervention.

The bull's-eye approach is an extension of previous systems that used semantic mapping (Holley & Dansereau, 1984). Conceived as an intervention to help students organize critical vocabulary and an assessment tool to determine if students could frame key vocabulary into correct context, semantic maps focus on which words (ideas) are related and how. Parker and Tindal (1990) reported a simple, easy classroom application, in which concept comparisons were used to

FIGURE 8.4

Bull's-eye chart for assessing student vocabulary

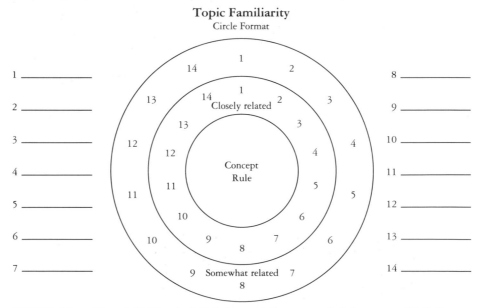

SOURCE: Adapted from S. W. Valencia, A. C. Stallman, M. Commeyras, P. D. Pearson, and D. K. Hartman. "Four Measures of Topical Knowledge: A Study of Construct Validity." *Reading Research Quarterly,* 26(3), 1991, 216.

determine how students associated key vocabulary. The following steps can be used to construct and analyze a concept map:

1. Identify a curriculum unit that takes no more than one to two weeks to teach.
2. Identify seven to ten key concepts that are emphasized in the material.
3. Pair each concept with every other concept (that is, pairwise comparisons) and list them.
4. Place a rating scale at the top of the list that has the following anchors: not related, distantly related, somewhat related, highly related.
5. Direct students to pick the level of relationship for each concept pair.
6. Identify concept pairs that are not systematically related, according to the text.

Variations on this technique include the use of distractors that are not from the content unit, use of a cause-effect relation or problem-solution relation, and comparison of student maps with teacher maps.

In addition to vocabulary knowledge, the student's familiarity with a topic or area of study can be assessed. After developing a clear definition of what they are teaching and what they would like the student to learn, teachers and consultants develop and present questions or prompts that would require the student to give oral or written responses. These responses would be used to determine the student's familiarity with a topic, concept, or rule and to develop specific academic interventions.

After giving an introduction and framework, topic familiarity can be assessed in two general ways. The first involves asking a series of "yes-no" questions that requires students to indicate whether an idea or piece of information would be found in the topic or concept and then to expand or justify their response. For example:

Teacher:	"Today, you are going to read a story titled . . .
	In this story, . . .
	Think about what you know about . . .
	Think about what the author might include in this kind of story. Below you will find several ideas that you might or might not find in such a story. For each idea, decide if you might find it in such a story."
No.	The idea would not be in a story like this one.
Maybe.	The idea could be in a story like this one.
Yes.	The idea would be in a story like this one.

Topic familiarity can also be assessed by presenting the student with open-ended questions or statements that require oral or written responses. Given the previous example, the teacher might ask students to respond to the following kinds of questions: (a) What might the author include in this kind of story? (b) What might happen in this kind of story? (c) What three ideas would the author include in a story of this kind? For written responses, students need to be told that spelling and grammar errors are not counted, because emphasis is placed on information about the student's familiarity with the story topic (Valencia & Pearson, 1988).

Developing Responsive Interventions

At the outset of any instructional program and before determining what to teach, consultants and teachers must establish the student's level of motivation, interest, and background knowledge. If interest and motivation are low and background knowledge is insufficient, the content of what is taught must be more restricted. Interest is easier to maintain when proficiency levels are high, and proficiency is more likely to increase when interest is high. In contrast, few people are motivated or reinforced by behaviors in which they are not fluent. Similarly, proficiency is more difficult to achieve when motivation is low. Therefore, consultants must attend to both motivation and background knowledge when interventions are developed. In particular, initial interest may need to be developed through external reinforcers. As skills, proficiency, and knowledge increase, the content material or information may become more interesting and motivating, creating less reliance on external reinforcers.

In this section, we look at interventions that are aimed at improving student motivation to learn and increasing their background knowledge. An emphasis is placed on teaching relationships and structures that address two problem types: when student interest and motivation (engagement) are low, and when the student exhibits problems with important vocabulary. We believe that the problem type must be identified so remediation efforts can be immediate, focused, and appropriate.

Interventions for students with low interest and motivation.   Students may have different motivations to learn. While some students have very short periods of engagement, others persevere for long durations. Level of engagement can be affected by a number of factors: (a) new, unfamiliar material, (b) negative experiences with the material, (c) an unpredictable lesson direction, and (d) absence of the functional utility of learning. Intervention guidelines for each of these problem types follows:

1. *The material is new and unfamiliar.* The novelty of instructional information may preclude significant student engagement. For students to learn new material, it must be anchored to what they already know. If material is new and unfamiliar, more attention should be devoted to providing a broader information context into which the content can be fitted. For example, in many social studies content areas, information usually has some relevance to current news; information in areas like physics or chemistry has less direct, obvious relevance to daily events and contexts. For instance, content dealing with the structure of molecules, the laws of motion and energy, or theories of nuclear reactivity has less obvious connections with daily school and home activities. Therefore, when student engagement is low, consultants and teachers should assess the relevance of the content for each student; it cannot be assumed.

2. *Negative prior experiences can influence student attention.* When there have been negative learning experiences, student attention and motivation are likely to be low. This situation removes the possibility of successful instructional engagement. At minimum, contingencies for learning new information should originate from within the classroom and be established by the teacher through classroom rules, social sanctions, and grading policies. Such contingencies, however, are often not sufficient for students who have a history of failure in similar experiences. These students quit trying and indicate that they "don't care" about negative outcomes. By the time a Request for Assistance has been made, a range of other undesirable behaviors—for example, not paying attention, talking out in class, and not completing assignments—are also being exhibited. Interventions should focus on gathering information about the student's interests and building change programs based on functional analysis data (on what happens when the student is engaged or not engaged). Positively reinforcing events should follow intervals of engagement.

3. *When students lack study skills and self-monitoring strategies, the likelihood of extended engagement is decreased.* Instruction designed to extend learning is often delivered in groups in which students are expected to complete assignments either in class or at home to extend their learning. For students with sufficient skills and information, such exercises are efficient and functional because they can complete assignments and receive appropriate feedback. However, students with poor self-management skills do not benefit because they are not engaged long enough to become proficient with the content. As a result, their engagement and motivation to learn is reduced. Consultants can help teachers identify and establish settings outside of instruction that enhance student study skills and self-management strategies, which, in turn, improves the student's motivation to learn. Consultants and teachers should embed these programs to improve the student's academic self-management skills and study skills within independent instructional activities.

4. *When students have not learned how to use concepts in solving problems or explaining principles, they have not learned the functional utility of what they have learned.* The major purpose for teaching concepts and principles is so students can manage the environment around them (that is, learn more, gain access to reinforcers, and avoid or escape aversives), not so they can complete assignments and receive good grades. Consultants and teachers must build instructional programs and interventions that emphasize the usefulness of the skills and knowledge being presented. These programs and interventions must emphasize teaching concepts and principles that can facilitate the transfer of what is being taught and learned to other contexts and environments.

Interventions for insufficient student background knowledge.   The previous interventions were designed for situations in which learning has a low reinforcement value for a student. Different interventions must be considered when motivation is present and sufficient but critical concepts are not well-developed or cohesive. Emphasis must focus on building a sufficient skill or knowledge base so new learning can be established and extended. Four types of problems should be considered: (a) when concept meanings have not been mastered, (b) when concepts are not hierarchically organized, (c) when critical concepts are not available and/or functional, and (d) when concepts are not linked into principles.

1. *Students may have partial or incomplete knowledge about key concepts but are mistaken in their full meaning.* Students may also not have mastered the full range of attributes that serve as the foundation for a concept. For example, in social studies, two important concepts involve government and economies. These two concepts, though related, involve different attributes (that is, the United States has a democratic government but a free-market economy). Unless these key attributes are organized clearly and presented systematically, the main concepts will not be mastered. For this type of problem, consultants and teachers should focus on determining how students define concepts and how they employ them in solving problems. In addition, and more important, they should identify and subsequently modify critical content that inadvertently reinforces and maintains misconceptions and ill-defined concepts.

2. *Although students may know concepts in terms of their critical attributes, they may not be linking them into a meaningful hierarchy or logical sequence of knowledge.* When deciding and assessing what to teach, consultants and teachers must understand that the ultimate instructional outcome is teaching students about the structure and interrelatedness of concepts and principles. However, structure and interrelatedness are often the very features that are incompletely developed. For example, a consultant and a teacher review a chapter on oceanography in a science book. They discover that it includes different forms of ocean life, but there is no discussion about tides, which is one of the most prominent characteristics of oceans. Understanding the concept of ocean tides requires learning about an organized network of interrelated phenomena: students must learn about (a) the influence of the moon and the sun on tides, (b) the subsequent effects on intertidal zones, and (c) seasonal and daily tidal patterns. When students lack information about knowledge form structures (concepts and principles) or their interrelatedness, consultants and teachers must identify the concept's critical attributes and the appropriate sequences of teaching examples and nonexamples, and develop a concept structure within teaching and curriculum materials.

3. *Although schools have divided teaching and learning into subject areas, considerable questions exist about the functional utility of these divisions.* Student performance may be affected by, and a function of, the manner in which subject areas are divided. For example, elementary schools often divide reading and language arts into different subject areas. Yet, for some students, the integration of reading and language arts into a single unit might result in a more functional alignment. For instance, while learning about story structure, they also learn how to convey a story in their own words. Most middle schools offer courses in biology, earth science, physics, chemistry, math, and English. The interrelatedness of these subject areas and their associated knowledge and skills is frequently overlooked. For some students, consultants and teachers may need to determine which concepts and principles can be integrated to become functional across content areas and problems.

4. *Instruction may not present any organized principles that can be used to integrate concepts.* Most of the concepts and principles discussed in the oceanography chapter are presented in isolation as discrete pieces of information. No attempt was made to reveal patterns of interrelationships that show how each concept and principle relates to a larger framework. With these kinds of problems, consultants may need to provide curriculum modifications that make essential relationships more overt and provide specific applications that illustrate and reinforce larger organizational principles. Specific procedures for identifying and organizing concepts and principles are described later in this chapter.

Summary

In this section, we discussed whether students are motivated and ready to learn. In particular, we examined ways to assess the student's interest and motivation to learn and his or her background knowledge. We emphasized that consultants and teachers must focus their attention on what is being taught. If the content of what is taught is positively reinforcing or "worth" learning, student learning and motivation will be affected. Consultants and teachers must consider two essential questions:

1. Is the learning environment sufficiently reinforcing to engage students and generate attention and participation?
2. Do students have enough requisite vocabulary to learn new concepts and principles?

Most research on human learning indicates that individual bits of information are not what is learned; rather, it is the structure and relationships used to organize this information that are learned. Learning involves rearranging relationships so students can use information, concepts, and principles to "explain" world events, manipulate information, and solve problems. Therefore, consultants must consider a broader view of learning based on student interest and interrelated organizations of facts, concepts, and principles. In the next section, we focus our attention on ways to manipulate instructional content to emphasize structure and relationships.

IDENTIFYING THE MAJOR STRUCTURAL CHARACTERISTICS OF THE CURRICULUM

When a Request for Assistance is received, consultants often discover that curricular options are limited. A specific basal program or set of materials has already been purchased and is being used. Therefore, consultants must understand this curriculum well. When analyzing curriculum, a number of factors can be considered, such as qualitative judgments of the material, the general skills sequence, and the use of supplemental materials and activities. In this section, we advise consultants to analyze the curriculum for specific structural elements and knowledge forms—that is, the type and arrangement of key concepts and principles. This focus addresses the following types of questions:

1. What elements of a story line are explicitly introduced?
2. Which elements are inferential?
3. When concepts are introduced, what and how many attributes are used in their definitions?
4. What kinds of examples and nonexamples are used?

5. How are concepts interrelated to form principles?

6. What principles are introduced and when?

7. How are these principles integrated to form an organized summary of the main idea?

By answering these kinds of questions, consultants can organize information in a curriculum, and, with the teacher, decide which details are central and which are peripheral. To illustrate this process, we separate narrative stories from expository material. However, in both types of material, the objective in the consultation process is to focus on structure, using the actual curriculum material as a medium to teach that structure. With narrative materials, we concentrate on story structure (story grammar) in which major story elements are identified. With expository material, we address major concepts and principles.

Story Structure and Story Grammar in Narrative Materials

Like road maps, story maps (Idol, 1987) have two characteristics that reflect the story's major features: a visual representation and an organizational (hierarchical) depiction. The visual display generally consists of an outline or graphic in which related information is boxed together. The organizational depiction reflects how the information is related. Using visual displays and organizational depictions, a story can be reduced to its essential structure, which is common to, or at least similar among, most narrative stories. Typically, stories have three setting characteristics (Idol, 1987): characters, time or era, and location or locale. In addition, stories usually (a) involve some type of problem or central plot, (b) unfold toward a goal or objective, (c) include actions on the part of characters in specific settings, and (d) result in some problem resolution or outcome. A visual graphic for displaying these elements is illustrated in Figure 8.5.

Story maps allow students to better organize information and to become proficient in looking for and identifying specific content. In Box 8.2, a sample is presented from "The Two Brothers" by Leo Tolstoy (1987), a story that appears in popular children's literature and major basals. In this story, most elements of a story map are present, including setting, characters, time, problem, action, and resolution. A completed story map for this example is illustrated in Figure 8.6.

Consultants and teachers should use story maps to help students develop story structures and understand the organization of a curriculum. Consultants can serve as resources by (a) creating story boards that can be used for preview or review, (b) providing practice in locating specific information to fill story boards, (c) presenting problems for students to complete using the story map structure, and (d) extending practice to new and different stories using the map.

Students need to understand the structure behind stories and, where appropriate, generalize this structure to new stories. If consultants find that such structure is implicit in teachers' instruction, it should become more explicit. If this structure is already explicit, it can be used to extend instruction as practice exercises. In either case, consultants need to ascertain the degree to which such structure is being emphasized and how it is being stressed.

FIGURE 8.5

Story map

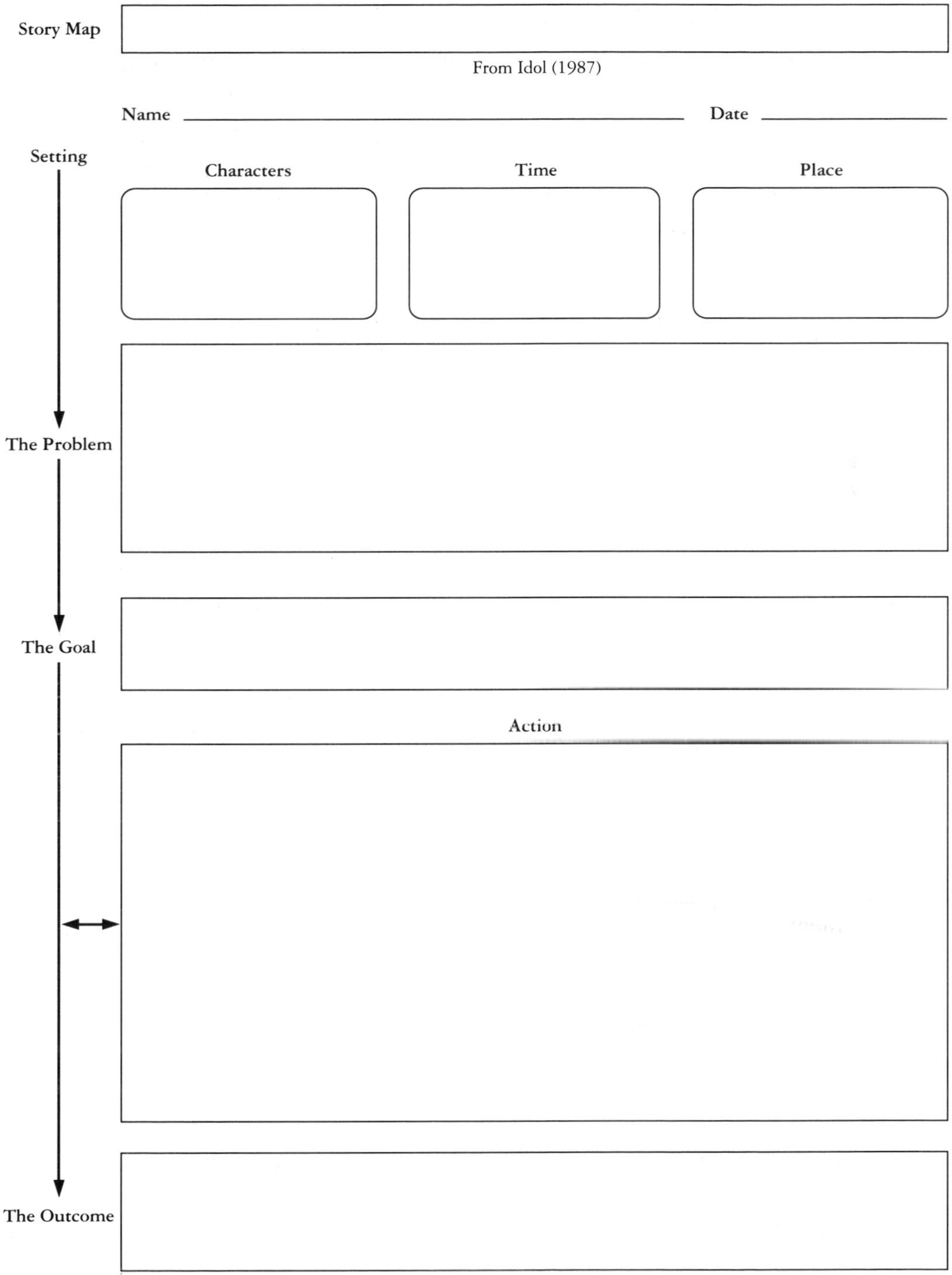

Story Map

From Idol (1987)

Name _____ Date _____

Setting

Characters   Time   Place

The Problem

The Goal

Action

The Outcome

SOURCE: L. Idol. "Group Story Mapping: A Comprehension Strategy for Both Skilled and Unskilled Readers." *Journal of Learning Disabilities,* 20(4), 1987, 199.

BOX 8.2

Sample of a story to be mapped

"THE TWO BROTHERS" BY LEO TOLSTOY

Two brothers set out on a journey together. At noon they lay down in a forest to rest. When they woke up they saw a stone lying next to them. There was something written on the stone, and they tried to make out what it was.

"Whoever finds this stone," they read, "let him go straight into the forest at sunrise. In the forest a river will appear; let him swim across the river to the other side. There he will find a she-bear and her cubs. Let him take the cubs from her and run up the mountain with them without once looking back. On the top of the mountain he will see a house, and in that house will he find happiness."

When they had read what was written on the stone, the younger brother said: "Let us go together. We can swim across the river, carry off the bear cubs, take them to the house on the mountain, and together find happiness."

"I am not going into the forest after bear cubs," said the elder brother, "and I advise you not to go. In the first place, no one can know whether what is written on this stone is the truth—perhaps it was written in jest. It is even possible that we have not read it correctly. In the second place, even if what is written here is the truth—suppose we go into the forest and night comes, and we cannot find the river. We shall be lost. And if we do find the river, how are we going to swim across it? It may be broad and swift. In the third place, even if we swim across the river, do you think it is an easy thing to take her cubs away from a she-bear? She will seize us, and, instead of finding happiness, we shall perish, and all for nothing. In the fifth place, even if we succeeded in carrying off the bear cubs, we could not run up a mountain without stopping to rest. And, most important of all, the stone does not tell us what kind of happiness we should find in that house. It may be that the happiness awaiting us there is not at all the sort of happiness we would want."

"In my opinion," said the younger brother, "you are wrong. What is written on the stone could not have been put there without reason. And it is all perfectly clear.

Knowledge Forms in Expository Materials: Concepts and Principles

Consultants may need to help teachers focus and modify expository material and information to improve student engagements with the curriculum. Several strategies can be used to make such modifications by focusing on what to teach. To illustrate the use of these strategies, we present a unit on oceanography. This topic is of high interest to some teachers and students and of low interest to others. Technical information found in this unit is too advanced for many low-achieving students. Therefore, it needs to be made appropriate (engaging and understandable) for all students, particularly those who are low achieving or "at-risk" for failing.

In this unit (from a Merrill Earth Science book by Bishop, Sutherland, & Lewis, 1981), the following topics are covered:

The Water Cycle
Composition of Ocean Water
Ocean Life
Life Processes in the Ocean

BOX 8.2   (*continued*)

In the first place, no harm will come to us if we try. In the second place, if we do not go, someone else will read the inscription on the stone and find happiness, and we shall have lost it all. In the third place, if you do not make an effort and try hard, nothing in the world will succeed. In the fourth place, I should not want it thought that I was afraid of anything."

The elder brother answered him by saying, "The proverb says: 'In seeking great happiness small pleasures may be lost.' And also, 'A bird in the hand is worth two in the bush.'"

The younger brother replied, "I have heard: 'He who is afraid of the leaves must not go into the forest.' And also, 'Beneath a stone no water flows.'"

Then the younger brother set off, and the elder remained behind. No sooner had the younger brother gone into the forest than he found the river, swam across it, and there on the other side was the she-bear, fast asleep. He took her cubs, and ran up the mountain without looking back. When he reached the top of the mountain, the people came out to meet him with a carriage to take him into the city, where they made him their king.

He ruled for five years. In the sixth year, another king, who was stronger than he, waged war against him. The city was conquered, and he was driven out.

Again the younger brother became a wanderer, and he arrived one day at the house of the elder brother. The elder brother was living in a village and had grown neither rich nor poor. The two brothers rejoiced at seeing each other and at once began telling of all that had happened to them.

"You see," said the elder brother, "I was right. Here I have lived quietly and well, while you, though you may have been a king, have seen a great deal of trouble."

"I do not regret having gone into the forest and up the mountain," replied the younger brother. "I may have nothing now, but I shall always have something to remember, while you have no memories at all."

SOURCE: L. Tolstoy *(1962)*. "The Two Brothers" (translated by A. Dunnigan), in *Fables and Fairy Tales*. New York, NY: New American Library.

Mapping the Ocean Floor
Ocean Floor Topography
Deep-Sea Deposits

These topics are not interrelated either within or among (sub)units by any guiding network of relationships. Rather, all information is equally presented, mostly as discrete facts. Concepts or principles are presented haphazardly and incompletely. For example, five concepts are presented in the water cycle topic; each concept has only one defining attribute, or maybe none. No principles are considered (see Box 8.3). After a brief coverage of the composition of water, the next topic deals with ocean life and life processes (see Box 8.4 for a list of more knowledge forms).

Clearly, even the best students will have difficulty learning such material. It is presented in a manner that emphasizes memorization with few structural or conceptual mnemonics available for organizing information. No connections are embedded between the different concepts. Finally, each concept is presented with only one attribute. Notice that algae is simply defined as a "dominant sea plant that lives attached to the bottom." No other attributes or distinguishing characteristics

FIGURE 8.6

Story map for "The Two Brothers"

Story Map	The Two Brothers by Leo Tolstoy

From Idol (1987)

Name _____ Date _____

Setting

Characters	Time	Place
Two brothers	At noon For six years	In a forest In a village

The Problem

Something written on a stone

"Whoever finds this stone," they read, "let him go straight into the forest at sunrise. In the forest a river will appear; let him swim across the river to the other side. There he will find a she-bear and her cubs. Let him take the cubs from her and run up the mountain with them without once looking back. On the top of the mountain he will see a house."

No one can know whether what is written on the stone is the truth. We shall be lost. Take cubs away from a she-bear. The stone does not tell us what kind of happiness we should find in the house.

The Goal

Find happiness

Action

The Outcome

The younger brother set off and the elder remained behind.

No sooner had the younger brother gone into the forest than he found the river, swam across it, and there on the other side was the she-bear, fast asleep. He took her cubs and ran up the mountain without looking back. When he reached the top of the mountain, the people came out to meet him with a carriage to take him into the city, where they made him their king.

One brother ruled for five years. In the sixth year, another king, who was stronger than he, waged war against him. The city was conquered and he was driven out. The elder brother was living in a village and had grown neither rich nor poor.

"You see," said the elder brother, "I was right. Here I have lived quietly and well, while you, though you may have been a king, have seen a great deal of trouble." "I do not regret having gone into the forest and up the mountain," replied the younger brother. I may have nothing now, but I shall always have something to remember, while you have no memories at all."

B O X   8.3

Topic introduction via knowledge forms

MAPPING THE WATER CYCLE

Concepts

Ocean	Continuous body of salt water that covers a little over 70% of the earth's surface.
Hydrosphere	The Earth's water portion.
Evaporation	Not defined or explicated.
Precipitation	Water in the air condenses and falls to earth; most of it returns to the ocean.
Transpiration	The process in which water escapes from the leaves of plants.

Principles

None presented

are considered; for example, it can be one-celled or multicellular; it has no true roots, stems, or leaves; or it usually contains chlorophyll.

In addition, the material contains useless information. One topic addresses how the ocean floor is mapped; this is a nonintegrated physics topic, not an oceanography topic. Also, the concept of sea level is touched on and then ignored (Box 8.5), even though it may fit better in a later section on topography and structure.

This type of approach has a number of advantages. First, consultants and teachers can ascertain the extent to which information is covered and identify those concepts and principles that are underdeveloped. Second, the approach focuses on curricular or environmental explanations for student learning and performance problems. Third, the variables that are emphasized are accessible to teachers and can be directly manipulated by them. Fourth, the approach enables consultants and teachers to take a more directive role in determining what to teach. Finally, they can assemble a list of relevant concepts and principles, which can be used to unify the information that is the focus of the next step.

IDENTIFYING ORGANIZING PRINCIPLES

Although consultants and teachers may be forced to use certain curricula that have been adopted by teachers or districts, they can rearrange the information by resequencing it, adding in new information, or deleting useless information. However, by modifying the information, they may create the same problem they are attempting to solve: an unorganized compilation of information that is not

B O X 8.4

Key knowledge forms

MAPPING OCEAN LIFE AND LIFE PROCESSES

Concepts

Plankton — Microscopic plants and animals that float at or near the ocean's surface.

Diatoms — Tiny, one-celled plants with a crystallike covering of silica; the main source of food for many sea animals; cover about half the ocean floor.

Algae — Dominant sea plant that lives attached to the bottom.

Nekton — All swimming forms (from herring to whales); can move from one depth or place to another; some like it cold, some like it warm; some roam the entire ocean; some are flesh-eating (like it cold); some surface feed at night.

Benthos — Bottom dwellers living in shallow water (on the sea floor); includes coral, snails, starfish, clams.

Buoyancy — Upward lift that makes movement in water easy.

Plants — Base of the food chain; use sunlight, carbon dioxide, and water to form sugar via photosynthetic process; most belong to floating plankton.

(Photosynthesis) — Not defined or explicated.

Principles

When storms mix the ocean waters, large amounts of nutrients are brought up from the deep and diatoms rapidly multiply; they cover the ocean's surface and form a great blanket of food.

When temperature ranges don't vary, little protection is needed against heat or cold.

As water depth increases, food becomes scarce.

---

systematic or based on interrelationships. Therefore, in this section, we present guidelines for selecting the information presented in a curriculum.

Frequently, the curriculum includes too much information to be presented in the time allotted. In addition, the number of supplemental activities is excessive. We advocate carefully limiting the amount of information presented. Although prepared students can efficiently move through an entire unit, students with learning problems will struggle or fail to keep up.

Teachers are already pressed for time and may not have the skill to focus and modify the curriculum. Therefore, consultants must help them identify the most critical, explanatory information. Ideally, consultants and teachers can work through this step together, so the burden of modification is not left to one person. Generally, the teacher should be viewed as the content expert; the consultant's responsibility is to place the content information into a well-framed perspective

BOX 8.5
Peripheral knowledge forms

MAPPING THE OCEAN FLOOR

Concepts

Sea Level — Elevation at which land and sea meet; defined as zero elevation; the average height of the sea without considering tides and waves.

(Echo sounding, sonar, radar) — Not defined or explicated.

(Seismographic, sonar detection) — Not defined or explicated.

Principles

$D = \frac{1}{2}t \times v$

When vibrations travel through rock of different densities, they travel at different speeds.

---

that facilitates and maximizes student learning. Ideally, this step would leave the teacher with a better instructional unit and, more important, with the requisite skills to apply the same strategy to different material with other low-performance students.

In our oceanography unit, too much material is being covered in the time allocated by the school, which is no more than six to ten days. Unfortunately, other units in the earth science curriculum have similar characteristics: numerous facts, complex concepts, limited example selection, nonhierarchial arrangement of concepts and principles, and little explication of interrelationships. The entire course has been "designed" to be covered in 10 to 12 weeks. Students with low motivation or poor background information are quickly and easily overwhelmed by the rapid accumulation of information.

When confronted with this type of problem, consultants must work with teachers to ascertain key knowledge forms that can be integrated into an organizing principle or a set of principles. For example, after examining the oceanography unit, the consultant and the teacher may find that the major topics involve life forms and topographical structures. They should then decide to use these two topics to develop an organizing principle that explains the most information with the fewest concepts and principles. Because the consultant and the teacher discover that most life forms are limited to those structural areas of the ocean where light can penetrate (that is, the continental shelf), they emphasize concepts and principles centered around life forms found on the continental shelf. In this unit, the consultant would also discover that two major questions (concepts) have not been addressed: (a) What is an ocean? and (b) How is the ocean defined and explicated by the movement of water? The consultant may need to help the teacher find supplemental information from videotapes, for example, that helps strengthen a more potent organizing principle.

If we assume that the topics ocean and water movement are included in the unit on oceanography with the topics life forms and topographical structures, we can develop an encompassing and organizing rule or principle:

> *Ocean type* (1) and *diversity of life forms* (2) depend on the availability of nutrients resulting from *physical structure* (3) and *water movement* (4).

In this example, we have italicized and numbered the major concepts in the order in which they might be presented. This organizing principle gives the teacher a framework for identifying and limiting instruction to the most pertinent information. In addition, low-achieving students can learn this information more easily. The major role of the consultant in this process is to identify key knowledge forms, provide assistance in supplementing the unit with other information, and assist in the development of an organizing principle.

DETERMINING IF ALL ELEMENTS ARE PRESENT

In previous steps, the consultant and the teacher have (a) defined the problem and instructional goals, (b) analyzed the curriculum to determine how it can be used to accomplish those goals, and (c) modified the curriculum to fit with the instructional goals. In this section, we discuss guidelines for determining if a curriculum provides information that defines and supports organizing concepts and principles.

Concepts and principles must be supported to prevent students from learning misrules or information that is highly stipulated. Multiple attributes for each concept and the relationship among these attributes must also be considered. The consultant's responsibility is to help teachers determine if appropriate multiple attributes are present and if they support an organizing principle. Typically, consultants can find and summarize relevant supplemental information, materials, and knowledge forms.

To illustrate, consider the oceanography unit in which topics are not covered adequately because too much information is presented. Most of the material is only partially covered. For example, although the ocean is presented as part of the water cycle, no descriptions of or information about the water cycle principle are presented. Without an organizing principle and clarification of key concepts, students must learn about oceans in a fragmented manner. When students look at a map, they see a variety of water references: gulf, bay, sea, ocean. Without an organizing principle and more information, students may create their own definitions for oceans, such as oceans are big bodies of water or oceans have salt water. For students with low motivation or interest and/or poor background information, learning about oceans under these conditions can be confusing and frustrating.

Consultants and teachers can remedy this problem by supplying missing information and providing linkages that bridge the major concepts and principles. However, consultants must carefully consider their modifications to ensure that they only add material needed to increase the student's familiarity and fluency with key organizing principles and major concepts. For example, if we define an ocean as a large body of salt water separated by continents and with its own circulation, we can then begin focusing on currents, which have a major impact on life forms and ocean structures. Rather than adding in more peripheral information, this definition continues our focus on the organizing principle. As such, we can say that there are six oceans: the South and North Pacific, South and North Atlantic, Indian, and Arctic. If we teach this definition explicitly and directly, we limit opportunities for confusion about bays, gulfs, and seas.

DETERMINING IF STUDENTS HAVE REQUISITE SKILLS TO EXTEND LEARNING

We have addressed three important features that define what should be taught: (a) the material must be interesting to students so they are motivated to learn more, (b) information must be within student reach (that is, it must include old and new concepts and principles), and (c) knowledge forms must be hierarchically structured and interrelated with other concepts and principles. If teachers ensured that what they taught was consistent with these three criteria, the amount of teaching could be reduced and the amount of student learning could be enhanced greatly. It is unlikely, however, that all students enter instruction with equal levels of motivation or background knowledge; thus, teachers must slow their pace of instruction to avoid overwhelming low-achieving students.

This problem can be reduced by explicitly teaching students how to manage their own academic learning. Thus, in this section, we address study skills. Assuming adequate interest or motivation, background information, and appropriate presentation of concepts and principles, students can learn information that is teacher directed. However, students can maximize their learning if they have behaviors or skills that maximize their engagement with instructional materials and curriculum. Gall, Gall, Jacobsen, and Bullock (1990) call these behaviors learning strategies (Box 8.6); we call them study skills because we consider them part of learning strategies.

Study skills or behaviors are useful for students when they study and can help them consolidate and extend learning. We have included them in this chapter because they are often omitted from direct instruction. Furthermore, these skills can be taught in any content area.

The behaviors are quite diverse, ranging from managing contingencies (self-evaluating, goal setting, keeping records, environmental structuring, and introducing self-consequences) to managing learning (seeking information, rehearsing and memorizing, asking peers or teachers for help, and reviewing textbooks or tests). Ideally, such behaviors can be taught before other content information and then reinforced during or after content instruction. The major goal is to get students directly involved in their learning and to make teaching more efficient.

Consultants can use these study skills in two ways. First, they can be part of an assessment checklist to determine the degree to which teaching and learning are maximized. For example, if many of these behaviors are being exhibited and learning problems still exist, the problem may not be associated with how students manage their learning but more directly with the content and method of

BOX 8.6

Self-regulated study skills

TYPE OF LEARNING STRATEGY

1. *Self-evaluating:* Student-initiated evaluations of the quality or progress of their work ("I check over my work to make sure I did it right.").
2. *Organizing and transforming:* Student-initiated overt or covert rearrangement of instructional materials to improve learning ("I make an outline before I write my paper.").
3. *Goal setting and planning:* Student setting of educational goals or subgoals and planning for sequencing, time, and completing activities related to those goals ("First, I start studying two weeks before exams, and I pace myself.").
4. *Seeking information:* Student-initiated efforts to secure further task information from nonsocial sources when undertaking an assignment ("Before beginning to write the paper, I go to the library to get as much information as possible about the topic.").
5. *Keeping records and monitoring:* Student-initiated efforts to record events or results ("I took notes of the class discussion.").
6. *Environmental structuring:* Student-initiated efforts to select or arrange the physical setting to make learning easier ("I isolate myself from anything that distracts me.").
7. *Introducing self-consequences:* Student arrangement or imagination of rewards or punishment for success or failure ("If I do well on a test, I treat myself to a movie.").
8. *Rehearsing and memorizing:* Student-initiated efforts to memorize material by overt or covert practice ("In preparing for a math test, I keep writing the formula until I memorize it.").
9. *Asking peers for help:* Student-initiated attempts to obtain assistance from peers ("If I have problems with math assignments, I ask a friend for help.").
10. *Asking teachers for help:* Student-initiated attempts to obtain assistance from teachers ("If I don't understand how to complete an assignment, I ask the teacher for more information.").
11. *Asking adults for help:* Student-initiated efforts to obtain assistance from adults ("When I write speeches for class, I ask my parents to be my audience so I can practice.").
12. *Reviewing tests:* Student-initiated attempts to reassess answers and questions on a test ("After I've answered all the questions on a test, I go over them to make sure that I've done my best.").
13. *Reviewing textbooks:* Student-initiated efforts to identify and organize important information in a textbook ("When I read, I highlight important information and then go through the chapter again and reread that information.").
14. *Systematically reviewing all materials to prepare for special projects or tests:* Student-initiated strategies for organizing quantities of information for final exams ("When I study for final exams, I review my textbook, handouts, and notes.").
15. *Other:* Learning behavior that is initiated by other persons, such as teacher or parents, and all unclear verbal responses ("I just do what the teacher says.").

SOURCE: M. D. Gall, J. P. Gall, D. R. Jacobsen, and T. L. Bullock (1990). "Theory and Reseach," *Tools for Learning.* Association for Supervision and Curriculum Development.

instruction. Second, consultants can select study skills to teach directly to students in preparation for eventually ending consultation.

Consultants can organize the process of preparing instructors to teach students to manage their own learning into five operations: (a) organizing materials and space, (b) managing time, (c) listening and participating in class, (d) completing reading assignments, and (e) writing school papers. We used the work of Gall, Gall, Jacobsen, and Bullock (1990) to develop most of the components within these areas.

Organizing materials and space.   Students frequently have problems organizing learning materials and supplies. They come to school with crumpled papers loosely arranged in bags, notebooks, jacket pockets, or lunch boxes. Their work is left in a variety of places as well. When the work must be turned in, teachers discover that students do not have their assignments *and* do not know where they are.

To help develop effective study habits, teachers must first give students a simple system for organizing their materials, including strategies that help them categorize their work, label its status, track its progress, and file it away. In addition, students should be taught how to organize a work space at home or in school so all necessary references and support materials are readily available when they need them. For example, having immediate access to supplies prevents students from wasting time looking for material, which interrupts both their concentration and their work. Finally, some type of storage system (a three-ring binder or notebook, manila files) should be developed for filing active and inactive work.

Managing time.   Students must also be taught how to use time efficiently. Students could benefit from many in-class and take-home tasks if they arranged for a specific time, place, and amount of time to complete their tasks and actually used the allocated time efficiently. Consultants and teachers can teach students a variety of strategies to use their time more efficiently and effectively: (a) using an assignment sheet to keep track of the required tasks and manage time lines and due dates, (b) developing a system to order assignments and tasks into a prioritized list, (c) setting reasonable goals and time lines that reflect priorities, (d) breaking small tasks into subtasks that can be completed gradually, successfully, and systematically, and (e) developing a calendar to schedule assignments relative to other activities.

In planning and teaching time management study skills, consultants and teachers should consider two important factors that affect completion of assignments and accuracy. First, assignment completion is typically affected and maintained by an interval schedule of reinforcement; that is, students are given a specific amount of time to complete a task. As a result, work on the task is relatively uneven and slow at the beginning of the interval; however, as the deadline approaches, work behavior increases dramatically. The result is rushed performance or incomplete assignments. Work performance could be more consistent if a ratio-type schedule of reinforcement was adopted. The assignment could be divided into subtasks or activities, and a time line could be established for the completion of a specified number of subtasks. This approach would provide more frequent opportunities for "task" completion and teacher feedback, and it would give a structure for more regular student performance and product completion.

Listening and participating in class.   Following suggestions made by Gall and colleagues (1990), consultants and teachers can help students become better listeners and classroom participants by teaching them to (a) maintain regular class attendance, (b) read assignments before class, (c) stay alert in class, (d) follow the rules of good listening etiquette, (e) attempt to answer every question, (f) ask questions when they are unsure about something, and (g) use the class time allotted for seatwork.

However, these general strategies alone do not guarantee that students will be successful in classroom activities. Other more specific study strategies are also needed. For example, students are required to complete work on their own, at home, or during study opportunities at school. To be successful, they must be able to work independently with class material. One useful strategy is to have the student take notes that can guide work completion when the teacher is absent. Thus, it is critical that students learn how to take notes that are informative, thorough, and accurate.

We consider note taking a critical study skill; unfortunately, students are rarely taught how to take notes. We believe that note-taking strategies must be taught directly, using a model-lead-test instructional sequence. Teachers should give students a set of model notes for a body of information (lecture or curriculum materials). They should highlight critical features or attributes of the notes and explain why certain information was written down. The instruction should emphasize four strategies: paraphrasing, highlighting, summarizing, and underlining. After the model or demonstration phase, students should be given practice trials, in which their notes are compared to some standard made by the teacher or another student, and then specific corrective or positive feedback is provided. Finally, they should be given a series of independent trials on new material.

When consultants and teachers are teaching students to take notes, they should consider highlighting the following strategies: (a) write down information immediately when it is important to remember what the teacher is saying, (b) use teacher cues to guide note taking ("This is important!" "In conclusion, . . ."), (c) take notes on definitions and examples, (d) take notes on assignments and test dates, (e) paraphrase and simplify larger amounts of information, (f) use abbreviations and symbols, (g) write legible notes, (h) stay alert at the end of class when important summary, concluding, and assignment information is given, (i) store notes in a three-ring binder, (j) label and date notes, (k) revise notes after class, and (l) review notes periodically.

Completing reading assignments.   Because reading skills are required across many academic tasks and activities, consultants should be well versed in strategies that facilitate student reading. One of the most well-known strategies for teaching students to summarize what they have read is the SQ3R system (Robinson, 1941): Survey, Question, Read, Recite, and Review. In general terms, the system provides students with a structure to interact with material frequently, in a predictable structured manner, and with opportunities for appropriate feedback. Using an adaptation of the SQ3R system proposed by Ekwall and Shanker (1985), we have developed a worksheet in which students write down their questions; in Steps 3 and 4, the answers are written as soon as they are found (Figure 8.7).

FIGURE 8.7
Worksheet for the adapted SQ3R strategy

Adapted SQ3R Worksheet

Step 1:   Survey the introductory statement, various headings, and summaries
             to grasp the main idea. Notice graphic aids and graphs.

Step 2:   Identify questions that arise from the survey that help define the
             purpose for reading the material. Write them down.

             _____

             _____

             _____

             _____

             _____

Step 3:   Read the material to answer the questions

Step 4:   Recite the answers to each of the questions (without reference to the
             text) and write your answers down.

             _____

             _____

             _____

             _____

             _____

Step 5:   Review the material using the text to check your answers and to
             seek additional information.

A host of other strategies, developed since SQ3R, represent variations of the SQ3R technique. Hoover (1989) compiled a list of these variations, as shown in Box 8.7.

Hoover's list includes strategies for improving a variety of student skills. Most strategies focus on reading, with an emphasis on helping students organize text as a whole and proceed in a systematic, goal-oriented manner. Other strategies are oriented around listening to teachers lecture and present information and taking notes for improving information retention. A few strategies extend the note-taking strategy to include student communication skills. Consultants should consider these strategies when working with content-related problems because they can be applied to any subject matter area and can be used with students of all ages.

B O X 8.7

List of SQ3R variations

AUTHOR(S) (DATE)	ACRONYM	DESCRIPTION
Smith & Elliott (1979)	PARS	Preview Ask questions Read Summarize
Thomas & Robinson (1972)	PQ4R	Preview Question Read, Reflect, Recite, Review
Norman & Norman (1968)	OK5R	Overview Key Idea Read, Record, Recite, Review, Reflect
Norman & Norman (1968)	OARWET	Overview Achieve Read Write Evaluate Test
Edwards (1973)	PANORAMA	Determine purpose for reading Survey material for organization Memorize material using notes/aids
Eanet & Manzo (1976)	REAP	Read Encode (use your own words) Annotate Ponder
Manzo (1969)	ReQuest	Reciprocal questioning (before reading)
Kelly & Holmes (1979)	GLP	Guided Lecture Procedure
Gearheart, DeRuiter, & Sileo (1986)	RARE	Review the questions at end Answer all questions you know Read the selection Express answers to the questions

In addition to the SQ3R strategy, consultants and teachers can teach students to gain more information from what they read by (a) using text structures or knowledge forms, (b) employing graphic organizers, and (c) developing appropriate question-generating and question-answering skills.

Writing papers and reports.   Because students must often complete assignments via written reports, they must be minimally proficient in writing. Unfortunately, they receive few writing strategies and practice opportunities to become fluent. Students most often receive instruction in creative writing, which is very different from technical or report writing.

Consultants and teachers, therefore, must be able to arrange occasions for students to learn how to write in a technical and functional manner. Specifically, students must acquire writing strategies that enable them to (a) develop main ideas,

B O X 8.7 (*continued*)

AUTHOR(S) (DATE)	ACRONYM	DESCRIPTION
Tonjes & Zintz (1981)	TQLR	Tuning in Questioning Listening Reviewing
Schumaker et al. (1981)	COPS	Capitalize Overall appearance Punctuate Spell correctly
Schumaker et al. (1981)	TOWER	Think Order ideas Write Edit Rewrite
Carman & Adams (1972)	SCORER	Schedule time Clue word search Omit difficult questions Read carefully Estimate answers Review the work
Fay (1965)	SQRQCQ	Survey the word problem Question identification Read the problem again carefully Question the process needed Compute the answer Question the answer
Tindal & Nolet (1992)	SORT	Select the words and ideas Order them in importance Reach a conclusion Tell about it and test it

SOURCE: Compiled by J. L. Hoover (1989), "Study Skills and the Education of Students with Learning Disabilities," *Journal of Learning Disabilities* 22:452-455, 461.

(b) sequence information, (c) use stylistic devices, (d) make clear, complete sentences, (e) connect sentences within paragraphs, (f) develop ideas across paragraphs, (g) create a first draft, and (h) edit and revise what they have written.

SUMMARY

In this chapter, we switched our focus from the management of social behavior to the management of academic behaviors and skills. Specifically, we addressed "what to teach." Of course, what to teach cannot be separated from "how" instruction is delivered; however, we believe that what is taught must be considered first. An analysis of the content of the curriculum must be systematic and broadly focused. We focused our attention on the answers to three questions:

1. Is the material interesting and are students motivated to learn?
2. Do students have the necessary background knowledge to learn new information and to integrate and extend that new information?
3. Can the content be used to teach structure and interrelationships?

We began this chapter with a problem case: Mike was having difficulty completing social studies worksheets and participating in class activities. Ms. Kimo's analysis of information from the Problem Identification Interview and her functional analysis observations revealed content and context issues that promoted Mike's problem behaviors. Specifically, the curriculum text was problematic. Based on this information, she developed an intervention, as shown in the completed Intervention Planning form illustrated in Figure 8.8.

The following is a list of the main ideas covered in this chapter:

1. Students are often required to perform and learn material in content areas that exceeds their skill development.
2. Assessments in three basic skills areas—reading, writing/spelling, and math—begin the instructional problem-solving process.
3. Emphasis must be focused on two levels: the specific tasks and behaviors that form the foundation of the skill area, and the fluent and automatic use of these tasks and behaviors.
4. Student interest (motivation) and background knowledge must be sufficient to sustain instruction.
5. Student interest and background knowledge are interrelated.
6. Direct observation should be used to assess interest, and comprehension probes of vocabulary and main ideas should be used to determine if students have sufficient background knowledge and topic familiarity.
7. Students must be taught from their current level to advance to higher-level skills, and interest (motivation) and background knowledge define the current level.
8. Consultants can be more effective in helping students and teachers with instructional problems if they can see the structure of what is being taught

FIGURE 8.8
Mr. Hagerty's completed Intervention Planning form

INTERVENTION PLANNING FORM	Teacher _Hagerty_ Date _6 / 19 / 91_ Consultant _Kimo_ School _Lower Lake Middle_

Student Information:
Name _Mike R._   DOB _7 / 24 / 79_ Sex: (M) F
Grade _7_ Age _12_ Room _107_ IEP: Y (N)

Review of Case Information. (4 minutes) (Check each area that has been reviewed.)

✓ Problem Behavior   ___ Current Level of Functioning
___ Replacement Response   ___ Required Level of Functioning
✓ Problem Context/Setting   ___ Long-Term Objective
✓ Testable Explanations

List four or five positive strategies to improve student performance. (4 minutes)

(1.) Adjust instructional setup   4. Change activity structure in classroom

2. Adapt curriculum materials   5. Refiance directions for completing assignments

3. Present supplemental handouts

Circle strategy (or strategies) to be implemented. (1 minute)

Name one strategy for managing unacceptable behavior. (2 minutes)

Establish response cost for incorrect answers on both in-class and take-home assignments.

FIGURE 8.8 (*continued*)

Identify what is needed/available to insure implementation. (2 minutes)

> Curriculum materials
> Access to computer lab at least 1-2 days/wk

Specify the steps for implementation of intervention. (6 minutes)

1. Present concept map prior to instruction to frame central concepts and their relationships
2. Provide overview of major principles for each unit
3. Make handout to show concepts/relationships graphically
4. Introduce material with current events to increase interest and show relevance
5. Intersperse lectures with more student engagement activities
6. Present more frequent reviews, particularly of assignments

---

Describe how student progress will be monitored and evaluated. (3 minutes)

> Performance on concept maps, in-class & take-home assignments, and final end-of-unit tests

---

Date for Starting Intervention 6/20/91

Next Meeting Date 7/1/91 and Time 2:30

Next Observation 6/21/91 and Time 9:45

Attach Additional Notes — see attached.

FIGURE 8.8 (*continued*)

> **NOTES:**
>
> — Reg. ed. Teacher will take responsibility for highlighting page #'s in chapters being taught (1 week in advance).
>
> — Within each chapter, important concepts will be highlighted; a graphic sketched to show important relationships.
>
> — Sp Ed. teacher will take responsibility to work w/ student on those concepts and relationships — 1 day/week: preview and review.
>
> — Student is responsible for attending class regularly.

explicitly   that is, using story structures with narrative materials and knowledge forms (concepts and principles) with expository material.

9. When working with knowledge forms, it is important to identify and integrate critical concepts and delete peripheral details.

10. After determining if a major structural proposition is in place, analyze the curriculum to see if all concepts and elements are well developed and supported by the proposition.

11. To elaborate and extend their learning, students must be taught study skills and learning strategies that will enable them to use materials on their own.

REFERENCES

ADAMS, M. J. (1990). *Beginning to read: Thinking and learning about print: A summary.* Champaign, IL: Center for the Study of Reading.

BISHOP, M. S., SUTHERLAND, B., & LEWIS, P. G. (1981). "Oceanography," Chapter 10 of *Focus on Earth Science.* Columbus, OH: Charles Merrill.

CARMAN, R. A., & ADAMS, W. R. (1972). *Study skills: A student's guide for survival.* New York: Wiley.

CARROLL, J. B. (1963). A model of school learning. *Teacher's College Record, 64*(8), 723–733.

CHEEK, E. H., JR., & CHEEK, M. C. (1983). *Reading instruction through content reading.* Columbus, OH: Charles Merrill.

DENMARK, T., & KEPNER, H. S., JR. (1980). Basic skills in mathematics: A survey. *Journal for Research in Mathematics Education* (March), 104–123.

EANET, M. G., & MANZO, A. V. (1976). REAP—A strategy for improving reading/writing study skills. *Journal of Reading, 19,* 647–652.

EDWARDS, P. (1973). Panorama: A study technique. *Journal of Reading, 17,* 132–135.

EKWALL, E. E., & SHANKER, J. L. (1985). *Teaching reading in the elementary school.* Columbus, OH: Charles Merrill.

FAY, L. (1965). Reading study skills. Math and science. In J. A. Figurel (Ed.), *Reading and inquiry* (pp. 93–94). Newark, DE: International Reading Association.

GALL, M. D., GALL, J. P., JACOBSEN, D. R., & BULLOCK, T. L. (1990). "Theory and Research, " *Tools for learning.* Alexandria, VA: Association for Supervision and Curriculum Development.

GEARHART, B. R., DERUITER, J. A., & SILEO, T. W. (1986). *Teaching mildly and moderately handicapped students.* Englewood Cliffs, NJ: Prentice-Hall.

HOLLEY, C. D., & DANSEREAU, D. F. (1984). *Spatial learning strategies: Techniques, applications, and related issues.* New York: Academic Press.

HOOVER, J. L. (1989). Study skills and the education of students with learning disabilities. *Journal of Learning Disabilities, 22,* 452–455, 461.

IDOL, L. (1987). Group story mapping: Comprehension strategies for both skilled and unskilled readers. *Journal of Learning Disabilities, 20*(4), 196–126.

KELLY, B. W., & HOLMES, J. (1979). The guided lecture procedure. *Journal of Reading, 22,* 602–604.

MANZO, A. V. (1979). ReQuest procedure. *Journal of Reading, 13,* 123–126.

MARTORELLA, P. (1972). *Concept learning: Designs for instruction.* Scranton, PA: Intext Educational Publishers.

NORMAN, M. H., & NORMAN, E. S. (1968). *Successful reading.* New York: Holt, Rinehart, & Winston.

PARKER, R., & TINDAL, G. (1990). *The reliability, sensitivity, and criterion-related validity of concept comparisons and concept maps for assessing reading comprehension.* [Research Report No. 3]. Eugene, OR: University of Oregon Resource Consultant Training Program.

PATTON, C. P., RENGERT, A. C., SAVELAND, R. N., COOPER, K. S., & CARO, P. T. (1985). *The world and its people: A world view.* Morristown, NJ: Silver Burdett Company.

ROBINSON, F. P. (1941). *Diagnostic and remedial techniques for effective study.* New York: Harper and Brothers.

SCHUMAKER, J. B., DESHLER, D. D., NOLAN, S., CLARK, F. L., ALLEY, G. R., & WARNER, M. M. (1981). *Error monitoring: A learning strategy for improving academic performance of LD adolescents.* Lawrence: University of Kansas Institute for Research in Learning Disabilities.

SMITH, C. B., & ELLIOTT, P. G. (1979). *Reading activities for middle and secondary schools.* New York: Holt, Rinehart, & Winston.

THOMAS, E. L., & ROBINSON, H. A. (1972). *Improving reading in every class.* Boston: Allyn & Bacon.

TINDAL, G., & MARSTON, D. (1991). *Classroom-based assessment: Evaluating instructional outcomes.* Columbus, OH: Charles Merrill.

TINDAL, G., & NOLET, V. (1992). Organizing knowledge forms to reflect critical thinking. Unpublished raw data.

TOLSTOY, L. (1987). "The two brothers" (translated by Ann Dunningan). In *Fables and Fairy Tales* (1962). New York, NY: New American Library.

TONJES, M. J., & ZINTZ, M. V. (1981). *Teaching reading/thinking study skills in content classrooms.* Dubuque, IA: William C. Brown.

VALENCIA, S. W., & PEARSON, P. D. (1988). Principles for classroom comprehension assessment. *Remedial and Special Education, 9*(1), 26–35.

VALENCIA, S. W., STALLMAN, A. C., COMMEYRAS, M., PEARSON, P. D., & HARTMAN, K. (1991). Four measures of topical knowledge: A study of construct validity. *Reading Research Quarterly, 26,*(3), 204–233.

WHITE, O., & HARING, N. (1980). *Exceptional teaching.* Columbus, OH: Charles Merrill.

CHAPTER NINE

How to Teach

INTRODUCTION

We know that teachers differ considerably in their backgrounds, training experiences, classroom histories, and orientations toward instructional tasks and
strategies. Yet, when looking into typical classrooms at any grade level and in
virtually any geographic region, we see many consistencies. Every room contains
desks, chairs, bulletin boards, and work tables; only the arrangements change
slightly from room to room. Although specific content, materials, and activity
sequences may vary, similarities in general expectations, activity structures, task
requirements, and operating procedures become apparent when students arrive
for class. Finally, in most classroom settings, teachers engage in similar kinds
of instructional behaviors, mostly verbal, interpersonal, and with noticeable
predictability.

But, in some classrooms, students are engaged in behaviors that conflict with
effective teaching and learning. They stare out the window, talk to each other about
nonschool and noncontent events, and play with their instructional materials. On
further investigation, we find that the teachers of these students also differ in the
way they instruct. Even well-developed material that is structured and selectively
organized can be delivered ineffectively and inefficiently.

Consultants must be skilled at helping teachers determine what to teach *and*
how to structure and deliver their teaching. In this chapter, we describe several
strategies for analyzing and modifying how to teach. We believe that consultants
must use these strategies so teachers can improve their delivery and students can
benefit from the instruction. Classrooms are divided activity structures that (a) represent events that demarcate the physical environment and the actions of
individuals within these environments and (b) control both the manner in which
teachers and students interact and the strategies used to deliver information.

The purpose of this chapter is to analyze "how to teach" and to provide a menu
of academic interventions that consultants and teachers can use to help students

succeed in academic contexts. We focus on how teaching is delivered, regardless of the specific content, which was addressed in Chapter 8. Before we begin this discussion, however, we need to describe the assumptions that underlie our approach.

Assumptions About How to Teach

We believe that classrooms have many consistencies that provide consultants with the basis for helping teachers analyze and modify their instructional behaviors and routines—that is, how they teach. These consistencies lead to general strategies for assessing academic learning problems and for building instructional interventions. We have made certain assumptions that are the basis for this approach to consultation:

1. *The major process is how teaching is delivered and the primary product is student achievement.* The strategies described in this chapter are built around the assumption that teachers deliver teaching through their instructional behaviors. The primary medium for analyzing the effects of this delivery is change in student behavior, or academic achievement. Oral and written responses are used to indicate the level of this academic achievement.

2. *Academic and social behavior problems are affected and maintained by similar contingencies.* Although we focus exclusively on academic behaviors in this chapter, distinctions between teaching and management strategies for academic and social behavior are artificial. In fact, many student problems may be the result of the combined effects of poor contingencies for managing behavior and ineffective strategies for delivering instructional content.

3. *The analysis of how to teach must focus on the overt instructional behaviors displayed by the teacher.* Assuming the consistencies described earlier, we emphasize the behaviors teachers use to deliver instruction. We are not ignoring the instructional features associated with the "before" and "after" of instruction (Kameenui & Simmons, 1991); however, teacher behaviors are accessible and modifiable and they have a direct, functional relationship with student learning.

4. *Verbal teacher behavior is the most common means of delivering instruction.* Although teachers use many gestures and express themselves through a variety of action behaviors, verbal behaviors dominate the classroom. Teachers continually give *mands*—words associated with commands, demands, and mandatory student responses—and *tacts*—verbal behaviors controlled by specific environmental antecedents (that is, discriminative stimuli) with established and conventional consequences (that is, reinforcements). Tacts include naming, assertions, and statements of association. In general, "the mand is an imposition on the hearer; the tact is a favor to them" (Winokur, 1976, p. 51). Obviously, teachers' verbal behavior is a complex combination of both mands and tacts that are considered links in a behavioral chain of teacher and student interactions.

5. *Modifications must be made to accommodate the student's learning and academic needs.* It is unlikely that consultants receive Requests for Assistance to help maintain the status quo; rather, requests are made because students are not learning under the prevailing instructional conditions. If the "what to teach" is appropriate, the delivery of instruction must be adjusted. The real problem is to identify what needs to be manipulated and how to make the modifications.

Given these assumptions, we discuss the analysis of instruction and how to teach from within an organizational scheme that reflects a three-step temporal perspective. The first step is to establish classroom environments that set the occasion for specific interactions among the teacher, the students, and the curriculum material. The second step is to organize and present the curriculum material; that is, teaching behaviors must be exhibited, new information must be presented (tacting), and students must be engaged with the material (manding). The final step is to provide follow-up and motivational techniques so students can maintain what they have learned and be productive (accurate and proficient) in other contexts. Obviously, all three aspects interact and should be considered in combination. However, we discuss each separately in order to address specific strategies. In summary, we focus on how to teach so "teaching methods or instructional means are viewed as classroom events within which students do academic work" (Doyle & Carter, 1987, p. 189).

Three Influences

Given these assumptions, our presentation on how to teach is based on three influences. First, we rely heavily on research found in the effective teaching literature (Berliner, 1987; Brophy & Good, 1987; Northwest Regional Educational Laboratory, 1990). We believe that these effective schooling practices and characteristics provide the essential foundation from which consultants and teachers must base their instructional activities and behaviors.

Second, we rely on a taxonomy of academic work and classroom organization, which was developed by Doyle (1983) and described by Doyle and Carter (1987), to characterize the activities presented and managed by teachers. Although classrooms can have a wide range of potential activities and organizational structures, they generally are characterized by a whole-class lecture or presentation, which typically takes up about 25% to 30% of the time, and independent seatwork, which accounts for approximately 60% to 70% of the time (Doyle & Carter, 1987). The basic premise of this scheme is that:

> Teachers organize groups of students for work by creating activities . . . (which) have two major dimensions. First, an activity has *organizational properties*, including (a) a pattern for arranging participants in the room (e.g., small groups versus whole-class presentations), (b) props and resources used (e.g., books versus films), and (c) duration, the time it takes for the activity to run (typically 10 to 20 minutes of class time). Second, an activity has a *program of actions* for teachers and students that guides behavior when an activity is set into motion. The program of action includes (a) roles, responsibilities, and action sequences for carrying out events (e.g., oral answering or writing workbook entries), and (b) rules of appropriateness that specify the kinds of behaviors that are allowed or disapproved (e.g., talking during snack time or silence during seatwork). [Doyle & Carter, 1987, p. 191]

Third, we have adopted an organization developed by Anderson and Burns (1989) to structure a classroom lesson. When a class begins, a wide range of behaviors are set in motion. We can expect to see a considerable amount of (a) verbal behavior displayed by students and teachers, (b) movement around the room by students and teachers, and (c) interaction and exchange between teachers and students. Somewhere in all this action lies a structure, which may or may not be systematically controlled and managed (Doyle & Carter, 1987). The Anderson and Burns model (Figure 9.1) focuses on three structural sources of influence on

FIGURE 9.1

Structural sources of influence on classroom interactions

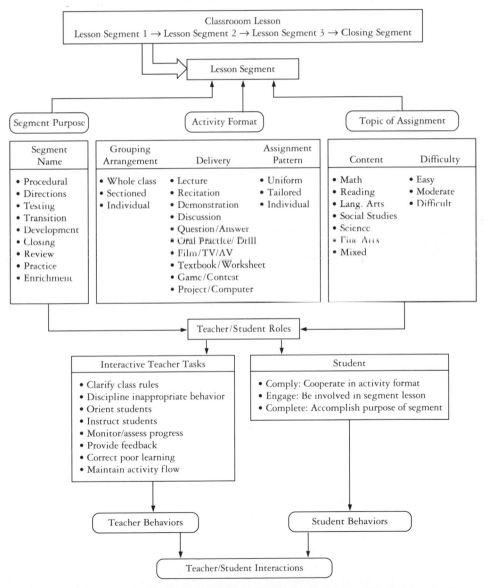

SOURCE: L. W. Anderson and R. B. Burns (1989). *Research in Classrooms.* Oxford: Pergamon Press.

classroom interactions: (a) lesson segments (consisting of a purpose, format, and topic), (b) teacher and student roles, and (c) teacher/student interactions. We use each of these components to discuss the effective teaching research and describe how consultants and teachers can use the major features of the taxonomy.

ANALYZING LESSON SEGMENTS TO STRUCTURE CONSULTATION

Classroom lessons often consist of minilessons or smaller segments that cumulatively lead the student toward some terminal learning objective. Each segment must be constructed and presented in an effective and efficient manner. In this section, we examine the segment's purpose, activity formats, and interactive teacher tasks. We illustrate how the Anderson and Burns (1989) model can be used to structure teacher and consultant activities, and we provide an example of how this analysis can be applied to a classroom problem.

Segment Purpose

The segment purpose is the aim of an activity or lesson segment and is defined specifically by the outcome established by the teacher. Definitions and examples for the nine different segment purposes are described below:

1. *Procedures:* Steps necessary for problem solving and achieving the expected outcomes.
   EXAMPLE: Mr. Musa, the science teacher, tells his students to "find an element in the periodic table, write its symbol on a green card, then go to the dictionary and find out where it can be found and for what purpose it is used."

2. *Directions:* Steps necessary for managing classroom behaviors.
   EXAMPLE: At the end of the lesson, Mr. Musa gives his students directions to "line up at the door and have your lunch ticket ready."

3. *Testing:* Activity designed to ascertain what students have learned.
   EXAMPLE: Mr. Musa gives an oral quiz in which Viktor must tell the symbol and one use of the presented element."

4. *Transitions:* Behaviors and time taken in changing from one activity structure to another.
   EXAMPLE: When switching from the lecture to the quiz portion of the lesson, Mr. Musa takes seven minutes, gathering and distributing materials, settling students, and arranging the desks for the quiz.

5. *Development:* Sequencing and delivering content designed to achieve some learning objective.
   EXAMPLE: To teach students about cesium, Mr. Musa discusses (a) the origin of the element name for cesium, (b) its atomic characteristics, (c) its molecular structure, and (d) its common uses in industry.

6. *Closing:* Activity used to complete teaching a segment lesson by providing summaries and reflections on information.
   EXAMPLE: At the end of the lesson, Mr. Musa restates the elements discussed during the lesson.

7. *Review:* Analysis or overview of previously presented information.
   EXAMPLE: Just before closing his lesson, Mr. Musa names other elements that have been discussed on previous days and discusses how they are related to elements from the current lesson.

8. *Practice:* Activity to provide students with an active opportunity to use information and skills that have been presented.
   EXAMPLE: Viktor is given a worksheet with a column of element symbols and another column with element names. He has to match the symbol to the name.

9. *Enrichment:* Activity whose purpose extends beyond the lesson's minimum requirements requiring advanced application of the information or resulting in additional skill development.
   EXAMPLE: Viktor finishes his worksheet before the end of the period and is allowed to go to the library and look in an encyclopedia for uses of cesium.

Each of these purposes is reflected at some time within a lesson segment. However, problems occur when segment purposes are missing, are not clearly defined, or are poorly executed. When confronted by a problem associated with a lesson, consultants and teachers should use the taxonomy to structure their analysis of the problem and determine the relationship between the segment and the student's performance. In Box 9.1, we have illustrated the kinds of questions consultants and teachers might examine for each segment purpose.

In the following example, we illustrate how a consultant and a teacher can analyze segment purpose and identify modifications to improve the execution of a lesson. Mrs. DeFuca asked Mr. Tombob, the building consultant, for help with three boys. She hoped he could make suggestions that would help organize her classroom so all her students were attending and learning at the same time.

When Mr. Tombob attended one of Mrs. DeFuca's lessons, he made several observations. At the beginning of the reading lesson, Mrs. DeFuca told all the students to get out their books and turn to page 154 to continue the story from the previous day so they could take the end-of-unit mastery test. While she was describing this plan, two students walked into the room and made some noise while getting into their desks. Ignoring these two students, she called on another student in the front row who was ready to begin reading (that is, his book was open and he was waiting quietly). After this student read for a couple of minutes, Mrs. DeFuca called on another student, who immediately picked up where the first student had left off. While individual students read, she corrected decoding errors and, every few paragraphs, made a comment or asked someone about the author's meaning. This routine continued for several minutes, until she called on one of the boys who had come in late. He had to ask where they were on the page. Mrs. DeFuca turned to the consultant with a "See, I told you so" look. She responded by walking over and pointing to the place in the book where they were reading, and then walked back to the front of the room, where she followed along on the passage from the teachers' edition. After about 30 minutes, the group finished the chapter.

Mrs. DeFuca then told the class that she was going to give a quick quiz on the last three chapters because they were at the end of the unit. She asked everyone to put everything away and not to touch their quizzes until she told them to begin. As she was getting the quizzes from her desk, a few students got up to sharpen their

BOX 9.1

Checklist of questions addressing segment purpose

Procedures	_____ Are all steps present? _____ Are the steps correctly sequenced?
Directions	_____ Are students listening to directions? _____ Are directions preceded by a statement of purpose? _____ Are there many steps?
Testing	_____ Are students prepared to take the test? _____ Have students been told the purpose of the test? _____ Are student protcols complete, clear, and easy to follow? _____ Do students know how their performance is being evaluated?
Transition	_____ Are transitions brief? _____ Is the classroom organized to minimize disruptions during transitions? _____ Are materials and resources readily accessible?
Development	_____ Is the context for learning (interest and motivation) established? _____ Are all concepts presented with appropriate examples and nonexamples? _____ Is important information highlighted? _____ Can the information be used to solve problems?
Closing	_____ Are students prepared to end the lesson? _____ Has the lesson purpose been summarized? _____ Have students been given feedback on their performance? _____ Do students know where the next lesson picks up?
Review	_____ Are highlights presented? _____ Are students given an opportunity to actively pratice what they've learned? _____ Have teachers solicited student reactions to their own works (samples)?
Practice	_____ Are students prepared to work independently? _____ Is all information presented on what to do? _____ Is material appropriate for practice (easy to moderate difficulty)?
Enrichment	_____ Are more materials available for students who want to learn more? _____ Are appropriate knowledge forms present (in type and diversity)?

pencils. On their way to the pencil sharpener, they slapped or teased others. Noticing these disturbances, Mrs. DeFuca told everyone to be quiet. Rather than causing any further delay, she asked the students to begin instead of reviewing the directions with the class. After the first few minutes, a couple of students raised their hands; they did not understand the first part of the test. Finally, after eight minutes of discussion and repeating directions, the room was quiet. Mrs. DeFuca settled in behind her desk, and Mr. Tombob's observation was over.

As a consultant, what questions should Mr. Tombob ask? What lesson segments were or were not activated? When Mrs. DeFuca gave directions, were all students clear (did they hear and understand the plan) about the reading and what they were expected to do? Were transitions between segments brief? Were the directions to the test clear? In finding answers to these questions, Mr. Tombob is assessing two major lesson segments—directions and transitions—and identifying a number of modification areas in order to improve the execution of the lesson.

Activity Format

An activity format defines how the segment purpose is accomplished. Teachers structure a medium or context for teaching and reacting to students through three major components: (a) the student grouping arrangement, (b) the delivery system, and (c) the assignment pattern.

Grouping arrangement.   Students can be taught in three types of arrangements: (a) whole class, (b) sectioned (small group), or (c) individually. The whole-class arrangement is efficient and easy for teachers to develop materials. Students have opportunities to learn incidentally from each other. For example, when students cannot answer a question that is presented by the teacher, they can listen to others give the correct answer and receive reinforcement or hear others receive a correction for an error. Whole-class instruction can be a problem for some teachers because it is difficult to monitor individual students and fewer students can actively participate.

Sectioned or small-group instruction is an excellent arrangement for maximizing student engagement. If students have been grouped on the basis of skill deficits, the lesson can be delivered more efficiently and with more feedback for individual performance. The advantages of incidental learning can be maintained if cooperative learning is used and student heterogeneity is structured. Student engagement is also likely to be quite high when the teacher provides opportunities for modeling, prompting, and reinforcement. Small groups can pose problems when teachers are unable to monitor other students who are not part of the group. These students may not be receiving optimal instruction; they may be given seatwork or "busy work" instead. In addition, grouping students may represent a form of tracking that unfairly keeps students from interacting with others and causes teachers to treat them based on their general grouping rather than on their individual strengths and weaknesses.

Individualized instruction is an effective arrangement for matching student skills with an appropriate instructional pace, curriculum, and delivery system. Feedback and corrections can be manipulated to fit every correct and incorrect response, the pace of instruction can be flexible, and high engagement rates can be maintained. However, students who are taught individually learn little from their peers and are isolated from their peers. This grouping arrangement is also very expensive and difficult to deliver, especially with respect to managing other students.

To weigh the advantages and disadvantages of the three types of grouping arrangements, consultants and teachers can ask the questions illustrated in Box 9.2.

In our example, Mrs. DeFuca has students reading in whole-class instruction. Is this arrangement the best choice? Is there a way to group the three boys who always seem to be on the wrong page so they can be monitored more closely and frequently? One solution, for example, might involve a sectioned arrangement. This type of grouping could be accomplished in several ways:

1. The boys can be placed together so more direct small-group management is possible. However, this new group might become a problem when Mrs. DeFuca has to work with other groups.
2. Each problem student can be paired with a more vigilant student who is likely to follow directions.
3. Grouping can be done on the basis of skill, instead of social behavior and compliance. Mrs. DeFuca would need to conduct reading assessments and place those with similar skills together to see if the boys could be placed in different groups.

Whatever Mrs. DeFuca does in this scenario, whole-class instruction does not seem to be the most effective and efficient activity format. The boys disrupt and distract the class. Because resources to individualize instruction, such as teaching assistants or parent volunteers, are limited, some type of sectioned activity format is justified.

Delivery.   Delivery refers to the system used as the medium to present explicit instruction. In the following list of ten delivery systems, we consider how each facilitates student responses or learning.

BOX 9.2

Checklist of questions addressing grouping arrangement

Whole Class	_____ What is the student learning from other students?
	_____ How disruptive is the student's presence in the group?
	_____ How engaged is the student?
Sectioned	_____ On what basis should students be grouped? And with whom?
	_____ What are other students doing during group instruction?
	_____ How long should groups be conducted? And where?
Individual	_____ Who can teach the student individually? And where?
	_____ How do skills and responses transfer and generalize to other (nonindividualized) settings?

1. *Lectures:* The most dominant format for delivering instruction in which the teacher directs all verbal interactions typically in a monologue and separated from the listener by several feet.
2. *Recitation:* Repetition of stock material by a student or students, directed entirely by the teacher or the curriculum materials.
3. *Demonstrations:* Presentation of models by the teacher so the students can see what they are learning and what they will eventually be demonstrating.
4. *Discussion:* An exchange with students facilitated by the teacher on a specific topic; gives both teacher and students opportunities to respond to each other's contributions.
5. *Question/answer:* A student-directed delivery system that provides opportunities for individual input and presents loosely guided parameters about what to say.
6. *Oral practice:* Like recitation, provides a structured delivery system in which students must devise responses.
7. *Film/TV/AV:* A third-party delivery system in which the teacher is usually proctoring in the room.
8. *Textbook/worksheet:* Presentation of information as a permanent product, which students must interact with in order to access new or review information.
9. *Games and contests:* Presentation of "problems" in game or contest situation; students must use some rule or algorithm to solve the problem.
10. *Project/computer:* Use of computers to deliver instruction with either a drill/practice activity or a game format; teachers can also assign projects in which students engage in independent study.

Because these different systems for delivering instruction can have a noticeable impact on how teachers and students interact, consultants and teachers should assess and modify them carefully and systematically, considering the questions illustrated in the checklist in Box 9.3.

In our reading lesson example, Mrs. DeFuca's basic delivery system consisted of oral practice in which (a) students devised responses by reading from a book, (b) Mrs. DeFuca described important components of the story after a few paragraphs were read, and (c) Mrs. DeFuca fielded comments and questions from students about the story. No lecturing, question-answering, or use of workbooks occurred, and demonstration and discussion represented a relatively minor amount of the instructional delivery.

What alternative delivery systems could be used to improve lesson delivery? What would happen if the lesson had been structured differently? What would the outcome have been if, for example, Mrs. DeFuca were to begin the lesson by directing students to listen while she reads the story to the whole class? They are then told that a map of the story will be handed out when she is done reading and that they will have to fill in the major elements of the plot, characters, setting, and so on. She then begins reading, stopping to define and describe key words and to ask questions after each paragraph has been read. When asking questions, she includes both literal (retell) and implication (prediction) types. While the students

BOX 9.3

Checklist of questions addressing instructional delivery

Lecture	_____ How long are the lectures?
	_____ What are the levels of engagement?
	_____ Are the knowledge forms within the lecture well balanced?
Recitation	_____ Is the material well suited (oriented toward facts) for recitation?
	_____ Do students recite individually or in groups?
	_____ How is the correctness of recitation monitored?
Demonstration	_____ Is the model well displayed?
	_____ Are the requisite steps explicated during the demonstration?
	_____ Is the information appropriate for demonstration?
Discussion	_____ Is the information appropriate (personal, evaluative) for discussion?
	_____ Do students stay on the topic?
	_____ Is the content monitored? Are interactions structured to ensure involvement by everyone?
	_____ How is the topic maintained?
	_____ Is a "conclusion" reached?
Question/ Answer	_____ Are the questions convergent or divergent?
	_____ What knowledge forms are represented in the questions?
	_____ How are students called on to answer questions?
	_____ Does the teacher exhibit an appropriate "wait time" after asking a question?
	_____ How are correct responses from students handled?
	_____ How are incorrect responses handled?

work on their story maps, Mrs. DeFuca walks among them to encourage and reinforce at-task behavior. When the students are finished, she pairs them up so they can read to each other. While these students are reading, she assembles a group of low-skill readers and conducts a round-robin reading, with students taking turns while she corrects decoding errors and comments about the plot, characters, setting, and so on. After about 15 minutes, she reassembles the whole class and finishes the story as she had begun—reading out loud. Using key words and phrases, she demonstrates how certain parts of the story fit together and then asks students to raise their hands to tell what they think are the most important components and meanings of the story.

This delivery system uses multiple systems, more than just oral practice, where only one student can respond at a time. The modified presentation allows more students to respond. It includes (a) a lecture-style system for everyone to get engaged, (b) a worksheet to provide structure and allow everyone a chance to respond, (c) an oral practice system so more students can respond and more small-group (sectioned) work with the students who need help can be conducted,

BOX 9.3   (*continued*)

Oral Practice/Drill	____ Is the material appropriate for oral versus silent practice? ____ How long are the responses? ____ How are they distributed among students?
Film/AV/TV	____ What is the reason for watching a film? ____ How does it fit into the lesson? ____ Does the information match the interactively taught information? The curriculum?
Textbook/ Worksheet	____ How does the textbook or worksheet extend the lesson? ____ What is the range of student responses represented? ____ What behaviors are exhibited? How long are students engaged? ____ What contingencies are present for feedback? For mistakes? For correct responses?
Game/Contest	____ How does the game fit into the lesson? ____ What types of student responses are necessary? ____ What decision-making skills are required? ____ What rules or algorithms are being learned? ____ What are the consequences for engaging? ____ How are students paced through the lesson? ____ What feedback is presented?
Project/ Computer	____ How does the textbook or worksheet extend the lesson? ____ What is the range of student responses represented? ____ What behaviors are exhibited? ____ How long are the students engaged? ____ What contingencies are present for feedback? For mistakes? For correct responses?

(d) a demonstration so all students can reach the conclusion at the same time, and (e) a discussion so students can respond to one another. This lesson format represents how the delivery system can be manipulated to allow students different engagements in a variety of tasks. The consultant's major problem is to determine which delivery systems are being used and not used.

Assignment pattern.   Assignment pattern refers to the manner in which students are given tasks to complete without teacher assistance. Students respond to teachers as a function of the manner in which tasks are given; that is, students complete assignments based on the contingencies in place. Consultants and teachers should consider three basic assignment patterns when assessing and modifying lessons. The first pattern is a uniform system in which everyone follows the same rules. For example, in most schools and classrooms, students are required to raise their hand if they want attention. Uniform sanctions maintain responses consistent with the rule.

In the second pattern, teachers tailor strategies that vary as a function of student grouping or skills. For example, students are given assignments or directions contingent on earlier responses: "Everyone who completed the first half of the worksheet in class today can turn it in; those who didn't get done must turn in the first and second halves of the worksheet at the beginning of class tomorrow." This contingency may be useful in getting students to stay on-task during class.

Finally, although assignments may be established as a function of classroom contingencies, student grouping, or skill level, teachers also assign instructional tasks on an individual basis. For example, at the end of the lesson, Ms. Brezchnov tells Mark to go to his desk and finish the worksheet, Rosa to work with Mr. Kavett to finish her worksheet, and Linda to put her worksheet away and finish it when she returns from science class.

Effective assignment patterns are needed if students are to be successful at extending their learning beyond the time spent with teachers in the classroom. This is especially true if students are at-risk of failure or exhibiting learning problems because of low "interest" or "motivation" or deficient skills. The questions illustrated in Box 9.4 can help consultants determine problems with extant assignment patterns or help them devise more effective ones.

In comparing Mrs. DeFuca's original delivery system and the consultant's modified version, the former system establishes a uniform assignment pattern in which everyone responds in the same manner. Contingencies for completion are primarily social with a focus on student compliance (that is, knowing their place in the story to begin reading when they are called on) and reading skill (actually reading the selection correctly in front of their peers). In the modified lesson, the contingencies are more individualized and tailored. For example, when students are working on the worksheet, Mrs. DeFuca can give individual contingencies to some students ("If you at least put down one word for each of the questions, I will consider the worksheet done."), while someone else can be given a social reinforcer ("Your answers sure are complete and thoughtful."). When the lower reading skill group works with her, she can give tailored (differential) attention within an oral practice situation. In summary, the original lesson had only one assignment pattern, whereas the adaptation allowed three types: a uniform pattern

BOX 9.4

Questions addressing assignment patterns

Uniform	_____ Are the tasks and required responses well described, with explicit time lines?
	_____ What are the contingencies for completing the work?
	_____ What are the reinforcers?
	_____ What are the time lines?
Tailored	_____ On what basis is the assignment differential?
	_____ Are assignments consistent with student skill level?
	_____ What are the contingencies for completing the work?
	_____ What are the time lines?
Individual	_____ Is the student's skill level appropriate for the assignment?
	_____ What are the contingencies for completing the tasks?
	_____ Can the student complete the work in the requisite time?

for everyone, a differential one for groups, and an individual one for specific students. These patterns do not occur in isolation but are controlled by the previous variables—lesson purpose, activity format, and delivery system—presented in this chapter.

Topics or Assignments

All lessons have a topic or assignment that defines the subject matter and its relative difficulty, which may vary across students. Consultants and teachers must consider two major topic or assignment issues: the nature of the content task(s) and the difficulty posed for students. Content refers to basic skill and content knowledge area addressed by a topic or assignment—that is, math, reading, language arts, social studies, science, fine arts, and mixed. Difficulty is differentiated into easy, moderate, and difficult. Consultants and teachers must examine the content and difficulty of tasks in their analysis of classroom activity structures (Box 9.5).

The content and difficulty of topics and assignments are covered in Mrs. DeFuca's lesson. However, because the material consists of narrative passages, decoding skills, vocabulary, and story grammar are important content components. Students need to have (a) phonetic skills to decode words and blend them together fluently and with expression, (b) synonyms and/or definitions of individual words, and (c) elements of a story to help structure the flow of events and integrate the different elements, such as characters and setting.

Unfortunately, this content does not represent the same level of difficulty for Mrs. DeFuca's entire group. For some students, the task is easy; these students are fluent readers and they have large vocabularies and considerable practice with narrative stories. With these skills, they can follow the plot and subplots without getting lost. However, others are not fluent readers and have to sound out individual words and blend them together slowly. By the time these students finish reading a selection, they have forgotten the story events or they are difficult to

BOX 9.5

Questions addressing content topics or assignments

Content	____ Do students have requisite skills to complete classroom tasks and assignments?
	____ Is reading proficient enough to gain information?
	____ Is spelling adequate to express information in writing?
	____ Is writing proficient enough to complete essays and reports?
	____ Is the content information organized into knowledge forms?
	____ Is the information presented with emphasis on major propositions?
Difficulty	____ Are assignments that are completed individually easy enough to preclude mistakes?
	____ When moderately difficult tasks are presented, is help available?
	____ Why are difficult tasks assigned?
	____ What feedback is presented? When?

recall. Furthermore, these students may have a more limited vocabulary and less experience reading. Thus, the same task is easy for some students and difficult for others. The only way out of this impasse is for the teacher to group students so that those who need extra help can get it while more successful students can move at their own pace. This grouping, however, should not be viewed as fixed; it is dynamic, occurring quickly and adaptively within the lesson.

Summary of Interactions Among Lesson Segments

Clearly, teachers' behaviors within a segment purpose, activity format, and topic or assignment do not occur in isolation or in a vacuum. Rather, students behave and learn in response to a complex learning environment that consists of a variety of setting arrangements and instructional antecedent and consequent manipulations. In the following sections, we discuss other considerations for facilitating and managing the interactions among lesson segments.

Establish systematic, routine classroom procedures.   In analyzing lesson segments, consultants need to consider how classroom procedures and lesson formats affect the potential for student improvement. The medium or context for actually delivering instruction must be well framed, consistent, and systematic and have clearly defined parameters. Such an arrangement maximizes teacher use of time and control over the eventual instructional sequence.

Teachers must be explicit in signalling the purpose of lesson segments. For example, Ms. Reissa prefaces a series of procedural steps with the following: "Now, I will describe the six steps you need to complete in making a model of an atom. Listen closely." Teachers may also need to review complex procedures while students are completing the task. Development, closing, and review must be well framed and clearly presented.

Transitions are an extremely important segment purpose and must be managed actively and overtly. Without efficient transitions, it is impossible to move from one activity structure to another. Transitions, rules, and procedures often seem unimportant to the content of a lesson; however, they may actually be the most important activity for creating and maintaining an academic focus (Doyle & Carter, 1987). Morine-Dershimer and Beyerbach (1987) indicated that pupil participation can be improved by establishing teacher routines, especially those dealing with classroom management and procedural issues.

Ideally, to shape and achieve smooth and efficient transitions, teachers should teach students about transitions at the beginning of the school year and then provide regular maintenance reminders. However, it is more likely that consultants will identify transition-related teacher and student problems after school has been in session. In either case, consultants and teachers should consider the following strategies for building and maintaining smooth and efficient transitions:

1. *Establish an individual student or classroom self-monitoring and feedback system.* Teachers and students can use a stopwatch to record the amount of time spent between lesson segments or write the beginning and ending times of each lesson and later compute the amount of time spent in lesson segments and transitions. Having data on the actual time spent in transition and making those data overt and public can be quite revealing and serve as a standard for comparison. Some of the graphing systems described in Chapter 6 can also help provide a visual display of transition data.

2. *Prepare all materials and resources well in advance of getting started on lesson tasks.* If teachers and students do not have the requisite curriculum materials ready at the beginning of a lesson, instructional time is lost. Placing specific and necessary materials in clearly designated places can reduce preparation. Students should be taught directly about the rules and routines for returning all materials to their appropriate places. They should also be given specific, positive feedback when they use and return materials appropriately.

3. *Provide clear advanced organizers and completion contingencies.* Consultants and teachers should provide students with clear information about what they are going to do and the consequences for making clear transitions. Setting contingencies may have the most immediate effect on getting students to minimize the time they spend disengaging from one activity and engaging in the next activity. For example, a teacher may state the following: "Everyone sitting at their desk with their book open to page 281 in the next minute can spend five extra minutes at lunch." Another teacher says, "In one minute, I will ask you to put your spelling workbook away, and ask you to get out your journals. I will give 'bonus' points to those students who make a quiet and on-time transition."

All strategies for managing transitions must be established systematically and implemented consistently. This is true of the other types of segment purposes as well. The critical notion is that the purpose should be so well established (automatic) that when students hear and see specific lesson cues, they know what is about to happen and what they should do. If this occurs, teachers can focus on the more important behaviors of teaching specific skills and content information. As Brophy and Good (1987) have noted:

> Higher achieving teachers had better managed classes even though they had more students. They spent less time in transitions and disciplinary activity, and their students called out more answers, asked more questions, and initiated more private academic contacts with the teachers. Classroom climate ratings and student attitudes were more positive in these classes, even though their emphasis was clearly on academics. [p. 347]

Use lesson segments that set the occasion for specific interactions.   Classroom environments must have lesson segments that are appropriate for the instructional delivery being used. In particular, they must maximize engagements between the students and what is being taught and between the student and the teacher. If a lesson segment is incompatible with the delivery method, instructional time will not be efficient and student learning will be slowed. For example, a demonstration delivery would have less impact if the procedural purpose was not clear. Similarly, grouping arrangements are highly related to specific segment purposes and delivery systems. Doyle and Carter (1987) present the following activity structures, which set the occasion for and facilitate specific delivery systems:

1. Whole-class presentations and recitations are often oriented around lectures using questions, answers, and teacher elaborations (QATE) (Korth & Cornbleth, 1982).
2. Whole-class or sectioned groupings need to occur for discussions and to stimulate student interest or generate complex analyses of a topic (higher-order operations), requiring a follow-up emphasis on closing or review.
3. Seatwork on textbooks or worksheets is often individual and characterized by infrequent and fixed opportunities for student responding and teacher feedback. Emphasis must be placed on giving students advance information or organizers before sending them to their seats and providing regular opportunities to receive feedback about their seatwork performance.
4. Small groups reflect differential grouping associated with basic skills instruction in elementary schools. Such grouping allows teachers to use recitation or oral drill and practice more than if they were teaching whole classes.
5. Individualized instruction is maximally responsive to student needs. The lesson purpose can virtually eliminate transitions and make all procedural and directional purposes very efficient. Lectures are seldom used, while all other activity formats can be implemented with maximum flexibility.
6. Instructional technology (primarily film and computers) often gives teachers time to catch their breath and diversify their delivery systems. However, teachers should develop and review instructional technology to increase the likelihood that content will fit with subsequent lectures, discussions, or question-and-answer sessions.

In summary, classroom lesson segments can be characterized as complex interactions among segment purposes, activity formats, and topics or assignments. As we have suggested in our descriptions of their interactions, they are not necessarily paired equally. However, consultants and teachers must realize two important features: (a) instruction can become efficient when these three components become established systematically and implemented as classroom routines, and (b) segment purposes, activity formats, and topics/assignments are not represented equally in a lesson segment but in specific combinations.

TEACHER/STUDENT ROLES

Continuing our use of the classroom lesson model developed by Anderson and Burns (1989), we see that segment purpose, activity format, and topic or assignment characterize a lesson segment and set the occasion for a range of possible teacher/student roles and interactions. Now, more specific interactions between teachers and students are likely to ensue and be maintained. Teachers and students assume roles that can be characterized, assessed, and modified. Given our focus on how to teach, we provide a brief overview of student roles and concentrate on teacher roles.

Student Roles

In every classroom lesson, students have three specific roles: to comply, to engage, and to complete. The degree to which students are successful in these roles is a direct function of the teachers' behaviors (interactive teacher tasks) and the segment purpose, activity format, and topic or assignment of the lesson segment. *Comply* is defined as the degree to which students cooperate in an activity format. Accomplishing maximum compliance is associated with efficient behavior, lesson, and classroom management. In addition, grouping arrangements, delivery, and assignment patterns must be structured appropriately and managed efficiently.

Engage is defined as the degree to which the student is actively involved in a lesson segment. Typically, engagement is defined by the amount of time that the student is actively interacting with the curriculum and satisfactorily progressing toward some learning objective. As with compliance, engagement is directly affected by segment purpose, activity format, and topic or assignment.

Complete is defined as the degree to which students accomplish the segment purpose. Achieving the purpose of a lesson segment is directly influenced by (a) the amount of student engagement and compliance, (b) the segment purpose, activity format, and topic or assignment features of the lesson segment, and (c) the interactive teacher tasks. In the next section, we focus our attention on interactive teacher tasks.

Interactive Teacher Tasks

Interactive teacher tasks are the teaching behaviors and interactions facilitated by teachers to present lesson segments and achieve student compliance, engagement, and completion. We have divided interactive teacher tasks into two general groups. First, teachers facilitate interactive tasks that establish environments conducive to learning. They clarify rules and present individual and group consequences for compliance or violation of these rules. Second, teachers engage in interactive tasks that are associated with teaching and learning of academic content. Given our emphasis on social behavior management in previous chapters, we now focus on the following interactive teaching tasks: (a) orienting students, (b) instructing students, (c) monitoring or assessing progress, (d) providing feedback, (e) correcting poor learning, and (f) maintaining activity flow. Each is defined and analyzed for use by consultants and teachers.

Orienting students.   Before presenting a lesson segment, teachers must first describe the context and frame or organize the content to be learned. Orientation is an active process made up of behaviors that can be observed. When students are oriented, they are looking at material and responding (talking, writing, listing, outlining). Orienting behaviors must be correct to facilitate learning and to minimize errors. Consultants and teachers should consider the following two strategies: create an anticipatory set to increase salience and interest, and use advance organizers to focus attention on terminal outcomes.

1. *Create an anticipatory set to increase salience and interest.* Few students learn when information is isolated and out of context with familiar or other learned information. Simply put, "whatever ways a teacher can use to tie in new ideas to old ones are likely to help students understand instruction better" (Berliner, 1987, p. 261). Teachers must create, or help students create, structures for integrating new information into what they have already learned. Although several cognitive constructs (such as schemata and ideational scaffolding) have been used to describe such structures, we refer to such phenomenon as previous learning.

Anticipatory sets heighten or focus student interest. Creating an anticipatory set consists of two parts. The first part is to determine the student's actual background knowledge and interests so that a context and relevance can be shaped for teaching new information. (Chapter 8 presented strategies for assessing background knowledge and interests.) The second part is to engage in tasks that relate new information to the student's background knowledge and interests. Consultants and teachers should consider overt strategies that use specific activity formats. For example, Mr. Nuthatch incorporates what has been learned with what is going to be learned in every development, closing, review, practice, and enrichment activity. When he previews the next lesson about the life cycle of the fruit fly, Mr. Nuthatch asks students if they (a) had ever seen small flies around a fruit bowl or at a fruit stand, (b) remember the flies that he had placed under the microscope to see insect wing structures, and (c) could tell him where flies come from.

2. *Use advance organizers to focus attention on terminal outcomes.* After the preparatory steps have been taken to analyze and organize the curriculum into a tight and connected body of information, teachers can begin setting up for teaching. Although some teachers actively and systematically prepare written plans, most teachers spend little time preparing their teaching. We believe that setting up must be systematic and complete so maximum instructional effectiveness and efficiency can be achieved. An old quotation clearly describes our position: "If you don't know where you are going, it's likely you'll never know when you get there." Knowing where you're going provides an overall understanding of what the unit is about and presages the content as well as the process. Students receive a general, organizing framework for all new information.

A clear setup for teaching provides an advance organizer (Ausubel, 1968) from which future information will be delivered and serves as the bridge between what students already know or think they know and what they will be learning. Many teachers view advance organizers as statements about what activities students will engage in during the lesson. We prefer to approach an advance organizer in terms of introducing the end goal of instruction and providing a conceptual overlay of the material to be presented.

> They are brief statements at a relatively high level of abstraction, generality, and inclusiveness compared to the material to be learned. These high level rules, propositions, and concepts help students to understand new instructional content by providing them with concepts on which to hang new ideas. That is, the advance organizer provides some way to structure the new knowledge that the teacher is trying to impart. [Berliner, 1987, p. 260]

In Chapter 8, we presented an example of an advance organizer that was used with an ocean unit. A proposition was used to encapsulate four major concepts (ocean, life forms, structure, and water movement) that were related and themes throughout this unit.

Using the example of an oceanography unit for middle school students, we may want to emphasize the connectedness of life forms. In Box 9.6, examples of two anticipatory sets are given. The anticipatory set in the excerpt from Jacques-Yves Cousteau (1981) introduces the study of oceanography in a much more interesting

BOX 9.6

Examples of two anticipatory sets

OCEANOGRAPHY

The ocean is a continuous body of salt water that covers a little over 70 percent of the earth's surface. Large as the ocean is, it is only part of the hydrosphere (HI druh sfihr), or Earth's water portion. Water in lakes and rivers and ice frozen in glaciers are all part of the earth's water supply. Water moves from ocean to land and back to ocean in a continuous cycle. Like the circulation of air, the water cycle is powered by solar energy. Evaporation of water depends on the sun's radiant energy. Transpiration (trans puh RAY shun) of plants also depends on sunlight. Transpiration is the process in which water escapes from the leaves of plants. Water in the air condenses, then falls to Earth as precipitation. Eventually, most of this water returns to the ocean. [Bishop, Sutherland, & Lewis, 1981]

THE OCEAN: A PERSPECTIVE

H_2O-Two atoms of hydrogen and one of oxygen. Water. The commonest, most abundant substance on the face of the earth, yet how rare this liquid is in the rest of the solar system and perhaps even in the galaxy.

Why should earth alone have been so lavishly gifted with this most precious of natural resources? Only minute traces of water in the liquid state have been found anywhere within reach of our telescopes or space probes.

The waves thudding on a distant shore are the heartbeat of man's ancestral home. The salt solution of the sea flows in man's veins, and—is it coincidence or part of nature's master plan—70 percent of man's body is water, the same proportion as the surface of the earth.

The great question today is: Can the sea help mankind survive? What is more, can it help man not only survive but also lead a full and rewarding life; in other words, live rather than exist?

I believe it can do both, in our quest for life's essentials. Since seawater covers so much of earth's surface, it is natural to look to the sea for our food, our energy, and, ultimately, our minerals. . . .

Space exploration has brought us the most precious gift of all, a global consciousness. However fragmented the world, however intense the national rivalries, it is an inexorable fact that we become more interdependent every day. I believe that national sovereignties will shrink in the face of universal interdependence. The sea, the great unifier, is man's only hope. Now, as never before, the old phrase has a literal meaning: We are all in the same boat.

That boat is the spaceship earth, a blue jewel glowing in the night of space, radiant and shining with the fluid of life the all-encompassing sea. [Cousteau, 1981]

manner than the actual curriculum unit presented by Bishop, Sutherland, and Lewis (1981).

Using the Cousteau excerpt, students can anticipate the kind of information that is forthcoming. They learn that (a) there is an emphasis on life forms and how they are interdependent on many different characteristics of the ocean, (b) interdependence is an important topic; and (c) there are implications associated with ignoring the ocean and its life forms.

In much of the current professional literature, an anticipatory set has been embedded into a problem-solving framework. Anchored instruction exemplifies this approach. Students are presented with a problem that serves as the advance organizer for the learning that follows. When teachers and consultants encounter learning failures, they should consider the impact of anticipatory sets and advance organizers. Students will not engage for long durations of time if learning is not reinforcing; that is, if outcomes and structure are unclear.

Instruct students using explicit instruction.   After orienting the student, instruction can be delivered as structured interactions between teachers and students. We believe that instruction is more than just telling; rather it involves systematically framing information so students can interact with it and solve relevant problems with minimal errors. This framing must be well established and planned so the interactions can involve active engagement with plenty of feedback. In addition, authentic tasks must be used to increase the likelihood of transferability outside the classroom.

We present three major components within this phase of instruction: (a) explaining and demonstrating, (b) using explicit language, and (c) supporting verbal presentations with graphic organizers.

Explaining and demonstrating refers to the transmission of information (tacts) by teachers or students. Recommendations from the effective teaching literature can help consultants and teachers with effective explanations and demonstrations.

In general, researchers have found that when effective teachers teach well-structured subjects, they

1. Begin a lesson with a short review of previous prerequisite learning.
2. Begin a lesson with a short statement of goals.
3. Present new material in small steps, with student practice after each step.
4. Give clear, detailed instructions and explanations.
5. Provide a high level of active practice for all students.
6. Ask a large number of questions, check for student understanding and obtain responses from all students.
7. Guide students during initial practice.
8. Provide systematic feedback and corrections.
9. Provide explicit instruction and practice for seatwork exercises and, where necessary, monitor students during seatwork. [Rosenshine & Stevens, 1987, p. 377]

These components provide an infrastructure within which teaching can best be framed and organized. Yet, specific verbal instruction is needed to actually carry out and deliver the information to be learned by students. Berliner (1987) includes the following steps:

STEP 1: Make sure you understand the question that a student has asked or that you raise in your explanation. Ask yourself what it is that most students who receive the explanation should be concerned about.

STEP 2: Identify "things" (elements, variables, concepts, events) involved in the relationship needing to be explained.

STEP 3: State the relationship between the different "things" you identified in step 2.

STEP 4: Show how the relationship identified in step 3 is an instance of a more general relationship or principle. [Berliner, 1987, p. 261]

Berliner (1987) indicates that explanations can be improved if teachers avoid using vague terms and use slower, longer, more expanded explanations. He also indicates that:

1. Teachers can do a better job of teaching how to comprehend written material by doing the following three things:
   a. "Focusing on specific mental process needed to do the task at hand" (p. 264). (The how to do, the process, is at least as important to communicate to students as the what to do, the product).
   b. "Making visible the mental process involved" (p. 264). (For example, the steps toward the solution of a problem can be verbalized, not left silent, allowing a teacher to model the way the relevant mental processes should be employed).
   c. "Making instruction cohesive and continuous across lessons" (p. 264). (It is hard to understand what is expected when instruction is disjointed and disconnected). [Berliner, 1987]

2. Teacher demonstrations and explanations should always include the rule-example-rule technique. "When compared to less effective communicators, the explanations of very effective communicators were found to contain more instances of a patterns of phrases called rule-example-rule" (Berliner, 1987, p. 265). In particular, liberal use of examples appears to be beneficial.

3. The verbal behavior of teachers is marked by explicit explanatory links using prepositions and conjunctions indicating cause, result, means, and purposes (for example, because, if . . . then, when . . . then, consequently, since, by, then, therefore).

4. Other verbal markers that serve as highlighting and transitional cues should be used explicitly. Specific

> cues to students that indicate what they should attend to most in an explanation. . . . Examples of such cues are phrases like "Now note this; . . . It is especially important to realize that . . .; It will help you to understand this better if you remember that . . .; Now, let's discuss the most crucial point of all, namely that . . ." [Berliner, 1987, p. 265]

In summary, Box 9.7 includes a list of guidelines for delivering clear explanations assembled by Rosenshine and Stevens (1987). Using these guidelines, we have

BOX 9.7

Guidelines for delivering clear explanations

1. Clarity of goals and main points
   ____ a. State the goals or objectives of the presentation.
   ____ b. Focus on one thought (point, direction) at a time.
   ____ c. Avoid digressions.
   ____ d. Avoid ambiguous phrases and pronouns.

2. Step-by-step presentations
   ____ a. Present the material in small steps.
   ____ b. Organize and present the material so that one point is mastered before the next point is given.
   ____ c. Give explicit, step-by-step directions (when possible).
   ____ d. Present an outline when the material is complex.

3. Specific and concrete procedures
   ____ a. Model the skill or process (when appropriate).
   ____ b. Give detailed and redundant explanations for difficult points.
   ____ c. Provide students with concrete and varied examples.

4. Checking for students' understanding
   ____ a. Be sure that students understand one point before proceeding to the next.
   ____ b. Ask questions to monitor students' comprehension of what has been presented.
   ____ c. Have students summarize the main points in their own words.
   ____ d. Reteach the parts of the presentation that the students have difficulty comprehending, either by further teacher explanation or by students tutoring other students.

SOURCE: Rosenshine & Stevens, 1987. "Teaching Functions," in *Handbook of Research on Teaching, Third Edition,* Wittrock (ed.). NY: Macmillan.

formed a checklist for consultants and teachers to use when analyzing and modifying their explanations and demonstrations.

Using explicit language refers to specific statements that (a) are understood by students, (b) focus on observable outcomes or performance, (c) give students specific direction in their learning, and (d) provide direct descriptions or explanations. Early comprehension instruction was dominated by teachers' asking students questions (Durkin, 1978–1979) in which, at best, "mentionings" of significant information from the text were provided. Now, more effort is devoted to teaching strategies explicitly so students can make meaningful interpretations and solve problems.

Consistent with Berliner's (1987) suggestions to use clear language, we emphasize highly specific verbal cues to help direct students in their learning. We cover two types of relationships: local (cohesion from sentence to sentence) and global (coherence to an overall topic). Although the terms *cohesion* and *coherence* are derived from the written expression literature, they are useful in describing any verbal behavior (oral or written). Consultants can use the resulting analysis to develop interventions that are (a) easily implemented without overhauling an entire teacher lesson and (b) helpful for all learners who are failing or at risk of failure.

Local relationships refers to the specific information that is found within and between sentences and is used to build connections and relationships. An analysis of local relationships focuses on the use of key positional words, vocabulary words, given-new principles (intersentence patterns), and finally, redundancies and stylistic devices. The following examples illustrate these terms:

1. Positional words.   A number of different positional words control readers' "expectations" of upcoming information. For example, Sloan (1983) identified the following relationships "with the words that can 'always' express the relationships given first, the 'synonyms' in parentheses" (p. 447): (a) coordination-and (furthermore, in addition, too, also, again), (b) observations-but (yet, however, on the other hand), (c) causation-for, (d) conclusions-so (therefore, thus, for this reason), (e) alternatives-or, (f) inclusions-"often expressed with a colon," and (g) sequences "first . . . second . . . third," or "earlier . . . later."

Ellis (1989) has called such key positional words *alert words* that signal important impending information. These words can be taught ahead of instruction as signals to help the learner with the lesson structure. Examples of alert words include:

1. *Offering reasons*: because, deduct, effect, explanation, purpose, reasons, since, therefore.
2. *Offering things/ideas*: example, instance, model, pattern, sample, type.
3. Presenting comparisons: associated, contrast, differences, with relation to, opposite, parallel, resemblance, similarities, on-the-hand.
4. *Expressing main ideas*: basically, driving at, drift is, in essence, in conclusion, in summary, key point, significance of this is, the gist is, the most important.
5. *Giving organizational information*: categories, characteristics, classes, divisions, features, first-second, third, groups, kinds, many members, parts, roles, several steps, stages, ways.

2. Vocabulary words.   Obviously vocabulary words directly control the reader's understanding of information, and many words are content specific. If an assessment is conducted prior to instruction, difficult or unknown vocabulary words can be identified and more precise words can be used in explanations and demonstrations.

3. Given-new principles.   When sentences are concatenated with new sequences of information, intersentence patterns (given-new principles) are formed. Notice in the following Oceanography Unit example, how the first sentence establishes the "given," and the remaining sentences present new and related information:

> Diatoms multiply rapidly when storms mix the ocean waters and bring up large quantities of nutrients from the deep currents. Then diatoms may cover the ocean surface and form a great blanket of food. Marine animals move in quickly and food is soon used up.

4. Stylistic devices.   Stylistic devices are used to create effects. Examples include metaphors ("the dawn of creation"), similes ("Like old bones, we have become rigid and brittle."), analogies ("It was similar to a free fall."), and various anaphoric structures ("It was both delightful and scary, exhilarating and frightening, and whimsical and serious."). At times, these stylistic devices can confuse the learner when pronouns are involved and require the learner to follow events in reference to a particular subject.

In summary, information proceeds within the lesson from one sentence to the next. By highlighting key words, particularly those that are positional and structural (describing relationships) and those that are associated with large amounts of content, consultants and teachers can help students interact with new information in a more successful manner.

In contrast to local relationships, *global relationships* refers to overall content organization that has been created through paragraph structure, organization devices (such as heading and subheadings), and implicit textual inferences. An example of global relationships is the writing style adopted by the American Psychological Association (APA), which is used by major educational publications. Information is structured into a standardized style in which major groupings are delineated by heading levels. Superordinate and subordinate relationships are reflected in the example shown in Box 9.8.

The APA style system stipulates how the text should look (for example, capitalization and underlining) so standard visual cues are given to the reader. In a similar fashion, most content area textbooks have structures that are reflected in chapter headings. Consultants and teachers should work to identify such global relationships and make them clear or more overt for students.

Graphic organizers are visual guides that reflect the structure of information; that is, how pieces of content (concepts and principles) are related. Rather than relying on words, typefaces, underlining, and the like, graphic organizers provide a single image or representation consisting of boxes, lines, arrows, and other figures. These visual displays are often superior to simply placing the content in text and trying to use words to explain relationships and associations; however, the type of organizer used should be compatible with the information being presented. For example, time lines best depict historical chronologies but may not work well for describing cause-effect relationships.

BOX 9.8

Example of superordinate and subordinate heading relationships

Introduction
    Overall theoretical focus or literature review
    Specific focus and purpose of study
Method
    Subjects
    Treatment or intervention
    Measures
    Procedures
Results
Discussion

Several types of graphic organizers—including maps, structural illustrations, hierarchical illustrations, and chronological charts—can be considered.

1. *Maps* are the heart of some subject matters like geography and related disciplines. A map, however, need not emphasize location alone; rather, the main idea may be more specific content (such as force, distance, or direction). For example, in Figure 9.2, a map is used to illustrate the ocean currents. The concept of circulation differentiates the oceans and is a critical attribute for the concept of ocean.

2. *Structural illustrations* are used to display information, but not necessarily to scale. All components are represented to show relationships and associations. In Figure 9.3, a structural illustration is used to present and display topographical ocean labels.

3. *Hierarchical illustrations* are used to reflect superordinate and subordinate relationships. In many cases, information is hierarchical and levels are nested within and across each other. Flow charts and other organizational charts are used to illustrate hierarchical relationships. In Figure 9.4, we use a hierarchical illustration to show information about ocean life forms (or any other phylic structure).

4. *Chronological charts* are used to organize sequences of events that are temporally related. Other kinds of information can also be included. For example, in Figure 9.5, information was taken from a science textbook about undersea life (Flemming, 1977). To reduce the confusion found in the narrative, we constructed a chronological chart.

FIGURE 9.2

A map depicting the concept of ocean

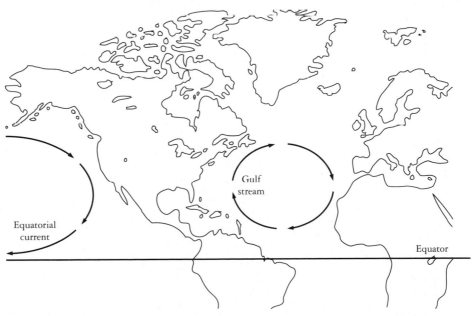

FIGURE 9.3
Structural illustration

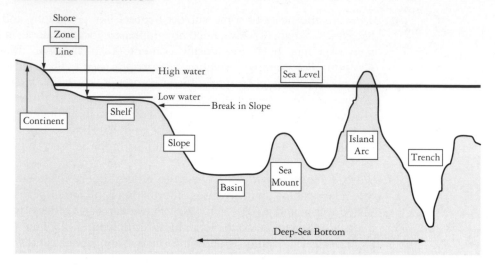

FIGURE 9.4
A hierarchical display

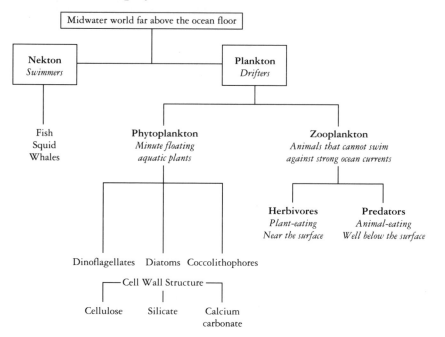

FIGURE 9.5

Chronological chart showing cycle of life, death, decay, and life in the ocean

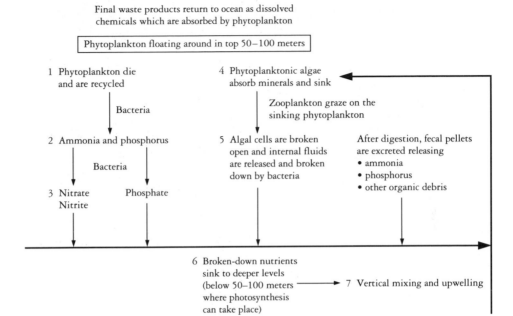

Final waste products return to ocean as dissolved
chemicals which are absorbed by phytoplankton

Phytoplankton floating around in top 50–100 meters

1 Phytoplankton die
  and are recycled

        Bacteria

2 Ammonia and phosphorus

        Bacteria

3 Nitrate   Phosphate
  Nitrite

4 Phytoplanktonic algae
  absorb minerals and sink

        Zooplankton graze on the
        sinking phytoplankton

5 Algal cells are broken
  open and internal fluids
  are released and broken
  down by bacteria

After digestion, fecal pellets
are excreted releasing
• ammonia
• phosphorus
• other organic debris

6 Broken-down nutrients
  sink to deeper levels
  (below 50–100 meters   7 Vertical mixing and upwelling
  where photosynthesis
  can take place)

Grossen and Carnine (1991) describe four other types of graphic organizers for displaying specific text structure patterns (see Figure 9.6). These organizers show relationships within information content and allow main ideas to be highlighted and structured visually. The first pattern or structure is descriptive or thematic, with emphasis on superordinate and subordinate relationships. Most content information can be organized into this structure if hierarchical relationships (similar to outlining) are reflected. The second type is comparative or contrastive, in which similarities and differences are highlighted on several dimensions or features. A third structure is sequential-episodic, in which major events are displayed in a chronological order and particular influences are shown under each event. Finally, a problem and solution map is the fourth structure, in which cause, effect, and solution are displayed in the order of occurrence. Grossen and Carnine (1991) note that these "four maps can form a basis for teaching students to use text structure patterns to identify main points and relationships among them . . . Any mapped text may vary from the skeletal form in a number of ways" (p. 49).

In summary, graphic organizers are useful tools for helping teachers convey information, support the delivery of instruction, and organize student independent practice. They are also useful in the consultation process because instruction can be manipulated while maintaining the central role of the teacher.

FIGURE 9.6

Four types of graphic maps for organizing information and analyzing specific text structure patterns

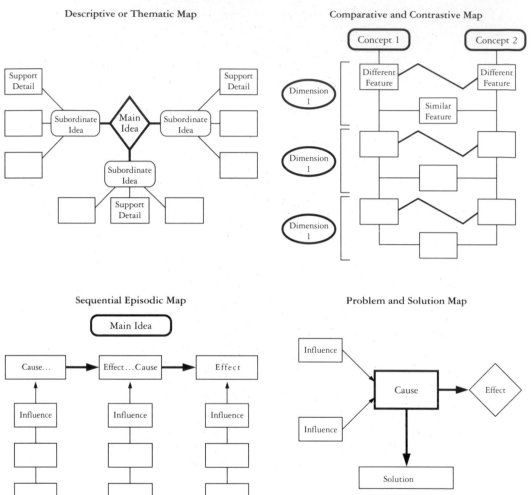

Descriptive or Thematic Map

Comparative and Contrastive Map

Sequential Episodic Map

Problem and Solution Map

SOURCE: B Grossen & D. Carnine. "Translating Research on Text Structure Into Classroom Practice", *Teaching Exceptional Children,* 24 (4), 1992, 48.

Given the need for explicit directions when initiating interactive reading tasks, Mrs. DeFuca should consider the following strategies:

1. Use an anticipatory set or an advance organizer that can be presented by using rich and elaborated information, modifying the tone of voice, or integrating initial information so relationships are highlighted.

2. Deliver instruction explicitly, in preparation for the distribution of worksheets. For example, specific directions can be read so that students know what and how to complete a story grammar task. The worksheet can include specific task completion directions and strategies.

In the questions below, use the main parts of the story to locate the sentence where the information is presented. Then summarize that sentence to answer the question. Remember the following to help you locate the sentences:

  a. *Characters:* People and animals that do things; usually have names (look for words that are capitalized).
  b. *Setting-Places:* Where the story occurs; sometimes have capital letters.
  c. *Era:* When the story takes place.

3. Use a range of graphic and advance organizers to present explicit instruction. For example, the story map can be created by the students or given directly by the teacher.

Monitor and assess progress during instruction.   At some time during the delivery of instruction, students respond. Then teachers must determine if the students are learning material at an appropriate level. We distinguish monitoring and assessment of progress during instruction from assessment that occurs following instruction. During instruction, most assessment is conducted interactively through a question-answer delivery system. No permanent record is maintained, and it is usually informal. Teachers use this information to determine pacing and focus instruction. In contrast, assessment that occurs after instruction emphasizes selection (or multiple choice) and production (or written essay) responses that leave permanent records for both immediate and delayed analysis.

During instruction, consultants and teachers must carefully attend to the planning and impact of question-answer strategies in the classroom. Information can be collected through anecdotal records or functional assessments.

> When a teacher asks a question, there are at least four possible reasons why a student may not respond (Winne & Marx, 1982): (1) The student is not attending, (2) the student is attending but doesn't understand, (3) the student understands what was intended but doesn't have the knowledge and cognitive skills to respond, (4) the student understands and has the knowledge and cognitive skills to respond but chooses not to (e.g., lacks motivation). Each of these conditions has important implications for pacing the lesson. What complicates the teacher's task further is that it is possible for all of these conditions to exist in a given classroom group at one time. And all of these conditions can characterize the same student over a period of time. [Morine-Dershimer & Beyerbach, 1987, p. 208]

What is important about question-asking within the instructional episode is that valid data are generated for making decisions about student performance. We use the term *valid* to reflect the accuracy and truthfulness of teachers' decisions as a function of the information they generate (Messick, 1989). For example, as implied in the four types of responses made by students, different decisions can be made. If students do not respond because of a knowledge deficit, then instruction needs to be parsed out, sliced back, repeated, or somehow reformatted. However, if their lack of response is because of inattention or noncompliance behavior, then contingencies for responding need to be reconsidered. Teachers must decide whether to buttress instruction or rearrange contingencies virtually on the spot. Fortunately,

> In the classroom, teachers' questions are about "known information" (the teacher knows the answer), and the teachers' reaction to the answer tells the student how well the answer met the teacher's expectations (Mehan, 1979). A positive evaluation of a response terminates the three-part question "cycle," whereas a negative evaluation continues or extends it, for the teacher may repeat or simplify the question or prompt the student to supply a more accurate response. [Morine-Dershimer & Beyerbach, 1987, p. 216]

To ensure that high-quality information is generated through questions and to maximize instructional effectiveness, consultants and teachers should consider research-based strategies that can be used to guide questioning and help students give sound answers. Gall and Rhody (1987) have suggested the following strategies:

1. Keep all students on task.
2. Phrase questions clearly.
3. Provide a wait time (typically three to five seconds is optimal for waiting after a question has been asked).
4. Respond to student answers positively and constructively.
5. Ask questions frequently.
6. Ask students questions in all phases (before, during, and after) of instruction.
7. Focus questions on academic content.
8. Focus questions on a variety of knowledge forms and in response to different text structures.
9. Consider a variety of learning tasks and student responses needed to answer the questions.
10. Be systematic and consistent in question-asking with controlled practice provided for strategies in answering the questions.
11. Ask questions that result in a high rate of success.
12. Encourage students to respond in some fashion, whether they are certain of the answer or not.
13. If students are incorrect, provide assistance or the correct answer along with an explanation.
14. Balance selection of respondents between students who volunteer and those who don't.

These 14 considerations can be distilled into at least one very important dimension: effective use of wait time (number 3). If that wait time is increased to an average of 3 seconds (Rowe, 1974), through relatively simple training procedures, ten beneficial effects occur:

1. The length of student responses increases.
2. The number of unsolicited but appropriate responses increases.
3. Failures to respond by students decreases.
4. Confidence, as reflected in decrease of inflected (question-like tone of voice) responses, increases.
5. The incidence of speculative responses increases.

6. The incidence of evidence-inference statements increases.
7. The incidence of student-to-student comparisons of data increases.
8. The frequency of student questions increases.
9. The incidence of responses from students rated as slow by teachers shows an increase.
10. The variety in types of actions taken by students increases. [Berliner, 1987, p. 269]

To summarize, if properly and carefully planned and implemented, questioning strategies can be used to monitor student progress and help students organize and select information. Questioning strategies also set the occasion for the delivery of feedback to students in classroom.

In our example with Mrs. DeFuca, her original instructional episode, which primarily consisted of oral practice, provided limited opportunity for monitoring student progress. Active student/teacher engagement and some type of student product or response are required to monitor student progress and to make judgments. Unfortunately, only a few students are able to respond, making it nearly impossible to determine how many of the other students are learning. However, if Mrs. DeFuca's lessons were revised as the consultant proposed, a number of opportunities would exist for monitoring student progress. During the whole-class story map worksheet exercise, each student generates a product, which would allow Mrs. DeFuca to monitor progress at the time it was being completed as well as over time and across successive exercises. By allowing students to pair up, Mrs. DeFuca could work with students who need more help and inspect their performance more closely. With a more concentrated rate of interaction, questioning of each student can be done more quickly and directly. If students were given a checklist to use during their peer reading, Mrs. DeFuca could monitor their progress to determine when it was time to move back into the whole-class lesson segment.

Finally, in the last phase of instruction (discussion), Mrs. DeFuca could improve student engagement and attentiveness by using some anticipatory set that is interesting and engaging. By structuring the activity at the beginning and ending of the reading, she would give all students access to the same requisite knowledge to participate in the discussion. Therefore, in the final segment, when a student does not answer a question, it is either because the question was not understood (presentation problem), the answer was not learned (acquisition problem), or a choice was made not to answer (compliance problem). In this approach, every attempt is made to structure instruction so an informed judgment can be made about the type of student response problem.

Provide feedback.   We define *feedback* as teacher responses that follow specific student academic responses or performance. In this context, feedback can be immediate or delayed in reaction to specific academic behaviors. Occasionally, feedback can take the form of praise in which it is used to confirm correct responding. At other times, praise serves more to correct, elaborate, and shape specific behaviors or to establish different controlling antecedent events (that is, discriminative stimuli). For example, when a student is reading orally and mispronounces a word), teachers can ignore the mistake, correct it, or halt the student and prompt a different response from the same or a different student. Each of these responses provides the students with specific feedback. To determine which response a teacher should make, it is important to conduct a thorough error analysis and functional assessment to discover if the error was a random error, a compliance problem, a missing prerequisite, or a systematic error (Haring & White, 1980). We offer the following suggestions to assist teachers and consultants in their analysis of errors and feedback types:

1. *Feedback, like reinforcement, should be precise statements referring to specific behaviors and not broad and vague statements about general performance.* For example, the information conveyed in the latter of the following two statements is more useful: (a) "I am very disappointed in how this class did on the test this week," or (b) "I was quite surprised that all but three students knew how to solve the addition math story problems but had trouble with the subtraction math story problems."

2. *Feedback, like reinforcement, should be immediate.* If it is delayed, it should be provided after a reminder or update of the behavior to which it is being associated. This strategy places the response in context with the appropriate antecedent or setting.

3. *Feedback should provide students with information.* When students answer correctly, teachers can elaborate and describe why the response is correct. For example, rather than saying, "Yes, Alfonse, the answer is thirty," the teacher could give more information by saying "Yes, Alfonse, you noticed that you had to carry the one when you added nineteen and eleven." If Alfonse were to give the wrong answer, the information contained in the teacher's answer becomes more important, "Alfonse, nine and one is ten . . . so, carry the one when you add nineteen and eleven."

4. *First efforts by the student to respond must be corrected, adjusted, or reinforced within one interaction; feedback should not follow guessing games or random answering.* If a response is clearly correct, provide specific praise and information. If a response is clearly incorrect, provide a simple and informative correction ("The answer is fifty-four; try again.") and move on to the next trial or student. If a student response is incomplete or partially correct, teachers should acknowledge what is correct and elaborate on completing the response correctly, for example, "Yes, squares have four equal sides, but remember that they also have ninety-degree corners."

In summary, consultants and teachers must understand the function of feedback within an instructional task and lesson format and relative to the learning history of a specific student. Feedback, like reinforcement or any other intervention, cannot be defined in abstract terms; it is defined based on its effect on the behavior. A functional analysis should be used to ascertain what effects are present and how new effects might be created.

For feedback to be effective, students must be engaged in high rates of responding, and opportunities must be provided within whole-class instruction so feedback is possible and useful for all students. Feedback can be given to any response presented during instruction and turned into a "teachable moment," especially for those students who are not actively responding. In fact, feedback may be more effective in larger groups, where a broader range of responses are available during teacher/student interactions. For example, if Mrs. DeFuca had structured a discussion during the final lesson segment, all responses by students could be elaborated, enriched, or extended with feedback that is specific, immediate, and informative.

Correct poor learning.   Many of the strategies discussed thus far can be used to correct poor learning. For example, the lesson segment purpose can be redefined, the grouping arrangement can be adjusted, different activity structures can be employed, assignment patterns can be rearranged, or alternative interactive teacher tasks can be attempted. However, within these strategies, a host of prosthetic strategies can also be implemented. We use the term *prosthetic* (Lindsley, 1964) to refer to their support function. A classic example of a prosthetic is the orthography used in the Direct Instruction materials (for example, Englemann & Haddox, 1981). For students who have difficulty learning to read, an orthography serves as a stronger visual prompt for certain responses than the typical English letter. As the child associates a response with an English letter in the presence of the orthography, the orthography is gradually eliminated.

In Box 9.9, we have organized strategies for correcting poor learning into major classes: (a) materials selection, (b) material adaptations, (c) opportunities for learning, and (d) contingencies for learning. More specific strategies are given for each class.

Maintain activity flow.   Teachers implement many strategies that work well for a short period. When strategies lose their effectiveness, students and/or teachers disengage from the lesson because the novelty of the activity has decreased; that is, the procedure or activity has lost its reinforcing qualities. Consultants must arrange the appropriate contingencies to maintain student and teacher interactive engagements and provide regular follow-ups so (a) learning will continue and (b) management of the program can be transferred fully from the consultant to the teacher.

In this last section, we concentrate on two strategies to maintain activity flow and student and teacher engagement in the classroom: (a) organizational techniques to monitor academic work so students are paced and provided feedback as they respond to teacher-presented tasks and (b) motivational strategies to manage accountability so students and teachers know the consequences associated with their behavior (Doyle & Carter, 1987).

Organizational techniques involve the management of time and space. Rather than focusing on specific teaching behaviors, consultants and teachers need to concentrate on their findings and on setting opportunities for maintaining positive interactions within the classroom. The best strategy to accomplish high rates of positive interactions is to ensure classroom contingencies distributed evenly over time and within lessons. These contingencies should be based on positive reinforcement (giving a positive outcome for a positive interaction) rather than on negative reinforcement (withdrawing an aversive outcome for engaging in a

BOX 9.9

Examples of strategies by class for correcting poor learning

MATERIALS SELECTION

1. Select special and supplementary materials or textbooks, such as lower-reading-level texts with the same content as the class text.
2. Provide instructional materials geared to the student's level of basic skills.
3. Use activities that do not demand as much reading skill.
4. Use "hands-on" activities as often as possible.

MATERIAL ADAPTATIONS

1. Adapt extant materials.
2. Leave extra white or blank space around questions or important information.
3. Provide a written outline or review sheet several days before the test is given.
4. Highlight main facts in the book.
5. Use self-correcting materials and programmed learning.
6. Provide a study guide.
7. Allow for the use of notes or the text in test taking.
8. Allow the student to have a sample or practice test.
9. Give assignments orally and visually.
10. Provide mimeographed material (legible).
11. Model the behaviors you expect—when talking to the student, show him/her an example of what you mean.
12. Use modeling of others.
13. Use adjunct media (computer programs, films, filmstrips) with the same content as the class.
14. Break complex tasks down into smaller steps and ensure successful completion of one level before progressing to the next.

OPPORTUNITIES FOR LEARNING

1. Change the number of opportunities for learning.
2. Reduce the quantity of material.
3. Provide an extra drill.
4. Enlist other students to work with the student who is having difficulty in a particular area.
5. Ask the student to repeat the directions and check for accuracy and understanding.

CONTINGENCIES FOR LEARNING

1. Rearrange the contingencies of reinforcement.
2. Provide immediate reinforcement of correct response.
3. Provide immediate correction of errors.
4. Use reflective statements.

positive interaction). For example, students working on their own frequently disengage from their activity because their work goes "unnoticed."

To increase the duration of their independent work, teachers must move more frequently and systematically among the students and provide positive statements about their work. When students require extended periods to complete larger tasks, teachers need to provide interim praise following a regular (fixed or variable) interval of time (interval schedule of reinforcement) or work (ratio schedule of reinforcement). When students ask teachers for assistance, opportunities for positive interactions are possible. To avoid missing a student, teachers must learn to scan students systematically, move regularly through the classroom, and teach students a clear attention-getting signal (such as a high handraise, placecard, help flag). To prevent students from disengaging when they must wait to obtain teacher attention, teachers and consultants should establish routines that keep students engaged (for example, have easy alternative activities available or teach students to ask a classroom assistant or peer tutor). All strategies should be designed to enable teachers to make brief contact with each student and provide more opportunities for reinforcing appropriate engagements.

Many classroom techniques involve the appropriate use of time. Consultants can devise strategies for maintaining activity flow by determining how teachers and students use time: (a) How much time do students have to complete assignments? (b) Is additional time available when work cannot be completed? (c) What are the contingencies associated with using time appropriately and inappropriately? (d) Are time limits used to pace students in their work?

Motivational techniques focus on identifying and developing "functional" reinforcers to maintain learning after teacher-directed instruction is done. Since many principles and strategies about reinforcement have been discussed in other chapters, we direct our discussion to a brief presentation on reinforcement and academic performance. Given this focus, we believe that instructional episodes must be developed and presented in such a manner that learning becomes a conditioned reinforcer for more learning. For example, the information that is gained in reading should maintain reading behaviors, and successful problem solving should become the reinforcing consequence for learning content information.

To accomplish this end, the high rates of positive reinforcement given initially for correct performance must be gradually decreased so more "natural" and functional reinforcers become controlling consequences. In the beginning, teachers may need to institute "artificial" reinforcers that are already controlling; that is, they are effective reinforcers. As students acquire academic responses and more natural reinforcers are included, the teacher can fade the artificial reinforcers, leaving the natural reinforcers to maintain the academic behaviors.

The consultant's and the teacher's challenge is to identify these controlling artificial and natural reinforcers. A functional analysis can be a useful strategy for noting (a) what reinforcers are present, (b) what consequences currently support other academic behaviors, and (c) what consequences need to be shaped into useful reinforcers. Efforts must be made to increase the reinforcing qualities of common school-based motivators, for example, daily progress reports, graphs and charts of student's progress, conferences with the student's parents or other teachers, grades and report cards.

Mrs. DeFuca needs to consider maintaining activity flow and using motivational techniques to make her instruction more effective. Her original lesson segment was dominated by a single purpose—oral practice—which limited the range of possible activities and reinforcers. By suggesting a diversification of the lesson segment, the consultant has created more opportunity for instruction to (a) be challenging to individual students, (b) allow the teacher to interact in different ways with students (one-to-one and large group), and (c) achieve different responses from students. By creating diversity, student engagement is enhanced and active.

OVERVIEW OF ENTIRE CYCLE USING EXPLICIT INSTRUCTION

In summary, we have discussed ways to structure, look at, and modify instruction so teachers and consultants can help students succeed in academic contexts. This discussion is based on the application or use of direct or explicit instruction.

> In direct instruction, the teacher attempts to convey content and skills through classroom dialogue in which he or she controls and directs the topic and actively involves students with content-related questioning. Students are asked a series of primarily factual questions related to the development of content. For the lesson to flow smoothly yet still convey new information, the questions must be at a level of difficulty that enables pupils to give correct responses about 85% of the time. The teacher provides corrective feedback for incorrect responses, probing and redirecting questions until correct responses are obtained, and reinforces students for correct responses. [Morine-Dershimer & Beyerbach, 1987, p. 212]

Specifically, in explicit instruction, we suggest that consultants and teachers consider three important phases of instructional structure: (a) presentation, (b) guided practice, and (c) independent practice. Presentation of new material must be controlled with respect to format, structure, and amount. Some students may have difficulty relating new information with existing knowledge and skills. Too much information is difficult to integrate into their behavioral repertoires. New information and skills need to be presented in small, controlled steps; continual opportunities for practice must be provided throughout the learning process.

Second, to incorporate new information and skills into existing behavioral repertoires, practice involving active engagement and rehearsal must be provided. Initially, teachers may need to guide practice by highlighting and structuring requisite skills and sequences. Gradually, students would assume greater control over the learning process.

Third, when learning new information or skills and working independently, students must have immediate access to previously learned verbal information and behavioral skills. To strengthen this information and these skills, overlearning must occur. If students systematically must task-analyze basic steps like sounding out a word or using various crutches in arithmetic, more advanced problem solving is hindered. The requisite steps in these skill areas must be automatic so students do not have to "think about them."

The most succinct summary of "direct instruction" has been organized around six major classes of teacher behavior: (a) review (check previous day's work and reteach, if necessary), (b) presentation of new content or skills, (c) guide student practice and check for understanding, (d) give feedback and correctives, and reteach, if necessary, (e) provide opportunities for independent student practice, and (f) schedule weekly and monthly reviews (Rosenshine & Stevens, 1987). This list is embedded within classroom activities (Box 9.10).

B O X 9.10
List of "direct-instruction" teacher behaviors (adapted from Rosenshine and Stevens, 1987).

1. *Daily review and check homework*
   - Check homework (routines for students to check each other's papers).
   - Reteach when necessary.
   - Review relevant past learning (may include questioning).
   - Review prerequisite skills (if necessary).
2. *Presentation*
   - Provide short statement of objectives.
   - Provide overview and structuring.
   - Proceed in small steps but at a rapid pace.
   - Intersperse questions within the demonstration to check for understanding.
   - Highlight main points.
   - Provide sufficient illustrations and concrete example.
   - Provide demonstrations and models.
   - When necessary, give detailed and redundant instructions and examples.
3. *Guided practice*
   - Conduct initial student practice with teacher guidance.
   - Use high frequency of questions and overt student practice (from teacher and/or materials).
   - Make questions directly relevant to the new content or skill.
   - Check for understanding (CFU) by evaluating student responses.
   - Give additional explanations during CFU or repeat explanation—where necessary.
   - Give all students a chance to respond and receive feedback.
   - Ensure that all students participate.
   - Provide prompts during guided practice, where appropriate.
   - Make initial student practice sufficient so that students can work independently.
   - Continue guided practice until students are firm.
   - Continue guided practice (usually) until a success rates of 80% is achieved.
4. *Correctives and feedback*
   - Follow quick, firm, and correct responses with another question or a short acknowledgement of correctness (e.g., "That's right").
   - Give process feedback following hesitant correct answers (e.g., "Yes, Linda, that's right because . . . ").
   - Give more practice with student errors.
   - Monitor students for systematic errors.
   - Give sustained feedback (e.g., simplifying the question, giving clues), explain or review steps, give process feedback, or reteach the last steps when giving corrections.
   - Try to elicit an improved response when the first one is incorrect.
   - Continue guided practice and corrections until the group can meet objectives of the lesson.
   - Use praise in moderation.
   - Give specific praise more often than general praise.

(continued)

SOURCE: "Teaching Functions," in *Handbook of Research on Teaching, Third Edition,* Wittrock (ed.). NY: Macmillan.

B O X   9.10   (*continued*)

---

5. *Independent practice (seatwork)*
   - Give sufficient practice.
   - Make practice directly relevant to skills/content being taught.
   - Practice until responses are firm, quick, and automatic.
   - Work toward 95% correct rate during independent practice.
   - Alert students that seatwork will be checked.
   - Hold students accountable for seatwork.
   - Actively supervise students, when possible.
6. *Weekly and monthly reviews*
   - Systematically review previously learned material.
   - Include review in homework.
   - Give frequent tests.
   - Reteach material missed in tests.

SUMMARY

The purpose of this chapter was to examine the "how to teach" aspect of classrooms in general and to develop a menu of academic interventions that consultants and teachers can use to help students succeed in academic contexts. We viewed classrooms in terms of activity structures organization so consultants and teachers could bring order to the range of instructional behaviors and contingencies that occur. Teacher and student behaviors were defined by the room arrangement, activity patterns, and time/sequence. In this model, a lesson segment was organized into three components: purpose, activity format, and topic or assignment. These three components, in turn, set the occasion for specific teaching behaviors and student responses, or teacher/student roles. We emphasized two points in this model: (a) behavior can be explained as arising from a number of different and complex classroom contingencies and (b) consultants have a broad menu of options for attempting different modifications. The following key points were covered in this chapter:

1. Lesson purpose depicts an intended outcome that must be clear, explicit, and consistent with the lesson segment.

2. Consultants can expect to see three dimensions of an activity format: (a) students interacting as a function of the grouping arrangement, (b) teachers using different delivery systems within any lesson segment, and (c) assignment patterns setting the occasion for students to perform.

3. Segment purposes and activity formats must lend themselves to better lessons.

4. Interactive teacher tasks are important and include (a) orienting students, (b) interacting with students using explicit instruction, (c) monitoring student progress within the lesson, (d) providing feedback to students on their performance, (e) correcting poor learning, and (f) generally maintaining the activity flow.

REFERENCES

ANDERSON, L. W., & BURNS, R. B. (1989). *Research in classrooms.* Oxford: Pergamon Press.

AUSUBEL, D. (1968). *Educational psychology: A cognitive review.* New York: Holt, Rinehart, & Winston.

BERLINER, D. (1987). But do they understand. In V. Richardson-Koehler (Ed.), *Educator's handbook: A research perspective* (259–294). New York: Longman.

BISHOP, M. S., SUTHERLAND, B., & LEWIS, P. (1981). Oceanography. In *Focus on earth science* (Chapter 10, pp. 134–154). Columbus, OH: Charles Merrill.

BROPHY, J., & GOOD, T. L. (1987). Teacher behavior and student achievement. In M. C. Wittrock (Ed.), *Handbook of research on teaching* (pp. 328–375). New York: Macmillan.

COUSTEAU, J. (1981). The ocean: A perspective. *National Geographic, 160,* 781–791.

DOYLE, W. (1983). Academic work. *Review of Educational Research, 53,* 159–199.

DOYLE, W., & CARTER, K. (1987). Choosing the means of instruction. In V. Richardson-Koehler (Ed.), *Educator's handbook: A research perspective* (pp. 188–206). New York: Longman.

DURKIN, D. (1978–1979). What classroom observations reveal about reading comprehension instruction. *Reading Research Quarterly, 14*(4), 481–533.

ELLIS, E. S. (1989). A metacognitive intervention for increasing class participation. *Learning Disabilities Focus, 5,* 36–46.

ENGLEMANN, S., & HADDOX, P. (1981). *Teaching your child to read in 100 easy lessons.* Columbus, OH: Charles Merrill.

FLEMMING, N. C. (1977). The undersea. NY: Macmillan.

GALL, M., & RHODY, T. (1987). Review of research on questioning techniques. In W. W. Wilen (Ed.), *Questions, questioning techniques, and effective teaching* (pp. 23–48). Washington, D. C.: National Education Association.

GROSSEN, B., & CARNINE, D. (1991). Translating research on text structure into classroom practice. *Teaching Exceptional Children, 24,* 48–53.

HARING, N., & WHITE, O. (1980). *Exceptional teaching* (2nd ed.). Columbus, OH: Charles Merrill.

KAMEENUI, E. J., & SIMMONS, D. C. (1991). *Designing instructional strategies: The prevention of academic learning problems.* Columbus, OH: Merrill.

KORTH, W., & CORNBLETH, C. (1982, March). Classroom activities as settings for cognitive learning opportunity and instruction. Paper presented at the annual meeting of the American Educational Research Association, New York.

LINDSLEY, O. R. (1964). Direct measurement and prosthesis of retarded behavior. *Journal of Education, 147,* 62–81.

MEHAN, H. (1979). "What time is it, Denise?": Asking known information questions in classroom discourse. *Theory into Practice, 18,* 285–294.

MESSICK, S. (1989). Validity. In R. L. Linn (Ed.), *Educational measurement* (3rd ed.) (pp. 103–104). New York: American Council on Education and MacMillan Publishing.

MORINE-DERSHIMER, G., & BEYERBACH, B. (1987). Moving right along. In V. Richardson-Koehler (Ed.), *Educator's handbook: A research perspective* (pp. 207–232). New York: Longman.

NORTHWEST REGIONAL EDUCATIONAL LABORATORY. (1990). *Effective schooling practices: A research synthesis 1990 update.* Portland, OR: Northwest Regional Educational Laboratory.

ROSENSHINE, B., & STEVENS, R. (1987). Teaching functions. In M. C. Wittrock (Ed.), *Handbook of research on teaching* (pp. 376–391). New York: Macmillan.

ROWE, M. B. (1974). Wait time and rewards as instructional variables: Their influence on language, logic and fate control—Part I. Wait time. *Journal of Research in Science Teaching, 11,* 81–94.

SLOAN, G. (1983). Transitions: Relationships among T-units. *College Composition and Communication, 34,* 447–453.

WINNE, P. H., & MARX, R. W. (1982). Students' and teachers' views of thinking processes for classroom learning. *Elementary School Journal, 82,* 493–518.

WINOKUR, S. (1976). *A primer of verbal behavior: An operant view.* Englewood Cliffs, NJ: Prentice-Hall.

Evaluating Academic Outcomes

Ms. Gatos and Mr. Hwang have been working on how to improve Kiyoshi's performance in social studies. Together, they have assessed and evaluated what Kiyoshi needs to learn and how previous instruction has been structured and presented. Now Ms. Gatos and Mr. Hwang must develop an intervention plan quickly and systematically Ms. Gatos knows that she must keep potential intervention acceptability and effectiveness in mind as she works with Mr. Hwang. However, it is difficult to determine the degree to which an intervention will work when it is actually implemented.

Given the number of factors—implementation integrity, program completeness, number and kinds of student skill deficits—that must be considered, Ms. Gatos will be hard pressed to predict the success of the intervention. In fact, many of us would be reluctant to place much money on this prediction. Would you bet your paycheck? Half your paycheck? A dollar? Although we may have reasons for selecting various academic treatments, most bets are off when predicting intervention success for specific individuals. Three factors provide the basis for understanding why there is this uncertainty regarding individualized intervention.

First, group research data only indicate general intervention effects and effectiveness. Most group research is based on performance averages in which individual differences are unknown. Some students improve greatly, others make no improvement, and some actually get worse. The relative effectiveness of any particular treatment can only be addressed in general terms, but this is still a great place to start. The real work begins once interventions have been introduced. In this chapter, we focus on individual contingencies, rather than group characteristics.

Second, every environment has unique features that interact differently with individual interventions. In this chapter, we discuss a number of strategies, guidelines, and decision rules designed to be used with specific assessment techniques and to be oriented around the individual student. The goal is to develop and use an integrated assessment strategy that (a) moves from survey levels to specific levels (Howell & Morehead, 1987), (b) is centered around the individual educational plan, and (c) ensures outcome measures that are sensitive to the student and the learning environment.

Finally, intervention plans are developed from hypotheses about potentially controlling variables. These hypotheses or testable explanations are derived from functional analyses, in which antecedents and consequences are assessed and postulated as relevant controlling variables. Implicit in this approach, however, is the assumption that these controlling variables cannot be defined as truly controlling until predictable changes in behavior are observed when the variables are manipulated. We believe this empirical approach to problem solving and intervention development is central to education and psychology and sets the occasion for using student outcome performance to make a host of educational decisions, including identification and eligibility for specialized programming.

In this chapter, we present general procedures for developing an assessment system designed to ascertain learning outcomes for academic interventions. More specifically, we focus on practices associated with curriculum-based assessment (CBA) and address three main topics: definitions and variations of CBA, operationalizing CBA, and decision-making in CBA.

CLASSROOM-BASED ASSESSMENT: DEFINITIONS AND VARIATIONS

To understand a CBA approach, consultants must consider what it is and its main features and variations. In its most general terms, CBA is a formative and standardized set of procedures that uses production responses to determine a student's level of functioning on basic skills and content knowledge from the classroom curriculum. Numerous different systems are available; some are quite unique and others are similar like "old wine in new bottles." We suggest that consultants refer directly to the extensive literature available for more information about the specific varieties of CBA:

DENO, S. L., & MIRKIN, P. K. (1977). *Data-based program modification.* Reston, VA: Council for Exceptional Children.

HOWELL, K. W., & MOREHEAD, M. K. (1987). *Curriculum-based evaluation for special and remedial education.* Columbus, OH: Merrill Publishing Company.

IDOL, L., NEVIN, A., & PAOLUCCI-WHITCOMB, P. (1986). *Models of curriculum-based assessment.* Rockville, MD: Aspen Press.

SALVIA, J., & HUGHES, C. (1990). *Curriculum-based assessment: Testing what is taught.* New York: Macmillan.

SHINN, M. (1989). *Curriculum-based measurement: Assessing special children.* New York: Guilford Press.

TINDAL, G., & MARSTON, D. (1990). *Classroom-based assessment: Evaluating instructional programs.* Columbus, OH: Charles Merrill.

ZIGMOND, N., VALLECORSA, A., & SILVERMAN, R. (1987). *Assessment for instructional planning in special education.* Englewood Cliffs: Prentice-Hall.

Consultants can help teachers understand CBA by emphasizing its nine primary characteristics, which are used to compare the different variations. Any system having all or most of these dimensions qualifies as CBA, and any system lacking these characteristics is probably something else.

1. *CBA samples items from the curriculum.* Although it seems obvious, this characteristic is more involved than it appears. Simply stated, curriculum is defined as the materials used in instruction. However, determining which curriculum items to use can be difficult. For example, Ms. Neuburger wants to measure and monitor Sally's progress in reading as she is moved from special education to the regular program. Sally is currently receiving instruction in Corrective Reading, but the regular education teacher uses Scott-Foresman. Which curriculum should be used to sample items and to monitor Sally's progress, either before placement to ascertain readiness or after placement to determine success? Tindal (1992) assessed students using items selected from two different curricula. The performance for some students in one curriculum predicted performance in the other. Using a substantive measure such as oral reading fluency, for these students, the curriculum was less important than the instructional focus on improving reading.

2. *CBA focuses on basic skills and content knowledge.* CBA generally has been confined to the basic skill areas of reading, spelling, writing, and math. However, content information like geography, social studies, and physical sciences may also be considered for assessment purposes (Tindal & Marston, 1990). The specific measuring procedures differ for each domain.

3. *CBA uses standardized procedures in test administration and scoring.* Many educators confuse the term *standardized* with *norm-referenced*. Standardized refers to the use of overt procedures that may be replicated by others or by the same person later in time. An example of standardized administration directions used in a recent study of written retelling of a story is illustrated in Box 10.1.

4. *CBA generates production responses.* In most CBA procedures, the student creates or produces something, rather than selecting the correct answer as in most multiple-choice criterion-referenced tests. For example, a production response is

B O X 10.1

Standardized administration directions for written retell

> I want to know what you think of the stories you read and how well you can re-tell them. I'm handing out a story that I want you to read silently. It is an unfinished story. When you are done reading the story, turn the page over and read the directions, which say: "Pretend you are telling this story to a friend. Describe the main idea and all the important details. Write down as much as you can about the story." Once you start writing, do not look back at the story, so be sure you have read it carefully before you turn over the page. Are there any questions? You should finish both reading and writing in about ten to fifteen minutes. I'll warn you when there are only five minutes left. If you finish early, please sit quietly at your desk, so others can finish without being disturbed. The story title is . . . (continues)

required when a student writes a story, reads a passage, or writes the correct spelling of dictated words. Although some authors (such as Idol, Nevin, & Paolucci-Whitcomb, 1986) have described selection-type procedures, we emphasize student production responses so that an error analysis step can be embedded into the decision-making process. Other selection responses, like the Maze technique (Parker, Hasbrouck, & Tindal, in press), may also be appropriate for monitoring student progress and improvement.

5. *CBA produces reliable and valid data.* We hope that all measures used in making educational decisions, whether academic or behavioral, are consistent (reliable) and useful (valid) (Messick, 1989). The best strategy for attaining reliability and validity is to employ standardized assessment procedures.

6. *CBA provides opportunities to use multireferenced data.* Consultants and teachers must have data that can be anchored or referenced to multiple points in the curriculum or environment. When making decisions about student performance, three types of reference or interpretive standards can be used. First, peer norms can be developed and used to compare the performance of a target student and others who are of the same sex, age, race, or cultural background. Expressed in terms of a percentile rank or standard score, the comparisons help place the student within the range of peer performance. Second, absolute standards derived from specific skill areas can be used as reference standards. For example, teachers frequently place students into one of three skill domain groups: mastered, uncertain of mastery, and not mastered. These levels also correspond to various grading systems in content area domains like geography and science: "A" and "B" indicate mastery, "C" is uncertain or marginal mastery, and "D" and "F" represent little or no mastery. Third, previous performance may be used as a baseline to evaluate current progress. Although it is preferred, few educators use this type of reference.

7. *CBA is repeated over time.* Regardless of whether the reference is norm-related, criterion-related, or individual, repeated behavior samples need to be collected to ascertain change over time. A common practice is to administer published achievement tests in the spring of each academic school year. This one-time testing provides a general snapshot of student progress. However, it does not allow teachers to determine how fast students are learning, what they are learning in the local curriculum, how variable their learning has been over time, and when and what curricular or instructional modifications need to be made. Teachers need to conduct repeated or formative measures to answer those questions.

8. *CBA uses graphs to display results.* Consultants and teachers can use a variety of charts and graphs (see Chapter 4) to display CBA data. Regardless of the type, graphs and charts should be selected and used so individual student progress can be monitored and evaluated on an ongoing basis.

9. *CBA guides many educational decisions.* Information collected through CBA procedures can be used to make educational decisions at a variety of levels: (a) screening and eligibility (for specialized programs like Chapter 1 and special education), (b) instructional planning and formative evaluation, and (c) program certification and outcome evaluations. Ideally, the data generated at one level of decision making can be extended and incorporated into other decisions and used to create an integrated system anchored to student performance on relevant classroom tasks.

Most CBA research has involved a specific type of measurement called curriculum-based measurement (CBM) (see Shinn, 1989, for a review of major components by key contributors). In CBM, sampling is confined to basic skill areas, involves brief tasks lasting one to three minutes, and employs rate-based outcomes. There is considerable research supporting the application of CBM in educational decision making. Although one criticism is CBM's narrow attention to limited behavior sampling (for example, reading aloud and counting the number of words read correctly per minute), scores of well-designed studies empirically support the use of these measures.

In summary, many CBA methodologies are available. CBM has the strongest empirical foundation and is confined to the use of one- to three-minute probes in basic skill areas. Other CBA types have addressed critical thinking skills (how to manipulate information) within various content areas and across diverse fields (such as speech or preschool).

OPERATIONALIZING CLASSROOM-BASED ASSESSMENT

Consultants need to develop proficiency in classroom-based assessment for two major reasons. First, many student problems are social and academic responses to poorly designed or executed instructional and management programs. Consultants need to ascertain information to answer three basic questions: (a) What skills does the student have? (b) How can programs be aligned to improve these skills? and (c) To what extent are program outcomes being achieved? Assessment data provide the foundation for answering each of these questions. Second, consultants need to train others to collect more reliable and valid classroom data. If teachers can acquire these skills and become fluent at them, there is an increased likelihood that they will make better intervention decisions and engage in more systematic program evaluations after the consultation relationship has concluded. Most teacher-training programs do not provide formal training in CBA-based assessment strategies.

In this next section, we discuss basic skills, content knowledge, and procedural knowledge. Although they are discussed separately, consultants and teachers should consider them along a continuum where emphasis varies depending on assessment or on instructional activities.

Basic Skills

Education provides students with the basic skills to communicate effectively. These basic skills are the building blocks of all subsequent learning. In most cases, students have learned these skills by the end of elementary school. Although some new skills may be introduced by design or accident in middle and high school, a major goal of education is to provide students with the basic skills to acquire content knowledge by manipulating information and to use procedural knowledge to solve problems.

In this discussion, we assume that consultants are familiar with teaching and assessing basic skills and will apply and generalize strategies from our examples to other examples and contexts. Given these assumptions, we (a) limit our discussion of basic skills to reading, spelling, writing, and math and (b) focus on minimal essential skills rather than on more complex skills. For example, in reading, we focus on the code; in spelling, on correct letter sequences; in writing, on production and word sequencing; and in math, on facts and minimal computation. These basic skills have five essential features:

1. They constitute the minimal unit of meaning in communication. Behavior cannot be broken down into anything more basic or meaningful.
2. They involve symbol manipulation. Emphasis is on format and structure.
3. They are tool movements, useful as a means to an end. Therefore, basic skills are the building blocks for more complex communication.
4. They are comprised of both content and procedural knowledge. Many facts, concepts, and principles support the symbol manipulation within any communicative act, and the skills are organized into well-developed routines unified by rules.
5. They become automatic with practice and application; that is, these skills are executed fluently and smoothly without planning and deliberation.

These five characteristics define the "basic" nature of basic skills. As a student's learning history becomes more sophisticated and varied, differences between a basic skill and either content or procedural knowledge become less distinct. Differences become measured in terms of degree. Content information (the substance of content knowledge) and procedural routines (the rules that organize information into sequential steps) are used to explicate basic skills. Once these basic skills are well developed (automatic), students engage in more elaborate communications. In the remainder of this section, each basic skill is described in terms of central issues and assessment strategies.

Reading.   More disagreement seems to exist in reading than in any other basic skill area. The major controversy focuses on how comprehension is defined. This issue is confounded by other factors, for example, the reader's background knowledge and interests, the manner in which the assessment is conducted, and whether comprehension and understanding are different or the same. Rather than attempting to resolve this controversy, we simply consider comprehension as a reaction to material that has been read.

A strong relationship exists between comprehension and reading fluency (decoding). Proficient readers tend to be better at understanding what they read. However, this relationship between reading fluency and comprehension is not perfect; it does not imply causation (that is, teach students to read fast and they comprehend better, or vise versa). Although it is unlikely that readers who are not fluent can become adequate comprehenders, every teacher seems to report a student who can read fluently but cannot comprehend. However, because reading is a basic skill and requisite for gaining access to information in other academic areas, consultants and teachers must consider the student's reading skills before examining less direct, high-inference academic problems.

Decoding fluency and comprehension should be considered essential features of reading. When students approach a reading task, they must decode the written message and translate it into speech (either vocal or subvocal) before any reactions can occur. Oral reading fluency serves as the major reading outcome measure; silent reading is impossible to assess reliably. Words read correctly and incorrectly per minute serve as the basic indicator of the student's basic skill of reading. This measure is easy to incorporate into consultation assessments and can be done quite efficiently by following these steps:

STEP 1: Select a representative passage; make a student passage (unnumbered) and a follow-along passage (numbered with a count of the cumulative words written after each line on the right margin).

STEP 2: Establish directions that emphasize careful reading, not speed-reading. These directions, for example, may state, "Begin reading at the top of this page, and read across the page. If you come to a word you don't know, just say 'pass.' If you take too long on a word, I'll tell it to you. Read at a comfortable rate. This is not a speed-reading test. When the time is up, I'll tell you to stop. Any questions? Begin."

STEP 3: Administer a one-minute timed probe to measure rate and accuracy.

STEP 4: Count specific errors—omissions, insertions, hesitations, and substitutions—as the student reads.

STEP 5: At the end of one minute, make a slash after the last word read.

STEP 6: Tell the student to read the remainder of the passage silently to assess a passage retell.

STEP 7: Count the words read correctly and incorrectly in the one-minute probe.

In summary, standardized administration and scoring procedures are employed to determine the student's oral reading fluency. As a general standard for helping consultants and teachers evaluate levels of student reading performance, we offer the oral reading fluency norms (correct words per minute) in Box 10.2 (Hasbrouck & Tindal, 1992). These norms have a variety of uses. Special education teachers can determine how discrepant their students are in reading fluency by administering a grade-level passage and comparing the student's rate to the levels on this chart. An individual education plan can also be written using the passage at the goal level and determining how much improvement needs to occur from current to expected levels over a given time period. Similarly, passages from earlier grade levels can be administered to find the level at which the student can (should) be taught. In summary, these normative data are most useful for three decisions: screening, goal setting, and instructional placement.

The main advantage of this strategy for assessing the basic skill of reading is its focus on the terminal behavior—that is, on decoding or oral fluency. Unlike many of the reading basals, where reading is indirectly assessed (for example, by identifying word parts using a multiple-choice response), this measure actually incorporates reading into the assessment process. If students can read the words correctly, then consultants can assume that they know the rules underlying the process. As a consequence, consultants can also be quite diagnostic by listening to the prosodic features of the reading (voice quality and rhythm) and identifying

BOX 10.2

Oral reading fluency norms (correct words per minute)

GRADE	PERCENTILE	FALL	WINTER	SPRING
2	75	82	106	124
	50	53	78	94
	25	23	46	65
3	75	107	123	142
	50	79	93	114
	25	65	70	87
4	75	125	133	143
	50	99	112	118
	25	72	89	92
5	75	126	145	151
	50	105	118	128
	25	77	93	100

SOURCE: Adapted from J. Hasbrouck and G. Tindal. "Curriculum-Based Oral Reading Fluency Norms For Students In Grades 2 Through 5," *Teaching Exceptional Children,* 24 (3), 1992, 42.

error types. The biggest disadvantage of the CBA system for assessing reading is that it may have limited utility for students beyond the elementary years. However, consultants should consider it an important tool in their assessment repertoire.

Spelling. Although spelling, defined as sequencing letters in correct order, has few major controversies, the (in)consistency of the English language has caused some discussion. If the English language is consistent, then teachers can present instruction and assessment strategies using phonically regular words. However, if it is inconsistent, then teachers should teach and assess student's spelling of high-use, high-frequency words. In the first approach, instruction and assessment emphasize phonological, morphological, and syntactical rules and a consistent scope and sequence reflecting phonological generalizations. The second approach focuses first on introducing high-use or high-frequency words, followed by words that are used less often. Given these two perspectives, consultants should determine which approach teachers are using before sampling words that would be used to assess student's spelling skills.

Given a system for sampling words, consultants must determine a sensitive scoring system that emphasizes production responses. We do not recommend an approach used by most norm-referenced spelling tests where students merely select the correct spelling of a word from several choices. This response does not approximate the spelling response students must make in typical classroom contexts—that is, to tell or write the entire word. Spelling performance is characterized by the number of entire words (or letter sequences) spelled correctly (for example, eight out of ten words, 70% of the words). The "entire word" approach to scoring spelling is easy and common. However, to provide an adequate reflection of student spelling skills and not confuse performance on similar sounding words (such as *blue* and *blew, hi* and *high, wait* and *weight*), targeted

B O X   10.3

Letters-in-correct-sequence spelling marks and scores

STUDENT	MARKED SPELLING	SCORE
Maria	‸‸‸‸‸‸‸ ___handle___	7 correct 0 errors
Ruth	‸‸‸ ‸‸‸ ___hanedle___ ᵛ ᵛ	6 correct 2 errors
Karen Lyn	‸‸‸‸ ___handel___ ᵛᵛ	4 correct 3 errors

words should be presented within sentences to provide appropriate clues on which variant of the word is being used. The major disadvantages are that this approach does not provide (a) information about the parts of words spelled correctly or accurate letter sequences and (b) useful data when a small number of words are being spelled.

An alternative scoring procedure emphasizes letters-in-correct-sequence and focuses on successive pairs of letters that correctly appear together. It is a simple procedure that gives the student credit for correct letter sequences within entire words. To illustrate this procedure, three students were asked to spell the word *handle.* The teacher's marking and scoring of each student's response is shown in Box 10.3. The following rules are used to score and mark:

1. Treat the blank space at the beginning and the end of the word as part of a letter pair.
2. Place a caret (inverted *V*) over correct letter pairs.
3. Place a *V* under incorrect letter pairs.
4. Count the number of carets to determine the number of corrects and the number of *V*'s to determine the number of errors. A correctly spelled word will have a correct count equal to the number of letters in the word plus one.

Consultants and teachers may have difficulty determining a plan for choosing words to assess a student's spelling skills. Although many curricula organize words into phonetic families, the English language has many exceptions for every generalization. Therefore, at minimum, some inclusion of frequently appearing words (especially exceptions) is often needed to supplement instruction and assessment procedures and to move students along. Sampling becomes particularly important as consultants interact with teachers who want to maximize the amount learned in the shortest possible time—that is, to increase the student's learning rate.

A useful sampling plan presents students with a random sample of words from the entire grade level. This presentation provides a preview of words that have not yet been taught and a review of words that have been taught. If these words are presented in a rolling dictation (every five to ten seconds for two minutes) at the beginning of the week, teachers can identify the words that students need to study. At the end of the week, the measure is repeated by presenting the words in the same manner but in a different order. Student performance is summarized using the number of correct letter sequences. This system has several advantages: (a) only the words that need studying are addressed, (b) growth is relatively easy to see, and (c) the student can move through the curriculum at an individually paced manner.

Written expression.   In a contemporary view, writing is conceptualized as a multiskill construct in which it is important to account for the type of writing required of the student. Three types of writing generally have been delineated: (a) expressive or narrative, which is writer oriented because the purpose is to express feelings, attitudes, and perceptions, (b) explanatory or expository, which is subject oriented because the aim of writing is to describe, explain, or present information, and (c) persuasive, which is audience oriented because the author takes a position on a topic and attempts to convince the audience. The purpose of narrative or descriptive writing is to present personal experiences. Expository writing is used to set forth an idea that either informs or explains by relating observations, presenting analyses, and conveying information. Persuasive writing is designed to convince others to adopt or endorse the writer's view. In all three types, a number of prompts—such as pictures, topic sentences, story starters, incomplete sentences, and reading passages—are available for generating such writing.

The major issue in written expression is whether the consultant's assessment uses a direct or indirect writing sample. With a direct measure, writers are typically presented with a stimulus and asked to write a response expressing themselves in a particular manner. For example, the writer may be given the following prompts: Describe an emotional reaction, recount an event, describe an object, explain a procedure, or defend a position. Direct assessment uses a specific and standardized administration format, scores student performance in a prescribed manner, and is reported according to a certain form. In contrast, indirect assessment requires no production response. Instead of writing, students select correct answers from a menu of options. In written communication, multiple-choice formats, with a focus on sentence structure, word usage, spelling, or punctuation/capitalization, are frequently used.

Although few norm-referenced measures use direct writing samples, these types of samples are preferred for most classroom purposes. Both direct and indirect types of measures can use objective or subjective scoring systems. Confusion arises because many direct assessments of written expression often use subjective criteria—that is, some form of rating scale on a dimension of quality. Similarly, most indirect writing measures employ an objective scoring format in which responses are coded as correct or incorrect without reference to either a judgment or inference of quality.

In general, direct assessments tend to focus on composition skills and indirect assessments on appropriate usage and convention. However, a direct assessment may be scored by objective means by using firm and consistent criteria, such as correct word sequences, for scoring a response as correct. Likewise, an indirect assessment may also employ subjective criteria, such as sentence order and word usage, on which judgments are made. Assuming the consultant has selected a direct assessment strategy, two other influences should be considered: what prompts are used in generating writing samples, and how those writing samples are scored. These influences determine what writing behaviors are emitted, how writing is expressed, and what kinds of interpretations are made.

Assessing written expression directly is difficult because of the varied writing stimuli presented and the chain of writing behaviors displayed. In other language arts areas, individual stimuli are presented and the student makes a single response. In the assessment of written expression, it is difficult to assess the correctness of response dimensions other than grammar or syntax. For example, teachers can control a reading task by the sequence of words or skills they present. In spelling, specific words are selected, ordered, and dictated to students to ascertain specific skills. But teachers have little control over their students' writing, other than to specify the topic and to prompt certain writing characteristics. Thus, the development and selection of proper scoring systems is important.

Consultants and teachers should consider two scoring systems: subjective and objective. All subjective scoring systems establish criteria for judging student writing samples by (a) matching the writing sample to another sample, (b) scoring it according to predefined quality markers, or (c) scoring it for the presence of critical features. Three different systems for subjectively evaluating writing have been identified: (a) general impression in which a holistic rating of composition quality is obtained, (b) analytic in which separate judgments are made of various components of the composition such as organization, style, or wording, and (c) primary trait in which judgments are made about the degree to which the composition expresses a certain type of writing. Most subjective systems rely on rating scales to score a written product. These rating scales have a low value of 1 and a high value of 4 to 7, with specific descriptions for each value. While subjective scoring systems are based on judgments of quality expressed through rating scales, objective systems are based on actual counts of specific characteristics. The most frequently used objective scoring systems assess fluency, syntactic maturity, vocabulary, content, and conventions.

If possible, all compositions should be assessed both subjectively and objectively. However, if the prompts are varied and the writing samples are brief, subjective and holistic scoring systems should be considered. If writing samples are comparable and the compositions are of sufficient length, an objective and more analytic scoring approach can be taken. More subjective judgments can be made of the changes observed in compositions over time. All compositions can be scored against three common objective criteria: words written, words spelled correctly, and words in correct sequence.

Math.   Math has the following features: numbers and numeration, variables and relationships, geometry (size, shape and position), measurement, probability and statistics, graphs and tables, and technology (for example, calculators and computers). Additionally, four cognitive process levels (Bloom et al., 1956) have been included: knowledge, skills, understanding, and application. Offering a different definition, elementary, middle, and high school teachers and academicians have defined the following areas as basic skills in mathematics:

1. *Elementary computation:* Skills normally introduced in grades 1–6.
2. *Advanced computation:* Skills normally introduced in grades 5–8.
3. *Applications:* Using mathematics in problem solving.
4. *Estimation:* Giving "ballpark" answers.

5. *Measurement:* Using English and metric systems, perimeters, areas, or volume.
6. *Algebra:* Applying formulas, solving equations, simplifying expressions.
7. *Understanding:* Describing rationale and logic for solutions or procedures.
8. *Geometry:* Constructing shapes or proving theorems.
9. *Probability and statistics:* Interpreting charts and graphs, making predictions.
10. *New math:* Applying set language, reading or writing nonbase 10 numerals.
11. *Calculator use:* Using a calculator to solve computation problems.
12. *Mathematics appreciation:* Incorporating math into a larger social context.

Unlike the language arts area, math is lawful and aids in the development of a hierarchy of learning and skills. Although most learning in the early grades focuses on sets, numbers or notations, the four basic operations, and the properties that govern them, later instruction addresses more complex and social applications, for example:

1. *Algorithms*, which express lawful relationships within a variety of contexts: algebra, geometry, trigonometry, calculus, and so on.
2. *Sentence solving*, which expresses mathematical symbols in problem forms as simple as basic computation skills ($15 + 31 = $ ___) or as complex applications of algorithms to solve novel problems ("Given that the area of a circle equals 9π, what is the area of a square that just surrounds the circle?").
3. *Problem solving*, which places a social context around a problem that must be translated into a sentence solution (If a bag of chicken pellets can feed 18 chickens for 54 days, how long will it last if only 12 chickens need to be fed?).

These taxonomies or definitions of math are "generally hierarchical," for example, students must first learn counting numbers before learning integers or understand integers and become fluent in their use before working with rational numbers. Sequential knowledge, understanding, and skill are needed in the following areas and order: number or notation system, operations, properties, algorithms, sentence solving, and problem solving. For example, it is unlikely that a student could determine the area of the square and circle problem without knowledge of real numbers or solve the story problem about chickens without knowledge of rational numbers. Furthermore, determining the area of a square simply requires application of an algorithm, while the story problem requires first setting up the problem and then applying the algorithm. Both problem types require knowledge of certain operations and the properties that govern them. The term *generally hierarchical* simply means that familiarity and minimal proficiency are needed with earlier content areas before such facility can be expressed in later content areas. However, the exact level of proficiency is not clear, so an absolute mastery sequence may be inappropriate.

Assessment strategies in math can focus on very complex procedural routines. However, since we have confined our discussion to basic math skills, the major issue is the manner in which consultants and teachers sample problems and score performance. Two different systems are available for evaluating student performance on computation problems: counting the number of problems completed correctly and counting the number of digits in the correct place value. Most systems score the entire problem as correct or incorrect; however, as in scoring letters-in-sequence in spelling, the number of digits in the correct place value may be more sensitive to changes in student performance. Digit scoring can be applied to all four basic operations with whole numbers, fractions, and decimal numbers.

Summary of basic skills focus.   To acquire information (content knowledge) and develop facility with various procedural routines (solving problems), students must have minimal skills within the basic language arts and math areas. All students, regardless of classification (for example, Chapter 1, LD, EMR, TAG), must become proficient (fluent) in manipulating symbols. However, for low-achieving students, curricula in language arts and math may have to be adjusted in order to make decisions about instructional level placement and to assess learning rates. For example, the curriculum for an area may need to be adapted or adjusted in order to present a narrower range of skills and cover more critical material in depth. In addition to basic skills, consultants need to look at the kind of information presented to learners and the responses that teachers expect students to make when this information is manipulated and when mastery is indicated.

The remainder of this section addresses two knowledge areas in which most instruction is likely to occur with older students or those who are more high achieving: content knowledge and procedural knowledge. However, consultants should not ignore the need for all students to have content knowledge of the world around them.

Content Knowledge

When consultants and teachers consider content knowledge, they must examine how the content is represented (content task or type of information) and the behaviors students use to transmit their knowledge of this content (intellectual operation).

Content task or type of information.   Regardless of whether the content knowledge is divided into separate domains (such as history or geography) or integrated across domains (such as combined health or home economics), consultants and teachers must organize information into discrete units to focus instruction and provide a learning framework. This information can be classified in a variety of ways. Bloom and associates (1956; Bloom, Madaus, & Hastings, 1981) have divided knowledge, comprehension, application, analysis, synthesis, and evaluation. Generally, latter forms on this continuum are assumed to represent higher levels of knowledge; however, differences between levels may be difficult to establish, and cumulatively, levels may be more complex than represented by individual levels (Seddon, 1978).

An alternative taxonomy was developed by Miller and Williams (1973), Williams (1977), Miller, Williams, and Haladyna (1978), and Roid and Haladyna (1982). They organized content information into three types: facts, concepts, or principles.

1. *Facts are associations between names, objects, events, and places that use singular exemplars.* The unique feature of a fact is that the association is narrow and not generalized across a range of events, names, places, and objects. The following examples represent history and literature facts that were part of a test administered to 686 American college seniors by the Gallup poll (reported in the Eugene *Register Guard* [Henry, 1989]):

   • William Shakespeare wrote *The Tempest* (answered correctly by 42% of the college seniors).
   • Karl Marx stated, "From each according to his ability, to each according to his need" (23% of college seniors answered that the phrase was part of the U.S. Constitution).
   • Mark Twain wrote *The Adventures of Huckleberry Finn* (answered correctly by 95% of college seniors).
   • Harry S Truman was president when the Korean War began (14% of college seniors answered John Kennedy was president).
   {Aside: Overall results from this survey were as follows: (a) 39% of the college seniors failed the 49-question history subtest, (b) 68% of college seniors failed the 38-question literature subtest, and (c) only 11% of college seniors would have received an "A" or "B" grade for the combined 87-question test.}

   A weakness of a test like this is that only facts were tested. Narrow questions were asked in isolation and required specific answers associated with single exemplar objects, events, dates, names, or places. Facts are difficult to remember without an organizing scheme. Yet, they are the basic building blocks for access to more advanced information. For example, basic facts are necessary to develop a key vocabulary that can be used to learn and apply concepts and principles.

2. *Concepts are clusters of attributes, characteristics of names, or constructs.* They may be "thought of as a category of experience having a rule which defines the relevant category, a set of positive instances or exemplars with attributes and a name (although this latter element is sometimes missing)" (Martorella, 1972, p. 7). In this definition, rules provide the formulas for organizing concept attributes that, in turn, provide the criteria for distinguishing exemplars from nonexemplars.

   Classrooms are full of concepts that form a major part of our daily vocabulary and, in turn, serve as the foundation for most teaching and learning in the classroom for all school-age children. To illustrate the complexity and confusion associated with concepts, consider the following examples:

- In a *National Geographic World* magazine, young elementary school students are asked, "What's it like to be a musher or sled dog driver?" In the same magazine, a story is presented about the Bermuda Triangle. In the first story, the concept about a particular type of person is addressed, and in the latter story, the concept of a geographic area is presented.
- In a high school math class, students are given the following examples for the concept of polygon: quadrilateral, rectangle, rhombus, trapezoid, square, and parallelogram.
- In a political science class, students learn about complex concepts like communism, socialism, and democracy.
- We use many labels to describe our students: talented and gifted, intelligent, learning disabled, or mentally retarded. The rules for specifying which attributes should be considered as exemplars and nonexemplars are often unclear and contradictory.
- Many objects in our daily life are examples of concrete concepts: trees, stools, automobile, desk, computer. However, when does a stool become a chair? And what is the difference between a car and a truck?

Test items must be constructed appropriately for concepts. For example, consider the following general knowledge questions of science concepts (Shapiro, 1983):

- An acid is any substance that
  <u>a</u>. is capable of donating a hydrogen (H+) atom to a reaction.
  b. is capable of donating a hydroxyl ion (OH−) to a reaction.
  c. has a pH between 7 and 13.
  d. can turn pink litmus a blue color.
- In geology, a nonconformity is
  a. a rupture in the earth along which movement has occurred.
  b. a fissure maintained by high pressure between two plates.
  c. a vertical fold in the earth's surface.
  <u>d</u>. a place where young material is deposited on an older, eroded surface.

3. *Principles are if-then or cause-effect relationships.* Principles describe relationships between and among different facts or concepts, more often the latter. Principles often reflect a dimension of time or space in which different concepts interact in predictable ways. The world of the classroom is full of principles, some focus on classroom behavior ("If you kids are noisy, we will not go out to recess") and others deal with content material ("When water reaches a certain temperature, it boils and turns to steam").

Many principles are emphasized in the science area. For example, after reading a short selection on the behavior of bacteria involved in the nitrogen cycle, students are asked the following principle-based question:

- What would result from the destruction of identifying bacteria over the whole world?
  <u>a</u>. Nitrogen-fixing bacteria would eventually die.
  b. Ammonia compounds would build up in the soil.
  c. Atmospheric nitrogen would increase.
  d. Soil would become depleted of nitrogen compounds.

Student behavior or intellectual operations.   Although the three types of content tasks provide the information that teachers present in classrooms, consultants and teachers also need to identify specific student behaviors that they expect to be acquired or changed. For example, what do teachers want students to do with facts, concepts, or principles? Write reports? Give speeches? Draw pictures? And even if teachers do ask students to engage in these behaviors, how do they know if students are correct or if they have "mastered" the content. Consultants and teachers must examine what behaviors students use to manipulate information appropriately.

Six different intellectual operations or student behaviors should be considered: reiteration, summarization, illustration, prediction, evaluation, and application. Each operation represents a different level of information control and a different manner of manipulation. Generally, these operations are successive with reiteration and summarization at the lower levels and prediction, evaluation, and application at the higher levels. Since they represent complex manipulations of information, differences between the last four operations may be slight.

1. *Reiteration* is the verbatim account of material that was instructed or read and can include facts, concepts, or principles. Verbatim or precise recall of information is emphasized. For example, Sammy Kay must restate the names of the planets as they were labeled in his science text.

2. *Summarization* is paraphrasing information presented in material being presented or read; the material can include facts, concepts, or principles. In contrast to verbatim recall, students can use different wording to reflect learning. For example, when her teacher gives her a novel example, Sarita must use new words to describe the "heat rises" principle.

3. *Illustration* involves (a) presenting new examples and requiring the student to provide a label or description or (b) asking the student to provide a new or unused example. Only concepts and principles can be assessed. For example, to show examples of the concept "over," Mr. Kerrigan held a pencil over his paper, put his hand over his head, and pointed to the light fixture over the floor. He also demonstrated noninstances of "over" by placing a book next to a pencil, and holding his hand under his chin. After handing Sammy Kay a crumpled piece of paper, Mr. Kerrigan asked him to show two new examples of "over."

4. A *prediction* is the use of a rule or principle to estimate or predict an outcome or consequence when given antecedent (preceding) information. Students are asked to say or write the rule leading to the outcome or apply the rule and provide or predict the outcome. Only concepts and principles can be assessed. For example, the teacher shows a videotape of a hot air balloon being filled with a propane heater and blower. When the blower is turned off, the teacher turns off the video player and asks the student to forecast what will happen when the holding ropes are released.

5. *Evaluation* is analysis of a situation by establishing or creating criteria to make judgments or decision. Generally, principles are applied to evaluation operations; however, concepts may be considered ("Is any form of government justifiable from an ecological/environmental view?"). Evaluation consists of analyzing a problem or situation to determine factors that should be considered in making a decision. It also involves anticipating consequences of an act and then judging whether those consequences are acceptable according to certain criteria. Evaluation items require three basic steps: (a) select the criteria, (b) operationalize the criteria, and (c) make a judgment based on these criteria. The judgment needs to be supported by the criteria. For example, after studying the pros and cons of capital punishment, Ms. Romeo presents a newspaper article about an individual who was found guilty of murder and sentenced to death; she asks her students to decide whether the death penalty was the best sentence and justify their answer.

6. *Applications* provide students with an outcome and require them to establish the conditions needed to attain that outcome. This operation is the reverse of prediction and is primarily applicable to principles. Again, concepts may be used if carefully considered. For example, Mr. Kerrigan asked his students to describe why the air in second-floor rooms of a building was cooler than the air in the third-floor room and warmer than the rooms on the first floor.

The wording of a question or request often gives a clue about the intellectual demands in which we are interested. Specific wording can be highlighted or taught so a specific operation category can be identified. For example, to ensure that the question focuses on reiteration, it is important that the student be directed to "restate exactly" or "repeat the statement." In contrast, when the question requires summarization, the directive may be to "summarize the results," "review the categories," "present the positions," or "describe or explain the material." Illustrations use phrases, such as "give an example" or "illustrate the point." Prediction employs directives like "predict the outcome," "anticipate the results," or "forecast the consequences." Evaluation includes terms such as "consider the criteria," "evaluate the positions," or "interpret the criteria needed." Finally, application may employ phrases like "establish the conditions," "vindicate the perspective," or "justify the outcome."

Summary.   The content tasks (facts, concepts, and principles) are identified and configured so that students can respond appropriately. Remember that a basic fact cannot be reduced to a simpler form, a concept reflects attributions or characteristics common to a set of objects or events, and a principle presents an if-then or cause-effect relationship. Also, specific types of wording can be emphasized or taught so students can learn the most appropriate and successful way to respond to instruction and materials.

Procedural Knowledge

In contrast to content knowledge, in which the focus is on what students know, procedural knowledge focuses on what students do when using a multistep manipulation of information (Gagne, 1985). Our definition of procedural knowledge is most like Gagne's learning hierarchies and cognitive strategies, in which multistep problems have prerequisite skills and reflect self-monitoring in reaching solutions. At the heart of procedural knowledge are rules that reflect established relationships that organize concepts and principles with other concepts and principles. Unlike content knowledge, in which the focus is on the manipulation of information in a single operation situation, procedural knowledge is based on a sequence of steps that are linked in either a linear or branching relationship. Rules provide the "glue" for interrelating these steps.

We can illustrate how rules are involved in procedural knowledge by giving examples from mathematics, which is one of the best sources of procedural knowledge. Most mathematics items or tasks, beyond those requiring simple computations, exemplify procedural knowledge. For instance, in a complex multiplication problem in which two 5-digit numbers are multiplied, a variety of skills are required: (a) successively multiplying each single value in the multiplicand by each single digit in the multiplier from right to left, (b) "carrying" the ten's digit for products greater than 9, (c) placing digits from the next product in its proper place, (d) adding numbers in each column, and (e) checking the answer by redoing each step or using an algorithm (such as checking by 9s).

This type of problem is more difficult to describe than to actually complete. When we read or describe the problem, we are focusing on content knowledge. When the student is directed to complete a series of problems, we are assessing the student's procedural knowledge of that problem type. Other math problem types are also characterized by their procedural knowledge. For example, multistep procedures are required to complete long division and story problems.

In each of the single and multioperation problems illustrated in Box 10.4, procedural knowledge is exemplified by a sequence of rule-based steps that must be used to solve the problem. The two story problems have four characteristics in common: (a) identification and discrimination of relevant from irrelevant information, (b) the setup of numbers for completion of computations, (c) compu-

B O X 10.4

Single and multioperation procedural knowledge problems

Problem
In 1880, 12,601,355 silver dollars were minted in Philadelphia, 5,305,000 in New Orleans, 8,900,000 in San Francisco, and 591,000 in Carson City. How many more silver dollars were minted in Philadelphia than in New Orleans?

Solution
$$\begin{array}{r} 12{,}601{,}355 \\ -\,5{,}305{,}000 \\ \hline 7{,}296{,}355 \end{array}$$

Problem
A box of 25 comic books sold for $2.75 and one comic book sold for $0.15. How much cheaper was it to buy a box of comic books than to buy 25 single comic books?

Solution
25/$2.75 (price per comic book when buying them by the box or $0.11)
$0.15 − $0.11 = $0.04
25 × $0.4 = $1.00
25 × $0.15 = $3.75
$3.75 − $2.75 = $1.00

tation of numbers, and (d) assignment of appropriate units. Whether computation or story problems, all math problems are similar in three respects: (a) several steps are required for solving the problem, (b) specific rules govern the manner in which a step is completed and the order in which steps are executed, and (c) links between the steps must be established to achieve independent problem solving.

Procedural knowledge need not be limited to mathematics. Subspecialties within the natural sciences also rely on procedural knowledge. For example, the effects of air pressure, gravitational pull, molecular reactions, chemical interactions, velocity, and force incorporate the use of procedural knowledge. Once the concepts and principles of a particular science are known, they can be used to work with other concepts and principles to solve more complex problems. For example, in Box 10.5 we illustrate an item from an economics class that focuses on the critical attributes of "profit" or "projections." In this problem, procedural knowledge is exemplified by (a) hierarchically arranging procedural steps so prerequisite

B O X   10.5

Example of a problem and solution requiring procedural knowledge

The concept of this item might be from an advanced placement economics class; it focuses on some critical attributes of "profit" or "projections." Solving the question requires procedural knowledge.

Use the data on the graph to answer the two questions below.
- In what year was the greatest increase in sales made? _____
- In what year was the greatest loss in sales made? _____

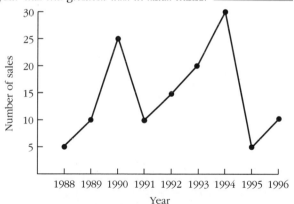

This item requires the student to complete the following three steps:
  a. Note the year in which the greatest difference exists between two successive years (not the highest or lowest absolute value).
  b. When that greatest difference is positive from one year to the next, rank these difference values from highest to lowest. The *highest* value is the answer to the first question.
  c. When that greatest difference is negative from one year to the next, rank these values from highest to lowest. The *lowest* value is the answer to the second question.

knowledge is incorporated into a problem solution, (b) using rules to organize and sequence these steps principles, and (c) sorting, relating, and linking relevant and irrelevant information to facilitate independent problem solving.

The social sciences can also be considered in the assessment and development of procedural knowledge. Concepts and principles are organized and interrelated into a problem solution in which rules govern their relationships and the sequence in which they are presented. For example, many essay questions require summarization of relevant information and an interpretation of the main ideas. Students are required to explain or predict various aspects of the content and to manipulate information; however, problem solving is more complex. First, students must include at least two intellectual operations: a summarization task and either a prediction or an application item. Second, these intellectual operations are interrelated in a rule-governed manner. The summarization must include a wide range of information, some of which is relevant for understanding the events leading to the main idea. Prediction or application must also utilize relevant information and be supported by earlier arguments. Third, interrelated relationships among arguments are reviewed so more independent problem solving can be fostered.

In summary, procedural knowledge focuses on how students perform rather than on what they know. It includes rule-based behavior in which information and skills are interrelated in an organized way to solve multistep problems. These rules guide behavior and provide an algorithm for solving problems. In the sense that a solution to the problem can be reviewed for its application of the rules, procedural knowledge can include a self-monitoring or independent functioning component.

CLASSROOM-BASED ASSESSMENT IN DECISION MAKING

The most complete view of CBA should incorporate all facets of classroom instruction and learning. Basic skills, content knowledge, and procedural knowledge all appear within the teaching/learning cycle. One version of CBA, curriculum-based measurement, focuses on basic skills. Nevertheless, many student achievement skills can and should be included within the assessment process; the only problem is that technical adequacy data may be limited (or nonexistent) with non-CBM measures. In this section, we discuss a system in which CBA and its variations can be incorporated into a consultation. We emphasize using CBA in a decision-making system that relates changes in student achievement and learning with educational decisions, which in turn shape the consultant's role.

We have organized our discussion about the decision-making process into four major sections: (a) administration of an academic checklist and determination of the general nature of the problem, (b) classroom observation and determination of the specific nature of the problem, (c) development of survey-level assessments, and (d) formative evaluation of instructional changes. In general, these sections focus on decision making that begins once a Request for Assistance has been initiated. Moving through the sections, the role of the consultant in defining and managing program changes increases, the decision-making focus shifts from a general management problem (compliance, attention, reinforcement) to a specific instructional problem (how instruction is delivered), consultants become more active in the management and direction of program modifications, and data-based decision-making is emphasized. The logic and theory behind this system comes from Deno and Mirkin (1977).

Administering an Academic Checklist to Determine the General Nature of the Problem

One objective of consultation is to determine effective, low-impact interventions that are easy to implement. Consultants and teachers should also identify academic interventions that have generalized applications across many students and settings. To accomplish these objectives, they must narrow the problem, placing the consultant in an advisory capacity. Specifically, data need to be collected to determine if the problem is specific to a particular student or is a general classroom problem. Checklists can be used to obtain information on the referring problem without conducting formal classroom assessments, such as direct observations or curriculum analyses.

Checklists.   A checklist is a simple tool for assessing the presence or absence of a specific classroom or instructional feature; it frequently provides respondents with opportunities to expand on any item. The primary function is to initiate the consultant and teacher interaction as the Request for Assistance is submitted. Although checklists are commonly used with social behaviors, few are present for academic behaviors. The main advantage is that little time is taken to focus the problem-solving process. However, like most checklist-based assessments, direct student assessments are eventually needed to ascertain or corroborate specific performance levels or problems.

The following checklists cover areas that consultants and teachers might consider in defining student problems. Rather than establishing a scale with specified anchors, the items on this list are simple prompts for considering the nature of the student's behavior. For example, under "Decoding Skills—Word Attack," a teacher can note that a student pauses, subvocally rehearses an unknown word, and then makes several false attempts to sound it out (that is, he or she makes several self-corrects). Any dimension of student performance (intensity, duration, frequency, or latency) can be considered. Additionally, the note may relate to the context in which the problem is exhibited. The main idea is to begin the assessment with information on the academic areas that are difficult for the student, then define the general nature of the problem and review possible controlling factors in the classroom.

A reading checklist should cover the broadest possible areas: general decoding skills, fluency, comprehension, and the context for reading. Decoding is separated from fluency, and comprehension is organized into overlapping categories like organization and story grammar. The different contexts for reading have equal importance as student performance variables. An example of a reading checklist is shown in Box 10.6.

In the area of written expression, three major skill areas need to be considered: penmanship, use of conventions, and organization. Organization may be one of the most difficult written expression areas to define, so it is important to obtain complete information at this step. Information about the context in which writing

BOX 10.6

Reading checklist identifying student problems

Directions: Please check (√) areas in which the student has deficits and provide a brief description that illustrates the problem or issue. Note type of materials and student responses.

_____ Decoding Skills
     _____ Word attack
     _____ Vowel sounds and digraphs
     _____ Consonant sounds and blends
_____ Fluency
     _____ Rate
     _____ Prosodic features
_____ Comprehension
     _____ Organization
     _____ Sequence
     _____ Main idea and supporting details
     _____ Story grammar and structural elements
     _____ Vocabulary
     _____ Content information
          _____ Concepts
          _____ Principles
_____ Context
     _____ Purpose for reading
     _____ Type of materials
          _____ Expository
          _____ Narrative
          _____ Descriptive
     _____ Independent worksheets
     _____ Following directions
     _____ Silent—oral reading
     _____ Spoken—written retell
     _____ Student/teacher read
     _____ Selection versus production behavior

occurs is an important aspect of written expression assessments. Such information helps consultants and teachers identify existing schedules of reinforcement that control student responding and develop new schedules. The checklist shown in Box 10.7 emphasizes the type of discourse and other conditions present within the assessment administration or behavior sampling.

Although a separate spelling checklist is presented, consultants and teachers must consider spelling as part of the writing process. In the spelling checklist shown in Box 10.8, it is possible to obtain preliminary information about both student performance and instructional programs by looking at the word structure (regularity and frequency) and the general contexts within which assessment samples are obtained (see Box 10.10).

Like checklists used in other academic areas, math checklists can be useful to assess student problems at the survey level. The sample checklist shown in Box 10.9 focuses on the conceptual learning that serves as the foundation for many math algorithms (sets, number type, specific concepts, specialized applications like

BOX 10.7

Written expression checklist identifying student problems

Directions: Please check (√) areas in which student has deficits and provide a brief description that illustrates the problem or issue. Note type of materials and student responses.

_____ Handwriting
      _____ Letter formation
      _____ Letter connections
      _____ Readability
_____ Conventions and Mechanics
      _____ Spelling
      _____ Sentence structure and grammar
      _____ Punctuation
      _____ Capitalization
_____ Organization, Coherence, and Cohesion
      _____ Topic ideas and paragraph setup
      _____ Intersentence connections
      _____ Stylistic devices (anaphoric structures, metaphors, similes)
_____ Context
      _____ Type of discourse
           _____ Narrative (1st person)
           _____ Expository/informative reporting (neutral)
           _____ Descriptive (3rd person)
           _____ Persuasive (2nd person)
      _____ Pacing and distribution of writing
           _____ Editions and drafts
           _____ Timed and untimed
           _____ Selection versus production behavior

BOX 10.8

Example of spelling checklist used to identify student problems

Directions: Please check (√) areas in which student has deficits and provide a brief description that illustrates the problem or issue. Note type of materials and student responses.

_____ Word families
_____ Frequent words
_____ Grapheme-phoneme relationships
_____ Context
      _____ Within—writing samples
      _____ Word lists
      _____ Timed/untimed
      _____ Dictation–copied
      _____ Selection versus production behavior

BOX 10.9

Survey-level mathematics checklist for identifying student problems

Directions: Please check (√) areas in which student has deficits and provide a brief description that illustrates the problem or issue. Note type of materials and student responses.

_____ Basic facts in four operations
  _____ Addition
  _____ Subtraction
  _____ Multiplication
  _____ Division
_____ Numbers
  _____ Counting—whole
  _____ Integers
  _____ Rational—positive and negative
  _____ Real—place value and decimals
_____ Concepts
  _____ Greater and less
  _____ Positive and negative
_____ Mental estimation
_____ One-step word problems (by operations)
_____ Two-step word problems (by operations)
_____ Geometry and spatial problems (area, volume)
_____ Algebra and equation problems
_____ Context
  _____ Timed and untimed
  _____ Singular versus multi operation format
  _____ Selection versus production behavior
  _____ Manipulative versus paper-pencil

geometry and algebra). This checklist is global in that it does not include many math subareas; it assesses a few applications for expressing the basic operations, such as one- to two-step word problems, geometry, and algebra. Items are not exhaustive because the checklist is designed to identify low-functioning students.

Rather than constructing individual checklists for specific content areas, a sample generic content-area information checklist is displayed in Box 10.10. In each content area, three dimensions are identified: (a) knowledge forms (facts, concepts, and principles), (b) response demands (reiteration, summarization, illustration, evaluation, prediction, and application), and (c) procedures (contexts) for gaining assessment information. The source from which information is obtained (in-class assignments, homework, reading, quizzes, tests, or projects) are important for validating the presence or absence of a problem.

Determining the general nature of the problem. Checklists are helpful for narrowing the type of student academic problem. However, consultants and teachers must also obtain information that characterizes the kinds of instructional programs being used in the student's immediate instructional environment or placement, usually the general education setting. Consultants and teachers must determine if the problem is based on immediate environmental explanations.

B O X   10.10

Generic content-area information checklist

CONTENT AREA	IN-CLASS	TAKE-HOME	READING	QUIZ	TEST	PROJECT
Social Studies						
Knowledge forms						
Response demands						
Procedures						
Psychological Sciences						
Knowledge forms						
Response demands						
Procedures						
Biological Sciences						
Knowledge forms						
Response demands						
Procedures						
Earth Sciences						
Knowledge forms						
Response demands						
Procedures						
Physical Sciences						
Knowledge forms						
Response demands						
Procedures						
Chemical Sciences						
Knowledge forms						
Response demands						
Procedures						

Having invested little time or effort to this point, the focus of problem solving is on taking inventory of programs and brainstorming alternatives. The information from the checklists can be viewed as a statement about the teacher's perception of student problems and their instructional organization and emphasis. For example, when a student is identified as having difficulty reading irregular words, the first question to arise may be the frequency with which students come in contact with such words. If the reading program is literature based, the likelihood is great; if it is a phonically based program, it may not be as serious. In another example, if a student is perceived as having difficulty in writing coherence and cohesion, it is important to determine what models are available and what kinds of directed instruction are received. If writing is being taught as a process, it may be difficult to find opportunities for explicit instruction, which is viewed as antithetical to a process approach.

In this early inquiry phase, consultants and teachers develop general classroom modifications, which offer a menu of variations that can be implemented with all students within the classroom. Interventions should not require extra resources and should fit within the instructional delivery model used with all students. Therefore, a critical feature of these modifications is that they are low impact and easy to implement. These strategies, described in previous chapters, often start and focus on the delivery aspects of instructional programs, for example, (a) incorporating information about a student's background knowledge and interest, (b) increasing student motivation, (c) rearranging the activity structure by manipulating the lesson segment, (d) making teacher behaviors more interactive, (e) decreasing transition time between and within activities, and (f) reducing the amount of time in nonacademic activities.

In summary, checklists are used to narrow our definition of student academic problems and get a glimpse at teacher programs. The general nature of the student problem is examined so consultants and teachers can consider low-impact and easy to implement rearrangement of the immediate instructional environment. If successful, the consultation need not go further except to implement a maintenance and follow-up strategy.

Conducting Classroom Observations to Determine the Specific Nature of the Problem

If general classroom modifications are unsuccessful, consultants and teachers must collect specific, direct information that enables them to determine the specific nature of the student problem and develop specific instructional-based interventions. For many student problems, the informal and general strategies described previously are adequate; however, for difficult-to-teach students, more direct and precise information must be obtained and instructional modifications need to be more specific.

If the problem is specific, consultants and teachers conduct classroom observations and analyze the curriculum to define the problem and give direction in developing an intervention. Therefore, at minimum, consultants and teachers should conduct (a) activity structure analyses to assess the aspects of what is being taught and how instruction is being presented and (b) functional analysis observations in problem contexts to develop environmentally based explanations. Since procedures for conducting a functional analysis were covered in detail in previous chapters, we focus our attention on activity structure analysis.

Information from classroom observations and activity structure analysis is used to sort out academic (learning) problems. Consultants and teachers must ascertain whether student performance problems are a function of deficits in specific academic skills or rule-governed behavior or of low motivation and interest; that is, is it a "can't do" or a "won't do" problem? They must identify the variables that contribute to or maintain the problem so they can develop specific explanations.

In analyzing classroom activity structures, consultants and teachers focus on instructional groupings and teacher management skills. In the sample observation form depicted in Figure 10.1, several activity structure dimensions are noted: (a) interactive teacher tasks, (b) student responses, (c) the class arrangement, and (d) tasks given to the student. In addition, we have superimposed a knowledge-form taxonomy to note the degree to which concepts and principles occur within instruction and the type of response that is modeled or required (reiteration-summarization, illustration). Information from this instrument provides an estimate of how many opportunities students have to learn and practice problem-solving skills. For example, if few opportunities exist and teachers mostly present facts and require students to reiterate them (Stiggins, Griswold, & Wikelund, 1989), problem-solving deficits can be identified and described. Outcomes from the activity structure observation form provide the consultant and the teacher with information about the kinds of reinforcement available for problem solving, for example, low rates of reinforcement, noncontingent reinforcement, or reinforcement of errors.

Survey-Level Assessments: Norm-Referenced Comparisons

Although it is useful to determine the general and/or specific nature of a problem, consultants and teachers must be able to use the information collected to develop and monitor the effectiveness of specific interventions. In this section, we focus on strategies designed to improve decision making and to help consultants become more directive in planning, implementing, and evaluating academic interventions. We emphasize the development and interpretation of norm-, criterion-, and individual-referenced standards of performance that allow the consultant to take a broad view of student performance and determine (a) performance discrepancies between a target student(s) and age-grade cohorts and (b) the range of skills within specific criterion domains, which in turn establish areas for delivering instruction and evaluating outcomes for individual students.

The term *survey-level assessment* (Howell & Morehead, 1987) refers to the use of a broad sampling plan in which students are presented with a maximum opportunity to exhibit errors and misrules within an academic area. For example, in beginning reading, the assessment materials may include different letter sounds, letter blends, and regular and irregular words (Carnine, Silbert, & Kameenui, 1990). In mathematics, the assessment may include all four operations, all the steps within them (such as carrying and borrowing), and the use of one- to three-digit numbers. Basically, the student is given many different reading and math problem types to solve so performance outcomes might reflect what has been mastered completely, partially, or not at all.

With a broad sampling plan, it is possible to assess an entire grade level; some items are appropriate for some of the students and everyone gets them correct. The norm-referenced approach is used in many CBM sites to develop normative standards for making a comparison between referred students and comparable

F I G U R E 10.1

Sample activity structure observation form

Date:	Time Begin:	Time End:	Page of
Observer:	Teacher:	Class:	Interval Length (sec): 10 20 30 60

Key Concepts							

Interval						Task	
Teacher						Inter. Inst.	OH/Board
lec	dem	led	obs	ask	ans	Textbook	Wksht
Student						Media	Activ/lab
lis	ask	ans	per	writ/cop		Test/Quiz	Other
Grouping Arrangements				**Demands Set By**			
Whl class	Indiv seat	Paired seat	Group seat	Task	Teacher	Student	Other
no code	**Reiterate**	**Summarize**	**Illustrate**	**Predict**	**Evaluate**	**Apply**	
Concept							
Princ							

Interval						Task	
Teacher						Inter. Inst.	OH/Board
lec	dem	led	obs	ask	ans	Textbook	Wksht
Student						Media	Activ/lab
lis	ask	ans	per	writ/cop		Test/Quiz	Other
Grouping Arrangements				**Demands Set By**			
Whl class	Indiv seat	Paired seat	Group seat	Task	Teacher	Student	Other
no code	**Reiterate**	**Summarize**	**Illustrate**	**Predict**	**Evaluate**	**Apply**	
Concept							
Princ							

Interval						Task	
Teacher						Inter. Inst.	OH/Board
lec	dem	led	obs	ask	ans	Textbook	Wksht
Student						Media	Activ/lab
lis	ask	ans	per	writ/cop		Test/Quiz	Other
Grouping Arrangements				**Demands Set By**			
Whl class	Indiv seat	Paired seat	Group seat	Task	Teacher	Student	Other
no code	**Reiterate**	**Summarize**	**Illustrate**	**Predict**	**Evaluate**	**Apply**	
Concept							
Princ							

peers. Because local norms can be established from items in the local curriculum, CBA can be used to help screen students who are at risk of failing. A series of academic tasks are established and then administered to a random population from the school or district. When a referral for special education or a Request for Assistance is received, the target student is given the same measures and his or her performance is compared to the norms. Different "discrepancy" rules have been used in the eligibility decision making. For example, four systems have emerged in the 1980s: (a) two times below the peer median (Pine County, MN), (b) one and one-half standard deviations below the mean of grade-level peers, (c) within a standard deviation of students who are two grades younger, and (d) the tenth percentile of grade-level peers.

These systems are embedded within a more encompassing problem-solving model that addresses other aspects, such as general cognitive functioning and environmental performance. In schools and districts that use norm-referenced CBA systems, students who have been identified as requiring special services have also been found using traditional measures based on an aptitude-achievement discrepancy. Mirkin, Marston, and Deno (1982) found students identified using CBA screening procedures more closely met the district's 20-point discrepancy on the Woodcock-Johnson than students who were identified with the Woodcock-Johnson alone.

Specific-Level Assessments: Formative Evaluation

Consultants need specific information to facilitate solving individual problems in the classroom. As we stated at the beginning of the chapter, it is not possible to predict with certainty what type of program works with individual students. Therefore, survey-level assessment needs to be followed by more specific-level assessment. However, we can use performance information from this survey task to help formulate specific-level tasks oriented toward particular student problems. For example, if results from several basic skill survey-level tasks indicate the student was very discrepant from peers in reading (but not math), we could develop more specific level measures in reading only. Furthermore, by inspecting his or her answers, we might find that the majority of problems come from vowel digraphs and suffixes. Now we can construct a reading measure that is linked directly to specific behavior samples and begin to look at the effects of instructional programs. In this process, we can begin to diagnose not only the student's problem, but also the solution. However, both steps must be linked to instructional programs and confirmed across more than one assessment situation.

In using such classroom-based assessments, consultants need to work closely with general education teachers to ensure the measures are aligned with the curriculum, and teachers need to provide instructional data about how teaching aligns with student performance. Similarly, it is important to determine the extent to which instructional modifications are effective in the general education classroom (that is, their impact on student performance deficits). By coordinating instructional modifications with regular summaries of student needs (performance on specific-level assessments), a decision to continue general education or move to a more restricted placement can be validated.

Probably the best use of CBA is in the instructional diagnostic process in which the domain is narrowed so it is possible to identify performance change in relatively brief periods. In Minneapolis, this process was operationalized and used to determine whether students needed special education services. Emphasis was placed on developing specific instructional plans and corresponding measurement systems. The instructional planning and measurement were applied concurrently for several weeks. Student performance was measured every other day or about three times per week, and the slope of improvement was used to determine how much learning had occurred.

For example, carrying and borrowing problems and all math facts for numbers 7, 8, and 9 are established as the instructional domain. A multifaceted, encompassing instructional routine is implemented; it consists of drill and practice on the math facts, using a computer game program, direct-instruction models for carrying and borrowing, systematic and immediate feedback in solving steps for problems (before completing the entire problem), a motivational system for correct performance on homework sheets, and self-monitoring of performance improvement on daily probes. A domain of problems is created for monitoring the student's learning. Every other day, a random sample of problems is selected and presented to the student. When performance change fails to occur on specifically designed items from a well-defined domain, even with intensive instruction from several individuals, we can begin considering placement into special education. For example, if improvement fails to occur in six weeks, we have evidence that the problem is related less to the curriculum and instruction and more to a learning problem. Because this decision is such a high stakes one and tends to generate considerable controversy, it is important to provide the most defensible system for labeling a student and ordering specialized instruction.

Because of the importance of size or adequacy of performance change, consultants need a systematic means of interpreting change and judging adequacy. We offer two strategies for assaying change. The first system is called *criterion referenced* because it focuses on mastery of specific skills; it is widely used in schools (c.f., curriculum mastery tests at the end-of-the-unit). The second system is called *individual referenced* because it is based on the rate of change for an individual by referring to their previous levels of performance. These two systems differ in the degree to which instruction and assessment are related. They represent different approaches to sampling behavior and interpreting whether learning has occurred. When we add in the element of time, we also can ascertain the pace at which learning has occurred.

Criterion-referenced evaluation.   In a criterion-referenced evaluation, the focus of assessment is on what the student actually can or cannot do on specific skills and knowledge tasks. Frequently, performance is interpreted in terms of mastery, connoting that learning has occurred. Criterion-referenced evaluations can be applied to many different arenas of learning and is not limited to academic tasks. An absolute standard of acceptance is implied with a focus on the rate at which different materials are being learned. Absolute criteria are used to make judgments. Interpretation is made in reference to a specific level of performance on a noncontinuous scale; that is, all levels of performance above a specified cutoff are

considered mastered and all levels of performance below it are considered nonmastered. The differences between scores within either side of this cutoff are less critical than those across the cutoff.

Individual-referenced evaluation.   Rather than using a specified level for mastery, an individual-referenced evaluation reflects change in material that is comparable over time. No specific minimum performance level is identified, rather change is noted on a continuous scale, from less to more, with emphasis placed on direction and rate of change over time. The materials are not qualitatively different and alternate forms are used to generate comparability across assessment tasks.

Although criterion- and individual-referenced systems should be considered as guides for assessing learning, they represent different interpretation standards for judging performance outcomes. For example, if you were told that a student in your class had received 35 points from an assessment, and were told nothing else, how would you interpret this score? Does the number 35 mean anything to you? Probably not. Even if you were told that this score was attained on a math story-problem test with 50 possible points on it, you would not be in any position to interpret the student's performance. The following section focuses on interpretation of student performance using each of these references.

Performance-based interpretation of student learning.   In a criterion-referenced approach, we are not concerned with the student's standing in a group, but we are interested in the student's performance on well-defined tasks. We are also primarily interested in the items used to develop the sample of student behavior. For example, this sample may be a random sample of single-operation math story problems from the first half of the book. Our student correctly answered these problems. In a criterion-referenced approach, we must always define the domain, including how we sampled the items. We also use a guideline for determining success, often referred to as mastery or proficiency. In most curricula tests or measures, the cutoff score for defining mastery is somewhere between 75% to 90% correct; however, this cutoff can be established anywhere.

In an individual-referenced approach, we interpret performance by comparing the student's score to his or her previous performance levels. Rather than comparing performance to other students or to some absolute standards of mastery, the important dimension is whether an individual's performance has improved over previous performance levels. This strategy is like the stock market's Dow Jones Average, which increases or decreases relative to the previous day's performance. A score of 35 out of 50 has more meaning if we are told that on previous weekly measures that sampled similar problems, the student had scored 20, 25, 21, and 30. With this information, we can interpret the score of 35 as definite improvement. Furthermore, we can see that improvement has been occurring quite consistently for the past month.

All student performance can be interpreted according to these two guides. However, they do carry different assumptions, and each has its own advantages and disadvantages. For example, a norm-referenced approach is generally inappropriate for evaluating change in performance, but it is the only strategy possible for other decisions like screening and placing students in specialized programs.

However, for our purposes, norm-referenced evaluation strategies have the following problems:

1. The items represented on the measure are broadly sampled because they have to accommodate students from a wide range of skill levels; very few items are instructionally useful.

2. Growth is difficult to ascertain, particularly at the extremes. Improvement on individual items can occur; that is, the student can get a raw score gain from the first to the second testing. However, since we use relative scores rather than raw scores to interpret change, it is likely that this raw score gain will be maintained when formatted correctly. That is, although the student may perform at the 98th percentile at time 1 and at the 98th percentile again at time 2, the student could have increased (or decreased) his correct performance without affecting his relative standing in the group from time 1 to time 2.

3. For consultants, a major purpose of assessment is to ascertain rate of progress across a range of items while controlling for practice effects. Therefore, assessment systems need to have many alternate forms that can be frequently implemented in the classroom. Whether they are survey-level CBA tasks or published tests, norm-referenced measures tend to have a limited number of alternate forms, thereby limiting their use to preassessment and postassessment.

In summary, only two options are available for ascertaining a student's progress or learning rate: criterion-referenced and individual-referenced evaluations. Each has its own unique characteristics, assumptions, uses, advantages, and disadvantages. In the material that follows, we examine each approach, consider implications for its use, and offer strategies for displaying results.

Criterion-Referenced Evaluation

Criterion-referenced evaluation closely matches assessment with instruction and is used predominately in the classroom and in most curricula (such as model-lead-test). We consider it a "nearsighted" approach because the focus is directed on closer objects, instead of those that are far away.

Procedures.   To implement this evaluation strategy, consultants need to complete three steps:

1. *Define a domain of items.* Items in this domain can be included within interactive observations, permanent products, or tests/measures. However, the boundaries of the domain must be clear—that is, they must specify which item types are in the domain and which are not. For example, the following domains are clearly specified: (a) addition math facts 1–9, (b) spelling words with a consonant-vowel-consonant (CVC) construction, (c) concepts from the instructional unit on the Civil War (in U.S. History, Chapter 9), and (d) principles relating to velocity and force. In each of these examples, the skill or knowledge content is clearly defined. Not all assessment domains are as clear, however, some only

provide a general picture of the content of instruction and assessment; for example, (a) fourth-grade math problems, (b) reading vocabulary words, (c) geography of the Far East, (d) the biomechanics of movement.

2. *Develop a strategy for sampling items from the domain.* The sampling strategy must satisfy the teacher and the consultant that the student's performance on the sample was representative of what he or she could have done on all items within the domain. Using the CVC construction and spelling example, it is not necessary to present all 100 words to determine whether the student can sound out or spell different consonants and vowels. Instead, the presentation of a smaller random sample (ten words that represent the range of CVC construction variations) would provide an indication of the student's spelling mastery of CVC words. An adequate random sample would support the assumption that performance on items not presented would have been similar. Item selection procedures are important because the quality of the assessment is directly affected, particularly with interactive observations and tests or measures; it is uncertain how the sampling system influences permanent product analysis.

3. *Determine mastery or proficiency.* Determining mastery or proficiency is typically included in most criterion-referenced assessments. Some level of performance is set; above this level student performance is deemed acceptable, below it is unacceptable.

The controversy associated with this practice has generated many journal articles and books, but little agreement is available on guidelines for setting and using mastery cutoffs. Although many tests or measures have as few as one or two items for making domain mastery decisions, we recommend a minimum of ten items to be certain of mastery. In general terms, more items are better than fewer, particularly with reference to a mastery measure; however, the number of items depends on the definition of the domain. With highly constricted domains, fewer items are needed; with broad domains, more items are needed to be certain that all those not included on the assessment are mastered.

Determining the "certainty of the mastery decision" should be considered within the context of three zones: (a) clear mastery, (b) uncertain mastery or nonmastery, and (c) clear nonmastery. The outside two zones (clear mastery and nonmastery) generally present no problem and high levels of agreement are obtainable. Greater disagreement is found in the uncertain mastery or indifference zone (Shepard, 1984). Given this dilemma, we recommend that all three mastery zones be considered in summarizing performance.

Implications.   The main advantage of a criterion-referenced evaluation approach is the proximity between instruction and assessment: They are well aligned. To borrow a phrase from personal computer jargon, "What you see is what you get." Furthermore, criterion-referenced measures are relatively easy to implement and follow an orderly four-step process:

1. Instructional goals are defined, and materials and activities are specified.
2. Instruction is implemented.
3. An assessment is completed. The materials and activities specified in step 1 provide the domain for sampling items.

4. A decision is made to determine if performance is sufficient to be considered mastered or acceptable. If sufficient, new materials and activities are organized for another set of instructional episodes. With each new set of materials and activities, new assessments are constructed.

Two serious drawbacks hinder efficient criterion-referenced evaluations. First, it is difficult to establish mastery or proficiency, because a proven technology does not exist. Given this limitation, teachers and consultants should include enough items or samples of behavior and consider all three zones when making decisions. Second, criterion-referenced evaluations are "nearsighted." Since instruction and assessment are closely matched, and assessment does not occur until instruction has been delivered, two types of errors can be made: (a) the student is paced no faster than instruction and assessment (no preview performance levels are ascertained) and (b) retention is assumed, since each assessment focuses only on the material that was taught (no review of performance is ascertained). Both problems can be overcome only by systematically including preview and review assessments, which are incorporated into the long-range sampling strategy of individual-referenced evaluations.

Displaying performance outcomes.   Because each assessment is based on qualitatively different material, comparison of performance across outcomes is confounded. For example, in an instructional unit on "peoples of the world," a student could master the information presented on subcultures in the United States but not be proficient on the Kurdish peoples of Turkey. Significant differences between material results in unrelated performance scores. Kinds of items and sampling strategies are also likely to be different. Therefore, the only way to display performance summaries is to describe mastery status only, for example, "Jon has mastered 90% of the facts about "subcultures of people in the United States." "Jon has also mastered 40% of the facts about the Kurdish peoples of Turkey."

Two record-keeping systems can be developed to record criterion-referenced performance mastery: a classroom gradebook and a graph. When using gradebooks (see Box 10.11) to record student mastery information, the following should be included:

1. A phrase or description of the instructional and assessment content.
2. Dates on which the content was presented and the assessments were conducted.
3. The type of assessment—an interactive observation, analysis of a permanent product, test/measure—that was conducted.
4. The number of items or opportunities presented or total possible score attainable.
5. The actual score of the student and whether the score is above or below the mastery or proficiency level.

The second strategy for depicting criterion-referenced performance data is to graph the mastery progress of the student. The graph (see Figure 10.2) should employ the following conventions (see also the graphing guidelines in Chapter 3):

B O X   10.11

Gradebook illustrating criterion-referenced evaluation

INSTRUCTIONAL CONTENT; DATES	TYPE OF ASSESSMENT; NUMBER OF OPPORTUNITIES	JOHN'S PERFORM-ANCE	SARAH'S PERFORM-ANCE
Geology Concepts; 12/5	*Interactive Observation*		
Bedrock	5	3	5
Continental drift	5	4	3
Continental shelf	5	5	4
Epicenter	5	5	5
Earthquakes	5	5	4
Richter Scale	5	5	5
Chemistry Concepts; 1/4	*Test/Measure*		
Atom	3	3	3
Atomic number	5	4	5
Atomic weight	5	5	5
Half-life	3	2	3
Chemistry Principles; 1/4	*Test/Measure*		
Fission	3	2	3
Fusion	3	2	3

1. Draw a vertical and a horizontal line so they intersect at 0. Label the vertical axis "Point Totals and Mastery Status." The horizontal axis can either use successive numbers (1 to N) to represent chapters or informational units or the phrase descriptor of the content (and type of assessment methodology). Label the horizontal axis with the dates that mastery was assessed.
2. Student data points (representing mastery or proficiency) are recorded as different symbols and a line is used to connect them over time. The only rule to follow is to move over and up when there is mastery and over (but not up) when there is no mastery. Since this graph communicates the same information as the gradebook, except the number of items or total score possible, this number may be placed in parentheses below the data symbol.
3. Successive values are recorded on the graph whenever an assessment is conducted.

Individual-Referenced Evaluations

Individual-referenced evaluation systems focus on performance change over time, with rate of improvement as the primary evaluation datum. Two important characteristics are considered: how much improvement has occurred in a certain period and what future rates can be predicted. In the following material, we describe critical features, outline implementation procedures, present an analysis of advantages and disadvantages, and describe procedures for recording and communicating assessment results.

FIGURE 10.2

Graphs illustrating criterion-referenced evaluation

● Cumulative Mastery Units

□ Geology Concepts (Interactve Observation)

△ Chemistry Concepts and Principles (Test/Measure)

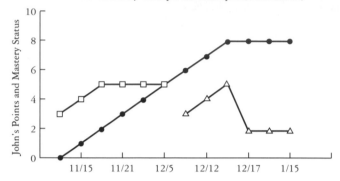

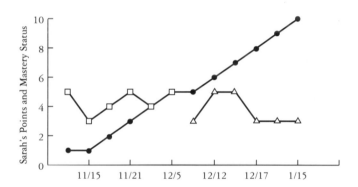

Features.   To compare a student's performance to previous levels and eventually calculate the rate at which learning is occurring requires comparability among all the data values. A criterion-referenced test or measure could not be used because each measure is unique and not directly comparable to other raw score values. However, when using individual-referenced evaluations, the sampling plan needs to be broader. Rather than matching the content of assessment with that of an instructional episode, the domain for assessment spans several instructional episodes; that is, it is a long-range goal assessment.

Unlike the nearsightedness and limited generalizability over time or across items found in criterion-referenced evaluations, the sampling plan of an individual-referenced evaluation includes preview and review components. As such, content information assessment is difficult to accomplish; however, the assessment of basic skills or procedural knowledge is improved. Individual-referenced evaluations are useful when there is knowledge or skill uniformity. Near examples (closely related to instruction) and far examples (appropriate generalizations not directly taught) can be included within any given assessment task. For example, in spelling, many words consistently follow standard phonetic rules; in reading, decoding rules have general application across many words; math computation rules are highly lawful across a range of problem types; and most math story problems and science problems include standard routines that generalize past the immediate items included on an assessment. Since content information is more specific and contains few far examples, individual-referenced evaluations are inappropriate.

Procedures.   The following steps should be followed in conducting an individual-referenced evaluation:

1. *Establish a domain that includes all material and activities from the entire instructional series,* from now until the end of instruction—that is, a long-range goal for the end of the year. For example, a teacher may indicate that students reading at the beginning of a book should have finished it by the end of the school year. Similarly, a math teacher may decide that one-step story problems with addition and subtraction computations are the long-range goal.

2. *Identify alternate assessment samples by selecting additional representative items.* For example, a teacher may randomly select passages that are typical of most others in the book and have students read from them and retell the story after each reading. A series of math problems may be collected that typify the type of problems the student will face during instruction.

3. *Collect assessments on a regular schedule,* weekly, biweekly, or monthly. To develop an adequate data base for viewing change in performance, a certain number of data values (7 to 12) should be generated.

In summary, an individual-referenced evaluation uses time-series information to ascertain how much improvement is occurring and the rate of this improvement. The student's performance is interpreted by looking at previous and recent performance levels (over time). If a program is working, a general trend of increased performance should be observed. To evaluate program effects, the general trend of improvement (referred to as slope) and the amount of variation or fluctuation (referred to as variability) should be considered.

Implications.   An individual-referenced evaluation considers a criterion that is based on determining if students are retaining the necessary information to solve a wider range of problems (including strategy generalizations) with greater automaticity or fluency. We believe that effective programs are not designed to increase a student's relative standing, which is the outcome of a norm-referenced evaluation. We also believe that nonmeasurable mastery states and lists of nongeneralizable skills, which are developed for criterion-referenced evaluations, are inappropriate educational goals. Individual-referenced evaluations provide us with meaningful indications of student improvement through trend analysis and within student comparisons. The student's performance is not compared to something that has been attained by others or interpreted using a list of skills having an absolute level of required performance; rather, the student is compared to himself or herself.

Any one data value has limited interpretative utility. Since the domain for item sampling is broad and the sampling strategy is often random, any one assessment may have a disproportionate number of items of a certain type. For example, in a reading assessment, an easy story may have been selected; or the story may have just been covered in class. In either case, the student's performance for that day may be high. The next measure may sample a more difficult passage or one that has not been taught. Consequently, performance levels are much lower. Therefore, to appropriately use this approach, the general data or performance trend must be considered. If a student is becoming a better reader, the number of words he or she reads correctly will generally improve over time.

Individual-referenced evaluations must be interpreted cautiously in relation to the material used for assessment. If a steep slope is observed, assessment items may be too easy, and actual performance improvement will no longer be visible (ceiling effect). In contrast, a very low slope, or no slope, may reflect assessment materials that are too difficult and are insensitive to change (floor effect).

Several other limitations should also be noted. The definition of the domain from which items are sampled can be problematic. Few standards exist for determining an appropriate amount of material from which to build an assessment sample. With a limited empirical data base, we suggest that attention be focused on realistic long-range goals from which items can be sampled. Individual-referenced evaluations are not appropriate for content information.

Displaying performance outcomes.   As in the criterion-referenced evaluation, two different record-keeping and communication systems may be employed: a gradebook and a graph (preferred). In developing the gradebook system, three components should be included: (a) a description of the assessment materials (where they were sampled from and how they were sampled), (b) columns that list the date and the score, and (c) the units for scoring performance. In Box 10.12, a gradebook system is depicted.

Graphs are constructed in the same manner used with a criterion-referenced strategy. Two axes are plotted; the vertical one depicts the performance scores and the horizontal one depicts time (successive days or weeks). Both axes should be

BOX 10.12

Gradebook illustrating individual-referenced evaluation

RANDOM SAMPLE OF PASSAGES FROM BASAL READER	DATES ASSESSED USING TESTS/ MEASURES	JANE'S ORAL READING: CORRECT AND INCORRECT	SUSAN'S ORAL READING: CORRECT AND INCORRECT
Page 105	Dec. 1, 1989	123 Cor/5 Inc.	103 Cor/1 Inc.
Page 210	Dec. 5, 1989	113 Cor/2 Inc.	93 Cor/3 Inc.
Page 190	Dec. 8, 1989	139 Cor/1 Inc.	113 Cor/5 Inc.
Page 35	Dec. 11, 1989	102 Cor/3 Inc.	123 Cor/3 Inc.
Page 240	Dec. 13, 1989	134 Cor/5 Inc.	128 Cor/5 Inc.
Page 113	Jan. 5, 1990	149 Cor/8 Inc.	119 Cor/1 Inc.
Page 188	Jan. 9, 1990	140 Cor/2 Inc.	130 Cor/2 Inc.
Page 56	Jan. 12, 1990	147 Cor/1 Inc.	125 Cor/1 Inc.

clearly labeled and include appropriate values or dates. At the top of the graph is a description of the student performance outcomes and in the graph are data values representing correct and/or incorrect scores. Successive values are connected with a line, except if (a) a large break occurs in time and no data have been collected or (b) an intervention change has been implemented (reflected by a vertical line). In these cases, the line connecting successive data values is broken and reestablished after the data collection is continued or after the vertical line.

In Figure 10.3, a graph is drawn for each student. The advantage of the graphs in Figure 10.3 is that slope and variability can be drawn into the picture. In this

FIGURE   10.3

Graphs illustrating individual-referenced evaluation

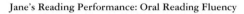

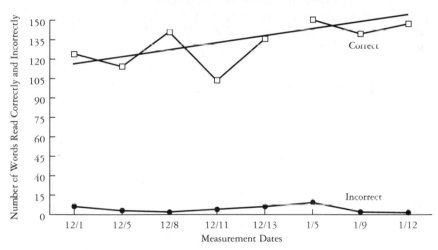

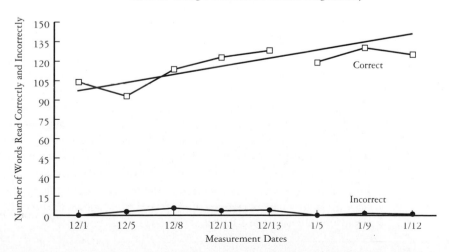

figure, a line of best fit (trend line) can be superimposed across the successive data values. By extending the line, an estimate of future performance levels and rates can be estimated. For example, in the first graph, projections indicated that in two months the student might be performing at a 175 word correct on the assessment. Variability of performance can also be drawn over the data array by drawing a line through the value farthest above the slope and parallel to it and a similar line through the value farthest below the slope and parallel to it. The band of values included within this envelope reflects the amount of variation present in the time series.

SUMMARY

The purpose of this chapter was to describe general procedures for developing an assessment system designed to ascertain learning outcomes for academic interventions. We began by arguing that each student needs to be assessed to determine if programs are effective. Although we may know about effective instructional programs, students react differently and programs need to be changed as students progress or falter. A classroom-based assessment program that is sensitive to instruction is needed. We described an assessment system that is flexible, can be applied across education settings, and is appropriate for basic skills with elementary and secondary students.

Great flexibility exists for assessing students. Rather than viewing this process as an extra burden, teachers and consultants must think of it as an opportunity to develop effective instructional routines and a confirmatory data base. Teachers and consultants must be actively involved in structuring appropriate assessment tasks for placing students into instructional levels and ascertaining learning rates. In developing a data base, teachers should first define the purpose of instruction: What are the performance outcomes that represent the material being taught? Second, they should develop a system for collecting this information. Finally, they should make assessment and instructional decisions, using either criterion- or individual-referenced evaluation procedures.

The main features of this chapter include the following:

1. Curriculum-based assessment is defined as a formative, standardized set of procedures that uses production responses to determine a student's level of functioning on basic skills and content knowledge from the classroom curriculum.

2. Curriculum-based assessment (a) samples items from the curriculum, (b) focuses on basic skills and content knowledge, (c) uses standardized procedures in test administration and scoring, (d) generates production responses, (e) produces reliable and valid data, (f) provides opportunities to use multireferenced data, (g) is repeated over time, (h) uses graphs to display results, and (i) guides many educational decisions.

3. Assessment information is needed to determine what skills students have, how programs can be aligned to improve these skills, and to what extent program outcomes are being achieved.

4. Basic skills (a) constitute the minimal unit of meaning in communication, (b) involve symbol manipulation, (c) are tool movements, (d) are comprised of content and procedural knowledge, and (e) become automatic with practice and application.

5. When considering content knowledge, consultants and teachers must examine how the content is represented and what behaviors students use to transmit their knowledge of this content.

6. Facts are associations between names, objects, events, and places that use singular exemplars.

7. Concepts are clusters of attributes, characteristics of names, or constructs.

8. Principles are if-then or cause-effect relationships.

9. Six different intellectual operations or student behaviors should be considered: reiteration, summarization, illustration, prediction, evaluation, and application.

10. Rules reflect established relationships that organize concepts and principles with other concepts and principles.

11. A checklist is a simple tool for assessing the presence or absence of a specific classroom or instructional feature.

12. When working with specific student academic problems, consultants and teachers should conduct (a) activity structure analyses to assess aspects of what is being taught and how instruction is being presented and (b) functional analysis observations in problem contexts to develop environmentally based explanations.

13. Norm-referenced approaches develop normative standards for making comparisons between referred students and comparable peers. Criterion-referenced approaches focus on the analysis of student performance relative to specific skills.

REFERENCES

BLOOM, B. S., MADAUS, G. F., & HASTINGS, J. T. (1981). *Evaluation to improve learning*. New York: McGraw Hill.

BLOOM, B. S., ENGELHART, M. D., FURST, E. J., HILL, W. H., & KRATHWOHL, D. R. (1956). *Taxonomy of educational objectives: The cognitive domain*. New York: David McKay Co.

CARNINE, D., SILBERT, J., & KAMEENUI, E. J. (1990). *Direct instruction reading* (2nd ed). Columbus, OH: Charles Merrill.

DENO, S. L., & MIRKIN, P. K. (1977). *Data-based program modification*. Reston, VA: Council for Exceptional Children.

GAGNE, R. M. (1985). *The conditions of learning and theory of instruction* (4th ed.). New York: Holt, Rinehart, & Winston.

HASBROUCK, J., & TINDAL, G. (1992). Curriculum-based oral reading fluency norms for students in grades 2 through 5. *Teaching Exceptional Children, 24,* 41–44.

HENRY, T. (1989, October 1). Christopher Columbus did what? Where? When? *Register Guard,* 1, 4a.

HOWELL, K. W., & MOREHEAD, M. K. (1987). *Curriculum-based evaluation for special and remedial education.* Columbus, OH: Charles Merrill.

IDOL, L., NEVIN, A., & PAOLUCCI-WHITCOMB, P. (1986). *Models of curriculum-based assessment.* Rockville, MD: Aspen Press.

MARTORELLA, P. (1972). *Concept learning: Designs for instruction.* Scranton, PA: Intext Educational Publishers.

MESSICK, S. (1989). Validity. In R. L. Linn (Ed.), *Educational measurement* (3rd ed.) (pp. 103–104). New York: American Council on Education and Macmillan.

MILLER, H. G., & WILLIAMS, R. G. (1973). Constructing higher level multiple choice questions covering factual content. *Educational Technology, 13,* 39–42.

MILLER, H. G., WILLIAMS, R. G., & HALADYNA, T. M. (1978). *Beyond facts: Objective ways to measure thinking.* Englewood Cliffs, NJ: Educational Technology.

MIRKIN, P. K., MARSTON, D., & DENO, S. L. (1982). Direct and repeated measurement of academic skills: An alternative to traditional screening, referral, and identification of learning disabled students [Research Report 75]. Minneapolis: University of Minnesota, Institute for Research on Learning Disabilities.

NATIONAL GEOGRAPHIC (1989). Go team go. *World, 172,* 3–7. Washington, D. C.: National Geographic Society.

PARKER, R., HASBROUCK, J., & TINDAL, G. (In press). The Maze as a classroom-based reading measure: Construction methods, reliability, and validity. *Journal of Special Education.*

ROID, G. H., & HALADYNA, T. M. (1982). *A technology for test-item writing.* New York: Academic Press.

SALVIA, J., & HUGHES, C. (1990). *Curriculum-based assessment: Testing what is taught.* New York: Macmillan.

SEDDON, G. M. (1978). The properties of Bloom's taxonomy of educational objectives for the cognitive domain. *Review of Educational Research, 48,* 303–323.

SHAPIRO, M. (1983). *Basic tips on the American College Testing Program: ACT.* Woodbury, NY: Barron's Educational Series.

SHEPARD, L. A. (1984). Setting performance standards. In R. A. Berk (Ed.), *A guide to criterion-referenced test construction* (pp 169–198). Baltimore: Johns Hopkins University Press.

SHINN, M. (1989). *Curriculum-based measurement: Assessing special children.* New York: Guilford Press.

STIGGINS, R. J., GRISWOLD, M. M., & WIKELUND, K. R. (1989). Measuring thinking skills throughout classroom assessment. *Journal of Educational Measurement, 26,* 233–246.

TINDAL, G. (1992). Evaluating instructional programs using curriculum-based measurement. *Preventing School Failure, 36,* 39–42.

TINDAL, G., & MARSTON, D. (1990). *Classroom-based assessment: Evaluating instructional programs.* Columbus, OH: Charles Merrill.

WILLIAMS, R. G. (1977). A behavioral typology of educational objectives for the cognitive domain. *Educational Technology, 17,* 39–46.

ZIGMOND, N., VALLECORSA, A., & SILVERMAN, R. (1987). *Assessment for instructional planning in special education.* Englewood Cliffs, NJ: Prentice-Hall.

CONCLUSION

CHAPTER ELEVEN

Working with Others

A few years ago, the staff at Pacific Elementary School developed a resource consultant program in which a teacher was released from classroom responsibilities for 75% of the day to provide assistance to other teachers. The teaching staff selected Mr. Freed as the resource consultant because (a) he was an effective teacher with most of his students, (b) he was respected by his peers, (c) he had a thorough knowledge of the operation of Pacific Elementary School, and (d) he could communicate effectively. Some of Mr. Freed's colleagues were equally qualified; in fact, some were more experienced in certain areas. However, Mr. Freed was chosen because he had one characteristic that separated him from the others: He was able to work effectively with others, from the principal to the bus driver.

The purpose of this chapter is to provide consultants with strategies and guidelines for working effectively with others. Inevitably, we also review strategies covered in earlier chapters; this reexamination is important because effective consultation is contingent on the use of effective strategies and procedures. This chapter is divided into six major sections: (a) rationale and assumptions for a behavioral approach to working with others, (b) strategies for preventing and responding effectively to roadblocks to working with others, (c) features of a basic problem-solving model, (d) strategies for communicating effectively with others, (e) strategies for specific problem situations, and (f) strategies for training others.

RATIONALE AND ASSUMPTIONS FOR A BEHAVIORAL APPROACH

Many people believe that Mr. Freed is a "natural" consultant because he has "innate" people skills. Teachers at Pacific Elementary School like working with him because he "empathizes" with them about their problems, works "collaboratively" with them in problem-solving sessions, and "respects" them as individuals with unique needs. They express great trust and confidence in Mr. Freed. Resource consultants in other elementary buildings frequently wish that they could take a pill that would help them build positive, empathetic relationships like Mr. Freed's.

One of the major challenges faced by consultants is determining how to develop the kind of trusting relationships that Mr. Freed has fostered with these teachers. In general, we might describe two basic approaches to working successfully with others. The first, which we refer to as a *process-oriented approach,* focuses on building positive working relationships. The assumption is that a trusting relationship must be established before it is possible to work on the particulars of a classroom or consultation problem. Consultants engage in nonthreatening activities that are directed toward meeting the teachers' personal needs, for example, (a) relieving stress and anxiety, (b) communicating feelings, expectations, and frustrations, (c) letting them know that they are good teachers and human beings, (d) letting them know that they are not alone, and/or (e) improving their self-esteem and self-confidence. Once these needs and goals have been met, the consultant and the teacher are ready to address the problem presented by the student's behaviors.

Consultants can actively work toward accomplishing these goals by practicing a number of process-oriented strategies. For example, they can apply "active listening" strategies that focus on letting teachers know that they are being heard. The consultant can respond to teacher statements by "parroting," paraphrasing, questioning, elaborating, confirming, or summarizing. An example of each of these strategies is given in Box 11.1.

The process-oriented approach to working with others offers many useful strategies, especially the oral communication techniques described in Box 11.1. Few would argue with the desirability of these goals; however, this approach also has several drawbacks. First, many of the outcomes and descriptors are difficult to describe in observable or operational terms. For example, *self-esteem, self-confidence,* and *good human being* are not defined in terms that enable consultants to determine when they have been achieved or when they are present. Second, a sizable amount of time may be required to engage in process-oriented strategies and to achieve goals. When consultant caseloads only allow one or two weekly visits with a teacher, every minute must be used effectively and efficiently. When a Request for Assistance is made, there is usually little room for delays in intervention development and implementation. Third, process-oriented strategies rely heavily on oral communications, which are used to infer the status of the teacher and the consultant/teacher relationship. Consultants must be experts at analyzing and interpreting what teachers say and at responding in a way that fosters positive personal relationships. Becoming fluent at these skills requires time and practice. Fourth, the process-oriented approach places the needs of the student in a secondary position behind the needs of the teacher. As a result, the student is often blamed for the academic or social behavior problem.

The second approach to working with others, referred to as the *outcome-oriented approach,* is based on the assumption that working relationships between consultants and teachers are facilitated by providing teachers with specific opportunities to experience success in solving a problem presented by the student. Instead of focusing directly on building a trusting relationship between the consultant and the teacher, the emphasis is placed on the outcomes of

BOX 11.1

Examples of process-oriented strategies

Parroting

Teacher: "Nikki is such a pain in my class."

Consultant: "Nikki is a real pain when she is in your classroom."

Paraphrasing

Teacher: "Every day I hope that she's sick so I won't have to deal with her disruptions and vulgar language."

Consultant: "If Nikki weren't at school, you wouldn't have to handle her misbehavior."

Questioning

Teacher: "I get extremely angry that I have to take so much time from other students to deal with Nikki's disruptions."

Consultant: "What do you feel like doing when you're so angry?"

Elaborating

Teacher: "It wouldn't be so bad if she'd show a little more interest in learning."

Consultant: "It sounds as if you're saying that you might be able to tolerate some of Nikki's misbehavior if she'd show more progress in her work."

Confirming

Teacher: "It really bothers me when she calls me names in front of the other students in the classroom."

Consultant: "I'd be upset too if a student called me names in front of the other students in my classroom."

Summarizing

Teacher: "I think you're beginning to see what I'm up against in this situation."

Consultant: "Yes, Nikki is displaying a number of extremely disruptive behaviors that put you in a difficult position. If she'd display some interest in her academic work, you would be less frustrated and angry. I can see how you'd find coming to work every day unpleasant."

consultation—for example, implementable interventions or functional and constructive change in teacher and student behaviors. These outcomes then serve as positive reinforcers that maintain and enhance the working relationship between consultants and the teachers; in turn, teachers engage in personal and interpersonal behaviors that suggest they are feeling better about themselves and their working situation. Thus, the goals of the outcome-oriented approach are (a) to structure the consultation process so it is efficient and effective, (b) to teach or strengthen teacher behaviors that can and will result in positive reinforcement, and (c) to establish and work toward predictable and significant changes in student behavior. Achievement of these outcomes enhances the working relationship between the consultant and the teacher.

We believe that to accomplish these goals consultants must take an applied behavior analytic and instructional perspective. More specifically, they must be able (a) to assess the teacher's behavioral strengths and weaknesses, (b) to assess the environmental or setting conditions that augment and/or hinder teacher functioning, and (c) to arrange contingencies so the teacher can systematically solve student

BOX 11.2

Behavioral assumptions behind the outcome-oriented approach

1. Teacher behaviors are learned.
2. The occurrence or emission of teacher behaviors is affected by antecedent and consequent events associated with the immediate environment.
3. Teacher behavior is purposeful.
4. Teachers can learn and be taught new behaviors.
5. Teacher behavior can be explained using behavioral principles.
6. Teacher behavior does not occur in a vacuum.

and classroom problems and learn and maintain new instructional skills and behaviors in the face of consultation roadblocks.

We prefer this approach because it addresses the disadvantages associated with the process-oriented approaches. First, emphasizing the behaviors and outcomes of the consultation relationship provides a clearly observable and definable focus for both the consultant and the teacher. Second, time can be used more efficiently when the focus is on solving the problem rather than on building an interpersonal relationship. With a collaborative and prescriptive structure, time is controlled, direction is clear, and definable outcomes are established as common goals for the consultant and the teacher. Third, although oral communication skills are important, the consultant is not burdened with trying to or learning how to interpret the meaning or intent behind teacher comments or behaviors. Finally, the focus of the consultant and the teacher is on changing the instructional environment so the student can be more successful. In many cases, this places the responsibility for the problem on the teacher or the classroom context.

The outcome-oriented approach to working with others is based on assumptions that are similar to those found in the behavioral perspective taken in this text; the difference is that the teachers' behaviors, not the students', are examined. Since these assumptions have been discussed at length in other sections, we have restated them from a consultant/teacher perspective but without elaboration in Box 11.2.

In the remaining sections of this chapter, we discuss roadblocks and strategies for working with others from an outcome-oriented approach that is based on behavioral principles and provides consultants with specific assessment and intervention strategies. Process-oriented strategies are useful; however, process and relationship building should not distract consultants and teachers from the main goal of consultation, which is to identify and implement specific ways for teachers to increase student success in academic and social contexts.

STRATEGIES FOR PREVENTING AND RESPONDING EFFECTIVELY TO ROADBLOCKS

At the district, building, and classroom levels, most consultants would like to believe that teachers (a) view them as valued and respected professionals who provide indispensable expertise and resources in solving instructional and social behavior challenges and (b) learn, implement, maintain, and generalize recommended interventions accurately and fluently without question or hesitation. In reality, teachers are unique. They differ in their biological predispositions, personal learning histories, cultural backgrounds, professional training, and behavioral repertoires. However, one feature that is common across all teachers (and consultants) is that, like the students they teach, they engage in behaviors that are responsive to environmental influences. Our analysis of roadblocks to working with others and presentation of strategies for preventing and responding effectively to these roadblocks is predicated on this commonality and on a behaviorally oriented outcome approach to consultation.

Before discussing assessment, analysis, and intervention strategies for working with others to reduce or eliminate roadblocks, we want to clarify what we mean by a *roadblock.* Piersel and Gutkin (1983) refer to failed or slowed consultation as being the outcome of "resistance to treatment" or "resistance to school-based consultation" (p. 311). They further elaborate:

> Resistance is said to occur when the consultant is unsuccessful in influencing the consultee to engage actively in a problem-solving process. . . . Resistance is conceptualized as resulting from a consultee's perception that consultation with a psychologist will lead to either inadequate reinforcement, excessive punishment, or both (Abidin, 1975). Although most psychologists might assume that provision of consultation services would act as a positive reinforcer for consultees, the situation is frequently complex, and many potential punishers are often implicitly and/or explicitly present. [pp. 311–312]

This description of the term *resistance* is useful; however, we prefer to use the term *roadblock* because it infers less internalized motivation or intention, tends not to associate cause with a person, and places an emphasis on environmental explanations. Thus, a *roadblock to consultation* is a situation or condition that inhibits or interferes with the attainment of consultation goals or objectives. This definition highlights the functional relationships that exist between behavior and setting or environmental influences.

Identifying and Assessing Roadblocks

Identifying the existence of a roadblock is relatively easy. Its presence is evident when progress toward consultation goals or objectives are inadequate or not achieved. The greater challenge is assessing the nature or features of the roadblock objectively without placing blame on the teacher or the student and, more important, so that effective consultation activities can be conducted. The process of assessing roadblocks is similar to analyzing student problems. Four basic steps should be considered when identifying and assessing roadblocks:

1. Determine that a roadblock condition is present and identify who is involved.
2. Identify the setting or context.
3. Conduct a functional analysis.

4. Identify and define observable behaviors that indicate the presence of a roadblock.

Step 1: Determine that a roadblock condition is present and identify who is involved.   The first sign that a roadblock to working with others *might* exist is student failure to achieve a desired level of functioning—that is, failure to demonstrate criterion functioning within a desired interval. The existence of the roadblock is confirmed if some factor inhibits the teacher's and/or the consultant's ability to implement a planned strategy. In contrast, a roadblock is not present if the consultant and teacher systematically and accurately implement a planned intervention that fails to solve a problem. In this case, the consultant and the teacher must revise the intervention. For example, Ms. O'Neill and Mr. Kim successfully complete the Problem Identification Interview and Intervention Planning forms. Together, they develop a flashcard strategy to help Wayne learn his Spanish vocabulary. Unfortunately, after three weeks, they find that it does not improve Wayne's use of Spanish vocabulary in conversations, so they change the intervention to include a daily 15-minute practice session with a peer. In this example, Ms. O'Neill and Mr. Kim worked together effectively; but their initial attempts to produce an effective intervention strategy were unsuccessful.

A roadblock *exists* if attempts to solve a problem are the result of either the consultant or the teacher failing to engage in best consultation practices. For example, Mr. Fuller dislikes working with consultants because he has to stay after school to discuss the problems he is having with his students and to develop classroom-based interventions. As a result, problem situations are not analyzed and interventions are not developed. The consultation process is inhibited by a roadblock—Mr. Fuller does not want to work extra hours. Thus, a roadblock exists when a student displays behavior indicating unsatisfactory progress *and* when the teacher and/or the consultant fail to engage in planned intervention strategies.

In addition to identifying a roadblock, it is important to determine who is involved in the roadblock, in particular, who is displaying roadblock behaviors. The behaviors or actions of the teacher and/or the consultant are the primary indicators. Other individuals, such as the student, administrators, or parents, often contribute to a roadblock situation; however, the teacher and/or the consultant are the focus of our functional analysis of roadblocks. The next step is to identify the setting or context in which the roadblock is observed. These contextual variables are critical considerations for interventions designed to reduce or eliminate roadblocks.

Step 2: Identify the setting or context in which the roadblock is observed.
Once it is determined that a roadblock exists, the next step is to identify and define where the roadblock is observed. Although roadblocks can occur in a variety of settings or conditions, consultants need to focus on school-related settings because teachers have direct access to these contexts, and it is within these contexts that students, teachers, and consultants must interact. More important, consultants can observe and intervene in these settings. For example, Mr. Waterson fails to implement a planned program accurately when his teaching assistant is not available; a consultant and a teacher write an incomplete intervention plan when

working in the faculty lounge; and when the vice-principal participates in the problem identification phase, Ms. Ramsey decreases her participation and contributions. Contexts can be defined narrowly (for example, whenever two individuals interact) or broadly (federal legislation, state funding). In the latter case, specifying the roadblock and developing a suitable intervention can be difficult and may require systems-level interventions.

Step 3: Conduct a functional analysis.   In previous chapters, we emphasized the importance of looking at behaviors within the context of immediate setting circumstances, especially antecedent and consequent events. Determining the possible relationships that exist between behaviors and immediate environmental events provides powerful information for explaining what is observed and for developing, implementing, and evaluating planned interventions.

The procedural steps and strategies for conducting a functional analysis were described and illustrated when we assessed the student's behaviors and their connections with classroom or school variables. For example, Mr. Kim's functional analysis data indicated that Jimmy's crying behaviors were affected by the frequency and intensity of the negative interactions between himself and his friends, Hisako and Alfonse. Based on this information, Mr. Kim developed an intervention in which Jimmy, Hisako, and Alfonse participated in social skills instruction that addressed being respectful and sensitive to the feelings of others.

Consultants should consider using the same functional analysis technology for examining consultation roadblocks. They should apply the same procedures used to analyze student problem behaviors. The difference is whose behaviors are being explained. When examining roadblocks, the teacher's or the consultant's behaviors are scrutinized, and the student's behaviors become the immediate antecedent and consequent events used to create testable explanations and functional relationship statements. A functional analysis for a teacher-based roadblock is illustrated in Figure 11.1. In this example, a decrease in teacher participation and verbal contributions is associated with a lack of positive reinforcement from the consultant.

A functional analysis is useful for assessing roadblocks because attempts are made to assess immediate environmental influences that are maintaining undesirable and inhibiting desirable consultation-related behaviors. When these influences are identified and confirmed, appropriate modifications can be made to remove the roadblock and facilitate the progress of the consultation process.

Step 4: Identify and define observable behaviors that indicate the presence of a roadblock.   After the roadblock context or setting is identified and a functional analysis is conducted, consultants should determine what specific behaviors indicate that a roadblock exists. Teachers and consultants engage in behaviors or actions that indicate the presence of a roadblock. These behaviors may be simple verbal statements ("This will never work . . . I've tried all that behavior modification stuff before") or more complex chains of behavior (a teacher does not implement the strategy as planned, a consultant stops visiting a classroom, an administrator does not provide the teacher with the required time and resources). These behaviors are the primary indicators of successful or unsuccessful attempts

FIGURE 11.1

A functional analysis of a teacher-based roadblock

Consultant = <u>Mr. Woodward</u>
Teacher = <u>Ms. Ramsey</u>

Antecedent	Behavior (Ms. Ramsey)	Consequence
Mr. W: "What do you think you might do when Candi talks out without raising her hand?"	Ms. R: "I think it would be a good idea to ignore Candi and her talkouts."	Mr. W: "Hmmm ... is that all you can think of doing?"
c *	"How about reminding Candi about the rule?"	"Well, ... I don't know. What else might be possible?"
c	"I don't know. What do you think?"	"You know what you can do better than I do. You tell me."
c	No answer.	"Think of anything."
c	"I can't think of anything."	"I think you might try focusing your attention on another student who is working appropriately."
c	"That's what I suggested earlier!"	"Not exactly. I think it would be better if you focused on something positive. What might that be?"
c	"You tell me." Slumps down in her chair...	

*c indicates that the previous consequence also functions as an antecedent for the next behavior.

to remove a roadblock. Types and examples of these roadblock behaviors are discussed in a later section.

Roadblock behaviors should be defined in observable terms using dimensional descriptors: frequency, latency, duration, topography, location, and intensity. For example, Mr. Freed observes that Boris's attendance has not improved after one week of a new intervention program. On further investigation, he discovers that Ms. Busselton is not following through with her part of the intervention program. She is calling Boris's home every three days instead of daily, and she is sitting in her classroom instead of meeting him immediately as he gets off the bus.

These four steps for identifying and assessing roadblocks are based on the same strategies and decision rules used in the problem identification and analysis phases of assessing a Request for Assistance. Although we are focusing on roadblocks, the outcome is the same—that is, information for developing and building interventions. The flow chart in Figure 11.2 provides a decision model for identifying and assessing roadblocks. In the next section, we examine the factors that contribute to maintaining roadblocks.

Factors that Maintain Roadblock Behaviors

Roadblocks can exist at the individual and/or systems level. In this section, we focus on roadblocks that occur at the individual level—that is, at the teacher and consultant levels. We prefer this level of analysis because the behaviors or actions of individual teachers and consultants denote the presence of a roadblock. Student and systems-level factors affect the behavior of the teacher and/or the consultant. We analyze the contributing factors that promote low rates of appropriate teacher and consultant behavior and describe general strategies for reducing roadblocks. Although both teacher and consultant behaviors can be affected simultaneously, we discuss them separately.

Factors contributing to low rates of desired teacher behavior.   The teacher is the primary agent for affecting change in student behavior. The consultant's role is to work with the teacher who requests assistance in order to bring about the desired levels of change. However, when the teacher fails to display the necessary intervention behaviors, the possibility of achieving a satisfactory change in student behavior is reduced. This failure can be explained within six contexts: (a) unlearned behavior, (b) no opportunity to engage in the desired behavior, (c) exhibition of desired behavior under inappropriate controls, (d) presence of competing behaviors, (e) ineffective reinforcement, and (f) existence of inhibiting aversives.

The first teacher-level roadblock is *not learning the skills needed to assist the student*. In this case, the teacher has not mastered specific intervention skills; that is, he or she is not accurate or not fluent. Ms. Ericson works with a consultant to develop a 10-minute social skills lesson to improve Alfonse's problem-solving skills. Unfortunately, she has never been taught how to set up and conduct role-play activities. As a result, Alfonse and the other students learn very little about problem solving and instead discover that being aggressive is an effective way to solve their problems. Ms. Ericson's inability to conduct effective role plays is a roadblock inhibiting the progress of consultation.

FIGURE 11.2

Flow chart for identifying and assessing roadblocks

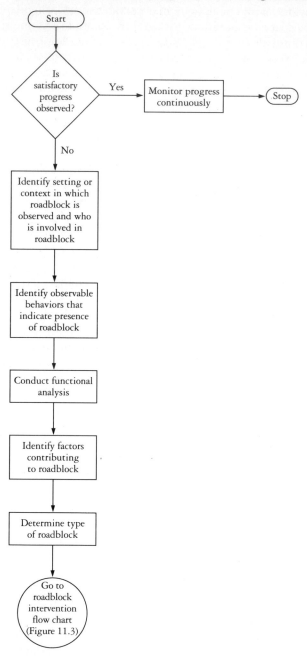

To avoid this type of roadblock or to reduce its consequences, consultants must be sure that teachers are accurate and fluent in their use of an intervention. Consultants can promote accuracy by directly training the teacher in the skill using specific verbal explanations, accurate modeling, and continuous positive reinforcement. We advocate a model-lead-test format in which the consultant models the skill, provides performance feedback as the teacher practices the skill, and checks for accurate implementation when assistance is not available. If lack of fluency is a problem, consultants need to provide informative and corrective feedback and practice. In Ms. Ericson's case, the consultant team-teaches a couple of morning social skills groups, so she can see how role-play activities are conducted.

The second teacher-level roadblock is a *lack of opportunity*. If a consultant and a teacher are unable to schedule meeting times or if a teacher is unable to engage in intervention activities because of a lack of time, competing school activities, or a lack of resources, consultation endeavors can be affected negatively. For example, Mr. Simon submits a Request for Assistance, but he has no time after school for the next two weeks to meet with the consultant to conduct problem identification and analysis activities. Ms. McRainy has decided to use computer time certificates as reinforcers for her program with Sidney, but there is only one computer, and it must be shared by all the primary students and teachers. Mr. Neuburger has his intervention developed and ready to go but is unable to implement it during Bruce's recess because he has to teach eighth-grade social studies during that time.

In each of these examples, the teacher is prepared and able, but time, resources, and competing activities interfere with opportunities to engage in the necessary tasks. The consultant's challenge is to help the teacher find opportunities or modify the consultation activities or interventions so time, resource, and activity obligations are less intrusive. Achieving this change may require the assistance of others. Mr. Neuburger may need to ask a fellow teacher to cover his social studies class for a few days. Ms. McRainy's consultant may need to help her identify and find different reinforcers for Sidney. Mr. Simon may need to arrange a meeting with the consultant before school, during lunch, or during his planning period.

A third teacher-related roadblock is when *inappropriate factors or influences control the teacher's behaviors*. This problem occurs when teachers learn to use a specific skill or strategy under a narrow range of conditions. Mr. Nelson has been helping Ms. Santiago give specific praise statements more frequently and contingently to her students. Together, they determined that praise must be given at least once every three to four minutes. To prompt Ms. Santiago, Mr. Nelson sits in the back of the room and raises his hand slightly. Ms. Santiago has no trouble when Mr. Nelson is present and giving signals, but when he is gone, she fails to provide specific praise statements. Ms. Santiago's behaviors are under the control of Mr. Nelson's prompts, not under the control of student behaviors—that is, when they raise their hands, use the appropriate tone of voice, or give the right answer.

Desired teacher behavior comes under the control of inappropriate contextual variables because consultants use training or extraneous prompts to help the teacher learn how to engage in a desired skill and then fail to remove the prompts as the teacher masters the skill. When this type of roadblock occurs, consultants should help teachers identify the relevant and natural features of the context that signal or set the occasion for the desired teacher behavior. Then they should systematically remove the prompts to increase independent teacher functioning. For example, Mr. Nelson should teach Ms. Santiago the relevant features of appropriate student behavior and the context in which they are required. He should also methodically remove the prompts he gives to her. In the beginning, he should give Ms. Santiago a prompt for every other praise statement. Later, he should give a prompt every third, fourth, and fifth opportunity. Over time, Ms. Santiago will become more independent of Mr. Nelson's assistance and begin to recognize the natural context cues that prompt her to provide verbal praise to her students.

A fourth factor that contributes to low rates of desired teacher behavior is the presence of *competing behavior*. In this roadblock, the teacher engages in behavior that competes with or occurs in place of desired behaviors. In most cases, the competing behaviors are maintained by reinforcers that are stronger, especially in the short term, than the reinforcers available for the desired behaviors. For example, Mr. Simon has learned that he should give his attention to other students who are behaving appropriately, rather than to Allie who is making noises. In the long term, he knows that removing his maintaining attention is the best strategy, but he has learned that a quick verbal reprimand ("Shhhh!") has an immediate effect on the behavior. Even though the noises eventually return, the instantaneous, but short-term, elimination of the problematic behavior is more reinforcing.

When consultants determine that competing teacher behaviors are affecting the progress of a consultation, they should attempt to provide stronger, more immediate and continuous reinforcement for the desired teacher behaviors. As required levels of teacher behavior are achieved, consultants can provide reinforcement on a more intermittent and delayed basis. In addition, natural reinforcers should be highlighted; that is, the beneficial outcomes of engaging in desired teacher behavior must be heightened. For example, the consultant provides Mr. Simon with large amounts of immediate positive reinforcement for (a) giving attention to Allie's neighbors when she is making noises and (b) providing her with specific verbal praise when she is working quietly. As Mr. Simon becomes more automatic in the implementation of this intervention, the consultant provides delayed positive feedback and highlights Allie's improved academic and social behaviors and Mr. Simon's effective teaching. By strengthening the desired teacher behaviors, competing teacher behaviors occur less often.

The fifth factor is *ineffective reinforcement for desired teacher behavior*. If desired teacher behavior is to be acquired and maintained, consultants must engage in effective reinforcement practices; that is, they must use reinforcers and schedules of reinforcement that are (a) effective, natural, and intermittent and (b) more powerful than competing reinforcers and schedules of reinforcement. Unfortunately, naturally occurring events may be difficult to develop into useful reinforcers; for example, the size of the change in the student behavior may be insufficient, the schedule of positive reinforcement from administrators or colleagues may be too thin, and few natural reinforcing consequences may be available. As a bus driver, Ms. Otis has few opportunities to interact with the teachers and administrators at Morrison Elementary School. When interactions do occur, only general acknowledgements and statements of appreciation are provided. As a result, most of Ms. Otis's specific attempts at managing problem student behaviors on the bus are unnoticed.

When desired teacher behaviors occur at low rates because of ineffective reinforcement, consultants must identify effective reinforcers and schedules of reinforcement in the same way they are identified and developed for students. Consultants can ask teachers what they would like to accomplish in a consultation; they can describe the successful outcomes of similar consultation cases; they can highlight the reinforcing aspects associated with a change in student behavior; they can solicit reinforcement from the natural environment; and of course, they can provide the teacher with effective reinforcement when desired behaviors are observed. In Ms. Otis's situation, the consultant arranged for Ms. Otis to present her behavior management plan to the faculty. In this presentation, Ms. Otis described what kinds of changes in student behavior she was expecting and how she was planning to accomplish these changes. The consultant also arranged for Ms. Otis to report to the principal on a regular basis so her progress could be acknowledged.

The last factor is *the presence of inhibiting aversives,* despite the availability or possibility of positive reinforcement. For example, Mr. Cougar has learned how to give specific praise to Timothy when he is behaving appropriately in the lunchroom. In fact, he has role-played the things he might say and has recognized the benefits of attending to Timothy's appropriate behaviors. However, when he actually supervises students in the lunchroom, he fails to provide specific praise because (a) Timothy tells him that he is being silly like his mother, (b) other lunchroom supervisors assert that praise will never work and that only weak teachers resort to bribery, and (c) Timothy's behaviors do not seem to be improving fast enough. Each of these factors inhibits Mr. Cougar's public use of praise.

To resolve this type of roadblock, consultants must focus on reducing the relative strength of the aversive setting factors. One strategy is to identify and make available strong reinforcers that will compete with the aversives. For example, Mr. Cougar must receive positive reinforcement from individuals he respects. A second strategy is to reduce the likelihood that the aversive events will occur; for example, use reinforcers that Timothy finds unique and age appropriate, rather than childlike, and that will produce more noticeable and immediate improvements in Timothy's behaviors. A third strategy is to show Mr. Cougar how the strategy has worked with other lunchroom supervisors. Each of these tactics is designed to reduce the aversive nature of the inhibitory events and increase opportunities for effective positive reinforcement for engaging in the desired teacher behavior.

Factors contributing to low rates of desired consultant behavior.   Ideally, consultants should receive preservice and inservice training that equips them with the requisite skills for effective consultation. However, the reality is that many consultants hone their skills on the job. This situation creates many potential roadblocks when they interact with teachers and other school personnel. We suggest that every consultation program include structured, objective feedback loops to help consultants assess their behaviors. This feedback could come from fellow consultants, teaching staff, and supervisors or through careful self-analysis of their behaviors and the impact they have on others.

Throughout this book, we have stressed that behaviors are learned and influenced by environmental events. Consultant behaviors are no less influenced by environmental events than teacher or student behaviors. However, when consultants do not display the necessary consultation skills, achieving satisfactory change in teacher and student behavior is impeded. If ineffective program features and teacher roadblocks can be eliminated, consultants must look at their own behaviors and environmental events that may be contributing to a roadblock.

Solving these types of problems can be difficult because consultants must first recognize that a roadblock exists and then arrange contingencies so its effects are minimized or eliminated. Functional analysis data should be used to evaluate consultant-level roadblocks. In general terms, consultants must look at the settings in which they are working, the behaviors they emit, and the events that precede and follow their behaviors. They must then examine the relationships among these elements. Six testable explanations or roadblock factors are possible: (a) unlearned behavior, (b) no opportunity to engage in the desired behavior, (c) exhibition of the desired behavior under inappropriate controls, (d) presence of competing behaviors, (e) ineffective reinforcement, and (f) existence of inhibiting aversives.

The first consultant-level roadblock is a *lack of mastery or fluency with a necessary consultation skill;* that is, the consultant has not learned a requisite behavior. Roadblocks are created if consultants have learned a narrow range of consultation skills or are not efficient and accurate in the strategies required in their interactions with teachers. For example, Ms. Bianca wants to use a written behavioral contract to help Cleo get to school on time, so she asks the resource consultant for assistance. Unfortunately, Mr. Marco is good at setting up and using verbal agreements but he has never written a contract. He must find a way to learn about writing a behavioral contract and then learn the skill well enough so he can work efficiently with Ms. Bianca. Mr. Marco's deficiency slows the consultation process and reduces his potential usefulness.

When consultants realize that they lack a skill or are not fluent in its use, the first step is to determine if they can acquire the required skill accuracy and/or fluency in a way that does not interfere with the progress of the consultation. If there is no potential for interference, they should learn the skill in a systematic and active manner; that is, they should (a) ask someone who is already fluent to demonstrate the skill, (b) arrange for opportunities to practice the skill and receive constructive feedback about its use, and (c) arrange all materials and procedures before presenting them to the teacher. If the time and/or effort required to learn a new skill might interfere with the consultation, efforts should be made to recommend an equally effective *and* appropriate alternative intervention or locate another person who is already fluent with the skill and can work with the consultant and the teacher.

The second roadblock occurs when there is *no opportunity to engage in the desired consultation skill or behavior.* In these situations, consultants have the necessary skills to engage in a consultation relationship but have no chances to implement or practice what they can do. Mr. Nelson is an expert at teaching social skills groups; in fact, he has written the social skills curriculum used by all middle schools in the district. However, his caseload has exceeded its maximum, he is training new consultants, he volunteers two mornings each week in a new elementary special education classroom, and he has been asked to conduct an evaluation of the district consultation program. Ms. Santiago needs assistance in presenting a daily 20-minute social skills group but is unable to schedule a time to meet with Mr. Nelson for the next four weeks. This roadblock is evidenced by an escalation in inappropriate student behaviors in Ms. Santiago's classroom, an increase in her use of aversive behavior management techniques, and a decrease in satisfaction in the consultation services.

When consultants find that their ability to work collaboratively and successfully with teachers is hindered by few opportunities to engage in required consultation behaviors and activities, they must find ways to make opportunities available or modify the way in which consultation services are provided. The first solution requires a careful evaluation and reordering of all consultation-related activities. Solving classroom problems must assume a high priority because problem resolution can be a powerful positive reinforcer of consultant and teacher behavior and can set the occasion for other successful and collaborative consultation relationships. Efforts must be made to eliminate or reduce engagement in activities that are not directly consultation related. If opportunities are limited despite reordering, consultants may need to modify the way they deliver consultation services. Even after eliminating his volunteer time in the special education classroom, Mr. Nelson finds that he is still unable to find time to assist Ms. Santiago. With the help of the building principal, Mr. Nelson frees Ms. Santiago from her classroom for two consecutive mornings to observe in another third-grade classroom where social skills are being taught. He calls the teacher and asks him to highlight the key features of the lesson for Ms. Santiago so she can learn more about teaching social skills.

Consultants may discover that their best consultation skills are *controlled by inappropriate factors or influences.* This roadblock situation occurs when consultants learn to use a specific skill or strategy under a narrow range of conditions. For example, as a new consultant for the district, Mr. Stevens was required to have every Problem Identification Interview form and Intervention Planning form that he developed approved by his immediate supervisor. His products were always of the highest quality and praised heavily by his supervisor. When his probationary period was over and he became a tenured staff member, Mr. Stevens continued to have his supervisor review his work even though it was not required. The resulting delays caused many teachers to stop working with him and several interventions to become ineffective. Instead of using the relevant features of the classroom problem and the student's performance data to dictate the appropriateness of each intervention, Mr. Stevens relied on extraneous factors, (such as his supervisor's approval).

Desired consultant behavior can come under the control of unsuitable environmental variables when the behaviors are first learned and practiced. Thus, consultants must learn the relevant and irrelevant contextual factors that should control or influence the use of a given consultation skill. In previous chapters, we attempted to provide strategies for identifying these factors and for building effective and relevant consultation relationships. In Mr. Stevens's case, his supervisor should have reduced his level of administrative control sooner, so Mr. Stevens could have become more independent in a systematic fashion. In addition, this roadblock might have been reduced if more attention was focused on the relevant environmental features and performance decision rules that contribute to choosing and evaluating a given intervention. If failures or roadblocks increase, functional analysis data should be assessed to determine whether relevant or irrelevant variables are affecting the consultant's behaviors.

A fourth type of roadblock occurs when *competing consultant behaviors* are present. With this type of roadblock, the consultant emits behaviors that are irrelevant or excessive to the immediate problem and its analysis and intervention. For example, Ms. LaRue finds that when she talks about her personal teaching experiences, teachers listen with interest. Unfortunately, she is frequently unable to complete specific problem-solving activities with her teachers. Mr. Baltic spends 75% of his time in a school building talking to the principal, secretary, and school psychologist. He engages in these off-task behaviors because many of the Requests for Assistance are from frustrated teachers who are challenged by extremely difficult student and classroom problems. In each of these examples, the consultant is engaging in behaviors that are not directly related to the identification and analysis of a problem, the development of an intervention plan, or the monitoring of intervention implementation. As a result, the consultation process is stalled or hindered.

This type of roadblock is observed when a consultant engages in behaviors that compete with desirable consultation behaviors. These competing behaviors occur for one, of two reasons: the consultant's competing behaviors are positively reinforced as with Ms. LaRue, or the consultant can remove or avoid an aversive condition by using competing behaviors, as evidenced by Mr. Baltic. To minimize the effects of this kind of roadblock, a functional analysis should be conducted to determine if the competing behaviors are associated with attention (positive reinforcement) or the avoidance or removal of an aversive situation (negative reinforcement). In the former case, efforts should be made to reduce opportunities for competing behaviors to be positively reinforced. For example, Ms. LaRue uses an agenda with specific times stated for each agenda task. She also uses a timer to set and signal the end of a task. These structures reduce opportunities for competing behaviors to be positively reinforced. When he observed that he was avoiding interactions with certain teachers or certain types of problem behaviors, Mr. Baltic set a specific time and day each week for working with each teacher, and he asked a colleague to assist him in some of the more difficult cases. In both of these cases, the solution required the consultant to be fluent with the necessary consultation skills and to make opportunities for these skills to be positively reinforced. Competing behavior roadblocks are difficult to remedy if desirable replacement skills are absent (the fair-pair principle).

A fifth consultation-level roadblock occurs when desirable *consultant skills are not enhanced or maintained by effective reinforcement.* Like student and teacher behaviors, consultant behaviors must be acknowledged or associated with some kind of positive outcome if they are to be maintained. For example, Ms. Johnsen graduated from her consultation training program with honors. In her new job, she quickly became a star resource consultant and was highly praised for her ability to change the behaviors of resistant teachers while maintaining collaborative relationships. However, over time, praise lost its reinforcing qualities and was not replaced by other effective reinforcers. As a result, many of Ms. Johnsen's skills are used less often.

When previous schedules of reinforcement or reinforcers are no longer effective in maintaining desired consultation skills, new schedules and reinforcers must be identified and new opportunities for positive reinforcement must be arranged. In Ms. Johnsen's case, her supervisor arranged new professional challenges for her (training other consultants, presenting at teacher in-services, developing creative solutions for recurring consultation problems) requiring new applications of her skills. Her supervisor also reassigned Ms. Johnsen to a new school with new teachers and a different working environment.

The last type of consultant-level roadblock is characterized by the *inhibition of desired consultation behaviors when in the presence of an aversive stimulus.* When consultants must constantly confront resistant teachers, violently aggressive student behavior, heavy caseloads, unsupportive administrators, or teachers who fail to follow planned intervention, they may be inclined to avoid or decrease their consultation behaviors. Ms. Morrisen dislikes Wednesdays because she is scheduled to work with Ms. Kane, who always complains about her unruly students and the lack of administrative and parental support. She also talks about getting out of teaching and into a profession where she is appreciated. Ms. Kane's behaviors are so aversive that Ms. Morrisen returns her telephone calls at the last minute and sometimes "forgets" to return a call. When meetings occur, Ms. Morrisen gives in to Ms. Kane's verbal complaints and unwittingly reinforces her complaints by nodding and consoling her. Frequently, Ms. Morrisen schedules other administrative meetings on Wednesdays so she can avoid interacting with Ms. Kane.

When aversive conditions inhibit consultants from engaging in effective consulting behaviors, all phases of problem solving are impeded. When consultants recognize the presence of this type of roadblock, they must arrange the environment so the aversive conditions are minimized and opportunities for engaging in desired consultation-related behaviors are more likely and positively reinforced. For example, Ms. Morrisen (a) instructs Ms. Kane to write down her concerns, (b) schedules specific starting times and durations for each meeting, (c) tells Ms. Kane that all nonconsultation-related concerns can be discussed during the last five minutes of each meeting, and (d) learns not to engage in off-task conversations. Ms. Morrisen changes the objectives of her meetings with Ms. Kane to reflect achieving reduced complaints. Ms. Morrisen's supervisor positively reinforces attainment of this objective.

Summary.   In this section, we presented a behavioral framework for characterizing the types of roadblocks that consultants are likely to encounter (Box 11.3). Although student- and systems-level roadblocks are possible, we focused on teacher- and consultant-level factors that contribute to roadblocks. Although we discussed these roadblocks separately, they probably involve the interaction of both teacher and consultant behaviors; that is, the behaviors of one person affect the behaviors of the other person. Consultants must learn to recognize when a roadblock is present and conduct a functional analysis to determine what situational factors are contributing to it. If they can develop testable explanations and functional relationship statements, then they will be able to devise a useful intervention for removing the roadblock. When the roadblock can be attributed to teacher behaviors, the consultant, in collaboration with the teacher, can analyze the

BOX 11.3

Type of teacher and consultant-level roadblocks, explanations, and general strategies

CONTRIBUTING FACTOR	EXPLANATIONS	STRATEGIES
1. Unlearned behavior	- Skill deficit - Lack of skill fluency	- Teach skill. - Provide structured practice and positive reinforcement.
2. No opportunity to engage in desired behavior	- Lack of time or resources - Other competing activities or behaviors	- Assess activities and rearrange priorities. - Secure resources. - Modify consultation activities and strategies.
3. Desired behavior under inappropriate control	- Failed generalized responding - Inappropriate training - Narrow range of exemplars - Ineffective fading of training prompts	- Teach behavior with multiple and full range of examples. - Systematically fade training prompts and teach situational prompts. - Teach for generalized responding.
4. Engaged in competing behavior	- Stronger reinforcers for competing behavior - Richer schedule of reinforcement for competing behavior	- Remove access to reinforcers for competing behavior. - Improve reinforcers and schedules of reinforcement for desired behaviors. - Remove setting factors that set occasion for competing behavior.
5. Ineffective reinforcement for desired behavior	- Reinforcer satiation - Thin schedule of reinforcement - Decrease in strength of reinforcer	- Thin schedule of reinforcement gradually. - Change reinforcer. - Switch to conditioned reinforcer. - Increase reinforcer deprivation. - Add (pair) new reinforcer.
6. Desired behavior inhibited by aversives	- Aversive given or present when desired behavior required - Lack of reinforcement for desired behavior	- Remove aversive. - Arrange setting so aversive is not present. - Increase positive reinforcement for desired behavior.

roadblock and develop and implement an intervention to remove it. If the roadblock is associated with consultant behavior, recognition and analysis may be more difficult. A supervisor, peer, or other staff member may need to provide an objective analysis of the roadblock and to develop and implement a valid intervention.

Once information about the type of roadblock and possible contributing factors has been collected and analyzed, interventions can be developed to remove or reduce its influence. Throughout this book, we have emphasized the importance of building interventions based on direct assessment information. A flow chart summarizing the relationships and decisions associated with problem type and general intervention focus is illustrated in Figure 11.3. This flow chart concludes with the recommendation to monitor the effect of an intervention on the progress of the consultation process.

FIGURE 11.3

Flow chart for determining type of roadblock and intervention focus

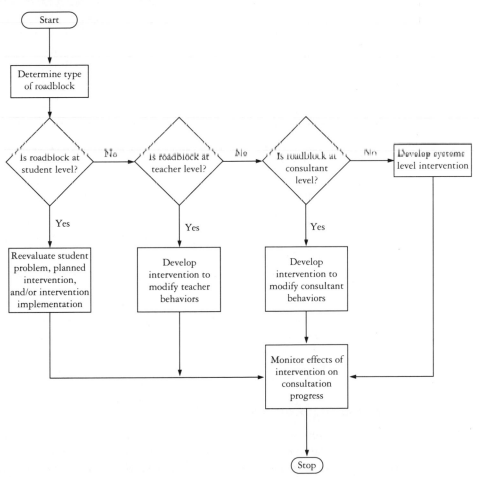

FEATURES OF A BASIC PROBLEM-SOLVING MODEL

In most sections of this book, we have discussed consultation as if individuals are willing and active participants in the process of solving student and classroom learning and social behavior problems. We also presented the removal of roadblocks as a relatively simple process of identification and remediation. However, whenever two or more people work together toward some common purpose or on a problem, conflicts or disagreements inevitably occur. Consultants must be fluent and efficient at solving problems, especially when they are involved in a conflict. In this section we discuss a problem-solving approach designed to assist consultants in resolving conflicts or disagreements.

In discussing this problem-solving or conflict-management strategy, we make three critical assumptions. First, the student's needs must be paramount in the problem-solving process. Of course, it is important to satisfy the needs of others as well, because their actions affect what happens to students and what they experience. However, at no time should we make decisions or engage in actions that fail to consider the student. The problem-solving and conflict-management structure should be viewed as a way to improve how we meet student needs.

Second, changing a person's attitudes, beliefs, or feelings is difficult and may not change their actions. Although we acknowledge the existence of these internal states or conditions, we strongly believe that consultants must focus on those elements that they can access (such as behaviors and environmental events and objects), can explain in observable terms (testable explanations and functional relationships), and can manipulate directly (environmental events and objects).

Third, people often have legitimate reasons for what they do. Although two people might display similar behaviors and strategies for solving a common problem, the contingencies that maintain or influence these behaviors and strategies might be different. For example, a consultant may respond to a Request for Assistance with the intent of maintaining the student in the regular classroom; however, the teacher may be seeking consultation assistance to facilitate a referral for special education and the eventual removal of the student from the classroom. Consultants must learn to avoid making subjective judgements about the merits of a person's behaviors or the motivations behind those behaviors and to focus on the environmental or setting-specific contingencies that affect the teacher's (or consultant's) behaviors and that can be manipulated.

Given these assumptions, we discuss (a) a simple definition for a conflict, (b) a basic problem-solving and conflict-management strategy, and (c) guidelines for facilitating the implementation of the overall problem-solving process. Since the problem-solving process frequently involves the resolution of conflicts, we integrate the two procedures.

Definition of a Conflict

Conflicts between individuals are common occurrences in everyday interactions. Most of the time, conflicts are minor and resolution occurs without significant losses or negative impact; in fact, problem solving and conflict resolution are informal and easily implemented. For example, Mr. Sanchez frequently finds himself in situations where his suggestions differ from what a teacher might propose. Usually, a suitable compromise is quickly proposed and accepted without excess behavior or emotion. In those situations, both Mr. Sanchez and the teacher adjust in the direction of the other person's position. However, there are times when problem solving and conflict resolution are difficult because no one can agree on a satisfactory solution. It is in these stalemate situations that consultants must have an effective, efficient, and objective strategy for responding.

Although a conflict can be defined in various ways, we prefer a simple definition that focuses on failed agreement. A *conflict* is a situation in which two or more people disagree about something. Acceptance of the other party's position and the development of an agreeable compromise position do not occur. A conflict is often indicated by the content of each person's verbal behavior ("I really can't go along with that." "How can you believe that something like that would really work?" "Who are you to tell me that I'm to blame?") and by displays of opposition behaviors (such as decreased verbalizations, failure to address the problem context, walking away). For example, Mr. Sanchez believes that Gracie's study skills could be improved with a simple increase in contingent praise by her teacher; however, Ms. Slick asserts that Gracie needs a quick and strong aversive consequence, like a parent conference or a few failing grades, to bring her around. Neither is willing to accept the other's position or agree on a suitable compromise. Ms. Slick questions Mr. Sanchez's classroom experience and repeatedly shakes her head whenever he makes a comment. Mr. Sanchez decreases his rate of positive verbal statements and threatens to involve the principal as a conflict resolution mediator.

People in difficult conflict situations display a variety of negative secondary or side effect behaviors, such as verbal or physical aggression, reduced conversation behavior, or walking away. Explanations for these behaviors fall into two categories: (a) people are denied access to positive reinforcement (that is, their position is not accepted by the other person or they are denied the opportunity to do something) or (b) people are presented with an aversive (the other person's position has loathsome qualities or they must do something that is unacceptable). People who display extremes of these behaviors are often characterized as unreasonable, withdrawn, hostile, or emotional. Consultants must evaluate these side effect behaviors to facilitate the problem-solving process and to predict the likelihood of successful conflict management.

Description of a Basic Problem-Solving and Conflict-Management Strategy

When a solution is needed for a difficult problem and a conflict occurs, the consultant must be fluent in two basic skills: conflict management and problem solving.

Conflict management.   Achieving an agreeable solution to a difficult problem is predicated on how well individuals are able to engage in an efficient problem-solving interaction. However, if one or both parties are engaged in relatively high rates of negative off-task behaviors, the likelihood of successful problem resolution is significantly reduced. Thus, one of the most important steps in the problem-solving process is determining whether a conflict exists and resolving that conflict. We suggest that consultants become fluent at a simple five-step conflict-management strategy that is designed to determine if problem solving can occur in an efficient and effective manner: (a) *stop* what I am doing, (b) *check* myself, (c) *pick* and *plan* the best action, (d) *go* with the action, and (e) *see* what happens.

When there is a conflict, the first step is for consultants to "*stop* what they are doing." This action prevents negative chains of behaviors from being shaped and avoids the possibility of conflict escalation. Consultants should identify and practice a specific behavioral response for stopping, such as sitting back and taking a deep breath, counting to ten covertly, looking away, taking a break for a drink of water. The function of this stop response is to break the sequence of behaviors and to set the occasion for assessing how to resolve the conflict.

After stopping, consultants should "*check* themselves." At this step, consultants should ask themselves if they can (a) avoid engaging in negative off-task behaviors and (b) increase their use of conflict resolution behaviors. If the consultant is not calm, he or she should ask for some time to think about the problem and set another time to discuss the matter. If the consultant is calm, he or she should determine if the other person is calm. If the other person is not engaging in on-task behaviors, the consultant should suggest meeting at another time.

If both parties agree to take some time and meet again, the specifics of that meeting should be set. In addition to deciding on a meeting time and day, both parties should agree to generate a list of possible solutions to the problem and be prepared to discuss the strengths and weaknesses of each solution.

If both parties can engage efficiently in a problem-solving sequence, they should do so immediately. A complete flow chart of the conflict-management steps and the decisions that must be made is illustrated in Figure 11.4.

Problem solving.   Like the highly structured formats for the Problem Identification and the Intervention Planning phases, we believe that conflict escalation and effective problem resolution is facilitated if the problem-solving process is objective and prescriptive. This approach can keep the consultant and the teacher focused on student needs, observable behavior, and the factors that affect their behavior. We also believe that conflicts must be resolved before effective problem solving can be conducted. If two people disagree and one or both are agitated, the efficiency of the problem-solving process can be affected. If Mr. Sanchez is focusing all of his attention and behaviors on Ms. Slick's failure to agree with him and if he is frustrated and angry and unable to calm himself, it will be difficult to engage in a process that requires oral explanations, listening to the other person's position, modifying and accepting an alternative solution, developing a plan for that position, and implementing that plan in a collaborative manner. If neither party is ready to problem solve, we suggest setting another time, day, and place to complete the process.

If conflicts are resolved and participants are calm and engaging, problem solving is possible. Many problem-solving sequences are available; however, they have five steps in common: (a) define/describe the problem, (b) generate multiple or alternate solutions, (c) evaluate solutions, (d) determine the best solution,

FIGURE 11.4

Flow chart of steps and decisions in basic conflict management sequence

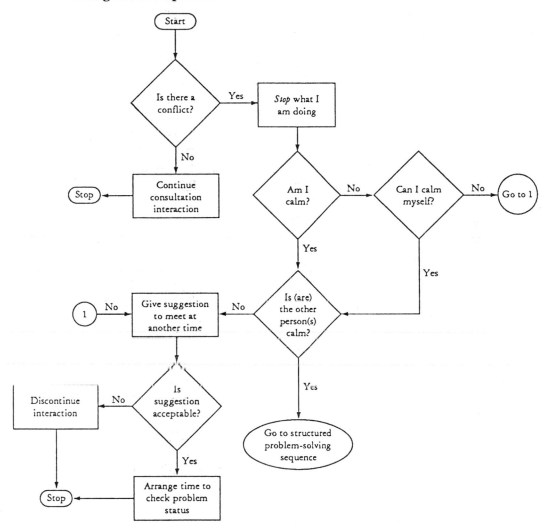

(e) develop a plan to implement the solution, and (f) implement the solution and evaluate the outcome (Christoff, et al., 1985; Robin & Koepke, 1990).

The problem-solving process should (a) be linked closely to the conflict resolution sequence; (b) respond to the differences that exist between the participants, and (c) include opportunities for close examination of the features of solutions and any contributions made by participants. We suggest a problem-solving process that expands the general five-step progression into a more comprehensive nine-step progression. A flow chart illustrating the 10 steps from a consultant's perspective is displayed in Figure 11.5. We also suggest that the problem-solving process be focused on completing a worksheet consisting of the

F I G U R E 11.5

Flow chart of steps in basic problem-solving sequence

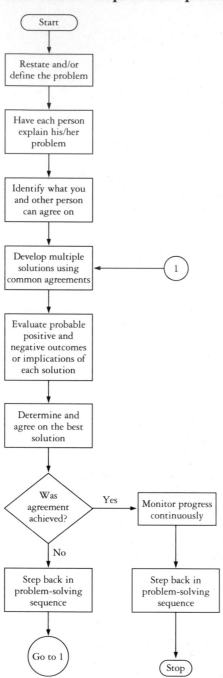

ten steps. Following a standard format and writing down information can make the exchanges between the two parties more objective and more focused. An example of problem-solving worksheet is illustrated in Figure 11.6.

Definitions and guidelines for each of the nine problem-solving steps are described in the following list. An example using the consultation case involving Mr. Sanchez and Ms. Slick is also presented.

STEP 1: *Restate and/or define the problem.*
1. Focus consultant and teacher attention on the observable features of the problem, such as the problem behaviors or the immediate context.
2. Follow the guidelines used in defining the problem on the Problem Identification Interview form.
3. Write the problem in the form of a question that needs to be answered.
4. Describe the problem relative to the student rather than to the teacher or the consultant.
   EXAMPLE: "What classroom-based strategies can be used to improve Gracie's study skills for and during biology class?"

STEP 2: *Have each person explain his/her position* .
1. Limit explanations to one or two sentences.
2. Listen without commenting.
3. List explanations.
4. Write in observable terms.
5. Use observable terms and explanations.
6. Accept all contributions.
   EXAMPLE: Mr. Sanchez
      a. Gracie must be taught study skills directly.
      b. Gracie has a skill deficit; she's not a compliance problem.
      c. Ms. Slick is a powerful reinforcer.
      d. Gracie has limited opportunities to learn how and when to use study skills.

   Ms. Slick
   a. Gracie must learn that there are consequences for her behaviors.
   b. Many teaching strategies have been tried.
   c. Ms. Slick has limited experience in teaching study skills.
   d. Gracie likes Ms. Slick.
   e. Ms. Slick has no other intervention options.
   f. Gracie has no study skills.

STEP 3: *Identify where there is agreement.*
1. Reword and task-analyze explanations to maximize the possibility of agreement.
2. Focus on objective, classroom-based explanations.
3. Avoid selecting explanations that are negative or subjective.
4. Where possible, use teacher wording.
   EXAMPLE:
      a. Gracie has no study skills and must learn them.
      b. Gracie likes Mr. Sanchez (positive reinforcer).
      c. Ms. Slick cannot provide the opportunities to teach study skills.

F I G U R E 11.6

A problem-solving worksheet

Problem-Solving Worksheet
Are we ready to problem solve?   No—Set another meeting date and time.   Yes—Continue to 1.
1.   Restate and/or define the problem.

2.   Have each person explain his/her position.
 	
        Teacher/Other:
 	
        Consultant:

3.   Identify where there is agreement.

FIGURE 11.6   (*continued*)

4.	Develop multiple solutions using common agreements.	
5.	Evaluate probable negative and positive outcomes or implications for each solution.	
6.	Determine and agree upon the best solution.	**Was agreement achieved?** No—Go to 4. Yes Continue to 7.
7.	Develop a plan to implement the best solution.	
8.	Implement the plan.	
9.	Evaluate implementation and outcome of intervention.	

STEP 4: *Develop multiple solutions using common agreements.*

1. Focus the process on the initial problem definition.
2. Write in observable terms.
3. Maximize use of teacher explanations and wording.
4. Avoid solutions that go beyond the immediate problem context.
5. Consider all possible solutions.
6. Avoid evaluating solutions as they are being developed.

EXAMPLE:

a. Arrange opportunities for Ms. Slick to teach study skills to Gracie and other students.
b. Schedule Gracie to spend one hour each day in Ms. Warberg-Ard's study skills class.
c. Teach Gracie to self-record when she engages in a study skill during biology class, and give her a free gift from the school store when she fills her recording card.
d. Send Gracie to the office when she fails to display appropriate study skills.

STEP 5: Evaluate probable negative and positive outcomes or implications for each solution.

1. State them in observable terms.
2. Consider the negative outcomes or implications first, then the positive.
3. Consider resource, training, material, and staffing needs.
4. Focus attention on problem definition.
5. Focus on short- and long-term benefits for student and teacher.

EXAMPLE:

a. No time to learn how to teach or to schedule study skills in Ms. Slick's class.
b. Gracie will get special attention for behaviors that are expected of other students without prompting or assistance.
c. Gracie might disrupt Ms. Warberg-Ard's classroom.
d. Gracie will learn skills that she has never learned before and that can be used in other subject areas.
e. Study skills instruction is a positive intervention.
f. Gracie's academic and subject area achievement will improve.

STEP 6: *Determine and agree on the best solution.*

1. If agreement is not achieved, go back to step 5 and develop other possible multiple solutions.
2. Focus on the problem statement.
3. Evaluate each solution separately.
4. Arrange the solutions in order of preference.

EXAMPLE:

a. Schedule one hour a day in Ms. Warberg-Ard's classroom.
b. Teach Gracie to self-record, and provide a choice in the school store when the criteria are met.

STEP 7: *Develop a plan to implement the best solution.*

1. Use the Intervention Planning form.

2. Consider guidelines and procedures covered in the development of Intervention Planning forms.

3. State individual responsibilities clearly and specifically.

EXAMPLE:

    a. Explain plan to Ms. Warberg-Ard and ask for her assistance.

    b. Prepare self-recording sheets.

    c. Identify what study skills need to be taught and emphasized.

    d. Develop a record-keeping system.

STEP 8: *Implement the plan.*

1. Follow the intervention implementation guidelines described in earlier chapters.

2. Initially, monitor implementation continuously.

STEP 9: *Evaluate implementation and outcome of intervention.*

1. Follow monitoring and evaluation guidelines described in earlier chapters.

2. Evaluate performance against criteria for acceptable performance.

3. Evaluate performance in collaboration with the teacher.

The latter steps of the problem sequence correspond closely with the activities associated with the Problem Identification and Intervention Planning phases discussed in the larger consultation process. Consultants should apply guidelines from these phases to the problem-solving process.

This nine-step problem-solving sequence is predicated on the consultant and the teacher being able to engage in a cooperative exchange. We believe that a structured problem-solving sequence can produce useful solutions. However, the greater the disagreement or conflict, the more structured and focused the process must become. If a proactive interaction is not possible, the consultant should use the conflict resolution process to determine the most appropriate action. If repeated conflicts and rescheduling of meetings occur, consultants should consider asking another person to assist in resolving the conflict and solving the problem.

STRATEGIES FOR COMMUNICATING EFFECTIVELY WITH OTHERS

Analyzing roadblocks, solving problems, and resolving conflicts can be made more effective and efficient with clear working structures, a behavioral focus, and an emphasis on manipulable environmental stimuli. However, each of these processes requires clear communications between the consultant and the teacher. For example, Mr. Sanchez is a highly competent consultant because he (a) has mastery of a wide range of knowledge, (b) is fluent at many academic and social behavior interventions, and (c) knows all the steps and components of problem solving and conflict resolution. Unfortunately, his communication skills are not strong, and he finds it difficult to work with others who do not communicate effectively. As a result, his ability to engage in necessary consultation strategies is hindered by his lack of effective communication skills. In this section, we briefly discuss the purpose of communications in consultation, communication forms, and strategies for communicating effectively.

Communication Purposes

Consultation depends on the exchange of information. Teachers and consultants must be able to describe effectively and efficiently what they see, give and obtain information, generate solutions, and express reactions and opinions. Communication content and strategies have three simple functions for the consultant. First, consultants use communication skills to get information from others. They ask questions, write requests, and conduct interviews. Second, consultants use their communication behaviors to give information to others. They make recommendations; write memos, letters, and reports; and give feedback to others. Third, consultants use communications to change the behavior of others; that is, to give others new skills, support or encourage certain behaviors, or discourage other behaviors or actions from occurring.

Communication Forms

Communication can take two basic forms. For the consultant, one of the most common forms is oral communication, such as face-to-face exchanges, meetings, and telephone calls. Written forms are much more varied and include permanent products such as, letters, reports, plan sheets, flow charts, memoranda, and agenda.

Strategies for Communicating Effectively

If consultants and teachers are to achieve successful consultations and collaborative interactions, they must be effective communicators. Regardless of their form, all communications should be professional in their content and presentation. For this simple rule to be useful, consultants must become fluent in strategies that make communications effective and efficient. The following strategies are designed to facilitate consultant and teacher communications.

Preparing professional written products.   All written products should be prepared in a professional manner. Although handwritten products can be perceived as more personal, neatly typed products communicate greater professionalism, emphasize the importance of their content, and make the presentation of material more accessible. An occasional handwritten note can reinforce personal relations; however, all letters, memoranda, and reports should be neatly formatted, typed, and errorless. To see the difference, compare the handwritten and typed versions of the same memo illustrated in Figure 11.7.

The following strategies can be helpful in developing professional written communications:

1. Use formats (agenda, letterhead, memoranda designs) that are routinely employed by building and district personnel. Avoid creating new forms that serve identical functions.

2. Proofread—then proofread again—each written communication, especially, material that will be placed in professional files or available to a number of readers. It is often helpful to have a colleague critically reread important communications. Particular attention should be directed toward correct spelling, proper grammar, professional vocabulary, neatness, and clarity.

3. Avoid informal fonts, notations, and graphics on formal written products. Although they may present a more relaxed document, they lower the professional nature of important written communications. For example, Mr. Sanchez draws happy faces on his memos, Ms. Ivanhoe inserts one of the 250 graphic images included with her word-processing program (an open book, an hourglass, or a schoolhouse), and Mr. Woo uses six different font styles and sizes (italic or bold and 10-point to 18-point type) throughout his letters.

4. Begin all written documents with a clear statement of purpose so the reader will have a clear understanding of the author's intent and content.

5. Use simple sentences and an active voice. While driving to and from schools, Ms. Umbell uses a small tape recorder to compose memos, reports, and letters. Unfortunately, her products include numerous conversational-style sentences that are complex in structure, content, and meaning; for example, "When I look at the problem very closely, it appears to me that Falko's current placement in Julio Estavez's third-period art class is placing unnecessary stress on everyone, and everyone would benefit if we could develop an alternative activity during that time of the day for Falko to receive more structured instruction." Mrs. Umbell might have written that sentence more succinctly as "Falko's behaviors have not improved in Mr. Estavez's third-period art class. I recommend that we consider an alternative placement during third period."

6. Treat all written products confidentially. Place and maintain all written materials in secure locations: (a) keep files in locked cabinets or offices, (b) avoid leaving materials in public places, such as staff rooms, desktops, car seats, (c) mail correspondence in sealed envelops, (d) limit the number of document copies to what is minimally necessary, and (e) clearly mark any sensitive material as "confidential" or "personal." If written documents are prepared on a computer, use appropriate security devices (passwords or access locks) and maintain all diskettes in a safe location. Dispose of all written materials in an appropriate manner: (a) black out names and other personal identifying information, (b) tear them up or incinerate them, and (c) erase diskettes completely. Without the details, the meaning of even the simplest written statement can be misconstrued. For example, Mr. Sanchez wrote a two-sentence memorandum to Ms. Slick that read, "Thank you for meeting with me last night and planning a strong intervention for eliminating Katrina's aggressive behaviors. I think we've got her figured out now." He folded it over and taped it to Ms. Slick's classroom door. Unfortunately, Katrina came by the room to pick up some extra worksheets to take home. Thinking that the note was for her, she read it. Believing that she was going to be suspended, she stormed out of the building, slamming doors, hitting lockers, and cursing Ms. Slick and Mr. Sanchez.

Preparing and presenting professional oral communications. Similarly, important oral communications should be prepared and presented in a professional manner; that is, they should include appropriate language, be concise and clear, and emphasize objective content. We also recommend that consultants use

FIGURE 11.7

Examples of handwritten and typed memos

January 15, 1992

To: Ms. Slick, Room 17

From: Mr. Sanchez, Resource Consultant

Re: Friday classroom observation

I want to thank you for letting me observe your third-hour social skills lesson. It can be difficult to teach when you are being observed.

I really enjoyed the improvements you've made in your presentation style and example selections. Your students seemed very attentive and enthusiastic.

I will see you next week when we can talk about Sonny's and Terry's progress in your group.

In the meantime, give me a call if you need anything.

Thanks again.

a strongoral cue that signals the listener that something important is about to be communicated. For example, Ms. Umbell begins all interactions with light conversation containing informal and nonthreatening content. However, when she is ready to discuss matters associated with a particular Request for Assistance or consultation case, she gives a clear signal that it's time to go to work.

FIGURE 11.7   (*continued*)

January 15, 1992

TO: Ms. Slick
             Room 17

FROM: Mr. Sanchez
             Resource Consultant

RE: Friday classroom observation

I want to thank you for letting me observe your third-hour social skills lesson. It can be difficult to teach when you are being observed.

I really enjoyed the improvements you've made in your presentation style and example selections. Your students seemed very attentive and enthusiastic.

I will see you next week when we can talk about Sonny's and Terry's progress in your group.

In the meantime, give me a call if you need anything.

Thanks again.

Ms. Umbell: "Thank you for sending me your lesson plan for building box kites. I can really use that activity at home when it's raining."

Ms. Thompson: "I hope you enjoy making the kites. Remember to use stiff paper on the back side of the kite."

Ms. Umbell: "I'll remember." (Pulling out her legal pad and uncapping her pen) "Let's get down to work."

In this example, Ms. Umbell communicates that it's time to work by preparing her work materials and giving a strong "time-to-work" statement. She uses this signal exactly the same way every time, so teachers have learned that it is time to work.

Strategies used to facilitate and maintain oral communications should also be used with written communications. Consider the following guidelines for both written and oral communications:

1. Use objective and professional vocabulary that requires minimum inferences. When Mr. Sanchez says, "We've got a helluva mess here. We might have had a chance to save Terry but this thing has gone way too long and far. I wonder why no one has done anything about this?" the teacher starts making excuses about how busy she's been, how lousy Terry's home situation is, and what a good teacher she is. Mr. Sanchez's comment could have been more objective and professional if he had said "Terry's situation is difficult. We will need to develop some specific classroom-based interventions to help Terry learn how to manage his anger more effectively. Let's start with listing the strategies that you have found to work in the past."

Objective and professional vocabulary also means using nonsexist and nondiscriminatory language, for example, "student with behavior disorders" rather than "behavior-disordered student," "boys and girls" instead of "boys and little girls," "Asian American" in place of "oriental," "child with at-risk behaviors" rather than "at-risk child."

Similarly, avoid using highly technical language or jargon except when commonly employed by the teacher. For example, *reinforcer, token, behavior,* and *event recording* are terms that are common to most educators. However, *discriminative stimulus, conditioned reinforcer, overcorrection,* and *contingent* are terms that are not familiar to many teachers. Consider common synonyms for technical jargon. For example, use "signal" or "prompt" for discriminative stimulus, "newly learned reinforcer" for conditioned reinforcer, "at the same time" or "in association with" for contingent.

2. Avoid making "you-statements." Focus on the student's problem behaviors, immediate environmental factors, collected data, and features of the intervention. You-statements can be threatening, imply personal deficiencies, or cause people to become defensive or disengage. For example, this statement, "You really are upset about not being able to help Sonny during lunch," might be stated in a less personal way as "Sonny's behaviors are sure difficult to figure out. Let's look at what seems to work at other times of the day."

3. Reinforce and expand all teacher contributions by parroting, paraphrasing, questioning, elaborating, confirming, and summarizing (see Box 11.1 for examples). The careful presentation of verbal praise following teacher contributions can be effective; however, praise statements must be sincere and, in fact, meaningful, useful, and reinforcing to the teacher.

4. Use concrete examples to illustrate and reinforce procedures and techniques. Although simple oral descriptions can increase efficiency, examples help clarify what is being said. For example, the following is a simple statement that assumes a great deal of prior knowledge for effective implementation: "When you give a token reinforcer, be sure to give a contingent verbal praise statement." The statement will carry more meaning if this example is added: "For instance, if I see Terry waiting quietly in line and keeping his hands to himself, I will say, 'Great job waiting quietly in line. Here's a pro-ticket that you can use for a free trip to the school store' as I hand him the pro-ticket."

5. When conversations become off-task or nonfocused, bring the conversation back to task by (a) asking questions that relate to the purpose of the interaction or (b) referring to task-related content that was discussed previously. For example, although the purpose of the conversation was to discuss Sonny's recess behaviors, Mr. Sanchez realizes that he and Ms. Slick are discussing how teacher-training institutions should teach more behavior and classroom management strategies for students with at-risk behavior. Realizing that they are off-task, Mr. Sanchez says, "What were we saying earlier about how a behavior contract worked with Sonny's behaviors during recess?" He might also have said, "I hear you, but let's go back to our immediate problem and see what things we said on the Problem Identification form trigger Sonny's chain of inappropriate behaviors."

6. Provide a clear statement of the purpose of an interaction or conversation and a strong advance organizer so the consultant and the teacher can identify what they are about to discuss and how the discussion is going to be conducted. For example, Ms. Umbell begins every review meeting in the same way: "The purpose of today's meeting is to review Sonny's progress now that he's using a new behavioral contract. First, it would help me if you could take three or four minutes to share your data on his classroom disruptions. Then I'd like to tell you what Sonny's dad and I talked about last night. I also want to make sure that we talk about ways to fade the token economy program when it's about three-twenty. Is that sequence okay with you?"

7. When anticipating a difficult or important conversation or interaction, write down and rehearse what needs to be said. Also, identify what controversial topics or problems might arise, and prepare specific responses or ways to prevent them from occurring. When a meeting involves making a recommendation to a teacher, the student's parents, the student, or an administrator, Mr. Sanchez writes a clear statement of what needs to be said, and he practices presenting the information to a colleague who tries to introduce potential roadblocks to which Mr. Sanchez must respond.

8. Use a written agenda or activity or task list to structure meetings and other gatherings where complex, difficult, or numerous issues must be discussed. These pieces of paper can serve a number of important functions: (a) a record-keeping device, (b) a prompt to return to or stay on task, (c) an advance organizer, and (d) a guide for sequencing topics. These written products can also serve as an objective third-party focus when conflicts occur between individuals. For example, when Ms. Umbell finds that she and a teacher are unable to solve a problem and that the conversation is becoming personal and defensive, she focuses her attention on taking notes on her agenda or filling out a worksheet ("Let's write down our ideas and look at them one at a time." "What was your idea about modifying the lesson? I'd like to write it down." "Let's step back and see what we've accomplished and what we need to do before four o'clock.").

STRATEGIES FOR SPECIFIC PROBLEM SITUATIONS

Despite their best efforts to facilitate and maintain effective and professional communications, consultants and teachers experience conversations and discussions that go awry. They discover that conversations are off-task, tasks are not completed, accurate information is not communicated, and descriptions are incomplete. Solving and managing these types of problems can be difficult; however, it is possible for consultants to respond in a way that is objective and responsible. In this section, we discuss an approach to working and communicating with others that focuses on identifying and manipulating what maintains problem behaviors in problem situations. Rather than inferring the motivation or intention (such as anger, frustration, or discontent) behind a teacher's or consultant's behavior, we look at the antecedents that set the occasion for a given behavior and the consequences that reinforce it. Although we focus on teacher behaviors, the same analysis and intervention strategies could be applied to consultant or administrator behaviors. In fact, whenever two people interact, each engages in behavior that is affected by and affects the behaviors of the other person. Many of the same strategies recommended for analyzing and solving student problem behaviors are also applicable.

We refer to teacher behaviors that are not associated with the direct achievement of consultation goals and product development as *off-task behaviors.* Examples of off-task behaviors include talking about unrelated topics, failing to complete tasks, challenging recommendations or comments made by others, or not participating or contributing in a discussion. *On-task behaviors* are what teachers do to facilitate the achievement of consultation goals and products. Examples include contributing to the completion of consultation forms and activities, staying on topic or issue, engaging in productive problem solving, and following through with commitments.

In this section, we discuss three kinds of problem situations and provide general strategies for responding to each problem type: (a) on-task behaviors have not been learned, (b) off-task behaviors are maintained by reinforcement, and (c) low rates of on-task behavior are maintained by a lack of positive reinforcement or the presence of aversives.

On-Task Behaviors Have Not Been Learned

Consultants may not find interactions to be productive because teachers have not learned how to engage in behaviors necessary for effective communications. For example, when Ms. Redhunt asks Ms. Ruburts to describe what Martha does at recess, she receives general statements that are not descriptive ("She's an angry little girl." "She's lonely and depressed." "She does whatever she wants."). Finally, Ms. Redhunt asks Ms. Ruburts if she knows how to describe Martha's behaviors in observable terms, and discovers that Ms. Ruburts has no idea how to respond.

When consultants discover that teachers have not learned or are not fluent at a skill required for a successful consultation, they should do the following:

1. Teach the teacher how to do the on-task behavior. For example, Ms. Redhunt explains to Ms. Ruburts what an observable and descriptive definition is and gives examples and nonexamples.

2. Provide a structure that leads the teacher toward displays of on-task behaviors. For example, we stress the use of forms and structures that guide the consultation process. Specific questions are asked in a predetermined sequence. When completed, a problem analysis or intervention strategy is developed.

3. Break complex tasks into subtasks that are easier to complete. For example, Ms. Redhunt asks Ms. Ruburts the following sequence of questions: (a) "Where on the playground do you see Martha having problems with her peers?" (b) "What does Martha do when her peers start talking with her?" (c) "When her peers do those things, what does Martha do?" and (d) "What would you like Martha to do instead of calling her peers names?"

Off-Task Behaviors Are Maintained by Reinforcement

Consultants may be unable to complete consultation activities or engage in productive communications because teachers engage in off-task behaviors; that is, they do not contribute directly to consultation goals and product. For example, whenever Ms. Redhunt meets with Mr. Honczycki, she must listen to conversations about poor administrative direction, degradation of American youth, and difficulties managing the nighttime behaviors of Mr. Honczycki's sons. The first step is to determine what kind of reinforcement is maintaining the off-task behaviors. Two types of reinforcement should be considered: positive reinforcement and negative reinforcement.

Off-task behaviors maintained by positive reinforcement.   High rates of off-task behavior can be maintained by positive reinforcement; that is, some reinforcing event follows occurrences of off-task behaviors. These reinforcing events can be an occasional nod, a verbal statement intended to empathize with the teacher, or a direct response to the off-task behavior. For example, whenever Mr. Honczycki says his son's nighttime sleeping problems are keeping him awake, Ms. Redhunt comments that it must be difficult to be the single parent of three boys. She frequently responds with general verbal acknowledgements ("I hear you." "That must be difficult." "Yes, I see." "Interesting.") and consenting physical movements (nods, smiles when he smiles, grimaces when he grimaces) that maintain Mr. Honczycki's off-task behaviors.

When consultants determine that off-task behaviors are being maintained or increased through positive reinforcement, they should take the following actions:

1. Completely and consistently remove any statements or actions that are positive reinforcers.

2. Provide an organizing statement at the beginning of the interaction that states the purpose and structure of the meeting or communication, and that provides a specific amount of time at the end of the meeting for discussing

"other" topics. For example, Ms. Redhunt begins her next conversation with Mr. Honczycki in the following manner: "Before we start, I'd like to spend ten minutes at the end of our meeting to tell you about some strategies that you might try with your son's nightmares. Don't forget to remind me when it is three forty-five. First, let's do three things: review Martha's homework performance, look at what we should be doing next, and write an agenda for the IEP meeting next week."

3. Use statements and actions that were positively reinforcing for off-task behaviors when on-task behaviors occur. For example, Ms. Redhunt nods when Mr. Honczycki offers a suggestion for the IEP meeting agenda, grimaces when he grimaces about Martha's homework grades, and says "that's interesting" when he gives a recommendation for a change in the current intervention.

Off-task behaviors maintained by negative reinforcement. Teachers may display off-task behaviors because these behaviors result in the removal or discontinuation of an aversive action or condition—that is, negative reinforcement. For example, off-task behaviors might be maintained because repeated requests by the consultant are removed, changes in current teaching practices are prevented, and talking about an aversive situation is stopped. For example, when Ms. Sarver repeatedly asks Ms. Redhunt questions about what it is like to be a consultant ("What is the hardest case you've ever had?" "What did you have to learn to be a consultant?" "Do you think I could be a consultant?") and Ms. Redhunt answers these off-task questions, less time is spent talking about changing seating arrangements and learning a new remedial reading program for Petur.

Strategies for decreasing off-task behaviors that are maintained by negative reinforcement include the following:

1. Providing stronger positive reinforcement for on-task consultation-directed behaviors—that is, positive reinforcers that are stronger than the negative reinforcers. Consultants may need to find individually specific positive reinforcers that can "motivate" teachers to engage in more on-task consultation behaviors. For example, Ms. Redhunt discovers that more on-task behaviors occur when the consultation activity is set up as a "consultation" training activity for Ms. Sarver—that is, taking advantage of her interest in becoming a consultant. When Ms. Sarver is on-task, Ms. Redhunt says statements like "That's an excellent suggestion. If you were a consultant, how would you arrange Petur's seating arrangement?"

2. Reducing the aversive qualities of previous negatively reinforcing consequences. This may involve engaging in aversive activities differently or less often, explaining the reasons behind an aversive activity, or providing more information or assistance to reduce the aversive qualities of an activity or event. For example, Ms. Sarver engages in off-task behavior because it results in less discussion about changing her reading program. To reduce the aversiveness of this potential change in curriculum, Ms.

Redhunt explains the advantages and positive outcomes of the new program before she makes her recommendation. She also indicates that the new program is not as different from other programs as Ms. Sarver may have thought.

3. Providing an advance organizer to prevent the use of off-task behaviors to remove an aversive event. For example, Ms. Redhunt begins the meeting with a statement designed to reduce the concern associated with changing reading programs and to make the discussion more collaborative than directive. She begins the meeting with Ms. Sarver in the following way: "I realize that a discussion about changing your reading program may be difficult; however, I'd like to give you about five minutes to list your concerns. Then I'd like to take another five minutes to describe how we might provide extra teaching assistant time or preparation time to ease the transition."

Low Rates of On-Task Behavior Are Maintained by a Lack of Positive Reinforcement or the Presence of Aversives

Consultation activities can be hindered when on-task behaviors do not occur at high enough rates to maintain effective interactions. Low rates of on-task behaviors can be explained in two ways: low rates of positive reinforcement or the presentation of aversive consequences.

Low rates of on-task behavior maintained by low rates of positive reinforcement. On-task behaviors must be maintained by effective positive reinforcement. If ineffective reinforcers, thin schedules of reinforcement, or delayed positive reinforcement are used, off-task behaviors are more likely to occur in place of on-task behavior. When this type of problem is determined, consultants should consider the following:

1. Changing to more effective reinforcers. Although nods and smiles were effective reinforcers with Mr. Honczycki, they were ineffective with Ms. Albertson. To increase Ms. Albertson's on-task behaviors, Ms. Redhunt switched to contingent verbal praise, which proved to be much more effective.

2. Enriching the schedule of reinforcement for on-task behaviors. In a 50-minute meeting, Ms. Redhunt provides about three positive verbal praises. When she gave ten or more verbal praise statements in the same 50 minutes, she found that Ms. Sarver's on-task behaviors increased noticeably.

3. Providing reinforcement more immediately after the on-task behaviors occurred. Ms. Redhunt usually waited until the end of her meetings or conversations before she provided any positive feedback to her teachers. For some teachers, like Ms. Sarver, Ms. Redhunt found that more immediate feedback was needed to increase and maintain acceptable rates of on-task behavior.

Low rates of on-task behavior maintained by the presentation of aversives.
When consultants engage in actions or make statements that others find aversive,
the effect can be a decrease in on-task behaviors. The behaviors needed to engage
in collaborative consultation are functionally punished. Teachers may find the
following consultant behaviors to be more aversive than reinforcing: maintaining
eye contact for long (or short) durations, physically sitting too close (or too far),
saying "you know" excessively, paraphrasing too often (or not enough), and
making too many (or not enough) corrections to statements made by others. For
example, Mr. Neil's supervisor observed him in a consultation meeting with a
teacher. She noticed that whenever the teacher made an appropriate contribution
to the conversation, Mr. Neil turned his face away. After experiencing two or three
of these responses, the teacher stopped making contributions because his
behaviors were being punished.

When an aversive consultant behavior follows an on-task teacher behavior, the
effect may be a decrease in on-task rates. In this situation, consultants should
consider the following:

1. Reducing the use of these aversive behaviors. After he learned about its
   effect on teacher on-task behaviors, Mr. Neil stopped turning away.
2. Increasing the contingent use of positive reinforcement for on-task
   behaviors. In Mr. Neil's case, turning away from the teacher was replaced
   with a short nod and an acknowledging verbal statement ("I agree." "I like
   that idea." "I hadn't thought of that.").

Summary

In this section, we attempted to provide a general approach to analyzing and
responding to interactions where high rates of off-task and low rates of on-task
consultation behaviors are being observed. We conclude this section with three
cautions. First, we focused on how consultants should respond to off-task teacher
behaviors. Consultants also engage in off-task behavior and must arrange
opportunities to analyze their own behaviors through observations by a peer or
supervisor or self-observation and evaluation. If a teacher is engaged in off-task
behavior, so is the consultant!

Second, one person's positive reinforcer can be another's aversive. There are
no universal reinforcers or aversives. We strongly recommend that a functional
analysis be conducted to observe the effect of a given event or action on the future
occurrence of on- and off-task behavior; only then can we make a reasonable guess
about whether a specific event is a reinforcer for a specific individual.

Third, consultation is an interactive, collaborative effort requiring behaviors
that must communicate respect, concern, enthusiasm, and empathy. We believe
that responsible consultation is possible; however, consultants must be honest and
sincere in their use of these techniques. All consultation efforts and actions become
functional aversives if conducted in a mechanical, condescending, or insincere
manner.

STRATEGIES FOR TRAINING OTHERS

Many times consultants find themselves having to teach others how to use a new technique or strategy. We believe that many of the strategies, procedures, and analyses described in previous chapters provide opportunities for direct and indirect training. For example, whenever consultants facilitate the completion of an Intervention Planning form, they provide a structured opportunity for teachers to learn about problem analysis and intervention development. Whenever intervention implementation strategies are described, teachers learn how to execute a strategy. In explaining a procedure, consultants provide a model for teachers to observe and learn new teaching or behavior management techniques. Each of these examples illustrates how consultants can affect the behaviors of others.

In this section, we provide a brief overview of different training opportunities and a basic format for presenting information both formally and informally to others.

Opportunities for Training Others

Whenever a consultant interacts with an individual or a group of people, there is an opportunity for training to occur, for example, through written products, oral explanations, demonstrations of a technique, practice sessions, or observation feedback. We describe three general opportunities available to consultants to train others: (a) large-group inservices, (b) small-group instruction, and (c) individual training.

Large-group inservice. Frequently consultants are asked to provide training for large groups of people. Large-group training sessions, however, have a number of disadvantages. First, it is difficult to individualize training with large groups of teachers and other school staff. Second, arranging instruction so staff members will generalize newly learned skills to other settings is relatively low. Third, it is difficult to select a range of training examples that will be sufficient for the range of skills and experiences found among individuals in a large group. Fourth, it is impractical to assess the strengths and weaknesses of each individual in a large group. Finally, "one-shot" inservices frequently occur because it is nearly impossible to schedule frequent, regular meetings.

However, large-group inservices also have some advantages. First, a large number of people are exposed to the same information, which, in turn, increases consistency and maximizes opportunities for discussion and independent follow-up activities, thus increasing the consultant's efficiency. Second, individual staff members have the opportunity to learn from and about other staff members with whom they may have little or no opportunity to interact. Third, the training needs of individuals can be addressed without singling out a specific individual.

Given these advantages and disadvantages, we suggest the following when planning and conducting large-group training sessions:

1. Distribute a needs analysis and conduct observations of the staff and their work setting. Use these data to construct activities, make examples, and formulate inservice outcome objectives.

2. Develop and prepare handouts and activities that maximize active participant engagement. For example, give out note-taking guides that require following along and filling in blanks with information. Prepare handouts that can be individualized according to the participant's position and responsibilities.

3. Schedule numerous participation activities that require physical involvement. For example, conduct role plays, arrange for small groups to engage in cooperative tasks, assign specific roles to individuals, require frequent reporting from different spokespersons.

4. Use a variety of formats (for example, overhead transparencies, videotapes, slides, audio tapes, scripted role plays, printed handouts) for the presentation of information.

5. Use small groups (three to five individuals) as the basic working unit. During the inservice, this unit would engage in collaborative activities and develop tasks and commitments for completion after the inservice is ended.

6. Identify an individual or a small team that can conduct and monitor follow-up activities after the inservice is completed.

Small-group instruction. Many consultants prefer small-group training opportunities because (a) individuals are more accessible, (b) training can be individualized, (c) more homogeneity can be arranged, (d) follow-up activities by the consultant are feasible, (e) presentation content (examples or role plays) can be focused on the needs of the whole group, (f) individuals have more opportunities for active engagement, (g) it is possible to assess the general strengths and weaknesses of individuals in the small group, and, in general, (h) the impact on students is improved. However, small-group training decreases (a) the overall impact a consultant might have over a larger group of individuals, (b) opportunities for interactions with new or other staff, and (c) the consultant's ability to interact with an entire building staff.

When consultants are planning for or presenting small-group training, they should consider the same guidelines used for large-group inservices, as well as the following:

1. Provide staff with opportunities for active practice and participation.

2. Work through activities as a group, using a staff person to lead the activity or summarize the outcomes.

3. Learn and use the names of participants.

4. If a lecture format is used, minimize the amount of passive listening required and maximize participation by asking frequent questions, giving examples and nonexamples, and utilizing frequent activities.

5. As each topic is discussed, ask participants to provide examples; then use these examples to model or demonstrate the topic.

6. At the end of the training, ask each individual to give an oral and, if possible, written commitment about what he or she will do differently tomorrow.

Individual training.   Consultants engage in individual training in formal and informal contexts. In the formal context, individual teachers may request training on a specific strategy, technique, or curriculum. For example, Mr. Neil learns that Ms. Redhunt is an expert on incidental teaching techniques, so he arranges for a special training session in which he will have her undivided attention. Consultants may also provide training as the indirect result of collaborative exchanges or the completion of consultation-related activities. These informal training opportunities arise when consultants make reference to a strategy in a conversation or written product, or when they are demonstrating a technique. For example, in working with Ms. Redhunt to complete the Problem Identification form, Ms. Tsuga learned about how to develop testable explanations and to determine whether the explanation is predictable.

Individual training sessions are effective when the goals are to (a) teach a specific and/or complex skill, (b) teach a skill that has limited generalizability or relevance to other staff members, (c) make maximum use of the available time and resources, (d) obtain specific assessment data about the individual's strengths or weaknesses, and (e) train a person to train others. However, the disadvantages of individual training sessions include (a) the high cost of repeated training of individuals, (b) the low influence or impact on others, and (c) the dependence on the trainer to provide support, remedial training, or follow-up.

When engaged in the training of individuals, the strategies described for large and small groups should be considered. Other guidelines include the following:

1. Use interactive training strategies so the individual is actively engaged.
2. Ask the individual to provide a specific example that can be used as a teaching example/model.

Basic Training Components and Format

Regardless of whether the training occurs in large or small groups or formally or informally, consultants must engage in effective training strategies. It should come as no surprise that we basically recommend the same strategies that teachers would use to teach skills, concepts, and strategies to students. The difference is in the complexity, presentation, and content of the instruction. The design of the instruction or training would not change. We recommend that consultants follow a basic model-lead-test format when training others. In this section, we describe the basic components of this format and useful strategies.

The model-lead-test format is well documented as an effective way to teach skills to others. Regardless of the level of formality, we highly recommend that the following components be included when training others. We also provide guidelines for each component.

1. *Introduction:* A brief overview of what is to be learned, the rationale for why the skill is important and/or useful, and a description of what will happen in the lesson.

    a. If appropriate, provide a brief review of what was covered in previous sessions and/or discuss any homework assignments.

    b. Provide concrete, relevant examples to help the trainee understand how this new skill might be useful.

2. *Outcome statement or objective:* A specific description of what will be learned in the present lesson; an exact statement of the outcome of the lesson.

    a. State in discrete and observable terms.

    b. Include measurable criteria for acceptable performance.

    c. Describe the specific conditions under which the new skill is required.

3. *Model or demonstration:* A presentation of the range of positive and negative examples of the skill by the trainer or other competent individual.

    a. Use positive examples to cover the range of instances that the trainee is likely to encounter.

    b. Use negative examples to teach when the new skill is not required.

    c. A model or demonstration should be presented by a respected, competent individual.

    d. Provide oral descriptions as the model is being presented so the trainee can learn the relevant features of the examples and the required skill.

4. *Role play or behavioral rehearsal:* Opportunities for the trainee to practice the new skill with corrective, reinforcing feedback from the consultant or trainer.

    a. Use positive examples to cover the range of instances that the trainee is likely to encounter.

    b. Use negative examples to teach when the new skill is not required.

    c. Trainees should not engage in a role play until they have had the opportunity to master the subcomponents of the new skill; that is, until they can display behaviors that can be reinforced or shaped.

    d. Provide oral descriptions as the role play is being conducted so trainees can learn the relevant features of the examples and the required skill.

    e. Provide frequent and informative feedback as the trainee engages in the new skill.

    f. Initially, provide written scripts or prompts to help trainees role-play accurately.

    g. Decrease coaching as the trainee becomes more fluent with a new skill.

5. *Review:* A brief statement describing the purpose of the lesson, what had been accomplished, and what the learning or outcome goal was.

    a. Emphasize the relevant features of the new skill and when it should be used.

    b. Briefly describe the range of positive examples.

    c. Probe the trainee's learning by asking questions.

6. *Test:* Opportunities for the trainee to demonstrate mastery of the skill on a new example and without feedback.

    a. Use untrained examples for test items.

    b. Request demonstrations of the skill rather than oral answers.

c. If possible, test in the natural context (for example, the classroom or playground).

d. Withhold feedback until the complete skill has been displayed.

7. *Homework:* Assignments to practice the newly acquired skill.

a. Get a written or oral commitment to practice the skill by a specific time and day.

b. Select assignments that correspond to the trainee's level of fluency on a new skill.

c. Require that all homework activities be turned in.

8. *Follow-up:* A brief event following the lesson to check on skill maintenance and reinforce generalized responding.

a. Send a letter, memo, or report to the trainee to prompt utilization of the new skill and to summarize and reinforce what was learned. A telephone call can serve the same function.

b. Provide opportunities for clarification and questions.

c. Identify a local person who can conduct follow-up activities.

SUMMARY

Successful consultation involves the collaborative interaction between two or more individuals. Consultants must learn to work effectively with others to remove roadblocks, manage conflicts, solve problems, communicate effectively, and train others. In this chapter, we cover formats, strategies, and guidelines to accomplish these outcomes. We emphasize a behavioral outcome-oriented approach that focused on teacher and consultant behavior, structured interactions, products, and immediate contexts.

The following is a list of the key features of this chapter:

1. An outcome-oriented approach to working with others is based on the assumption that working relationships between consultants and teachers are facilitated by providing teachers with specific opportunities to experience success in solving a problem presented by a student.

2. Goals of an outcome-oriented approach are to (a) structure the consultation process so it is efficient and effective, (b) teach or strengthen teacher behaviors that can and will result in positive reinforcement, and (c) establish and work toward predictable and significant changes in student behavior.

3. An applied behavior analytic and instructional approach must be taken in an outcome-oriented approach.

4. A roadblock to consultation is defined as a situation or condition that inhibits or interferes with the attainment of consultation goals or objectives.

5. To identify and assess roadblocks, consultants should (a) determine that a roadblock condition is present and who is involved, (b) identify the

setting or context in which the roadblock is observed, (c) conduct a functional analysis, and (d) identify and define observable behaviors that indicate the presence of a roadblock.

6. A variety of factors can contribute to low rates of desired teacher or consultant behaviors: (a) unlearned skills, (b) lack of opportunities, (c) inappropriate controlling factors, (d) ineffective reinforcement, and (e) inhibiting aversives.

7. An efficient and effective approach to problem solving and conflict management is needed because (a) students are important, (b) people's attitudes, beliefs, and feelings are difficult to change and there is no guarantee that behavior will change, and (c) people have different reasons for doing what they do.

8. A conflict is a situation in which two or more people disagree about something.

9. One of the most important steps in problem solving is determining whether a conflict exists and then resolving that conflict.

10. Conflict management begins with stopping to determine if the consultant and teacher are calm and can engage in problem solving.

11. Clear communication behaviors and strategies are needed to facilitate roadblock analysis, problem solving, and conflict resolution.

12. Communications can take one of two basic forms: written and oral.

13. Some teacher/consultant interactions are problematic because (a) on-task consultation and communication skills have not been learned, (b) off-task behavior is maintained by reinforcement, (c) low rates of on-task behavior are maintained by low rates of positive reinforcement, and (d) low rates of on-task behavior are maintained by the presentation of aversives.

14. Consultants can train others in large groups or small groups, or individually.

15. A basic training format includes (a) an introduction, (b) an outcome statement or objective, (c) a model or demonstration, (d) a role play or behavioral rehearsal, (e) a review, (f) a test, (g) homework, and (h) follow-up.

REFERENCES

ABIDIN, R. R., JR. (1975). Negative effects of behavioral consultation. *Journal of School Psychology, 13,* 51–56.

CHRISTOFF, K. A., OWEN, W., SCOTT, N., KELLEY, M. L., SCHLUNDT, D., BAER, G., & KELLY, J. A. (1985). Social skills and social problem training shy young adolescents. *Behavior Therapy, 16,* 468–477.

D'ZURRILLA, T. J., & GOLDFRIED, M. R. (1971). Problem-solving and behavior modification. *Journal of Abnormal Psychology, 75,* 107–126.

JOHNSON, L. J., PUGACH, M. C., & HAMMITTEE, D. J. (1988). Barriers to effective special education consultation. *Remedial and Special Education, 9*(6), 41–47.

PIERSEL, W. C., & GUTKIN, T. B. (1983). Resistance to school-based consultation: A behavioral analysis of the problem. *Psychology in the Schools, 20,* 311–320.

ROBIN, A. L., & KOEPKE, T. (1990). Behavioral assessment and treatment of parent–adolescent conflict. In M. Herson, R. M. Eisler, & P. M. Miller (Eds.), *Progress in behavior modification, 25,* 178–209.

WITT, J. C., & MARTENS, B. K. (1988). Problems with problem-solving consultation: A re-analysis of assumptions, methods, and goals. *School Psychology Review, 17,* 211–226.

NAME INDEX

SUBJECT INDEX

ABAB withdrawal design, 229, 230
Abscissa, 113
Academic achievement, 40–42, 301
Academic behaviors, 268–269, 301
Academic checklist, 361–366
Academic engaged time, 137, 268, 269
Academic learning time, 137, 268
Accountability, 144–150
Achievement, 40–42, 301
Acquisition, 183, 250
Acquisition problem, 132–133
Active listening, 386
Active voice, 415
Activity, 302
Activity flow, 333–336
Activity format, 307–313
ACT preparation test, 359
Adaptation, 176, 183, 251
Adaptation problem, 134
Advance organizers, 315, 318–320
Advocacy consultation, 5
Agenda, in oral communication, 419
Aim lines, 240–246
Aim star, 240–241
Algorithms, 352
Allocated time, 137
American Psychological Association (APA) style, 324
Analogies, 323
Analytic consultation, 15–20
  assumptions of, 19–20
  key features of, 16–18
  rationale for, 16
  steps in, 18–19

Anaphoric structures, 324
Antecedent
  behavioral, 86, 87, 88, 96
  instructional, 132–133
Antecedent manipulations, 143
Anticipatory set, 317–318, 319
APA style, 324
Application, 357
Applied behavior analysis, 17, 126, 127
Artificial reinforcers, 179, 249, 335
Assertive discipline, 126
Assessment, 56
  of basic skills, 264–267
  classroom-based, 39–42
  ecobehavioral, 63
  ecological, 62–64
  of interest, 267–273
  of intervention implementation, 224–228
  of motivation, 267–273
  norm-referenced, 367–369
  of progress, 156, 329–331
  of roadblocks, 389, 393, 394
  of setting, 61–62, 134–135
  specific-level, 369–372
  strategies for, 224–226
  survey-level, 367–369
  systematic, 42–46
  See also Curriculum-based assessment
Assignment(s), in lesson segments, 313–314
Assignment patterns, 311–313
Assistance, specialized, 247–248.
  See also Request for Assistance

Aversive stimulus, 144, 186, 188–189
  consultant behavior and, 401, 402
  on-task behavior and, 424
  teacher behavior and, 397

Background knowledge
  anticipatory sets and, 318
  assessing, 271–273
  interventions for, 275–277
  motivation and, 267–268
Back-up contingency, 197
Bar graphs, 112, 115
Baseline, 229–232
Basic skills
  in curriculum-based assessment, 345–353
  determining, 264–267
  math, 266–267, 351–353, 358–359, 362, 364
  reading, 265, 290–293, 346–348
  spelling, 348–350, 362, 363
  writing, 266, 293–294, 350–351, 362, 363
Behavior(s)
  academic, 268–269, 301
  antecedent of, 86, 87, 88, 96
  competing, 396, 400, 402
  consequence of, 86, 87, 88, 96
  consultant, 397–401, 402
  definitions of, 164–165
  dimensions of, 56–57
  discrete, 56–57
  externalizing, 43
  instructional, 301, 393–397
  internalizing, 43

437

CREDITS

These pages constitute an extension of the copyright page. We have made every effort to trace the ownership of all copyrighted material and to secure permission from copyright holders. In the event of questions concerning the use of any material, we will be pleased to make the necessary corrections in future printings.

Instructors of classes using *Effective School Consultation: An Interactive Approach* by Sugai and Tindal may reproduce blank forms from this publication for classroom use.

Chapter 2: 27, Excerpts reprinted with permission from *Placing Children In Special Education: A Strategy for Equity* by K. A. Heller, W. A. Holtzman, and S. Messick. Published by the National Academy Press, 1982. Reprinted with permission. **44,** Figure 2.4 from *Systematic Screening and Identification of Behavior Disorders,* by H. M. Walker and H. H. Severson. Copyright © 1990 by Sopris West, Longmont, CO. Reprinted by permission. **Chapter 5: 136,** Box 5.4 from *Effective Schooling Practices: A Research Synthesis (1990 Update).* Copyright © 1990 by Northwest Regional Educational Laboratory, Portland, OR. Reprinted by permission. **136,** Box 5.5 from *Effective Schooling Practices: A Research Synthesis (1990 Update).* Copyright © 1990 by Northwest Regional Educational Laboratory, Portland, OR. Reprinted by permission. **Chapter 6: 187,** Box 6.5 from *Effective Teaching: Principles and Procedures of Applied Behavior Analysis with Exceptional Students,* by M. R. Wolery, D. B Bailey, Jr., and G. M. Sugai. Copyright © 1988 by Allyn & Bacon Publishing Company. Reprinted by permission. **204,** Figure 6.8 from *Effective Teaching: Principles and Procedures of Applied Behavior Analysis with Exceptional Students,* by M. R. Wolery, D. B. Bailey, Jr., and G. M. Sugai. Copyright © 1988 by Allyn & Bacon Publishing Company. Reprinted by permission. **Chapter 8: 262,** Box 8.1 from *The World and Its People: A World View* by C. P. Patton, A. C. Rengert, R. N. Saveland, K. S. Cooper, and P. T. Caro. Copyright © 1985 by Silver Burdett Company, Morristown, NJ. Reprinted by permission. **272,** Figure 8.4 adapted from S. W. Valencia, A. C. Stallman, M. Commeyras, P. D. Pearson, and D. K. Hartman. "Four Measures of Topical Knowledge: A Study of Construct Validity." *Reading Research Quarterly,* 26 (3), 1991, p. 216. Reprinted with permission of Sheila W. Valencia and the International Reading Association. **279,** Figure 8.5 from "Group Story Mapping: A Comprehension Strategy for Both Skilled and Unskilled Readers" by L. Idol, 1987, *Journal of Learning Disabilities,* 20, p. 199. Copyright 1987 by PRO-ED, Inc. Reprinted by Permission. **281,** Box 8.2 from "The Two Brothers," from *Fables and Fairy Tales* by Leo Tolstoy, translated by Ann Dunnigan. Translation copyright © 1962 by Ann Dunnigan; Foreword copyright © 1962 by New American Library. Used by permission of New American Library, a division of Penguin Books USA Inc. **288,** Box 8.6 from "Theory and Research," by M. D. Gall, J. P. Gall, D. R. Jacobsen, and T. L. Bullock, 1990, *Tools for Learning.* Copyright © 1990 by Association for Supervision and Curriculum Development, Alexandria, VA. Reprinted by permission. **Chapter 9: 303,** Figure 9.1 reprinted with permission from L. W. Anderson and R. B. Burns, *Research in Classrooms.* Copyright 1989, Pergamon Press Ltd. **319,** Box 9.6 (bottom) from "The Ocean: A Perspective" by J. Cousteau, December 1981, *National Geographic,* 160 (6), pp. 781-782. Copyright © 1981 *National Geographic.* Reprinted by permission. **321, 330, 331** Quotes excerpted from *Educators' Handbook: A Research Perspective* by Virginia Richardson-Koehler (ed.). Copyright © 1987 by Longman Publishing Group. Reprinted by permission. **322,** Box 9.7 from Barak Rosenshine and Robert Stevens, "Teaching Functions." Reprinted with the permission of Macmillan Publishing Company from *Handbook of Research on Teaching, Third Edition,* M. C. Wittrock, editor. Copyright © 1986 by the American Educational Research Association. **328,** Figure 9.6 from "Translating Research on Text Structure into Classroom Practice" by B. Grossen & D. Carnine, *Teaching Exceptional Children,* 24 (4), 1992, p. 48. Copyright © 1992 by The Council for Exceptional Children. Reprinted with permission. **337,** Box 9.10 adapted from Barak Rosenshine and Robert Stevens, "Teaching Functions." Reprinted with the permission of Macmillan Publishing Company from *Handbook of Research on Teaching, Third Edition,* M. C. Wittrock, editor. Copyright © 1986 by the American Educational Research Association. **Chapter 10: 348,** Box 10.2 adapted from "Curriculum-Based Oral Reading Fluency Norms for Students in Grades 2 Through 5" by J. Hasbrouck and G. Tindal, *Teaching Exceptional Children,* 24 (3), 1992, p. 42. Copyright © 1992 by The Council for Exceptional Children. Reprinted with permission. **319,** Box 9.6 (top) from *Focus on Earth Science* by M. S. Bishop, B. Sutherland, and P. G. Lewis. Copyright

TO THE OWNER OF THIS BOOK:

We hope that you have found *Effective School Consultation: An Interactive Approach* useful. So that this book can be improved in a future edition, would you take the time to complete this sheet and return it? Thank you.

School and address: _____

Department: _____

Instructor's name: _____

_____

1. What I like most about this book is: _____

_____

2. What I like least about this book is: _____

_____

_____

3. My general reaction to this book is: _____

_____

4. The name of the course in which I used this book is: _____

_____

5. Were all of the chapters of the book assigned for you to read? _____

   If not, which ones weren't? _____

6. In the space below, or on a separate sheet of paper, please write specific suggestions for improving this book and anything else you'd care to share about your experience in using the book.

_____

_____

_____

_____

_____

_____

_____

Optional:

Your name: _____ Date: _____

May Brooks/Cole quote you, either in promotion for *Effective School Consultation: An Interactive Approach* or in future publishing ventures?

Yes: _____ No: _____

Sincerely,

George M. Sugai
Gerald A. Tindal

BUSINESS REPLY MAIL

FIRST CLASS   PERMIT NO. 358   PACIFIC GROVE, CA

POSTAGE WILL BE PAID BY ADDRESSEE

ATT: *George M. Sugai & Gerald A. Tindal*

Brooks/Cole Publishing Company
511 Forest Lodge Road
Pacific Grove, California 93950-9968